Abraham's Children

Abraham's Children

Jews, Christians and Muslims in Conversation

Edited by

Norman Solomon, Richard Harries and Tim Winter

t&t clark

Published by T&T Clark
A Continuum imprint
The Tower Building, 11 York Road, London SE1 7NX
80 Maiden Lane, Suite 704, New York, NY 10038

www.tandtclark.com

British Library Cataloguing-in-Publication Data
A catalogue record for this book is available from the British Library

Library of Congress Cataloging-in-Publication Data
Abraham's Children : Jews, Christians and Muslims in Conversation / edited by Norman Solomon, Richard Harries, and Tim Winter. -- 1st ed.
p. cm.
ISBN 0-567-08171-0 (hardcover) -- ISBN 0-567-08161-3 (pbk.)
1. Christianity and other religions. 2. Judaism--Relations. 3. Islam--Relations.
I. Solomon, Norman, 1933- II. Harries, Richard. III. Winter, Timothy J.
BR127.A27 2006
201'.5--dc22

2005020666

Typeset by Free Range Book Design & Production Ltd
Printed on acid-free paper in Great Britain by MPG Books Ltd, Cornwall

ISBN 0567081710 (hardback)
0567081613 (paperback)

Contents

Acknowledgments

Quotations from the Christian Bible are taken from the New Revised Standard Version unless otherwise stated.

The extract from 'That Nature is a Heraclitean Fire and of the Comfort of the Resurrection' from W.H. Gardner and N.H. Mackenzie (eds.), *The Poems of Gerard Manley Hopkins* (London: Oxford University Press, 4th edn, 1970), p. 105, is reproduced by permission of Oxford University Press on behalf of the British Province of the Society of Jesus.

CONTRIBUTORS

The Revd Professor John Barton teaches Old Testament studies at the University of Oxford, as Oriel and Laing Professor of the Interpretation of Holy Scripture. He has written a number of books about the Bible, and is joint editor of *The Oxford Bible Commentary* (Oxford: Oxford University Press, 2001). He is an Anglican priest and lives in Abingdon, near Oxford, where he assists in several churches.

The Revd Dr Marcus Braybrooke is President of the World Congress of Faiths, and until 2005 was vicar of the Baldons with Nuneham Courtenay near Oxford. He has travelled widely and been involved in interfaith work for over thirty-five years. A former Director of the Council of Christians and Jews, he was one of the founders of the Three Faiths Forum and of the International Interfaith Centre, of which he is now a Patron. His books include *Christian-Jewish Dialogue: The Next Steps* (London: SCM Press, 2000), *What We Can Learn from Islam* (New Alresford: John Hunt, 2002), and *A Heart for the World* (New Alresford: John Hunt, 2006).

The Revd Jonathan Gorsky is Education Advisor to the Council of Christians and Jews. He studied history at Liverpool and Manchester Universities and Jewish Studies at Jews College, London. He is a former Education Director of Yakar, a Jewish cultural centre in London, and a minister to the Orthodox community in St. Albans. He has worked in Christian-Jewish relations since 1992.

The Rt Revd Richard Harries has been Bishop of Oxford since 1987. Before that, he was Dean of King's College, London. For nearly nine years he chaired the Council of Christians and Jews. When he came to Oxford, he convened the Abrahamic Group, of which this book is a product. He is the author of many books, including *Art and the Beauty of God* (London: Mowbray, 1993), which was selected as a book of the year by the late Anthony Burgess in *The Observer*; *After the Evil: Christianity and Judaism in the Shadow of the Holocaust* (Oxford: Oxford University Press, 2003); and *The Passion in Art* (Aldershot: Ashgate, 2004). In 1996, he was elected a Fellow of the Royal Society of Literature. He is active in the House of Lords and since 1972 has been a regular contributor to BBC Radio 4's *Today* programme.

Dr Paul Joyce is a Roman Catholic Christian, who taught Old Testament Studies at Ripon College Cuddesdon, an Anglican theological college, before moving to teach in the University of Birmingham. Since 1994, he has been a University Lecturer in the University of Oxford and a Fellow of St. Peter's College, Oxford. His doctoral studies were on the book of Ezekiel, and he has written particularly on the literature of the Exile and also on the place of the Bible in the modern world.

Dr Annabel Keeler is a Research Associate at Wolfson College in the University of Cambridge, where she works in the field of Islamic mysticism and Qur'ānic hermeneutics, on which subjects she has published a number of articles. Her doctoral dissertation, on a twelfth-century Persian Sufi commentary on the Qur'ān, is currently in preparation for publication in early 2006 by Oxford University Press in association with the Institute of Ismaili Studies. She participates as a Muslim in a number of interfaith initiatives in Cambridge.

Professor Yahya Michot, since 1998, has been a Fellow of the Oxford Centre for Islamic Studies and the Islamic Centre Lecturer in the Faculty of Theology in the University of Oxford. His main field of research is classical Muslim thought, principally Avicenna (d. AH 428/1037), his sources, and his impact on Sunnism. This has led to a growing interest in the theologian Ibn Taymiyya (d. AH 728/1328) and the time of the Mamlūks.

Dr Basil Mustafa is Bursar and Nelson Mandela Fellow in Educational Studies at the Oxford Centre for Islamic Studies; Associate Tutor at the Department for Continuing Education in the University of Oxford; and a member of Kellogg College, Oxford. He is an educationalist with a special interest in the educational needs of Muslim minorities in Europe, and an active participant in interfaith dialogue.

Dr Lutfi Radwan is an environmentalist, lecturer and organic farmer, who graduated in 1992 with a doctorate from the University of Oxford on irrigation in rural Egypt. He has subsequently lectured on, and undertaken consultancy relating to, social and environmental sustainability in arid regions. More recently, he has been involved in organic farming in the UK where, in Oxfordshire, he and his wife manage a smallholding.

Dr Alison Salvesen is University Research Lecturer at the Oriental Institute in the University of Oxford, and Fellow of the Oxford Centre for Hebrew and Jewish Studies. She specializes in early Jewish and Christian translation and exegesis of the Bible. She has published books on minor Jewish Greek versions of scripture and on an early mediaeval Christian version of Samuel in Syriac. She has also worked in the field of Classical Hebrew lexicography.

Rabbi Sybil Sheridan is a rabbi of the Wimbledon Reform Synagogue and a Lecturer in Bible and Life Cycle and Festivals at the Leo Baeck College Centre for Jewish Education in London. She is the author of *Stories from the Jewish World* (London: Macdonald, 1987), and editor of *Hear Our Voice* (London: SCM Press, 1994) and *Taking up the Timbrel* (London: SCM Press, 2000), two anthologies of work by the women rabbis of Great Britain.

Rabbi Norman Solomon was born in Cardiff, south Wales, and educated at St. John's College, Cambridge. He has served as rabbi to several Orthodox congregations in Britain, was founder-Director of the Centre for the Study of Judaism and Jewish-Christian Relations in Birmingham, and was Fellow in Modern Jewish Thought at the Oxford Centre for Hebrew and Jewish Studies. He has published several books on Judaism.

The Revd Professor Keith Ward was Regius Professor of Divinity at the University of Oxford, and a Canon of Christ Church, Oxford. Before that, he was Professor of the History and Philosophy of Religion at the University of London. He is a Fellow of the British Academy, and among his publications is a four-volume comparative theology, published under the titles *Religion and Revelation*, *Religion and Creation*, *Religion and Human Nature* and *Religion and Community* (Oxford: Oxford University Press, 1994–2000).

The Rt Revd Kallistos Ware is an Assistant Bishop in the Orthodox Archdiocese of Thyateira and Great Britain, and also a monk of the Monastery of St. John the Theologian on the island of Patmos. He was Spalding Lecturer in Eastern Orthodox Studies at the University of Oxford from 1966 to 2001, and is an Emeritus Fellow of Pembroke College, Oxford. His books include *The Orthodox Church* (Harmondsworth: Penguin, 1963), *The Orthodox Way* (London: Mowbray, 1979) and *The Inner Kingdom* (Crestwood, NY: St. Vladimir's Seminary Press, 2000). He is co-translator of *The Philokalia* (London: Faber and Faber, 1979) and of Orthodox liturgical books.

Tim Winter is currently University Lecturer in Islamic Studies at the Faculty of Divinity in the University of Cambridge. He has studied under traditional authorities in Egypt and Morocco, and is an active member of the British Muslim community, leading the weekly Friday prayers in the mosque at Cambridge. He has published a series of translations of mediaeval Arabic ethical and mystical texts, together with a number of academic articles.

INTRODUCTIONS

Richard Harries

Until I came to Oxford in 1987, I was for many years a member of the Manor House Group, based in London. This sought to encourage harmony between Judaism and Christianity by bringing together Jewish and Christian theologians to discuss subjects of mutual interest. We used to meet twice a year and then go away for a weekend together. One fruit of that group was a book, published in 1992, *Dialogue with a Difference: The Manor House Group Experience*.[1] The 'difference' was that we got to know each other very well, sharing much laughter together, and became able to share strong disagreements as well as what we had in common; and we have remained friends after the group ceased to exist.[2]

When I came to Oxford, it seemed an opportune moment to initiate a similar group, this time including Muslims; and the presence in the city of the Oxford Centre for Islamic Studies was a great help in this regard. So the Oxford Abrahamic Group began in December 1992, and has been meeting ever since: usually twice a year, but sometimes three times, for the best part of a day at my house in north Oxford. At each meeting, three short papers are given on an agreed subject, one from each of the three Abrahamic faiths, followed by extensive discussion. It has usually been possible to take two subjects in a day, one in the morning and one in the afternoon. Initially, the intention was for the group to number twelve scholars, four from each faith, though in practice the overall membership has been larger in order that around a dozen scholars might be available to attend any one meeting. In addition to the contributors to this book, the present membership includes Ron Nettler, Farhan Nizami and Bassam Saeh. Past members have included the late Peter Hebblethwaite, Julian Johansen, Penelope Johnstone, David Marshall, Tariq Modood, Sohail Nakhooda, Jonathan Romain, James Walker and Jonathan Webber.

It was as far back as May 1998 that Tim Winter suggested that some of our papers should be published. Reflection on this soon made clear that not only

1. T. Bayfield and M.C.R. Braybrooke (eds.), *Dialogue with a Difference: The Manor House Group Experience* (London: SCM Press, 1992).

2. At about the time I came to Oxford, the original group disbanded. Some members formed a new group to include Muslims.

would the group's papers on a variety of subjects – old as well as new ones – be valued by a wider audience, but also the group's discussions, if there was some way in which they could be crystallized and recorded. We achieved this by using, for the basis of our discussions, a commentary on each subject, prepared in advance by myself from the first drafts of the papers, indicating those points which the three religions had in common, those points where the religions diverged in their understanding of the subject under discussion, and those issues which needed further exploration. These commentaries were revised, in the light of discussion at the meeting, by a representative of each of the faiths – myself, Norman Solomon and Tim Winter – before being presented finally to the whole group once more; and they are printed in this book at the end of each section. In this way, not only are the essays themselves framed in the context of dialogue (as each essay was revised in the light of its reception at our meetings), but also the commentary sections are distillations of, and attempts at, conversation between the three faiths. The aim has thus been not only to present treatments of subjects which have been forged in dialogue with all the sensitivities and sympathies which that involves, but also to offer ways forward for dialogue through practical examples of the same by a group of some years' experience.

One of the main blessings of a group like this, indeed one of the purposes in setting it up in the first place, is the building up of relationships of respect and trust, so that there can be a frank, as well as a polite, exchange of opinions. For this, continuity in group members is fundamental. This was initially difficult to achieve, due to people moving on from Oxford to new jobs elsewhere, but the group has remained fairly stable in recent years, so it has not just been a seminar with academics reading papers, but a group of believers who from their different standpoints have wanted both to share insights with others and also to learn from different perspectives. One, not surprising, feature of our discussions is that sometimes there has been as much of a debate between the adherents to a particular religion as there has been between members of different religions. In all three religions today, there can be found not only long-established, traditional understandings of particular beliefs, but also an openness to modern questionings and insights; and all three religions today exhibit something of the tension between these two sympathies.

In the time that the group has met, of course, the unprecedented terrorist attacks on America of 2001 have occurred, with the ensuing wars in Afghanistan and Iraq and further terrorist attacks in Europe and around the world, bringing fundamentalist readings of religious traditions into the spotlight, and heightening the tensions between ordinary communities of different faiths. In this new landscape, the task of dialogue is ever more urgent and we have felt more keenly the importance of what we have been trying to achieve. It is particularly in this spirit that we offer our conversations to be overheard.

A note about a practical feature of the book, to help the reader: while each author has tried to be true to the religion to which they belong, the individual essays represent the views of the author; they do not generally attempt to be neutral surveys. Nonetheless, it is hoped that each essay will acquaint the reader with a basic introduction to the features of that religion's treatment of the subject concerned, and to basic relevant texts; hence it has not been felt necessary to provide a final bibliography or suggestions for further reading. In one sense the book will be a success if it leads readers – both the serious academic researcher and the general reader – not so much to further reading as to actual dialogue.

Readers will also notice that while the treatments of most subjects are arranged in chronological order, that is to say, first the Jewish perspective, then the Christian, then the Muslim, it seemed appropriate in the case of the founders of the religions to give first place to the essay from the perspective of the religion founded: thus the essay from a Christian perspective comes first in the section on Jesus, and the essay from a Muslim perspective comes first in the section on Muhammad. In the section on Moses, the Jewish perspective comes first again.

Two people require special thanks: first of all, my chaplain, Michael Brierley, who has done a very great deal of the detailed editorial work which has proved necessary; secondly, my wife, Jo, who has provided hospitality for the group, with its variety of dietary requirements, from the start.

Norman Solomon

Like Richard Harries, I was a member of the Manor House Group. After the group published *Dialogue with a Difference*, I helped reconstitute it into a group including Muslims, in which form it still functions today. Several other 'Abrahamic' groups, both in the UK and other countries, not least Israel, now meet regularly and provide for the exchange of views between Jews, Christians and Muslims.

The Oxford Abrahamic Group, which I joined only when it was already well established, is distinctive not only for its cohesion and persistence but also for its broad range of academic expertise. Indeed, it is precisely this broad range of expertise that has enabled it to achieve new and fruitful perspectives on the relationships of Jews, Christians and Muslims. On the Jewish side, for instance, we have not ignored the variety and development of Judaism within Sasanian, Byzantine and Islamic cultures as well as in the West. Considerations of Christian and Islamic teaching and experience have been equally broad, and are reflected in this volume.

In working together, members of the group have learned that no faith community is monolithic, and that the range that exists within each faith reflects personal, social and cultural differences that cut across faith barriers. There are liberals and conservatives within each camp: Islam has no monopoly of fanaticism, Judaism no monopoly of justice, Christianity no monopoly of love. The constancies and commonalities of doctrine and vocabulary that define each faith group allow for considerable divergence in the actual expression of each; I would not necessarily agree, for instance, with all the interpretations of Judaism offered in this volume by my Jewish colleagues.

Paradoxically, the air of academic detachment that pervades Oxford has aided rather than undermined our understanding of the realities that underlie the conflicts that still bedevil interfaith and intra-faith relations. All of us know what it is like to live within a closed community, but in meeting together in a relaxed atmosphere of mutual confidence and trust, we can stand back a little, accept each other as we are, and dare to engage in self-criticism as well as in mutual questionings. The apologetics are there – no one wants to 'let the side down', to provide ammunition for detractors from his or her faith – but at the same time, each is ready to admit to a certain selectiveness, to doubts about at least some of the forms in which that faith has been couched.

We are all conscious of living within modernity, and that this to some extent shapes our understanding of our faiths. Adherents of all three religions have helped shape modernity, yet all three faiths, in their 'traditional' forms, which are essentially those achieved in the Middle Ages, conflict with aspects of modernity. Much of the dynamic of the group has arisen from addressing these conflicts together, giving the lie to those who see contemporary conflicts in terms of Islam versus the West, or versus Christendom.

A wise teacher once explained to me that he had not published anything, saying, 'I was unable to capture in writing the movements of my hands.' It is certainly true that much that appears in this volume lacks the 'movement of the hands', the attitudes and facial expressions of the participants: subtle forms of expression have occasionally been sacrificed in the interests of clarity; here and there, a sub-text has been lost as the living dialogue has given way to the written page. A dialogue is, after all, an engagement of persons, not a dry scholarly report, however great its scholarly pretensions; ultimately, you cannot write it down.

I very much hope that readers will nevertheless capture something of the dynamic which this group has enjoyed under the able leadership of Richard Harries, and be inspired by the spirit of understanding and peace that I, for one, feel privileged to have experienced.

Tim Winter

The Oxford Abrahamic Group is the best example known to me of a group of people who are simultaneously friends, scholars and practising members of religions that in the past have been capable of bitter rivalry. A congenial, quizzical, erudite circle, the group gathers twice a year for the better part of a day, taking a break for lunch. Although the themes are introduced with a formal presentation, often in the form of papers which are read out to the group, the seminar atmosphere soon dispels, as factual queries are cleared up and participants probe the relevance of the presentation to their wider personal understanding of the three traditions. Scholarship, conviviality and theology quickly become inseparable, to produce a very distinctive group ethos.

A frequent outcome of these encounters has been the discovery that themes which in briefer, more formulaic, dialogue sessions are ritually invoked as 'shared symbols', turn out to be metaphors of what most deeply divides the respective faiths. The figure of Jesus might seem a good starting-point for a mutual affirmation between Christianity and Islam; but investigation reveals how profoundly different are the Christologies which are scripturally and theologically embedded in the two faiths. At times, the group has turned to issues where one or two of the traditions have little to fall back on historically other than polemic: the issue of the founder of Islam is a case in point. Conversely, the discussion of a topic such as 'divine action in the world' might begin with well-worn assumptions about the fatalism of some religions and the free-will convictions of others, but end with the realization that all three traditions have developed similar internal spectrums of belief, reflecting ways in which human minds wrestling with paradox, and informed by a shared belief in a benign and omnipotent creator, can converge dramatically, despite scriptural and dogmatic differences.

Once frankly acknowledged, the realization that one's own co-religionists have seldom fully agreed on anything liberates the discussion by revealing how each tradition is confronted by large, broadly analogous challenges: tradition against modernity, scripture against rationalism, exoteric against esoteric. New solidarities thus emerge as participants identify and sympathize with thinkers who have analogous inclinations in the other faiths. Orthodox Jews and conservative Muslims, for instance, are frequently struck by the depths of rapport which can suddenly become manifest when discussing how the modern conscience is challenged by a traditional revealed law. Feminists may find that they comfortably speak to other feminists across religious borders. Spirituality, a more frequently cited basis for inter-religious understanding, can also provide moments of empathy, as when a poem cited during a presentation suddenly recalls a strikingly exact parallel in the treasured memories of a participant from a historically rival religion.

The comparative informality of the encounters, and the genial hospitality of the host, also allow the formation of friendships across denominational lines through the discovery of less intellectual but no less personal affinities and interests. To launch a passionate defence of the Cappadocian view of the Trinity, and then to find that one's interlocutor has children at the school where one's spouse is a teacher, provides a calming reminder that one never disputes with doctrines; one disputes with those who hold them, and that no belief which is important to evidently good people can be undeserving of respect. It is to this that one should attribute the persistent courtesy of the encounters, helped by what one can only describe as a kind of English reserve.

The mood of the group is sometimes hesitant, if the subject is unfamiliar to most present, or where participants are wary of treading carelessly on ground which someone evidently hallows. On a few occasions, however, the debate has grown wonderfully heated, to the alarm of those who feel that the future of the world somehow depends on who emerges from the exchange with most credit.

Can such a community offer a lesson for a wider public? Evidently, it is important for faith communities to know that their representatives are engaging seriously with thinkers in other faiths. Evidently, too, the great mass of believers in the three families of Abraham wish for conviviality with other believers. There have been times in history when this was not the case, but today, despite the headlines, and the heated rhetoric of fundamentalist preachers on all sides, it is reasonable to claim that most Abrahamic believers find themselves on slowly convergent paths. Multiculturalism and a world of mass communication have been far more active in this transformation than the interfaith project, but perhaps a book such as this, with all its evident limitations, and the necessarily partial quality of its reflection of the original conversations, can show how the living together in practice of different religious groups can find support in theology and the habits of its advocates. I think I speak for all members of the group when I add that this is most likely to succeed where the theology insists on the integrity of each religion, and refuses the logic of syncretism or relativism. Abraham's God, after all, is a God of truth, whose demands are absolute.

Part I:

Foundations of Faith

Chapter 1: Abraham

Abraham from a Jewish Perspective

Sybil Sheridan

> Now the Lord said to Abram, 'Go [*Lekh lekha*] from your country and your kindred and your father's house to the land that I will show you.'[1]

In this manner, the long narrative opens that relates the events of the patriarch's life. In the course of this paper, we will look at these events through the medium of Jewish Midrash and literature, and see how Abraham became the foil to Moses, the founder of Judaism, the formulater of prayer and the ultimate man of faith. Abraham's relationship to his two sons will then be examined to see if there is a textual basis for today's dialogue between Jews and Muslims.

Abraham, Moses and Noah

A close look at the text above immediately presents a problem to the Jewish reader. The command *lekh lekha* translates literally as 'go for yourself' – a phrase open to many interpretations. Does it mean, 'Take yourself?' 'Go it alone?' 'Go for your own sake?' If the vocalization is removed, the phrase could be a double command: 'Go, go!' With each understanding, a world of different interpretation opens itself up, concerning the motive and circumstances of God's call.

What appeared clear to rabbinic interpreters of the phrase is the presence of a prehistory – one not recorded in the text, but necessary to its meaning: a Midrash explaining why it is that Abraham is not surprised to be addressed so suddenly by God, why it is that he obeys without demur – one that explains the precise meaning of our phrase.

Midrash is a multifaceted system, utilizing myth, mores, tradition and imagination to illustrate a point that links linguistically to the text in hand. The silence over Abraham's early years is filled with stories of a star in the east, a prophecy and an evil king who sets out to find and kill the child.[2] If this

1. Genesis 12.1.
2. For a summary of the many stories about Abraham, see L. Ginzberg, *The Legends of the Jews* (Philadelphia, PA: Jewish Publication Society of America, 1909), I, pp. 185–89.

sounds suspiciously Christian, one must bear in mind that the narrative is one that prefigures the birth of Moses in just the same way that the birth stories of Jesus echo those of Moses. In Jewish theology, Abraham is the precursor to Judaism's greatest prophet and so in his life he parallels all that Moses will later come to do. He leaves Ur to become a wanderer, and he goes down to Egypt so that he can leave Egypt. At his death, he is possessor of only one small field – as tantalizingly close to, yet distant from, the promise of a country for his descendants, as is Moses dying on Mount Horeb. Abraham is only surpassed by Moses himself. Abraham is seen as the first Jew;[3] Moses becomes the greatest Jew.[4] Abraham is perceived *par excellence* as the man of faith;[5] Moses sees God face to face.[6] Abraham undergoes ten tests of his belief; Moses is the agent of ten plagues – and issues ten commandments.[7] Abraham founds a family; Moses founds a faith.

Abraham's realization of God's presence, in Midrash, parallels Moses' burning bush experience. Having been hidden in a cave, Abraham emerged and

> wondered in his heart: 'Who created heaven and earth and me?' All that day he prayed to the sun. In the evening, the sun set in the west and the moon rose in the east. Upon seeing the moon and the stars around it, he said: 'This one must have created heaven and earth and me – these stars must be the moon's princes and courtiers.' So all night long he stood in prayer to the moon. In the morning, the moon sank in the west and the sun rose in the east. Then he said: 'There is no might in either of these. There must be a higher Lord over them – to Him will I pray, and before Him will I prostrate myself.'[8]

Abraham's young life is spent trying to convince people of the futility of idolatry, culminating in smashing his father's idols to demonstrate their powerlessness.[9]

This violent action indicates a clear break with the past. Midrash compares him to Noah. There are ten generations between Adam and the flood,[10] in which one sees the gradual corruption of humanity from its first ideal creation. The flood marks a catastrophic event that breaks with the past and starts a new creation in the family of Noah. There are another ten generations from Noah to Abraham during which time, again, the bright hope for the future of the world becomes tarnished. Once again, God focuses on one person, but this time God does not destroy the rest of humanity. Mindful of the covenant with Noah, God chooses Abraham and his descendants, not as a surviving remnant of humanity, but as the agent of the divine will to be communicated to all people.

3. Babylonian Talmud, *Hagiga* 3a.
4. Deuteronomy 34.10.
5. Genesis Rabba 39.1, Song of Songs Rabba 4.19, etc.
6. Deuteronomy 34.10.
7. Exodus Rabba 15.27, 30.16 and 44.4.
8. This version is from W.G. Braude's translation of N. Bialik and C. Ravinsky, *Sefer ha-Aggada* (New York: Schocken Books, 1992), p. 31, based on Genesis Rabba 42.8.
9. Genesis Rabba 38.13.
10. Mishnah Avot 5.2–3.

Abraham's Blessing

Abraham is seen as the first proselyte, the first to declare the unity of God, who wanders around setting up altars,[11] proclaiming the name of God and converting others to this belief. To this day, the convert to Judaism takes the patronym *Avraham Avinu*, the child of 'Abraham our Father'. Thus it is demonstrated that Abraham is the spiritual progenitor of all who take up the faith as well as being the physical ancestor of Isaac, Jacob and the subsequent Jewish nation. Thus the blessing at the end of God's call to Abraham declares: 'in you all the families of the earth shall be blessed'.[12] Abraham leaves Haran with the 'souls that he had made' there[13] – a clear reference to converts, according to rabbinic commentary,[14] providing a model of missionary activity for which Judaism was at one time famous.[15] However, because of mediaeval beliefs of supercessionism by both Christianity and Islam, Judaism was forced to abandon the practice until the modern era, and no longer claims a mission to proselytize.

The blessing has elicited other interpretations, however. One idea that is currently popular among liberal Jews is that the blessing has been fulfilled through the spread of Christianity and Islam – daughter religions of Judaism which also proclaim monotheism and a spiritual descent from Abraham. Another view removes the suggested missionary element, stating instead that the blessings God metes out to the other nations of the world are dependent on their treatment of the Jews in their midst.[16] Whatever the interpretation, the blessing implies a universalism which is very much part of the message of Judaism. However, it is counterweighed by God's covenantal promise given at the time of the circumcision: 'I will establish my covenant between me and you, and your offspring after you throughout their generations, for an everlasting covenant, to be God to you and to your offspring after you.'[17]

This suggests a relationship based on birth, compounded by the particularist assertion, 'And I will give to you, and to your offspring after you, the land where you are now an alien, all the land of Canaan, for a perpetual holding; and I will be their God.'[18] Thus the life of Abraham sets up a tension between the universal and the particular which continues to play its part in Judaism.

One solution of this tension is the rabbinic interpretation of the first covenant with Noah and all of humanity as one that demanded obedience to seven basic laws which included belief in the divine, prohibition of murder, theft and

11. Genesis 12.8.
12. Genesis 12.3.
13. Genesis 12.5.
14. Genesis Rabba 29.14.
15. Cf. Matthew 23.15: the Pharisees 'cross sea and land to make a single convert'.
16. S.R. Hirsch, *Commentary on Genesis* (trans. I. Levy; Gateshead: Judaica Press, 1963), pp. 226–27.
17. Genesis 17.7.
18. Genesis 17.8.

incest, and the establishment of a judicial system. By following these, 'The righteous of all nations will have a share in the World to Come.'[19]

On the other hand, the 'children of Abraham' have a different covenant. God's promise to them is sealed by the sign of circumcision. A child may be born a Jew, but it is by the rite of circumcision that he enters into that special relationship with God from which all non-Jews are excluded. Such an interpretation may not seem politically correct for many reasons today,[20] but there is no doubt about the strength of the conviction for most Jews of the importance of the practice. From the decrees of Antiochus, through the persecutions of Christianity, the sign of the covenant of Abraham was seen as an act of defiance, an act of loyalty and a reason for martyrdom. The parting of the ways between Judaism and Christianity seems to have been focused on this issue,[21] the rejection of circumcision by Christianity being perceived by Jews as the embracing of Hellenism and its implicit idolatry. For a non-Jewish male who wishes to convert, circumcision is a prerequisite in all denominations of Judaism.

The Aqeda

Tradition has it that Abraham was given ten tests to demonstrate his faith, of which the first was his readiness to leave his family and country and follow God to an undisclosed land. Commentators differ as to what constitutes the next eight, but the overriding sense is that despite all evidence to the contrary, Abraham continued to believe in the seemingly impossible promise of numberless progeny and a land of his own. That faith was most strongly tested in the last trial, the *Aqeda* or binding of Isaac.

'After these things God tested Abraham.'[22] As with the call, the command is multifaceted: 'Take your son, your only son Isaac, whom you love.'[23]

As with the call, the place to which he should go remains unclear, and as with the call, the words *lekh lekha*, 'go for yourself', are used. But there is a difference. Abraham responds to God's initial words with the word '*hinneni*' ('here I am') – a simple response implying a trusting readiness to do whatever God commands – and it is this that gives rise to a variety of interpretations.

19. Midrash Yalkut Shimoni, Neviim 296.

20. As well as a possible implied racism, one must today raise the question of whether a woman is part of the covenant of Abraham since she is not circumcised. If a woman is to be considered part of the Abrahamic covenant, what makes her so? Her birth? Her marriage? If the former, can a man also be part of the covenant without circumcision? Such questions are only now beginning to be addressed. See, for example, L. Hoffman, *Covenant of Blood* (Chicago, IL: University of Chicago Press, 1996).

21. Acts 11.1–18.

22. Genesis 22.1.

23. Genesis 22.2.

Does Abraham have faith that God will not allow the death of his son, or is his faith so strong that even the death of his son will not shake it? Does trust in God mean a blind faith? A questioning faith? A reasoned faith? Does Abraham pass the test, or fail it? In the Middle Ages, under the influence of Christian persecution, a cult of martyrdom developed which saw the *Aqeda* as a model for *kiddush hashem*, or dying for the sanctification of the divine name. The following *piyyut* or liturgical poem, read on *Rosh Hashana* in Sephardi synagogues, is based on a number of Midrashim that demonstrate not only Abraham's willingness, but also Isaac's, to do God's will. Isaac says, 'Through the knife my speech faltereth; yet sharpen it father, I beseech thee. Have courage and bind me strongly! And when the fire shall have consumed my flesh, take with thee the remains of my ashes and say to Sarah, Behold, this is the savour of Isaac.'[24]

Another version also popular in that period has it that Abraham in fact did sacrifice Isaac. The ashes of the sacrifice mentioned above were then gathered up and given to Sarah. They later served as an atonement for Israel's sins and were the ashes placed on the head at times of national mourning.[25] Further versions have him sacrificed and then resurrected, at which point Isaac utters the benediction said three times daily, '*Barukh 'ata ... mehaye ha-metim*.' 'Blessed are You ... who gives life to the dead.'[26]

Yet in most periods, the trust in God has implied that whatever is asked, God would never go back on his promise and allow Isaac to die. It becomes 'the very loftiest summit of spirituality reached, not only in Jewish, but in all events which show human greatness'.[27]

Thus Midrash sees Abraham battling against reason, storms and everything that Satan can hurl at him as he attempts to climb Mount Moriah to fulfil God's command.[28] Here, determined faith – strongly held against all opposition – seems to be the message. Other interpretations have treated the narrative symbolically. The *Aqeda* and the story of Job are pitched against each other, as God and Satan argue as to which character is the more steadfast in his faith. Some would say that there was no question of intended filicide. For some, the incident was to demonstrate the evils of human sacrifice. What Abraham thought was God's command was his own mistaken idea of what God requires, based on the practices of the Canaanite faiths that surrounded him. This

24. Judah ben Samuel Ibn Abbas of Fez (d. 1167), *The Book of Prayer and Order of Service according to the Custom of the Spanish and Portuguese Jews* (trans. D.A. de Sola; Oxford: Oxford University Press, 1957), II, p. 106.

25. Based on 'the ashes of Isaac', mentioned in Babylonian Talmud, *Ta'anit* 19a.

26. Ephraim ben Jacob of Bonn (twelfth century) composed a *piyyut* on the *Aqeda* as part of his *sefer zekhira* based on *Pirqei d'Rabbi Eliezer* 31 and *Midrash ha-Gadol* 1.323 and other late Midrashim.

27. S.R. Hirsch, *The Pentateuch* (trans. I. Levy; Gateshead: Judaica Press, 1976), I, pp. 373–74.

28. *Midrash Tanhuma*: Vayera 22.

returns us to the idea of Abraham as innovator of faith in God. As well as being the first to call upon God, he becomes the first to reject human sacrifice.[29]

Whatever the interpretation, the *Aqeda* holds a significant position in Judaism.

> The role of the man of faith, whose religious experience is fraught with inner conflicts and incongruities, who oscillates between ecstasy in God's companionship and despair when he feels abandoned by God, and who is torn asunder by the heightened contrast between self-appreciation and abnegation, has been a difficult one since the time of Abraham and Moses.[30]

Thus writes Rabbi Joseph B. Soloveitchik. He finds help for the human condition in the lives of our forebears. 'It would be presumptuous of me to attempt to convert the passional antinomic faith-experience into a eudaemonic harmonious one while the Biblical knights of faith lived heroically with their very tragic and paradoxical experience.'[31]

It is this personal connection to the trials of Abraham that explains the dominant place the *Aqeda* holds in Jewish ritual. Not only is it the fixed reading for *Rosh Hashana*, where the *shofar*, the ram's horn sounded during the service, is associated with the ram caught in the thicket, but the text also forms part of the daily morning service.

Abraham and Liturgy

Abraham figures greatly in the liturgy. Moses may be associated with *halakha* (Jewish law), but he is rarely mentioned in prayer. We do not pray to the God of Moses, but to the God of Abraham, who along with Isaac and Jacob are in prayer the *Avot* – the forefathers, patriarchs or ancestors.

The first blessing of the *tefilla* (the main prayer said by observant Jews three times each day) begins by addressing '*Elohenu vElohe Avotenu; Elohe 'Avraham, Elohe Yishak vElohe Ya'akov*', 'our God and the God of our ancestors: God of Abraham, God of Isaac, God of Jacob'.

The specification of 'our God', and the God of each patriarch individually, gives rise to the understanding that while we share the same God, the experience of Abraham, of Isaac, of Jacob and indeed of ourselves of the Deity has been very different. So while Abraham stands as the first to encounter God, and while his life may be an example to the rest of us, we can learn, not only from him, but from his descendants' lives as well as our own inevitably different

29. First declared by Abraham Geiger, this view finds modern expression in W.G. Plaut, *Torah: A Modern Commentary* (New York: Union of American Hebrew Congregations, 1981), p. 149.
30. J.B. Soloveitchik, *The Lonely Man of Faith* (New York: Jason Aaronson, 1996), p. 2.
31. Soloveitchik, *Lonely Man of Faith*, p. 2.

experience.[32] Nevertheless, all those experiences derive from the first divine encounter, and so the blessing ends, '*Barukh 'ata ... magen 'Avraham*', 'Blessed are You ... the shield of Abraham.'[33]

In Midrash, the three patriarchs become initiators of daily prayer.

> It has been taught according to R. Jose b. Hanina: 'Abraham established *shaharit* [the morning prayer,] as it says, [Genesis 19.27] "And Abraham got up early in the morning (and went) to the place where he had stood." There is no standing except in prayer as it says, [Psalm 106.30] "And Pinchas stood and prayed." Isaac established *minha* [the afternoon prayer,] as it says, [Genesis 24.63] "And Isaac went out to meditate (*shuah*) in the field towards evening." There is no meditation except in prayer as it says, [Psalm 102.1] "A prayer for the afflicted, when he faints and pours out his complaint (*siho*) before the Eternal." Jacob established '*aravit* [the evening prayer,] as it says, [Genesis 28.11] "And he came upon (*vayifga*) the place." There is no meeting (*pegia*) except in prayer, as it says, [Jeremiah 7.16] "Now, do not pray for this people neither lift up cry nor prayer for them, and do not intercede (*tifga*) with Me."'[34]

In some circles, Abraham becomes a direct intercessor with God;[35] in others it is through his merit that our prayers are heard.[36]

Abraham's Relationship with his Sons

Today, in the context of trialogue between the Abrahamic faiths, the focus moves to a different aspect of Abraham's life, namely the births of his two sons and their relationships with him. Traditionally, Ishmael has not figured greatly, or in very positive terms. The Bible tells of how Hagar was initially the surrogate mother, whose son, Ishmael, was to be adopted by Sarah. However, after his birth, Hagar seemed to take on airs and Sarah retaliated by humiliating her until

32. Cf. the saying of Israel Baal Shem Tov, in *Forms of Prayer* (trans. J. Magonet; London: Reform Synagogues of Great Britain, 1977), p. 357: 'Why do we say "Our God and God of our fathers?" There are two sorts of person who believe in God. The one believes his faith has been handed down to him by his fathers; and his faith is strong. The other has arrived at faith by dint of searching thought.'

33. Cf. Genesis 15.1.

34. Babylonian Talmud, *Berakhot* 26b; cf. *Berakhot* 6b.

35. Cf. Babylonian Talmud, *Bavli Eruvin* 19a, where Abraham brings up the circumcised from Gehenna, and *Bava Batra* 17a, where 'the Angel of death has no dominion over Abraham'. Abraham's death was directly from God, and therefore he remains in close proximity to, and supposedly has influence with, God.

36. Cf. the *piyyut* by David ben Bekoda for the second day of *Rosh Hashana* ('*yaane b'vor avot*' – 'for the sake of the pure lives of the patriarchs'), de Sola (trans.), *Book of Prayer*, II, p. 94 and *Tehine* of the Matriarchs for the Shofar ('May the merit of the four matriarchs, and the three patriarchs and Moses and Aaron stand by us in judgement for they have arisen to plead for us') (E. Umansky and D. Ashton [eds.], *Four Centuries of Women's Spirituality* [Boston, MA: Beacon Press, 1992], p. 53).

she fled. Later, after Isaac's birth, Ishmael is seen to mock or menace him and Sarah urges Abraham to send both mother and son away. In both stories, an angel of God speaks to Hagar during her exile, assuring her of Ishmael's future as a father of nations. However, it is his birth that introduces conflict into the household, and in order to justify the actions of Sarah and God's approval of her deeds, it becomes necessary in the Midrash to paint Ishmael as shameless and immoral.[37] Though God blesses Ishmael, though he too becomes a father of nations with twelve tribes to his name, there is no doubt that it is Isaac who is the son of the promise.[38]

> 'And he shall be a wild ass of a man' [Genesis 16.12]. Rabbi Johanan and Rabbi Shimon ben Laqish: R. Johanan said: 'All other people grow up in settlements, but he will grow up in the desert.'
>
> Resh Laqish said: 'Indeed a wild ass of a man. For all other people plunder wealth, but he plunders lives. His hand will be against everyone, and the hand of everyone against him. He and his dog are the same. Just as his dog eats carrion, so does he eat carrion.'[39]

Nevertheless, Ishmael is never seen as quite as evil as Esau, the mythological ancestor of Rome and thus of Christianity.[40] He remains steadfastly a worshipper of God, despite the idolatry of his mother and wives. There are stylistic similarities in the biblical text between Hagar's flight into the desert and the *Aqeda*. Both children are at the point of death when an angel intervenes. Abraham 'looked up and saw a ram, caught in a thicket by its horns', while God opened Hagar's eyes 'and she saw a well of water'.[41] Both children are therefore part of the divine plan, being progenitors of nations whose destinies appear to run in parallel. Moreover, whatever the sins of Ishmael were, Midrash suggests that he repented of them, enabling the two brothers to bury their father together.[42]

The story of these two brothers, who had had their battles, who lived separately, but who could come together to mourn their father, was quoted by President Clinton at the funeral of Israeli Prime Minister Yitzhak Rabin in 1997, in the presence of King Hussein of Jordan and representatives of the Palestinian people alongside Israelis. This text, often overlooked by Jewish commentators, may well found the basis for a new look at the role of Ishmael.

37. Bereshit Rabba 53.11.
38. Genesis 17.18–20.
39. Bereshit Rabba 45.9.
40. One of the most commonly quoted Midrashim in this context is Bereshit Rabba 63.10: '"And the boys grew ..." [Genesis 25.27]. R. Phinehas said in R. Levi's name: "They were like a myrtle and a wild rose-bush growing side by side; when they attained to maturity, one yielded its fragrance and the other its thorns. So for thirteen years both went to school and came home from school. After this age, one went to the house of study and the other to idolatrous shrines."'
41. Genesis 22.13 and 21.19.
42. *Bava Batra* 16b.

Another would be the Midrash on the *Aqeda* where between each of God's commands, Abraham inserts an objection, rather in the vein of their encounter at Sodom.

> God said: Take your son.
> I have two sons!
> Your only one.
> Each is the only one of his mother!
> Whom you love.
> I love them both!
> Isaac![43]

Here, it becomes clear that Abraham loved both his sons and regarded them as equal; and in the same spirit, the Israeli poet Shin Shalom wrote the following:[44]

> Ishmael my brother,
> How long shall we fight each other?
> My brother from times bygone,
> My brother – Hagar's son,
> My brother, the wandering one.
> One angel was sent to us both,
> One angel watched over our growth –
> There in the wilderness, death threatening through thirst,
> I a sacrifice on the altar, Sarah's first.
> Ishmael my brother, hear my plea:
> It was the angel who tied thee to me ...
> Time is running out, put hatred to sleep,
> Shoulder to shoulder, let's water our sheep.[45]

43. Sanhedrin 89b.
44. Shalom Joseph Shapiro (b. 1904).
45. J. Magonet and L. Blue (eds.), *Forms of Prayer* (London: RSGB, 1985), III, p. 891.

Abraham from a Christian Perspective

Paul Joyce

Abraham in the New Testament

Although the book of Genesis, as part of the Christian Bible, has down the centuries exercised its own direct influence upon Christianity, it has been above all through the mediation of the Abraham tradition by the New Testament that it has had its distinctive theological impact. The major themes that emerge in the New Testament treatment of Abraham (particularly as expressed by Paul) are faith, universalism and covenant. These form a cluster of interrelated motifs, which together represent an important means by which early Christianity expressed its identity. These themes potentially represent a positive resource for inter-religious dialogue but, as we shall see, they can also be problematic, especially in relation to Judaism.

The themes of faith, universalism and covenant need to be illustrated in some detail. Paul was probably the earliest of the New Testament writers and had the task of articulating for the first time the meaning of Christianity in relation to its Jewish background. For Paul, Abraham became a central point of reference in this task, serving as a representative and embodiment of faith and trust in God, prior to the giving of the law to Moses. He was at pains to emphasize that Abraham's relationship with God was one in which he received blessing and promise without earning them by his own actions. The fourth chapter of the letter to the Romans develops this theme. In Romans 4.2–3, we read: 'For if Abraham was justified by works, he has something to boast about, but not before God. For what does the scripture say? "Abraham believed God, and it was reckoned to him as righteousness."'[1] The setting of Paul's work is one in which he was arguing with his fellow Jews that for the follower of Jesus what matters is faith rather than obedience to the law. In the same chapter, Paul related this theme to that of circumcision, making the point that Abraham was reckoned righteous by God before circumcision was introduced, as recounted in Genesis 17:

1. Citing Genesis 15.6.

> How then was [righteousness] reckoned to [Abraham]? Was it before or after he had been circumcised? It was not after, but before he was circumcised. He received the sign of circumcision as a seal of the righteousness that he had by faith while he was still uncircumcised. The purpose was to make him the ancestor of all who believe without being circumcised and who thus have righteousness reckoned to them.[2]

The second major theme is that of universalism, by which is here meant the notion that salvation is for all humankind and not Jews alone, another central concern for Paul. Romans 4.16–17 refers to the promise being guaranteed to all the descendants of Abraham, 'not only to the adherents of the law but also to those who share the faith of Abraham (for he is the father of all of us, as it is written, "I have made you the father of many nations")'.[3] Paul wrote in similar vein in Romans 9: 'not all Israelites truly belong to Israel, and not all of Abraham's children are his true descendants; but "It is through Isaac that descendants shall be named for you." This means that it is not the children of the flesh who are the children of God, but the children of the promise are counted as descendants.'[4]

In the letter to the Galatians, we encounter the same themes of faith and universalism. Chapter 4 presents a striking allegory about Abraham's two sons, born of two women, polemically contrasting the followers of Jesus (represented by Isaac) and Paul's Jewish opponents (represented by Ishmael). Ishmael is born of the slave Hagar, from Mount Sinai (which corresponds to the present Jerusalem), whereas Isaac is born of the free woman Sarah, who corresponds to the heavenly Jerusalem.[5] The previous chapter argues that those who believe – explicitly including all gentiles – are the descendants of Abraham by virtue of their faith.[6] And at the end of that chapter, we find a famous text that expresses this theme of universalism in classic form: 'There is no longer Jew or Greek, there is no longer slave or free, there is no longer male and female; for all of you are one in Christ Jesus. And if you belong to Christ, then you are Abraham's offspring, heirs according to the promise.'[7]

Paul's third main theme in connection with Abraham, that of covenant (frequently expressed in terms of promise), comes out most clearly in this same chapter: 'My point is this: the law, which came four hundred and thirty years later, does not annul a covenant previously ratified by God, so as to nullify the promise. For if the inheritance comes from the law, it no longer comes from the promise; but God granted it to Abraham through the promise.'[8] Paul thus exploited the theme of a pre-Sinai covenant that antedates the giving of the law.

2. Romans 4.10–11.
3. Citing Genesis 17.5.
4. Romans 9.6–8, citing Genesis 21.12.
5. Galatians 4.22–26.
6. Galatians 3.7–8.
7. Galatians 3.28–29.
8. Galatians 3.17–18.

The gospels, broadly speaking, feature the same central themes in relation to Abraham. A recurrent question in the gospels is that of who is a true child of Abraham. In Luke 19, the concern is with how a Jew might live up to their descent from Abraham. Jesus says of Zacchaeus, 'Today salvation has come to this house, because he too is a son of Abraham';[9] Zacchaeus has, it seems, been reintegrated into the people of God. Elsewhere, John the Baptist is presented, more polemically, as challenging the people in the words: 'Do not presume to say to yourselves, "We have Abraham as our ancestor"; for I tell you, God is able from these stones to raise up children to Abraham.'[10] The related theme that gentiles have access to salvation is expressed elsewhere in the gospels. In Matthew, Jesus says of the centurion: 'Truly I tell you, in no one in Israel have I found such faith. I tell you, many will come from east and west and will eat with Abraham and Isaac and Jacob in the kingdom of heaven.'[11]

Within John's Gospel, chapter 8 is dominated by the figure of Abraham. Here we find the familiar theme of true sonship of Abraham as a matter of being in right relation with God rather than just a matter of physical descent, and here again the polemical edge is evident, probably reflecting acrimonious relations between church and synagogue late in the first century CE. We read that Jesus' audience says to him, 'We are descendants of Abraham and have never been slaves to anyone. What do you mean by saying, "You will be made free"?' The passage continues: 'I know that you are descendants of Abraham; yet you look for an opportunity to kill me.' The answer comes back, 'Abraham is our father', and then Jesus says to them, 'If you were Abraham's children, you would be doing what Abraham did, but now you are trying to kill me, a man who has told you the truth that I heard from God. This is not what Abraham did.' And again, 'You are from your father the devil, and you choose to do your father's desires.'[12]

The covenant theme features in a number of the references to Abraham in the Acts of the Apostles. In Acts 3.25, Peter is presented as saying to the people in the temple at Jerusalem: 'You are the descendants of the prophets and of the covenant that God gave to your ancestors, saying to Abraham, "And in your descendants all the families of the earth shall be blessed."'[13] In Stephen's review of the history of Israel in Acts 7, we hear that Abraham is 'our ancestor', to whom both the land and the 'covenant of circumcision' were given.[14]

Turning now to the remainder of the New Testament, the letter to the Hebrews is particularly important when considering Abraham, and here too the now familiar themes emerge. In chapter 6, for example, Abraham appears, with the motifs of faith and promise highlighted: 'so that you may not become

9. Luke 19.9.
10. Matthew 3.9; cf. Luke 3.8.
11. Matthew 8.10–11; cf. Luke 13.29.
12. John 8.33, 37, 39–40 and 44.
13. Citing Genesis 22.18.
14. Acts 7.2–3 and 8.

sluggish, but imitators of those who through faith and patience inherit the promises ... And thus Abraham, having patiently endured, obtained the promise.'[15] The theme of faith is highlighted strongly in Hebrews 11, in which Abraham is presented as a model of obedient faith: 'By faith Abraham, when put to the test, offered up Isaac. He who had received the promises was ready to offer up his only son, of whom he had been told, "It is through Isaac that descendants shall be named for you."'[16]

The letter of James takes a contrary line on faith and works when compared with most of the rest of the New Testament, James being concerned to emphasize that faith alone is not enough; it has to be demonstrated in action. James writes:

> Was not our ancestor Abraham justified by works when he offered his son Isaac on the altar? ... Thus the scripture was fulfilled that says, 'Abraham believed God, and it was reckoned to him as righteousness,' and he was called the friend of God. You see that a person is justified by works and not by faith alone.[17]

Ironically, James is here perhaps closer than Paul to the actual concerns of the Genesis narratives, which do seem to understand Abraham as acting virtuously. Also of interest here is that Abraham is presented as the friend of God,[18] a theme much emphasized in Islam.[19]

The importance of the interrelated motifs of faith, universalism and covenant has been highlighted. A further theme linked with Abraham in the New Testament is that of resurrection. Surprisingly often and in a variety of ways, resurrection and Abraham occur together in the New Testament, to a degree that seems more significant than can be accounted for by the general assumption of resurrection hope that pervades the New Testament. In Romans 4, reference is made to those who share the faith of Abraham 'in the presence of the God in whom [Abraham] believed, who gives life to the dead and calls into existence the things that do not exist'.[20] In Mark 12.26–27 (interestingly the only reference to Abraham in Mark), we read: 'And as for the dead being raised, have you not read in the book of Moses, in the story about the bush, how God said to him, "I am the God of Abraham, the God of Isaac, and the God of Jacob"? He is God not of the dead, but of the living.'[21] In Luke's parable of the rich man and Lazarus, the rich man says to the patriarch in the afterlife: 'No, father Abraham; but if someone goes to them from the dead, they will repent.' Abraham

15. Hebrews 6.12–15.
16. Hebrews 11.17–18, citing Genesis 21.12.
17. James 2.21–24, citing Genesis 15.6.
18. As in Isaiah 41.8 and 2 Chronicles 20.7.
19. For a useful popular reflection on the figure of Abraham within Christianity and Islam, see J. Kaltner, 'Abraham's Sons: How the Bible and Qur'an See the Same Story Differently', *Bible Review* 18.2 (2002), pp. 16–23 and 45–46.
20. Romans 4.17.
21. Cf. Matthew 22.31–32 and Luke 20.37–38.

responds: 'If they do not listen to Moses and the prophets, neither will they be convinced even if someone rises from the dead.'[22] Throughout the same passage, Abraham figures centrally (presumably because he is the archetypal faithful man of God), for while the poor man dies and joins Abraham in heaven, the rich man calls out to Abraham from Hades, begging him to relieve his agony.[23] In the letter to the Hebrews too, Abraham is linked with the theme of resurrection: '[Abraham] considered the fact that God is able even to raise someone from the dead – and figuratively speaking, he did receive him back.'[24]

Before leaving the New Testament, we should note two other uses of the Abraham tradition in the letter to the Hebrews. Chapter 7 has six references to Abraham, focusing particularly upon the encounter between the patriarch and Melchizedek in Genesis 14. The main point of the passage is that Melchizedek, a type or anticipation of Jesus, is greater than Abraham or his descendant Levi, of whom the priestly line came. This is unusual in that Jesus is more generally in the New Testament aligned with Abraham over against Moses, whereas here, Abraham (as well as Moses, who was descended from Levi) is subordinated to Melchizedek, the mysterious antecedent of Christ. Finally, Abraham is presented as a model of hospitality in Hebrews 13: 'Do not neglect to show hospitality to strangers, for by doing that some have entertained angels without knowing it.'[25] The allusion is to his entertaining three mysterious figures at Mamre.[26]

Abraham in Later Christian Tradition

We shall return to consider the implications of the New Testament legacy, but before that, let us review briskly some features of Abraham in later Christian tradition. Not surprisingly, the main New Testament themes remained dominant in the patristic period of Christianity, with newer motifs also developed alongside older ones.[27] Fathers such as Clement of Rome, Ambrose and Augustine exalted Abraham's obedience in leaving his homeland, while his willingness to sacrifice his son Isaac in Genesis 22 provided them with a model of perfect obedience to the will of God. It is interesting and characteristic that the Fathers should have developed Abraham as a model of virtue, notwithstanding Paul's influential emphasis on faith; with this may be compared the way in which Gregory the Great made Job above all a moral exemplar. The sacrifice of Isaac was taken to prefigure the death of Christ, and many writers, for example Tertullian,

22. Luke 16.30–31.
23. Luke 16.22–24.
24. Hebrews 11.19.
25. Hebrews 13.2.
26. Genesis 18.
27. See M. Sheridan (ed.), *Genesis 12–50* (Ancient Christian Commentary on Scripture, Old Testament, 2; Downers Grove, IL: InterVarsity Press, 2002).

Origen and Cyril of Alexandria, elaborated on the similarities. Parallel to Christian reflection on Genesis 22, there is a Jewish tradition of lively speculation upon this so-called 'binding' of Isaac. Of possible relevance to the shaping of Christian theology is that some scholars have entertained the possibility that Jewish thinking about the sacrifice of Isaac influenced the Christian development of the theology of the cross, though more have thought it probable that any influence runs the other way. Of course, it is also likely that there was a good deal of independent reflection upon these themes within the two traditions.[28]

The Fathers highlighted other features too. For example, they were interested, positively, in the dating of Abraham (to prove the superior antiquity of Christianity compared with pagan religions) and, negatively, in his multiple marriages (to warn against polygamy). They also made much of the divine appearance to Abraham at Mamre, under the guise of three men; not surprisingly, this was taken as a premonition of the divine Trinity. Indeed, Christian reflection on this passage as a model of the Trinity has played a significant part down the centuries, not least in that great icon of the eastern tradition, *The Holy Trinity*, by Andrei Rublev (c. 1370–1430). This justly famous icon, now in Moscow's Tretyakov Gallery, shows the three angels who appeared to Abraham as a portent of the Trinity of Father, Son and Holy Spirit.

Abraham has an important place in Christian liturgy. For example, from Anglican morning prayer, in the words of the 1662 *Book of Common Prayer*, the Benedictus proclaims God's saving action:

> To perform the mercy promised to our forefathers: and to remember his holy Covenant; To perform the oath which he sware to our forefather Abraham: that he would give us; That we being delivered out of the hands of our enemies: might serve him without fear; In holiness and righteousness before him: all the days of our life.[29]

And within evening prayer, the Magnificat declares: 'He remembering his mercy hath holpen his servant Israel: as he promised to our forefathers, Abraham and his seed for ever.'[30] In the Roman Catholic tradition, both in the canon of the mass and in the sequence 'Lauda Sion', the sacrifice of Isaac in Genesis 22 is described as prefiguring the eucharist. In the modern Roman Catholic mass, the first eucharistic prayer calls on God to 'Look with favour on these offerings and accept them as once you accepted the gifts of your servant Abel, the sacrifice of Abraham, our father in faith, and the bread and wine offered by your priest Melchisedech.'[31]

28. See further E. Kessler, *Bound by the Bible: Jews, Christians and the Sacrifice of Isaac* (Cambridge: Cambridge University Press, 2004). More generally, there has been a growing recognition that the relationship between Judaism and Christianity over the centuries has been one of complex interaction, involving influence in both directions. See, for example, M. Hilton, *The Christian Effect on Jewish Life* (London: SCM Press, 1994).

29. From Luke 1.72–75.

30. From Luke 1.54–55.

31. *The Sunday Missal: A New Edition* (London: HarperCollins, 1984), p. 42.

Abraham has remained part of the life-blood of literature too, albeit sometimes in a vestigial and confused way, as in Shakespeare's *Henry V*,[32] where the Hostess declares that the lately dead Falstaff is not in hell, but rather 'in Arthur's bosom', which echoes 'Abraham's bosom', the phrase used to denote the heavenly resting place of Lazarus in the Lukan parable of the rich man and Lazarus.[33]

In the modern period, Christian reading of the Bible, at least in some circles, has been significantly influenced by the historical-critical approach to the Bible. The Abraham narratives have been subjected to much critical study. In this context, it is typical to ask about the original meaning of biblical material. The question naturally arises as to whether Paul (who has so shaped Christian perceptions) manipulated and even distorted the Abraham story. It was noted above that in his use of Genesis 15, Paul was keen to interpret 'reckoned as righteousness' in verse 6 to mean that Abraham had in fact not earned merit but rather had merit attributed to him. However, a plain reading of Genesis 15 would seem to suggest that the original does indeed view Abraham as having acted in a virtuous way, and to this extent one might describe Paul's use of the passage as a distortion (we earlier suggested that the letter of James might be closer to the original meaning of Genesis here). Should we on these grounds (of apparent deviation from original meaning) disown such a use as Paul's? While in the past some historical critics would have described Paul's interpretation as a serious misunderstanding, many scholars are now more ready to see Paul's handling of scripture as a legitimate re-reading in his own context. It is important to ask in such a case what interpretative interest is being served: if the quest were for the original meaning of Genesis 15.6 (the typical preoccupation of most historical critics of Genesis), the criteria to be applied might well be different from those relevant to an assessment of Paul's theological use of the passage in his attempt to articulate his understanding of the Christian gospel. We shall return later to the issue of Paul's handling of scripture.

Although many assume that the historical-critical approach is a value-free secular phenomenon, it was pioneered and long remained dominated by German Protestant Christians. Indeed, what many Christians have perceived as a neutral academic approach is regarded as distinctively Christian by many Jews. This is well illustrated in Chaim Potok's novel *In the Beginning*,[34] in which reference is made to Julius Wellhausen's documentary analysis of the Pentateuch as a destructive work wrought upon the Jewish scriptures by Christians.[35] Turning specifically to the historical-critical study of Abraham, one might argue that the emphasis on the gracious nature of the covenant granted to

32. II.3.9–10.

33. Luke 16.22–23.

34. C. Potok, *In the Beginning* (London: Heinemann, 1976).

35. J. Wellhausen, *Prolegomena zur Geschichte Israels* (Berlin: G. Reimer, 1883), translated as *Prolegomena to the History of Israel* (trans. J.S. Black and A. Menzies; Edinburgh: A. & C. Black, 1885).

Abraham is a fair reflection of the biblical text of Genesis,[36] but it is also undeniably reminiscent of Paul's characterization of Abraham as the model of faith in the era before the giving of the law. Could it be that under the guise of disinterested academic study, some Christian historical critics in fact invest Abraham with elements of their own theological tradition?

The story of Abraham has continued to be a rich source of Christian theological reflection, figuring centrally, for example, in the work *Fear and Trembling*, by the nineteenth-century Danish thinker Søren Kierkegaard.[37] Kierkegaard took the story of the sacrifice of Isaac in Genesis 22 and made it the vehicle for extended reflections upon the human condition and ultimate truth. Abraham is portrayed as a great man, who chose to sacrifice his son in the face of conflicting expectations and in defiance of any conceivable ethical standard. This challenged the dominant view of Hegel's universal moral system: for Kierkegaard, the suffering individual must alone make a choice 'on the strength of the absurd'. This work has played a key role in the background to twentieth-century existentialist philosophy. It is also of interest in the history of biblical interpretation: Kierkegaard used the story of Genesis 22 with extraordinary freedom and yet nevertheless remained remarkably faithful to it. Jolita Pons has recently written of Kierkegaard's multiple retellings of the story of Abraham in *Fear and Trembling* as profound interpretation in the 'subjunctive mood' (picking up Kierkegaard's own fascination with the notion of the subjunctive): what might have happened, how characters might have responded.[38] We might here see Kierkegaard as anticipating later developments in biblical interpretation in which readers have felt the freedom to explore possibilities within narratives. Such trends in the late twentieth century and early twenty-first owe much to secular literary studies in English, French and other modern languages, but also stand in some continuity with important Jewish traditions of reading, including the tradition of Midrash.

The social anthropologist Carol Delaney has written powerfully about the social legacy of biblical myth, focusing upon the narrative of Genesis 22 and considering its reception and influence in Judaism, Christianity and Islam. She argues that the pervasive ideal of the willingness to sacrifice one's own children is one that has had a pernicious effect on all three traditions and indeed on the modern secular world.[39] Feminist biblical criticism has focused a good deal on the patriarchal narratives, with Sarah and Hagar featuring prominently.[40] Given that feminist criticism has done so much to highlight the 'patriarchy' both

36. See for example R.E. Clements, *Abraham and David: Genesis XV and its Meaning for Israelite Tradition* (Studies in Biblical Theology, 2nd series, 5; London: SCM Press, 1967).

37. S. Kierkegaard, *Fear and Trembling* (London: Penguin, 1985).

38. J. Pons, *Stealing a Gift: Kierkegaard's Pseudonyms and the Bible* (Perspectives in Continental Philosophy, 3; New York: Fordham University Press, 2004).

39. C. Delaney, *Abraham on Trial: The Social Legacy of Biblical Myth* (Princeton, NJ: Princeton University Press, 1998).

40. P. Trible, *Texts of Terror: Literary-Feminist Readings of Biblical Narratives* (Overtures to Biblical Theology, 13; Philadelphia, PA: Fortress Press, 1984); cf. T.J. Dennis, *Sarah Laughed: Women's Voices in the Old Testament* (London: SPCK, 1994).

of biblical societies and our own, it is perhaps not surprising to be reminded that the New Testament presents the wife of the archetypal patriarch, Abraham, as the model of subservient wifely obedience:

> Wives, in the same way, accept the authority of your husbands, so that, even if some of them do not obey the word, they may be won over without a word by their wives' conduct ... It was in this way long ago that the holy women who hoped in God used to adorn themselves by accepting the authority of their husbands. Thus Sarah obeyed Abraham and called him lord. You have become her daughters as long as you do what is good and never let fears alarm you.[41]

Among those who have reflected recently on the role of Abraham within the Christian Bible is Walter Moberly, who is critical of the legacy of the historical-critical approach and seeks to give greater weight to literary and, more especially, theological concerns.[42] Moberly takes as his particular focus of reflection the profound narrative of Genesis 22. Although he gives attention to both Jewish and Muslim treatments of this passage, he is straightforward about the distinctively Christian approach he adopts. He sees as the central theme of the story an emphasis not unfamiliar to other traditions, namely 'fear of God' (understood as trusting openness and responsiveness to God that is ready to relinquish everything); but he also sets the passage within its context in the Christian Bible as a whole and within the constructive tasks of Christian theology. He writes, for example, that 'Attention to the narrative portrayal of the nature and development of the "love" between God and Abraham in Genesis 22, and between Father and Son within Matthew's Gospel, is therefore an element in the continuing task of articulating a trinitarian understanding of God and humanity.'[43]

Abraham and Inter-religious Dialogue

In modern times, Abraham has been highlighted very much as a symbol of inter-faith unity, as the father in faith of Jews, Christians and Muslims. The figure of Abraham is indeed one revered by all three traditions. Reference is often made to 'the children of Abraham' and to 'the Abrahamic faiths'. In various attempts to secure a Middle Eastern peace settlement in the late twentieth century and even in the context of the Western Alliance's campaign against Al-Qaeda after 2001, rhetorical reference to this shared heritage has had a place.

It was hinted earlier that the primary New Testament themes in connection with Abraham (faith, universalism and covenant) might potentially represent a positive resource for inter-religious dialogue. The emphasis on salvation

41. 1 Peter 3.1 and 5–6.
42. R.W.L. Moberly, *The Bible, Theology and Faith: A Study of Abraham and Jesus* (Cambridge Studies in Christian Doctrine; Cambridge: Cambridge University Press, 2000).
43. Moberly, *Bible, Theology and Faith*, p. 237.

being a matter of faith (all are accepted, without the need to earn acceptance), the stress on universalism (all are included in the purposes of God) and the notion of a covenant that includes all humankind: these are indeed themes that might reasonably be thought to have the potential to contribute to a positive interfaith solidarity between Jews, Christians and Muslims, and that might, moreover, even beyond these three traditions, provide resources for humanity as a whole.

However, uncritical optimism is inappropriate. Rhetorical appeal to a shared tradition is not always immune from the charge of manipulation and exploitation. In the context of international relations and especially the waging of war, such rhetoric should certainly be viewed with wary scepticism. Also it should be remembered that an emphasis on Abraham as father of Jews, Christians and Muslims alike, while it may be a powerfully inclusive motif, may also exclude other faith communities, for example adherents of Hinduism or Buddhism. Moreover, it is important to remember that the Abraham themes that Paul made so central for Christianity were forged in the polemical struggle of early Christianity to define itself. They are profoundly and inescapably christocentric, born of the era of the parting of the ways between nascent Christianity and emergent rabbinic Judaism. Moberly's readiness, in his study of Abraham and Jesus, to be entirely open about the fact that he is concerned with constructive Christian theology as well as with historical exegesis is a welcome sign of the times. However, especially after the Shoah or Holocaust of the twentieth century, all Christian theologians should be sensitive to the charge that the appropriation of the Jewish scriptures by the Church and the supersessionist reading of them to serve Christian theological ends is potentially problematic and indeed (to put the point more strongly) may not be completely unrelated to attempts to exclude the Jewish 'other' in more practical ways, even indeed genocide. These issues pose a major ongoing challenge for Christian theologians.[44]

The Abraham tradition may indeed hold treasures that can serve the quest for genuine inter-religious dialogue, but it offers no short-cuts and no easy answers. Only through a sober and self-critical sifting of these resources will Christians prove fit partners for a realistic dialogue with adherents of the other Abrahamic religions.

44. Among recent creative attempts to take up this challenge may be noted J.D. Dawson, *Christian Figural Reading and the Fashioning of Identity* (Berkeley, CA and London: University of California Press, 2002).

Abraham from a Muslim Perspective

Tim Winter

Abraham in Muslim Scripture

The Qur'ānic recasting of Bible stories reveals much about its author's expectations of Muslim readers. The evolving doctrine of *ʿiṣma*, prophetic infallibility, took its cue from the noticeable (to Bible readers) intensification of the ethical and exemplary qualities of the prophets and patriarchs. In the new telling, the Hebrew ancestors are still living, breathing creatures, worthy forerunners of the Final Prophet; but have been stripped of the sins which supply, in the eyes of many, much of the richness and moral ambiguity of the Bible stories. Lot, now, does not sleep with his daughters; David does not seduce Bathsheba; Solomon does not incline towards foreign gods. The stories are told not to illustrate God's providence towards Israel, but rather to personify virtues which Muslim believers are urged to adopt. Thus Moses is God's 'interlocutor' (*kalīmu'Llāh*); Jesus is God's 'spirit' (*rūḥu'Llāh*); and Noah is the 'one saved by God' (*najiyyu'Llāh*). Their lives are abbreviated and turned into homilies, allowing later tradition to identify particular virtues or spiritual orientations with various prophetic archetypes.

This is hagiology, but it is still salvation history, rooted in an ambitious optimism about God's desire to perfect God's servants in the context of their earthly careers. The ideal types are infallible, but they enter entirely into our humanity: they marry, beget children, take up arms, experience intense vulnerability and know the complexity of human relationships. The proliferation of earthly but perfected individuals in scripture brings readers the joyful knowledge of the accessibility, diversity and power of grace.

Abraham's story is characteristic of this Qur'ānic intention. He is the archetype of the Muslim *par excellence*, not only in his ties to Mecca and his fatherhood of Ishmael, but in the Muhammadan anticipations of exile from an idolatrous city, desert wanderings, angelic experiences, and paternity to a blessed, privileged line: in the Prophet's case, the *ahl al-bayt*, the People of the House who have some, always disputed, share in God's gift of protection from sin and from final frustration. There is, as the Qur'ān states, 'an excellent example for you in Abraham and those who followed him'.[1]

The pagan Arabs, sure of their Abrahamic ancestry, were introduced to Qur'ānic monotheism through stories such as the narrative of the youthful Abraham who contemplated the unchanging bodies of heaven, and was moved to search for God. The Qur'ān had urged the heathen Quraysh to consider the marvellous signs of God's creation:

> The sun and the moon are made punctual,
> The stars and the trees are prostrate to Him …
> Which, then, of your Lord's blessings would you deny?[2]

In a passage rich with haggadic resonances,[3] traditionally dated to the Meccan period, the Qur'ān recounts the boyhood confusion of Abraham. The Harranian cult of the stars probably recalled aspects of Meccan paganism:

> Thus did We show Abraham the kingdom of the heavens and the earth, that he might be of those who possess certainty.
>
> When the night grew dark upon him he saw a star. He said: 'This is my Lord!' But when it set, he said: 'I love not things that set.'
>
> And when he saw the moon rising in splendour, he said: 'This is my Lord.' But when it set, he said, 'Unless my Lord guide me, I surely shall join the ones who are astray.'
>
> And when he saw the sun rising in splendour, he cried: 'This is my Lord! This is greater!' And when it set he exclaimed: 'O my people, I am free from all that you associate with Him.
>
> Assuredly I have turned my face toward Him who created the heavens and the earth, as one by nature upright, and I am not of the polytheists.'[4]

At the end of the sequence, which broadens to name many of the great prophetic figures of its vision of history, the Qur'ān's audience is told: 'Those are they whom God guided; so take their guidance as your model.'[5]

'One by nature upright', in Arabic *ḥanīf*, denotes a non-Jewish, non-Christian monotheist.[6] Abraham, who was 'neither Jew nor Christian',[7] is the archetype

1. Qur'ān 60.4. For a mediaeval list of parallels between Abraham and Muhammad, see Ismāʿīl ibn Kathīr, *Dalā'il al-nubuwwa* (Beirut and Cairo: Dār al-Kitāb al-Lubnānī, AH 1420/ 1999), pp. 509–24.
2. Qur'ān 55.5–13.
3. L. Ginzberg, *The Legends of the Jews* (Philadelphia, PA: Jewish Publication Society of America, 1913), I, p. 189, and V, p. 210. Some such Midrashim are late, and themselves seem to originate in the Qur'ānic text (Ginzberg, *Legends*, V, pp. 212–13).
4. Qur'ān 6.75–79.
5. Qur'ān 6.90.
6. U. Rubin, 'Ḥanīfiyya and Kaʿba: An Inquiry into the Arabian Pre-Islamic Background of the *dīn Ibrāhīm*', *Jerusalem Studies in Arabic and Islam* 13 (1990), pp. 85–112; N.A. Faris and H.W. Glidden, 'The Development of the Meaning of the Koranic Ḥanīf', *Journal of the Palestine Oriental Society* 19 (1939), pp. 1–13.
7. Qur'ān 3.67.

of Muhammad, who is told, 'Set your face for religion as a *ḥanīf*; this is the original disposition [*fiṭra*] of God, by which He has created humanity. There is no altering God's creation; that is the right religion, but most of the people do not know.'[8] True, primordial religion is thus unpolluted by schism and egotistic dispute,[9] which are the consequences of a wilful falling away from simple monotheistic values until 'corruption appears on land and sea'.[10] Islam thus vaunts itself as a return to *fiṭra*, to a prelapsarian virtue, and much of its self-perception is framed as a human repentance from the errors which divided Jews and Christians, and also the Arabs, descendants of Ishmael who, as idolators, had descended still more grievously into factionalism and error. The Qur'ān's Abraham, then, is a reproach to every religious category with which it is concerned, and an almost proleptic anticipation of the *ḥanīfiyya*, the simple monotheism, to be announced by the Ishmaelite prophet. As a *hadīth* puts it: 'I created My servants as Muslim *ḥanīfs* [*ḥunafā' muslimīn*]; but then demons came unto them, and dragged them from their religion, forbidding that which I had made lawful, and commanding them to worship that for which I had revealed no authority.'[11]

The Jewish error was to over-elaborate the law,[12] while that of the Christians was to worship the Messiah as an incarnated logos. Islam, by implication, is to be a *via media* between exoteric and esoteric, and this is the virtue associated with Abraham the *ḥanīf*.

The Meccan Arab who wished to repent in this way frequently clashed with his or her family; and the Qur'ān tells how Abraham argued with his people,[13] and particularly with his father, who in Muslim tradition, as in the oral Torah, was a maker of idols.[14] His most ingenious argument turns out to be his undoing:

> 'By God, I will play a trick upon your idols after you have gone away and when your backs are turned.'
>
> Then he broke them all into pieces, all except the large one, so that they might turn to it.
>
> [The pagans returned and] they said: 'Who has done this to our gods! Surely it was some evildoer!'
>
> They said: 'We have heard a youth speak of them; his name is Abraham.'

8. Qur'ān 30.30.
9. Qur'ān 30.32.
10. Qur'ān 30.41.
11. Muslim, Janna, 63.
12. Cf. n. 11 of my chapter 'Pluralism from a Muslim Perspective' in this volume.
13. Qur'ān 6.80–84; 19.42–48; and 21.51–57.
14. Ginzberg, *Legends*, I, p. 195; for the breaking incident, see I, p. 124. The Terah of Genesis is known to the Muslim exegetic tradition (Ismāʿīl ibn Kathīr, *Qiṣaṣ al-anbiyā'* [ed. Muṣṭafā ʿAbd al-Wāḥid; Cairo: Dār al-Kutub al-Ḥadītha, AH 1388/1968], I, p. 173), which is unsure whether the Qur'ānic Āzar (6.74) refers to his father or to his father's votary idol.

> They said: 'Then bring him before the eyes of the people, so that they may witness.'
> [When he came] they said: 'Is it you who has done this to our gods, O Abraham?'
> He said: 'Nay, this one, who is their chief, has done it; so ask them, if they can speak.' ...
> Then they were confounded, and said: 'O Abraham! You know that they do not speak.'
> He replied: 'Do you then worship, besides God, things that cannot profit you at all, nor harm you?'[15]

This returns us to the Prophet's argument against the idols around the Abrahamic shrine of the Kaʿba.

Like the Prophet, too, Abraham was persecuted: the story of Nimrod's furnace seems to prefigure the surrender of the will to God in the face of apparently certain destruction that awaits the lone defier of established religion. His experience of salvation by God in the midst of the furnace,[16] which could burn only his fetters,[17] teaches him that reliance upon God's commandments must take precedence over fallible human assessments, a lesson which readies him to make the right decision when ordered to sacrifice his son.

Abraham is also the archetype for angelic visitations to the Prophet: he was visited by warners who instructed him to leave the community of Lot;[18] and was given 'good tidings of a clement son'.[19] His Egyptian bondsmaid Hagar, given to him by Pharoah,[20] is an anticipation of the Egyptian Marya, given to the Prophet by the Coptic governor of Egypt.

Apparently next in chronological order comes the Binding.[21] This is recounted only once in the Qur'ān:

> And when he was of an age to walk with him, [Abraham] said: 'O my dear son, I have seen in a dream that I must sacrifice you; so look, what do you think?'
> He replied: 'My father, do as you are commanded. God willing, you will find me to be steadfast.'
> Then, when they had both surrendered unto God, and he had cast him down upon his face,
> We called unto him: 'Abraham!
> You have made the vision true. Thus do We reward the doers of good.'

15. Qur'ān 21.57–67.
16. Qur'ān 37.97–99.
17. W.M. Brinner (trans.), *The History of al-Ṭabarī (* Tārīkh al-rusul wa'l-mulūk*), Volume II: Prophets and Patriarchs* (Albany, NY: State University of New York Press, 1987), p. 61; Ibn Kathīr, *Qiṣaṣ*, I, p. 183.
18. Qur'ān 15.51–56 and 51.24–34. These are identified with Gabriel, Michael and Raphael; cf. Ibn Kathīr, *Qiṣaṣ*, I, p. 219, as in Ginzberg, *Legends*, I, p. 242, and V, p. 237.
19. Qur'ān 37.101.
20. Ṭabarī, 63. For some of the rabbis, she was Pharoah's daughter (Ginzberg, *Legends*, V, p. 231); this was too much for the Islamic tradition to assimilate.
21. For a substantial collection of mediaeval retellings, see Ṭabarī, 82–105; for modern reflections, see M. Talbi, 'La foi d'Abraham', *Islamochristiana* 8 (1982), pp. 1–11; and S. Bektovic, 'The Doubled Movement of Infinity in Kierkegaard and Sufism', *Islam and Christian-Muslim Relations* 10 (1999), pp. 325–27.

That was indeed a clear trial.
Then We ransomed him with a tremendous sacrifice.[22]

There are some obvious reasons why this incident is less important for Muslim commentary than for the traditions of Judaism and Christianity. It is not a sign of the superior destiny of one son. In fact, for at least two centuries after the Qur'ānic text was delivered, Islam was unsure which of the sons was the intended victim: so late a voice as Ṭabarī (d. 923) preferred Isaac,[23] and there is no strong reason why this would damage Ishmael's claim to prophetic and patriarchal status; Ishmael, after all, was also sentenced to a near-certain death by his expulsion into the wilderness as a child. Exploiting the story to give categoric preference to one son over the other was therefore not attempted.[24]

The commentaries, instead, moralize about prophetic submission (*islām*) to God. The binding episode encapsulates what Islam understood to be the utter appropriateness of its Abrahamic affiliation. The dominant school of Sunni theology, Ashʿarism, adopted a command ethic which denied that values might exist prior to God's commands. Infanticide is wrong because God forbids it; God does not forbid it because it is wrong.[25] Granted that the establishment of the 'prior' with relation to a timeless God raises its own complexities, this theology, which seeks to defend the utter independence and sovereignty of God, found in Abraham's abandonment of his own will an ideal of human behaviour. To question such an order, even one which seems to challenge the Qur'ān's own vehemence about pagan infanticide among the

22. Qur'ān 37.102–107.

23. Ṭabarī, 82. Cf. N. Calder, 'From Midrash to Scripture: The Sacrifice of Abraham in Early Islamic Tradition', *Le Muséon* 101 (1988), pp. 375–402 (375); and R. Firestone, 'Abraham's Son as the Intended Sacrifice (*al-Dhabīḥ*, Qur'ān 37:99–113): Issues in Qur'ānic Exegesis', *Journal of Semitic Studies* 34 (1989), pp. 95–132 (117).

24. Many redaction critics have concluded that the Ishmael material in Genesis originated as an Ishmaelite initiatory hero legend which later was assimilated into Israelite traditions. This would account for the high praise and quasi-martyr status of Ishmael and Hagar in the larger biblical narrative that is committed to the idea of the unique covenantal privilege of the heirs of Isaac. The prioritizing of Isaac may be dated to the late Elohist redaction phase. See H.C. White, 'The Initiation Legend of Ishmael', *Zeitschrift für die alttestamentliche Wissenschaft* 87 (1975), pp. 267–305. C. Westermann, *Genesis 12–36* (London: SPCK, 1985), p. 344, concludes that the promise of separate destinies to the sons is a late insertion.

25. The *ḥadīth* literature, however, suggests that the Prophet often adopted a more intuitionist view. See, for instance, the *ḥadīth* of Wābiṣa ibn Maʿbad: 'I came to God's Messenger (may God bless him and grant him peace), and he said: "You have come to ask about goodness and sin." "Yes," I replied. And he said: "Ask for a verdict [*fatwā*] from your heart. Goodness is what the soul and the heart find peace in, and sin is that which causes abrasion in the soul, and a hesitation in the breast; even if people have given you verdict after verdict"' (Ibn Ḥanbal, *Musnad*, cited in Ibn Rajab, *Jawāmiʿ al-ʿulūm wa'l-ḥikam* [ed. Wahba al-Zuḥaylī; Damascus: Dār al-Khayr, AH 1417/1996], II, p. 22).

Arabs,[26] would be idolatry itself, an exalting of the human will above that of God. Here Islam sets itself against what some might see as the Promethean self-glorification of Kant, and the subsequent tradition which holds Abraham culpable.[27] There is a stark absolutism here, which makes absolute love lead logically to absolute obedience:

> He who settles down in the domain of belief in One God,
> Becomes free of the bonds of wife and children.
> He turns away from all other than God,
> And he puts a knife to the throat of his son.[28]

'God tried Abraham with commands,' the Qur'ān states, 'and he fulfilled them.' God then says, 'I have appointed you an example [*imām*] for mankind', to which the patriarch replies: 'And of my offspring?' 'My covenant shall not include wrongdoers.'[29]

After recording this momentous but very conditional promise, the text turns to a description of the building of the Kaʿba by Abraham and Ishmael,[30] who offer up one of the most famous of all Qur'ānic prayers:

> Our Lord! And make us submissive unto Thee, and of our seed a nation submissive unto Thee, and show us our ways of worship, and relent towards us. Truly Thou, only Thou, art the Relenting, the Merciful.
>
> Our Lord! And raise up in their midst a messenger from among them who shall recite unto them Thy revelations, and shall instruct them in the Scripture and in wisdom, and shall purify them. Truly Thou, only Thou, art the Mighty, the Wise.
>
> And who forsaketh the religion of Abraham save him who befooleth himself? We chose him in the world, and truly in the Hereafter he shall be among the righteous.[31]

A distinctive feature of the Muslim Abraham, then, is that he has a destination. Lévinas hailed the patriarch as the Semite *par excellence*, the migrant from ontology to alterity, whose nomadism denies the aggressive Hellenic trap of final resolution and restoration of Self against Other, represented in the figure of Ulysses.[32] The Qur'ān's Abraham is more Mosaic, he is a migrant and not simply a nomad; but his migration is not to a city, but to a barren nowhere which enshrines the House of the Great Covenant, the earthly representation of the infinity of God. This migration is represented by the ḥajj, many of whose

26. Qur'ān 6.151 and 17.31.
27. G. Rabel, *Kant* (Oxford: Clarendon Press, 1963), pp. 334–35.
28. M. Iqbāl, *Asrār-i Khūdī*, translated as *Secrets of the Self: A Philosophical Poem* (trans. R.A. Nicholson; London: Macmillan, 1920), p. 42.
29. Qur'ān 2.124.
30. Qur'ān 2.127. Some pre-Islamic Jews also regarded the Kaʿba as the 'house of Abraham'; see Rubin, 'Ḥanīfiyya', p. 109.
31. Qur'ān 2.128–30; cf. 14.35–41.
32. Cited in C. Davis, *Levinas: An Introduction* (Cambridge: Polity, 1996), p. 33.

practices are seen as Abrahamic, and which takes place amid the pilgrim chant of *Labbayk*, 'Here I am!', surely an echo of Abraham's *hinneni*. The Muslim is indeed the nomad; but the eternally wandering Ishmaelite predicted by Genesis has a homeland in God, represented in the earthly temple at Mecca, where the pilgrim, like Ishmael, receives his initiation.[33] The covenant and promise, then, are for all the descendants of Abraham, who becomes exemplary in his own fulfilment of its demands, and in his experience of the miraculous divine protection which results. It is thus that he is *khalīlu'Llāh*, 'God's intimate', God's friend and protegé.

Abraham as Patriarch of Reconciliation

If such is the Qur'ān's Abraham, how comfortable should we be with the recently recommended category of 'the Abrahamic religions'? Kenneth Cragg is deeply suspicious of this, preferring the One God as our starting-place. Abraham, for him, has been too differently received by the three traditions:

> He is, for Judaism, the fount of the right 'seed,' the progenitor of the faithful by his free exile but only, also, by the proper lineage after him. For Islam he is the great iconoclast, the breaker of false gods and, only via Ishmael, the founder of the Ka'ba and the great Hanif who was 'neither Jew nor Christian.' The New Testament possesses him as having exemplified a 'faith-relationship' with God which antedated the Mosaic covenant and so could be a precedent for the grace that obviated Law.[34]

Cragg's depiction of Christianity and Judaism seems reductive; and his image of Islam is dangerously deficient. For Muslims, the Abrahamic category is a precious one precisely because the Qur'ān reveres *both* sons as heirs to covenant

33. Cf. White, 'Ishmael', p. 301: 'it is significant that the larger group of rituals which constitute the Hajj, when taken as a whole, form a rite of passage for the Moslem which embodies many features of the ritual initiation' (of Ishmael, in the pre-Elohist material embedded in Genesis). Modern geographers of the Pentateuch seem to have identified an important ancient cult-centre to the south of Beersheva, associated with Hagar and Ishmael, and also with the Elijah legend of 1 Kings 19.1–18. It may be significant that the Meccan sanctuary is associated not only with Ishmael, but with Elijah (Ilyās), in a number of *hadīths*; see U. Rubin, *Between Bible and Qur'ān: The Children of Israel and the Islamic Self-Image* (Princeton, NJ: Darwin Press, 1999), p. 41.

34. A.K. Cragg, 'Isma'il al-Faruqi in the Field of Dialogue', in Y.Y. Haddad and W.Z. Haddad (eds.), *Christian-Muslim Encounters* (Gainesville, FL: University Press of Florida, 1995), pp. 399–410 (401). The sequencing of religions here is typically Craggian. Ishmael is not necessarily a negative type for the rabbis; see for instance B. Lewis, 'An Apocalyptic Vision of Islamic History', *Bulletin of the School of Oriental and African Studies* 13.2 (1950), pp. 308–38 (321), for an early Abbasid rabbinical vision in which an angel describes the Kingdom of Ishmael (Islam) as a deliverance from the wickedness of Edom.

and promise.[35] 'We make no distinction between any of His prophets.'[36] Isaac is the prophet and patriarch who begets the no-less-venerated Jacob, and then the entire Hebrew lineage which culminates (in Islam's view) in Jesus of Nazareth. Ishmael is ancestor of the Arabs, and thus of Muhammad. Jesus is Messiah because he 'seals' and vindicates the Jewish story, while Muhammad is the Final Prophet (*al-ʿĀqib*) because he brings to a culmination the larger story of Abrahamic monotheism. While Jesus was sent to the Israelites,[37] as the Messiah figure whose mission was not to encompass gentiles,[38] Muhammad, son of the half-gentile Ishmael, is 'sent to all mankind', a theme which is taken up in a separate chapter in this collection.[39] As part of this universal, caliphal duty, the Ishmaelite is under the obligation to protect his younger brother. As an Ottoman patriot remarked a century ago in a lecture to the Cardiff Zionist Association, during a more hopeful era of Jewish–Muslim relations: 'As in ancient times the little boy Ishmael protected Isaac his younger brother, so to-day as one of the humble descendants of that elder brother I extend to you my hand. In return we only ask that you will repay that kindness by loyalty to us.'[40]

For Islam, then, the category of the 'Abrahamic' is a welcome one, because it is properly hospitable. For liberal Judaism, Jonathan Magonet is evidently comfortable with the term.[41] In Christianity, too, there are signs that Cragg's hesitations are not widely shared. In 1985, Pope John Paul II, addressing a vast crowd of young Muslims at a stadium in Casablanca, told them: 'Your God and ours is the same, and we are brothers and sisters in the faith of Abraham.'[42]

35. Genesis 17.10–11 and 23–26 note that Abraham and Ishmael were circumcised on the same day. For biblical hints in favour of an inclusive covenant, see R.W. Maqsood, *The Mysteries of Jesus: A Muslim Study of the Origins and Doctrines of the Christian Church* (Oxford: Sakina Books, 2000), pp. 160–61: for instance, the promise of the land 'from the river of Egypt to the river Euphrates' has only been fulfilled in Ishmael (for this, see Ibn Kathīr's treatment of the promise of the land: 'this is a glad prediction which relates to this [Islamic] community, for the promise has not been perfected by any community other than that of Muhammad' [Ibn Kathīr, *Qiṣaṣ*, I, p. 199]). But the eminent fulfilment of the promise in Ishmael does not exclude or even marginalize Isaac.

36. Qur'ān 2.285.

37. Qur'ān 61.6.

38. This forms part of Muslim polemic against Christian universalism; on occasion, Matthew 10.5 and 15.24 are also invoked; cf. G. Parrinder, *Jesus in the Qur'an* (London: Sheldon Press, 1965), pp. 39–40.

39. See my paper 'Muhammad from a Muslim Perspective', in which this *ḥadīth* is discussed.

40. A. Quilliam, 'Islam and Christian Conceptions of the Jew', *Crescent* 31 (1908), pp. 27–28 (27).

41. This is implicit throughout his *Talking to the Other: Jewish Interfaith Dialogue with Christians and Muslims* (London: I. B. Tauris, 2003); see, for instance, the prayer on p. 191.

42. Cited in J. van Lin, 'Mission and Dialogue: God and Jesus Christ', in G. Speelman, J. van Lin and D. Mulder (eds.), *Muslims and Christians in Europe: Breaking New Ground. Essays in Honour of Jan Slomp* (Kampen: Uitgeverij Kok, 1993), pp. 142–60 (153).

Abraham in Jewish, Christian and Muslim Thought

Norman Solomon, Richard Harries and Tim Winter

After surveying the multiple ways in which Abraham has been interpreted in the three traditions, it would be possible to ask, 'Will the real Abraham please stand up?' Assessment of Abraham, who is a foundational figure for all three religions, poses basic questions of scriptural interpretation and theological method. None of the essayists here would be happy with a purely 'reader-response' theory of interpretation, in which each reader is free to suggest his or her own meaning of a text. All three not only recognize a controlling authority in the texts, but also believe that those texts have a meaning in themselves, which we have a duty to elucidate. Nevertheless, it is also clear from these essays that the meaning and significance of Abraham has been sought in different contexts, and with different aims, resulting in an immense variety of ways in which he has been understood. Sometimes biblical texts have been interpreted polemically, in such a way as to divide one religion from another. Sometimes, however, their interpretation brings the religions together. One example of the latter, used by Sybil Sheridan and Tim Winter, is that for both Judaism and Islam, Abraham is first and foremost a believer in the one true God and therefore an opponent of all forms of idolatry. They both refer to a story, told slightly differently in the two traditions, of how Abraham looked beyond the created order, however beautiful, as exemplified by the sun and moon, for the true creator. This struggle against idolatry has been one of the crucial themes for both Judaism and Islam, and not only in their beginnings. An example of a rather different handling of Abraham, illustrated in Paul Joyce's paper, is the use of Abraham in Paul's letter to the Romans, where Paul argued that a right relationship to God depends entirely on faith and not on obedience to the commandments. It is an argument worked out in a specific, polemical context, against the Judaism of his time, as he perceived it.

The priority today, for members of the Oxford Abrahamic Group and for many others who share their concerns, is to find in Abraham the things that unite us, while not being dishonest about where the differences lie. In relation to this, Tim Winter ends on a hopeful note when he writes, 'For Islam, then, the category of the "Abrahamic" is a welcome one, because it is properly hospitable.'[1] He also quotes John Paul II addressing a large crowd of young Muslims in Casablanca in 1985 with the words, 'Your God and ours is the same, and we are brothers and sisters in the faith of Abraham.'

One context for the interpretation of Abraham has been the mainstream understanding of the religion in question. For Judaism, Abraham is the first Jew, prefiguring in many ways the story of Moses. Sybil Sheridan brings out the fact that if Moses is the central figure for Judaism, with Abraham prefiguring him in the Midrash in a number of ways, Abraham is no less important a figure in his own right and is associated with some of the defining qualities of Judaism. So 'Abraham is seen as the first Jew; Moses becomes the greatest Jew. Abraham is perceived *par excellence* as the man of faith; Moses sees God face to face.'[2] So it is that to this day, the convert to Judaism takes the patronym, the child of 'Abraham our father'. For Islam, Abraham is the first Muslim, the one who truly submits to God and whose story prefigures the defining aspects of the life of the Prophet Muhammad. So perhaps the important point is to be aware of these mainstream contexts, as well as one's own assumptions and purposes, not being frightened of allowing the two to interact in a mutual questioning.

Abraham plays an important role in the liturgy of Judaism, not just in the important festival of *Rosh Hashana*, but in the daily morning service. Within Christianity, Abraham is an important figure in the liturgy of both East and West: he occurs in the Benedictus and the Magnificat recited in the daily offices, in the canon of the Roman Catholic mass, and in the Orthodox liturgy of St. Basil the Great. Each of the five daily Muslim prayers concludes with an invocation of blessings upon Abraham. So obtaining more convergent theologies should shape the way people pray and believe in a very direct way.

The *Aqeda*, or binding of Isaac,[3] raises a number of issues. To begin with, Sybil Sheridan brings out the great variety of very different ways in which the story has been understood within Judaism. In the Middle Ages, for example, under the influence of Christian persecution, a cult of martyrdom developed, which saw Isaac as willing to do God's will in order that the divine name might be sanctified. He was actually killed and his ashes, gathered up and given to Sarah, later served as an atonement for Israel's sins, being placed on the head at times of national mourning. In the modern period, the story is more a pointer to the fact that conflicts are commonly experienced by a person of faith. Within Christianity, there is a strong and fairly consistent interpretation of the story as a prefigurement of the sacrifice of Christ, and the story is thereby linked to the eucharist. So, for example, in early Christian iconography, this is one of the scenes which is depicted on one side of the altar.

Then there is the ancient philosophical question, raised by Tim Winter in his paper, above, about whether something is right because God commands it or

1. Quotations from Tim Winter's paper, 'Abraham from a Muslim Perspective', above.
2. From Sybil Sheridan's paper, 'Abraham from a Jewish Perspective', above.
3. Genesis 22.1–18.

whether we judge God's commands to be ethical or unethical by a standard independent of that command. This dilemma is present in the Bible, as, for example, in Abraham's response to God's intention to destroy everyone in Sodom and Gomorrah completely, 'Shall not the Judge of all the earth do what is just?'[4] Tim Winter is quite clear that, from an Islamic point of view, it is God's commands that are definitive for our understanding of right and wrong. From a Christian point of view, this problem is focused in a more existential way in Kierkegaard and his teleological suspension of the ethical, the idea that the journey of faith may lead us into an awesome area where ordinary standards of right and wrong do not apply. However, for many people, there can be no suspension of the ethical even when the ethical is brought to bear on what is claimed to be a command of God.

There is also a wider context for Abrahamic interpretation today, which affects all three religions, and that is the crisis of religious faith experienced by many people: the sheer difficulty of believing in God in a world which seems to pose many questions about the possibility of such belief. Within this wider context, as well as the more specific one of keeping greater common ground between the three religions, we might be able to affirm at least two things.

First, Abraham is a person of faith, one who believes in the one true God. His faith is a tested faith, as Judaism brings out in its Midrash of ten tests. It is a surrendering, obedient faith, as Islam emphasizes. It involves going out into the unknown, as Hebrews 11 stresses, drawing on the story of how Abraham was exiled from his home country into unknown lands, a story also central to the Qur'ān.

Secondly, Abraham is a universal figure. God's call to Abraham declares, 'in you all the families of the earth shall be blessed'.[5] But in what way is this to come true? There has been a lively debate in Judaism, with some taking the view that a wider humanity is blessed through Judaism's offshoots of Christianity and Islam. For Christianity and Islam, the emphasis tends to be on those who are blessed by coming to have a faith like that of Abraham.

In Judaism, the covenant is with Abraham and his descendants. There is also a covenant with all creation and the whole of humanity, the Noahide covenant, a theme which is taken up in this book in the later section on pluralism. But it has always been an essential feature of Judaism that while there is no limit to God's mercy to the rest of humanity, God has called the Jewish people into a quite specific, binding relationship with God's self. This covenant is first made with Abraham and is passed on through his physical descendants.

This raises a question about the role of Ishmael, crucially important for Islam, but ignored and overlooked in Christianity and perhaps also in Judaism. The only significant exception in Christianity has been some modern feminist

4. Genesis 18.25.
5. Genesis 12.3.

writing which has drawn attention to the suffering of Hagar.[6] Is it possible for Judaism and Christianity to retrieve the figure of Ishmael and make more of him? Sybil Sheridan points to how this has been done in one Midrash, where however much the two brothers, Isaac and Ishmael, quarrelled, Ishmael repented of his sins, enabling them, as in Genesis 25.9, to bury their father together. This Midrash was quoted by President Clinton at the funeral of the Israeli Prime Minister Yitzhak Rabin in 1997. There is also another Midrash which makes it quite clear that Abraham loved both his sons and regarded them as equal; a theme which has been taken up by the modern Israeli poet Shin Shalom in one of his poems:

> Ishmael my brother,
> How long shall we fight each other? ...
> Time is running out, put hatred to sleep,
> Shoulder to shoulder, let's water our sheep.[7]

Thus the figure of Abraham can set the tone for dialogue between Jews, Christians and Muslims by offering the premise that we treat each other on an equal footing; indeed, it is only on this assumption, under which the Oxford Abrahamic Group has operated, that genuine dialogue can proceed.

6. T.J. Dennis, *Sarah Laughed: Women's Voices in the Old Testament* (London: SPCK, 1994), pp. 62–83.
7. From Sybil Sheridan's paper, 'Abraham from a Jewish Perspective', above.

Chapter 2: Moses

Moses from a Jewish Perspective

Jonathan Gorsky

Moses, the dominant figure of much of the Pentateuch, plays the central role in the foundation narrative of the Jewish people, the story of the exodus from Egypt. As intermediary between God and Israel, he is also teacher of the Torah, which was revealed to him alone on Mount Sinai, and is the sole source of Israel's understanding of the divine will and purpose. Moses is both charismatic leader and intercessor who stills God's anger when the people succumb to temptation. His relationship with God is uniquely intimate, and contrasted as such with even the greatest of the later prophetic figures, who are deemed not to have attained Moses' degree of spiritual clarity and understanding.[1] But his role in what was to become normative Judaism, the Judaism defined by the rabbis in the centuries following the destruction of the temple in Jerusalem in 70 CE, is not quite as exalted as one might expect, particularly in comparison with the writings of the Samaritans or the Hellenistic Jewish philosopher Philo Judaeus. There are also distinctions between the rabbinic Moses and the image that emerges from the apocrypha and pseudepigrapha. The study of these literatures provides an important comparative focus for understanding the development of the normative tradition.

This paper examines the different images of Moses developed respectively by the Samaritans, Philo Judaeus and the teachers of rabbinic Judaism. Each image was derived from biblical narratives held in common by all of the figures concerned, who brought their own cultural and theological assumptions to their foundational stories and read them accordingly. Traditional Jewish reading does not merely replicate the text; paradoxically, this most conservative of endeavours turns out to be remarkably innovative.

1. For current discussion about the historicity of the Moses narratives, see J.K. Hoffmeier, *Israel in Egypt: The Evidence for the Authenticity of the Exodus Tradition* (New York and Oxford: Oxford University Press, 1997), pp. 135–63. The Sinai account is in Exodus 19–20. For Moses as intercessor, see Exodus 32–34 and Numbers 14.11 as well as the striking reference in Psalm 106.23, 'He would have destroyed them, had not Moses, his chosen one, stood in the breach ... to keep his wrath from destroying them' (my translation). For Moses as unique prophet, see Numbers 12.6–7, Mekhilta de Rabbi Shimon Bar Yochai to Exodus 20.18, and Babylonian Talmud, *Yevamot* 49b.

Moses according to the Samaritans

The most important Samaritan documents are the Pentateuch and the Memar Markah, which is usually dated from around the fourth century CE. As the Samaritans rejected the greater part of the Old Testament, it is not surprising that Moses was their central figure, with several books of the Memar Markah also being devoted to him. While the Samaritan Moses was clearly developed from the Pentateuch, it has been pointed out that there are striking similarities with Christian images of Jesus; the important difference between the two figures is that the Samaritans never went as far as establishing Moses as either divine or the 'Son of God'. In the Samaritan liturgy, Moses is addressed as 'exalted man, lord of all the world, the crown of humanity who was sent as saviour of Israel', and he is given a wide range of titles, in contrast to the more restrained 'Moses our teacher' of the rabbinic tradition.[2]

The rabbinic tradition associated the light of Moses' countenance with the light said to be hidden by God at the beginning of creation, but far more was made of this in the Markah, where Moses became the light of the world who inspires humanity to turn to God in penitence. The rabbis did not attach such significance to the phenomenon of the light, which indicated personal, rather than cosmic attainment.

The Samaritans also had high regard for Moses as teacher of Torah: he was given a role which could sometimes be creative, rather than that of a simple amanuensis, and he was described in – again – recognizably Johannine terms, as the incarnate logos, rather than as the faithful servant of the biblical and later Jewish tradition.

In the biblical narratives, Moses is several times portrayed as intercessor who saves Israel in times of divine anger, and this was developed by the Samaritans, who saw him eternally fulfilling this role and continued to seek his intercession on their behalf. While the Samaritan focus on Moses appears to have drawn to some extent on Christian imagery and is remarkably exalted, there are striking parallels in the pseudepigrapha, particularly with reference to

2. For copious material on the Samaritan Moses, see J. Macdonald, *The Theology of the Samaritans* (London: SCM Press, 1964), pp. 147–224. For the comparison with Jesus, see pp. 420–46; Moses as intercessor, pp. 211–14; Moses' titles, p. 201; comparison with John's Gospel, pp. 150–51; Moses as saviour of Israel, p. 199; Moses as lord of the world, p. 171; Moses as lawgiver, pp. 200–203; and Moses and the primordial light, pp. 165–72. For a more restrained rabbinic reference, see for example Babylonian Talmud, *Soṭa* 12a. The identity of the Samaritans is disputed. They claimed to be descendants of the biblical tribes of Ephraim and Manasseh. The assumption that they were descended from the people living in Samaria when it was conquered by Assyria in the eighth century BCE and other peoples were brought in by the Assyrians, is based on the account in 2 Kings 17. The Memar Markah is a work of theology and exegesis based on the Pentateuch. The author, Markah, was a venerated Samaritan scholar and poet who flourished in the fourth century CE. For an English translation, see J. Macdonald (ed. and trans.), *Memar Marqah: The Teaching of Marqah* (Berlin: Alfred Töpelmann, 1963).

intercession, which is noticeably less prominent in rabbinic Judaism. In the *Testament of Moses*, for example, Moses' role as intercessor is more important than that of lawgiver, and in the pseudepigrapha, Pseudo-Philo's *Biblical Antiquities* has Moses say in his farewell speech that future generations will lament his death and say in their heart, 'Who will give us another shepherd like Moses ... to pray always for our sins and to be heard for our iniquities?' God responds by taking Moses' rod into his presence, as a covenantal sign, like Noah's rainbow, to remind himself of his desire to be merciful. This is clearly different from the Samaritan notion of eternal intercession, but the intercessive role is very significant for both sets of readings.[3]

Philo Judaeus

Philo Judaeus was likewise preoccupied with a most exalted portrayal of Moses, who is said to have attained a divine nature via his identity with the logos: Moses became a divinity on Mount Sinai, and in Philo's biography of him we learn that God gave the entire world into his hands, and that the elements obeyed him as their master. It is important to place Philo, and perhaps other first-century Jewish authors who ascribe divinity to human beings, in the context of remarks in his discussion of Genesis, where he differentiated the ultimate likeness of God, which is beyond all replication, from the logos, which he described as '*deuteros theos*'. Moses' divinity is derived from his identity with the logos, and not the ultimate essence of God, so it is possible to attain divinity without participating in the Godhead, which remains beyond human perception. Nevertheless, the transcendent exaltation of Moses is the ultimate human possibility of being transformed into the divine, as Philo understood it. For Philo, Moses' journey up the mountain was an allusion to his ascent beyond the heavens, where there was no place but God – and his holy soul was made divine in the process of its ascension.[4]

3. For sources and commentary, see S.J. Hafemann, 'Moses in the Apocrypha and Pseudepigrapha: A Survey', *Journal for the Study of the Pseudepigrapha* 7 (1990), pp. 79–104, especially pp. 89–104 for sources on intercession. The Pseudo-Philo reference is 19.11.

4. There is a useful discussion on Philo and Moses, as well as other relevant Hellenistic material, in A.F. Segal, *Paul the Convert: The Apostolate and Apostasy of Saul the Pharisee* (New Haven, CT and London: Yale University Press, 1990), pp. 44–45. For relevant Philo material, see, for example, *Sacrifices 1–10*, and *Moses* 1.155–58. For the '*deuteros theos*', see *Questions on Genesis* 2.62; but also, more moderately, Philo's *On the Change of Names* 22. For an excellent survey of Moses in Hellenistic Judaism, see J.M.G. Barclay, *Jews in the Mediterranean Diaspora: From Alexander to Trajan (323 BCE – 117 CE)* (Edinburgh: T&T Clark, 1996), esp. pp. 127–38 and 426–28. See also W.A. Meeks, 'Moses as God and King', in J. Neusner (ed.), *Religions in Antiquity* (Festschrift E.R. Goodenough; Leiden: E.J. Brill, 1968), pp. 354–71. For a small anthology of pertinent primary sources, see J.L. Kugel, *The Bible as It Was* (Cambridge, MA: Belknap Press, 1997), pp. 544–47.

Rabbinic Judaism

In briefly introducing the rabbinic responses to the Moses narratives, it must be stated at the outset that very frequently there were different schools of thought, and even the best-known citations do not necessarily express a complete consensus of opinion. Nevertheless, these citations were formative of religious culture, and tended to marginalize dissenting opinions, at least in popular perception.[5]

In a curious but polemical discussion, Rabbi José asserted that the divine presence never descended to earth, nor did Moses or Elijah ever ascend to heaven.[6] Biblical verses were then adduced to the contrary and the conclusion was that nevertheless a minimal – but highly significant – distance was maintained in each case; Moses indeed went up to God, but stopped when he was ten handbreadths from heaven. The intent was clearly to maintain a distinction between the human and the divine: the small measurement was sufficient to establish a boundary, at the same time as indicating unsurpassed intimacy between Moses and God, but the boundary remained crucially intact.[7]

Even in statements that appear to contradict Rabbi José's assertion, the distinction of humanity and God still remained. For example, the notion of the divine presence resting upon people of outstanding spiritual attainment was derived by Rabbi Yochanan from the exemplar provided by Moses,[8] but even here the divine presence was not synonymous with the Godhead, and it was not regarded as a '*deuteros theos*'. Also, distinction was intrinsic to the image; the divine presence 'rested upon' the figures concerned, but they did not, in consequence, become divine beings. Nor was the phenomenon confined to Moses,

5. For introductions to rabbinic culture and beliefs, see G.F. Moore, *Judaism in the First Centuries of the Christian Era: The Age of the Tannaim* (Cambridge, MA: Harvard University Press, 1927–30). This is most readable, as is C.J.G. Montefiore and H. Loewe (eds.), *A Rabbinic Anthology* (London: Macmillan, 1938) (or later editions), which is avowedly selective and non-analytical, but still useful. These works might be compared with E.E. Urbach, *Hazal: Pirke 'Emunot Ve-De'ot* (Jerusalem: Magnes Press, 1969), a massive analytical survey of rabbinic ideas and beliefs, which in turn has been subject to debate and emendation, but remains an outstanding and deeply learned achievement, and is essential reading. For translation, see E.E. Urbach, *The Sages: Their Concepts and Beliefs* (trans. I. Abrahams; Jerusalem: Magnes Press, 1979).

6. Babylonian Talmud, *Succah* 5a.

7. For further discussion of the rabbinic concept of the divine presence, see Urbach, *Hazal*, pp. 29–52. The Rabbi Jose passage is somewhat elaborated in the Midrash to Exodus 19.20. See Mekhilta Bahodesh 4.224, and also paragraph 9, where Rabbi Akiva roots the discussion in the apparent contradiction between Exodus 20.22 ('I spoke with you from heaven') and Exodus 19.20 ('the Lord descended upon Mount Sinai'). Kugel, *Bible as It Was*, p. 374, aptly cites Nehemiah 9.13 ('You came down also upon Mount Sinai, and spoke with them from heaven'). Kugel's anthology has a variety of different ways of handling the tension, which were profoundly important for later theological discussion, albeit that Midrash operated within literal narrative boundaries and expressed ideas accordingly.

8. Babylonian Talmud, *Nedarim* 38a.

for it was associated with saintly figures down the ages. A Midrash sought to distinguish Moses and the patriarch Isaac:[9] Isaac asserts that when he was bound on the altar at Mount Moriah, he had a vision of the divine presence; Moses responds that he, Moses, had gone further, and spoken with the divine presence face to face. But he claims no more than that, and in further Midrashic sources on Exodus 25.8, when Moses is told by God that God's presence will rest in a small, earthly sanctuary, Moses expresses astonishment that this could be the case: 'Master of the universe, even the highest heavens cannot suffice to accommodate your presence and you instruct us to make you a sanctuary.'[10]

Several rabbinic homilies emphasized Moses' constant awareness of his human limitations, even when he ascended to the highest heavens: for Rabbi Joshua ben Levi, when Moses went up to God, the angels said, 'What has a son of a woman to do among us? How can the Torah be given to flesh and blood?' Moses responded that the Torah is full of material that pertains only to humankind, and has no relevance to angels. The angels then praised God and became friends of Moses. The rabbis emphasized Moses' humility time and again: the Bible described him in these terms (Numbers 12.3), and the rabbis saw his humility, his fearfulness in the presence of God (Exodus 3.6), as being the source of his spiritual distinction. In proportion to one's self-effacement in the presence of the divine, so is one's spiritual development. The divine presence rested upon Moses precisely because, in his own self-abnegation, he was able to comprehend what can be known of God in the greatest plenitude conceivable for a human being.[11]

With regard to Moses' role in the revelation of the Torah, the rabbis again differed from some first-century and earlier literature, such as the *Letter of Aristeas* in which Moses is far more than an amanuensis; he is the author of the law, albeit that God puts thoughts into the hearts of lawgivers, so safeguarding the notion of divine origin, and we learn that Moses drew up 'his laws' to aid 'the quest for virtue and the perfecting of character'. Josephus also implied that Moses should be seen as a lawgiver, rather than an amanuensis, and so did Philo Judaeus.[12]

For the rabbinic tradition, it is important to note how little Moses added from his own understanding, and that even the three matters in question were given

9. Devarim Rabba 11.3 and Vayikra Rabba 31.9.

10. See Urbach, *Hazal*, p. 39, for further discussion of these sources.

11. For Rabbi Joshua ben Levi, see Babylonian Talmud, *Shabbat* 88b–89a. For Moses' humility and the relation of this quality to bringing the divine presence into the world, see Mekhilta to Exodus 20.18. See also Midrash Tanchuma, Genesis 1.

12. Material from the *Letter of Aristeas* is cited in Hafemann, 'Moses in the Apocrypha and Pseudepigrapha', pp. 87–88. For Josephus and Philo, see Barclay, *Jews in the Mediterranean Diaspora*, pp. 426–28. For Josephus, see particularly *Contra Apion* 2.151–54. Barclay also notes (p. 426) that in Moses, Diaspora Jews discerned the skills of a lawgiver comparable to Solon, Lycurgus or Minos of Crete. For Philo's description of Moses as lawgiver, see the early pages of *On the Life of Moses* 2 (*The Works of Philo: Complete and Unabridged* [trans. C.D. Yonge; Peabody, MA: Hendrickson, 1993], pp. 492–94).

divine approval. If the Torah is linked with Moses and described as Torat Moshe, this was because Moses was reluctant to take any credit at all, even to the point of refusing to acknowledge that God had given it to him: 'What am I that God should have given the Torah to me?' he responded, when questioned about its location. While several traditions extolled Moses' learning, a famous passage has Moses hearing one of the greatest of the early rabbis, Rabbi Akiva, teaching Torah and not being able to understand Akiva's creative reasoning.[13] Moses is only reassured when Rabbi Akiva's disciple asks his teacher for his source, and Akiva responds that 'this is a teaching which was given to Moses on Mount Sinai'. The story is usually taken in the context of underlining the massive development of the oral tradition, but it is inconceivable outside the rabbinic perception of Moses: one cannot imagine it occurring in the writings of Philo or the teachings of the Samaritans.[14]

In terms of the role of Moses in Jewish tradition, the story illustrates both Moses' ultimate authority and its limitations. Rabbis did not merely repeat what they had learned from him; they expounded and developed the tradition with great creativity. Furthermore, the Targumim on Deuteronomy 30.11–14, which tells all of Israel that the world of the Torah is very near to them, and neither in heaven nor beyond the sea, counsel the ordinary reader that it is not necessary to have Moses' attainments in order to study it: 'The Torah is not in heaven, that one should say, if only we had someone like the prophet Moses who might go up to heaven and take it down for us.' Moses' self-effacement had already been made graphically clear in the biblical text where two otherwise unknown figures, Eldad and Medad, prophesy, and Joshua is alarmed that this will compromise Moses' authority. Moses allays Joshua's fears, and expresses the hope that the spirit of God would indeed rest upon all Israel.[15]

Moses did not become a great figure of intercession in the rabbinic tradition. As the Torah is given to all Israel, so is the way of prayer, and the rabbis who so determinedly maintained the distinction between the human and the divine likewise elaborated the intimacy of God and Israel, albeit with some trepidation. The Talmud has God appearing to Moses as the leader of a congregation,

13. Babylonian Talmud, *Menachot* 29b.

14. For Moses' three additions, see Babylonian Talmud, *Shabbat* 87a. On his own initiative, he had the Israelites keep an added day of sanctity before revelation broke the tablets of stone that he had received from God and separated him from his wife in perpetuity. For his humble refusal to take credit and the Torah consequently being associated with him, see Babylonian Talmud, *Shabbat* 89a and its comment on Malachi 3.2, 'Remember the Torah of Moses, my servant.' For a contrast to Babylonian Talmud, *Menachot* 29b, see Babylonian Talmud, *Nedarim* 38a, where we learn that fifty gates of understanding were created in the world and all but one were given to Moses. See also Babylonian Talmud, *Sota* 19b and Babylonian Talmud, *Berakhot* 5a for the extent of the knowledge that Moses received on Sinai, and Midrash Tanhuma, Yitro in similar vein.

15. The Targumim to Deuteronomy 30.11–14 referred to are Targum Neophyti and Targum Pseudo-Jonathan. I am grateful to Kugel, *Bible as It Was*, p. 526, for the references. For Eldad and Medad, see Numbers 11.24–30.

drawing his prayer shawl around himself, and showing Moses the order of prayer.[16] 'He said to him, whenever Israel sin, let them carry out this service before me, and I will forgive them.' Several rabbinic sources encourage people to turn to God and not to emissaries in their time of need. One of the later rabbis of the Talmud, the Amora Rabbi Yudan, compared people who pray to angels to those who have a powerful patron, but are afraid to disturb him, and send a message via his servant. He assured his hearers that God is not like this, and if they are troubled they should cry out before God, and God will answer them.[17]

Finally, Moses was rarely seen as a political exemplar or liberation figure. While the exodus is the major narrative of the tradition, it was usually retold or recast in terms of the intervention of God on behalf of God's people, with little attention paid to the role of Moses and his leadership. The Passover Haggadah, the narrative of the exodus recited in Jewish houses every year, is entirely focused on the divine redemption of Israel from Egypt, and Moses is mentioned only once, and then incidentally. The roots of this are biblical, particularly in the use of the exodus narrative by the prophets, and perhaps also reflect the end of the Babylonian exile, the foundation narrative of Second Temple Judaism, when some of the people returned from exile to Jerusalem, but with the sanction of Cyrus, king of Persia, who was a very different divine instrument. Finally, Jewish messianic hope is usually focused on a David figure rather than a Moses exemplar.[18]

16. Babylonian Talmud, *Rosh Hashana* 19b.

17. There are famous rabbinic passages that speak of major figures interceding for Israel: see particularly the introduction of Lamentations Rabbah, paragraph 24, cited in Montefiore and Loewe, *Rabbinic Anthology*, pp. 247–49. The rabbis eloquently elaborated Moses' intercession in the biblical narratives; see Montefiore and Loewe, *Rabbinic Anthology*, pp. 76–77 for examples. See also the example of Esther Rabba, the Midrash on Esther 3.9, cited in Montefiore and Loewe, *Rabbinic Anthology*, p. 99. At one point, Elijah turns to Moses to intercede and Moses responds, 'Is there no upright man in this generation?' Elijah replies in the affirmative, citing Mordechai, and Moses agrees to join with Mordechai in prayer. These passages, however, do not imply that Israel should pray to the figures concerned as intercessors, and Moses' response to Elijah is of interest in this context. The Amora Rabbi Yudan is cited in Babylonian Talmud, *Berakhot* 9.12, and Babylonian Talmud, *Yoma* 52a includes the observation that the people of Israel are precious, for they require no intercessor (literally, 'emissary'). These references are in Urbach, *Hazal*, p. 160 (at the end of his important chapter on the heavenly host).

18. For prophetic use of the exodus narrative, see J.D. Pleins, *The Social Visions of the Hebrew Bible: A Theological Introduction* (Louisville, KY: Westminster John Knox Press, 2000), p. 75, where the discussion is primarily on the covenant and legal traditions. For Cyrus as divine instrument, see Isaiah 44.28–45.1. See also Isaiah 63.9, which refers to angelic rather than Mosaic redemption during the exodus, although not as sharply as the 'neither messenger nor angel but his presence' of current translations which are based on the Greek Septuagint rather than the Masoretic text; vv. 11–12 have Moses as shepherd in the context of God as redeemer; see also vv. 16–17. See also Jeremiah 16.14–15 and 23.7–8 for the apparent replacement of the exodus model by a future redemption, which seems entirely dependent on

Moses, for the rabbis, was neither a divine being, nor a lawgiver, and he did not become an intercessor or a political exemplar as might have been expected given the biblical narratives. In the orthodox Jewish sabbath liturgy, Moses rejoices in his portion, for God has called him a faithful servant, the humblest and most anonymous of his prospective titles, especially by comparison with the much discussed 'godly man' (*Ish HaElohim*) of Deuteronomy 33.1.[19] But this diminution does not indicate a lack of Mosaic significance in the development of the tradition.

Conclusion

First, Moses remains a challenge for all future Jewish leaders, especially those with grandiose or royal ambitions. His presence is clearly manifest in several biblical critiques of Jewish leadership, and the good shepherd image elaborated by the rabbis is an effective critique of those who seek only power and status. Leadership signifies self-effacing devotion to the well-being of one's community, and the stature of its greatest exemplar is sufficient to subvert the worldly ambitions of lesser claimants. Prophets – and rabbis – were uninhibited by kings because their greatest figure was likewise so.[20]

Secondly, the Moses narratives create a community which is not dominated by a dynastic hierarchy, but which, at its finest, is a place where everyone is equal before God. The priestly structure centred around the temple has always

God; and Jeremiah 32.20–22 and Ezekiel 20 and 36.24–28 for further examples. For a useful and cautionary discussion of this trend in Second Temple and rabbinic literature, and particularly the 'neither by messenger nor angel' phrase, see W. Horbury, *Jewish Messianism and the Cult of Christ* (London: SCM Press, 1998), pp. 78–83. The first century CE certainly saw some Jewish groups who took Moses and Joshua as exemplars of redemptive political action. See R.A. Horsley, 'Like One of the Prophets of Old: Two Types of Popular Prophets at the Time of Jesus', *Catholic Biblical Quarterly* 47 (1985), pp. 435–63. See also J.D. Crossan, *The Historical Jesus: The Life of a Mediterranean Jewish Peasant* (Edinburgh: T&T Clark, 1991), pp. 168–206. The rabbis derived the Messiah's Davidic lineage from, for example, Isaiah 9.7, Hosea 3.5 and Jeremiah 30.9. See also Babylonian Talmud, *Soferim* 13.13 for the formative images of David as Messiah in the traditional liturgy.

19. Together with Exodus 7.1, this has been taken as indicating divinity, particularly by Philo; but see Philo's rarely quoted *On the Change of Names* 22 (*Works of Philo*, p. 352), where clearly Philo's notion of the divine person is more circumscribed than some of his material has led scholars to believe, and is very different from classical Christianity. See also Kugel, *Bible as It Was*, p. 376, where Pesikta de Rabbi Kahana, a Midrashic source, is quoted to the effect that Moses was 'human' in the heavens and 'God' on earth. The Hebrew 'Elohim' need have no divine meaning, as Rashi, the greatest of the Jewish commentators explained on the Exodus verse. See also Nahmanides on Deuteronomy 33.1. Moses is described as faithful servant in Numbers 12.7. His rejoicing in the title of servant is a rabbinic gloss.

20. For the shadow of Moses in biblical critiques of leadership, see for example 1 Samuel 12.1–13, Ezekiel 34 and Nehemiah 6.14–15 (cf. Numbers 16.15). For a rabbinic description of Moses as shepherd, see Exodus Rabba 3.1.

to be in dialogue with the unmediated relationship with the divine that is granted to all Israel via Torah study and prayer.

Thirdly, the Moses narratives' emphasis on humility are the *sine qua non* of Jewish spiritual life, and neither biblical narratives nor rabbinic traditions gloss over Moses' human frailties. Moses' relation with God is characterized by a reticence in the face of the divine that is present even in moments of extraordinary intimacy. The sense that there is that of the divine which lies beyond human grasp, and that to approach God is a fearful and awe-inspiring encounter where the only proper response is to hide one's face, remains with Jews, who, to the occasional chagrin of their dialogue partners, are reluctant to 'discuss theology' in the manner of the West, even to this day.[21] The distinction between the human and the divine, even if it is only ten handbreadths, is the great intuition of the Moses narratives, which are pervaded by a sense that God is at once transparently immanent and utterly transcendent. Even for Philo Judaeus, who did not hesitate to affirm Moses' divinity, this great intuition was ever present and it will always be at the heart of Christian-Jewish conversation. Today, Jews are wholly unfamiliar with the Samaritan literature, and the works of Philo Judaeus have few readers apart from specialist scholars. The rabbinic Moses has triumphed, and Philo especially would be regarded as having alarming affinities with Christianity.

21. For Moses hiding his face, see Exodus 3.6. For rabbinic comment, see Midrash Tanhuma, Genesis 1, cited in Montefiore and Loewe, *Rabbinic Anthology*, p. 171. For Moses' human frailties, see for example Numbers 20.7–13, and rabbinic discussion in Babylonian Talmud, *Shabbat* 55b, and Babylonian Talmud, *Yoma* 86b, where Moses insists that his failings should be recorded in the Torah.

Moses from a Christian Perspective

John Barton

Christian attitudes to Moses have often been ambivalent. On the one hand, he is the great lawgiver, and his name stands as a symbol for the law in the New Testament, which speaks of 'Moses and the prophets' as a designation for scripture.[1] On the other hand, Jesus is sometimes presented as a new Moses, for example in the Sermon on the Mount, and this may have the effect of making him the *true* 'Moses' for Christians, so that the old one is no longer needed. Much debate among Christians has centred on these two contrasting ways of thinking about the Jewish dispensation, one affirming it as essential, the other treating it as superseded in Christ. The importance attached to Moses varies as between these two different ways of thinking.

There is clearly a strain in Christian thought which from early times has regarded Moses as a superseded figure. John's Gospel says, 'The law indeed was given through Moses; grace and truth came through Jesus Christ',[2] relegating Moses to a past order, so that whatever was good in him is now to be found in Jesus Christ, and whatever was bad in him is superseded. However, this Johannine strain of thought has not been the majority view within Christianity, which honours Moses and regards him as an essential figure in God's self-revelation. Moses has been important in three ways for Christians: as mystic, as liberator, and as lawgiver.

Moses as a Mystic

Christians have often seen Moses as a great spiritual personality. His mysterious sojourn on the mountain for forty days and forty nights makes him the prototype of all mystics who have encountered God in solitude and silence. Especially in the early Greek fathers of the Church, he appears as the model for anyone who wishes to seek God by the mystical path. This is already his role

1. See Luke 16.29, in the parable of the rich man and Lazarus.
2. John 1.17.

in Philo, and it is at least partly from Philo that patristic ideas of Moses derive.[3] Classically in Gregory of Nyssa, in the fourth century, Moses is our guide as we approach the mountain at the top of which God is to be encountered, the pioneer in pursuing the vision of God which all religious believers strive to possess.[4] Reading the text of Exodus 19 rather literally gives one the impression that Moses keeps going up and down the mountain. Thus if Moses went up the mountain in verse 9, how can God have told him to come up the mountain in verse 12? He was already there. Then again, if he went up in verse 15, how can he have gone up again in verse 18? Modern biblical scholarship has explained this plausibly as the result of weaving together several originally independent accounts of Moses' ascent.[5] But for Gregory the complications of the story in Exodus are fruitful in pointing to the complexity of the mystical ascent, with its frequent setbacks and hesitations, even though at its end lies the knowledge of God's own self.

Moses as a Liberator

The second role of Moses in Christianity is as the one who led the exodus from Egypt. Christianity has been rediscovering the exodus in the last thirty years or so – not simply as a 'typological' parallel to salvation in Christ, as traditionally in Christian thought, but in its own right as an example of how God rescues the oppressed. In liberation theology, especially in Latin America, the exodus has become for Christians, and above all for poor Christians, the supreme symbol of God's willingness to intervene on behalf of God's people – understanding 'God's people' here to mean neither Jews nor Christians as such, but the poor and oppressed of whatever race or creed.[6] Liberation theologians stress less the ethnic identity of the people Moses led out of Egypt and more their social status as poor, downtrodden and enslaved. This follows a particular trend in modern biblical scholarship which is by no means undisputed, but clearly does have some anchorage in the biblical text itself, according to which it was indeed the social status of the 'Hebrews' rather than their ethnic identity that led them to revolt against their overlords.[7] For liberationists, Moses is the saviour sent by God to rescue the poor, whom God particularly values; he is their champion and their helper. He is therefore a model to be imitated by all Christians. Christians have a sacred duty not to stand idly by

3. See Philo, *On the Life of Moses*, especially section 35.

4. Gregory of Nyssa, *Life of Moses*, chapters 167 and 227.

5. On Exodus 19, see for example B.S. Childs, *Exodus: A Commentary* (London: SCM Press, 1974).

6. Cf. C.C. Rowland (ed.), *The Cambridge Companion to Liberation Theology* (Cambridge: Cambridge University Press, 1999), for a survey of major trends in this influential movement.

7. See above all N.K. Gottwald, *The Tribes of Yahweh: A Sociology of the Religion of Liberated Israel 1250–1050 BCE* (Sheffield: Sheffield Academic Press, 2nd edn, 1999).

when faced with injustice and oppression, but to intervene and act as God's own agents in helping to overcome socio-economic oppression and exploitation.

Moses as the liberator, and the exodus as the decisive act of divine salvation, have become important also in strands of Christianity unconnected with liberation theology. The Church of England, in its *Alternative Service Book* of 1980 (now superseded by *Common Worship*),[8] had a special 'Moses Sunday', the sixth Sunday before Christmas. Its collect ran: 'Lord God our Redeemer, who heard the cry of your people and sent your servant Moses to lead them out of slavery: free us from the tyranny of sin and death, and by the leading of your Spirit bring us to our promised land.'[9] This represents a spiritualization of Moses' mission. What for Christians corresponds to Moses' victory over Pharaoh is the conquest of sin and death, and 'our promised land' is presumably what used to be called heaven; though the prayer could also be interpreted in the manner of liberation theology as asking God to overcome all that enslaves the human beings God has made and give them peace, *shalom*. However it is meant, Moses certainly becomes an important figure as the prototype of all God's acts of salvation; and this is repeated when much is said of him in the celebration of Easter, understood again as giving Christians something analogous to what Passover gives to Jews, a celebration of release and salvation. One of the most dramatic elements in the celebration of the Easter vigil, in the dark hours before Easter Day, is the reading of Exodus 14, the story of the crossing of the Red Sea. The reader ends with an unfinished sentence: 'Then Moses and the people of Israel sang this song to the Lord, saying' – and the congregation stand and sing the Song of the Sea (Exodus 15), 'I will sing to the Lord, for he has triumphed gloriously …' What is happening in this celebration is not necessarily about Christ superseding Moses, though it could also be taken in that way. Christians are making bold to appropriate the salvation history of Israel in the Hebrew Bible, and share in the same sense of liberation and exhilaration.

Indeed, what Moses did becomes basically a model for all experiences of liberation, which can potentially be appropriated by any human being who experiences oppression or enslavement, literal or metaphorical. This process had already begun in the book of Isaiah, where the coming liberation from the yoke of the Babylonians is described as a new exodus.[10] What Christianity does is to describe the experience of salvation in connection with Jesus as likewise a new exodus. In either case, the figure of Moses takes on a more universal significance, but at the cost of making him matter less as a historical person. He turns into a symbol for freedom from oppression.

8. *The Alternative Service Book 1980* (London: SPCK, 1980); *Common Worship: Services and Prayers for the Church of England* (London: Church House Publishing, 2000).

9. *Alternative Service Book 1980*, p. 413.

10. See, for example, Isaiah 52.11–12.

Moses as Lawgiver

A third aspect takes Moses much more literally by concentrating on his role as the lawgiver. There has been much debate in the history of Christianity as to which of the laws in the Bible are binding on Christians (or indeed on everyone), and which are to be seen as not in force for non-Jews. The general consensus has been that they all derive from God, but that they differ in their scope and permanence (in recent years, as also happened in the very early Church, some people have started to suggest that certain of the laws are not of divine origin at all).[11] For example, except for a very few types of Christianity, such as some in North Africa, circumcision is not practised. Similarly, the food laws are usually seen as no longer binding, though there are Christian groups such as the Seventh-Day Adventists who do still observe them in a modified form, just as they keep the sabbath rather than observing Sunday. Notoriously contentious in relation to Judaism has been the Christian idea of distinguishing 'moral' or ethical laws from 'ceremonial' or ritual laws, and keeping only the first: a distinction I understand Judaism to resist.

Even within the so-called moral laws, however, there is no doubt that pride of place goes to the Ten Commandments, which all Christians regard as the core and basis of their ethical code. In the eighteenth century, it was normal in the Church of England for there to be two clearly legible tablets on the wall behind the altar, one with the Creed and the Lord's Prayer, and the other with the Ten Commandments. They are repeated at the beginning of every communion service according to the *Book of Common Prayer*, as they are also in the Calvinist tradition, and examining one's conscience by reference to them often takes the place of confession to a priest. There are many manuals which analyse moral obligations by attaching them all to one or other of the commandments, not always very plausibly: spending too much money on clothes, for example, was often included as one of the offences against the commandment 'Thou shalt not commit adultery.' But the very implausibility shows how important it was felt to be to relate all of human conduct to the commandments.

Within Christian tradition, Lutheranism has been less enthusiastic than either Catholicism or Calvinism about placing the commandments at the centre of Christian life. While agreeing that they certainly are binding on Christians and indeed on everyone, Luther stressed that they were not God's first word to the human race, but God's second: God's first word was a declaration of love and blessing, or what Christians call 'gospel', using that term as a generic. One might put it by saying that Abraham came before Moses, the covenant of promise and of God's free choice of Israel before any demand God might make. Lutherans have tended historically to present this as a novel Christian

11. Cf. H. von Campenhausen, *The Formation of the Christian Bible* (London: A. & C. Black, 1972).

insight and even as part of the superiority of Christianity over Judaism, but recent studies by New Testament scholars and specialists in the literature of Second Temple Judaism, especially E.P. Sanders, have shown decisively that it was a normal way of seeing the relation of grace to law in the Jewish world within which early Christianity came into being.[12] Indeed, it is already there in the Hebrew Bible, in the way Moses speaks to the people in Deuteronomy:

> So now, O Israel, what does the Lord your God require of you? Only to fear the Lord your God, to walk in all his ways, to love him, to serve the Lord your God with all your heart and with all your soul, and to keep the commandments of the Lord your God and his decrees that I am commanding you today, for your own well-being. Although heaven and the heaven of heavens belong to the Lord your God, the earth with all that is in it, yet the Lord set his heart in love upon your ancestors alone and chose you, their descendants after them, out of all the peoples, as it is today.[13]

Moses here is not just a lawgiver, but someone whose job it is to remind the people of what God has done for them, and only within that context to make sure they know what it is they have to do for God. So, in the verse from John, 'The law indeed was given through Moses; grace and truth came through Jesus Christ', the implied 'but' should at least be replaced by an 'and'. Better still, we might say that grace, truth and the law were given through Moses. What a Christian might want to add is, 'and also through Jesus Christ'. But to set Moses as the lawgiver *against* Jesus as bringer of salvation is certainly a travesty.

Conclusion

Moses has thus been important for Christians, although usually with a sense that Jesus improved on his work and gave it a new direction. In the story of Jesus' transfiguration,[14] Moses is one of the two ancient figures who appears, talking to Jesus (the other is Elijah), and Luke tells us that the three discussed Jesus' 'departure' (Greek *exodos*), 'which he was about to accomplish at Jerusalem'.[15] Here the parallels between Jesus and Moses are made overt: Jesus like Moses is to accomplish an 'exodus' – only it will be his own exodus from the world, not that of the Israelites from Egypt. Yet that exodus like the original one will be also an act of liberation, in which Moses' original mission to save his people is taken up and generalized to include the salvation of the

12. E.P. Sanders, *Paul and Palestinian Judaism: A Comparison of Patterns of Religion* (London: SCM Press, 1977); *idem*, *Paul, the Law, and the Jewish People* (Philadelphia, PA: Fortress Press, 1985).
13. Deuteronomy 10.12–15.
14. Matthew 17.1–8, Mark 9.2–8 and Luke 9.28–36.
15. Luke 9.31.

whole world. Yet, from the very fact that Moses was placed at the centre of this scene, we see how far Christians felt the need to continue to relate to him, the founding figure in the Judaism from which they ultimately derived.

Moses from a Muslim Perspective

Annabel Keeler

The prophet Moses is known in Islam by the name of Mūsā (which, according to Islamic tradition, is derived from two Egyptian words: *mū*, meaning 'water', and *shā*, meaning 'tree') because the basket in which the infant Moses floated came to rest by trees close to Pharaoh's residence.[1] Moses is defined in the Qur'ān as both prophet (*nabī*) and messenger (*rasūl*), the latter term indicating that he was one of those prophets who brought a scripture and law to his people. He has, moreover, the status of being one of the '*ūlū'l-ʿazm*', that is, those apostles who were endowed with special determination, constancy and forbearance in obeying the commands of God.[2]

Among prophets, Moses has been described as the one 'whose career as a messenger of God, lawgiver and leader of his community most closely parallels and foreshadows that of Muhammad',[3] and as 'the figure that in the Koran was presented to Muhammad above all others as the supreme model of saviour and ruler of a community, the man chosen to present both knowledge of the one God, and a divinely revealed system of law'.[4] We find him clearly in this role of Muhammad's forebear in a well-known tradition of the miraculous ascension

1. *The History of al-Ṭabarī* (trans. W.M. Brinner; Albany, NY: State University of New York Press, 1991), III, p. 35. The Old Testament (Exodus 2.10) provides a different etymology: his name is Moses (or *Moshe*) because Pharaoh's daughter drew him from the water. However, the article on 'Moses' by M. Greenberg *et al.* in the *Encyclopedia Judaica* points out that the popular etymology which is presented in Exodus 2.10 would logically have required the form *mashui* ('one that has been drawn out'), not *moshe*, which actually means 'one that draws out', and that therefore the name *moshe* may be understood as a pointer to his future destiny.

2. The *ūlū'l-ʿazm* are mentioned in Qur'ān 46.35: 'Then have patience [O Muhammad], even as the *stout of heart* among the messengers of old had patience' (translations in this paper are from M. Pickthall, *The Meaning of the Glorious Qur'an* [London: Allen and Unwin, 1930], with numerous reprints from various publishers thereafter). The prophets Noah, Abraham, Moses, Jesus and Muhammad are usually included among the *ūlū'l-ʿazm.*

3. W.M. Brinner, 'An Islamic Decalogue', in W.M. Brinner and S.D. Ricks (eds.), *Studies in Islamic and Judaic Traditions* (Atlanta, GA: Scholars Press, 1989), II, pp. 67–84 (68).

4. A.H. Johns, 'Moses in the Koran', in R.B. Crotty (ed.), *The Charles Strong Lectures 1972–84* (Leiden: E.J. Brill, 1987), pp. 123–38 (123).

(*miʿrāj*) of the Prophet, where Moses advises Muhammad from his own experience as messenger and lawgiver. According to a tradition narrated from the Prophet, after the Prophet had ascended through the seven heavens and been taken into the divine presence, the duty of fifty prayers a day was placed upon him. As he descended through the heavens, he encountered the prophet Moses, who inquired about the number of prayers that had been prescribed for his people. On hearing the number fifty, he warned Muhammad that this would be too heavy a burden to place on people who are weak, and advised him to return to the divine presence, and request a reduction. Muhammad did so, and was granted a reduction of ten prayers. As he passed by Moses the second time, he was again questioned about the number of prayers, and again Moses advised him to have the number reduced. This continued until only five prayers remained for each day and night. Even then, Moses advised him to go again to the divine presence and have the number reduced, but this time Muhammad refused, saying that he was ashamed to go back any more.[5]

It is perhaps because of his special role as Muhammad's predecessor that Moses is mentioned far more than any other prophet in the Qur'ān.[6] Most of the key events in his life that are narrated in the Bible are to be found dispersed through the sūras of the Qur'ān, with, in addition, a story which is not found in the Bible, that of Moses' journey to the meeting of the two seas, and his encounter with Khiḍr.

Moses in the Qur'ān

The Qur'ānic versions of events in Moses' life sometimes differ in their details from their biblical counterparts. For example, Moses is adopted by Pharaoh's wife, and not by his daughter; it is Moses rather than Aaron who addresses Pharaoh and demonstrates before him the miracles of the rod turning into a serpent and the hand becoming leprous white and then returning to its normal state. Sometimes these variations bring their own nuances of meaning. For example, in the Qur'ān, Moses' mother does not hide him in the basket in the bulrushes; she is commanded by God to place him in an ark and cast him on the waters of the Nile, thus abandoning him completely to God's protection and demonstrating her total trust in God. There is also a significant shift of emphasis in the stories. The mission with which Moses is charged, when God addresses him from the burning bush, is not so much the liberation of the children of Israel

5. One of the best-known accounts of the Prophet Muhammad's *miʿrāj* is to be found in Muhammad Ibn Isḥāq's biography of the Prophet, *The Life of Muhammad: A Translation of Ibn Isḥāq's Sīrat Rasūl Allāh* (trans. A. Guillaume; London: Oxford University Press, 1955), pp. 181–87. On the *miʿrāj* in various branches of Islamic literature, see M.A. Amir-Moezzi (ed.), *Le voyage initiatique en terre d'Islam* (Paris and Louvain: Peeters, 1996).

6. According to Johns, 'Moses in the Koran', p. 123, there are 502 verses in the Qur'ān relating to Moses as compared with 93 relating to Jesus, 131 to Noah and 235 to Abraham.

from oppression by the Egyptians, as their salvation, and equally that of Pharaoh, through acceptance of the divine message. In the seventy-ninth ṣūra of the Qur'ān ('Those Who Drag Forth'), the story is related as follows: 'Hath there come unto thee the history of Moses? How his Lord called him in the holy valley of Tuwa [saying], Go thou unto Pharaoh – Lo! He hath rebelled – and say [unto him]: Hast thou [will] to grow [in grace]? Then I will guide thee to thy Lord and thou shalt fear [Him].'[7]

Likewise, the few cursory references in the Qur'ān to the exodus seem to be more concerned with the punishment of Pharaoh (for his imperviousness to all God's attempts to convince him of the truth) than with the triumphal escape of the Israelites. In the following passage, taken from ṣūra 10 (Jonah), the focus is clearly not on the salvation of the children of Israel, but on Pharaoh's ultimate end:

> And We brought the Children of Israel across the sea, and Pharaoh with his hosts pursued them in rebellion and transgression, till, when the [fate of] drowning overtook him, he exclaimed: I believe that there is no God save Him in whom the Children of Israel believe, and I am of those who surrender [unto Him]. What! Now! When hitherto thou hast rebelled and been of the wrongdoers?[8]

Thus, while in the Qur'ān Moses certainly acts as a leader and lawgiver to the children of Israel, his prophetic role, like that of Muhammad, is shown to extend to all of humanity. In the Qur'ān, as in the Bible, we find many references to Moses' continuing struggle with the intransigence and disobedience of his people. Such accounts may well have been intended as an admonition to Jews who were exposed to the Islamic revelation, and it is interesting to note in this regard that stories in the Qur'ān about the children of Israel are sometimes addressed to them in person, for example: 'And remember when We made a covenant with you and caused the mount to tower above you', or 'O Children of Israel! We delivered you from your enemy, and we made a covenant with you on the holy mountain's side, and sent down on you the manna and the quails.'[9] But the reminder of Moses' experiences with the children of Israel

7. Qur'ān 79.15–19.

8. Qur'ān 10.91–92. Most commentators have understood the end of this passage to be an indication that Pharaoh's last-minute attestation of faith on seeing the inevitable approach of death was too late to save his soul, while Pharaoh's body being raised to the surface of the water (10.92) was a clear sign to the children of Israel of their salvation from his oppression. The twelfth to thirteenth-century mystic Ibn ʿArabī, however, held that Pharaoh's attestation of faith was accepted, and therefore may be understood as a sign of God's overriding mercy (Ibn ʿArabī, *The Bezels of Wisdom* [trans. R.J.W. Austin; Classics of Western Spirituality Series; London: SPCK, 1982], pp. 250 and 264–65). See also the *Mathnawī* of Jalāl al-Dīn Rūmī (trans. R.A. Nicholson; London: Gibb Memorial Trust, 1968), II, pp. 411–12. A Ph.D. dissertation on the figure of Pharaoh in the works of Ibn ʿArabī and Rūmī is currently being prepared by Amer Latif at the State University of New York.

9. Qur'ān 2.63 and 20.80.

would also have given Muhammad an idea of the kind of difficulties he might face in galvanizing the community of early Muslims. On the other hand, stories of Moses' confrontation with Pharaoh, like that of Abraham with Nimrod, must have provided encouragement for Muhammad in his struggle with members of his own tribe who were vehemently opposed to his monotheistic message.

Apart from his Qur'ānic role as prophet, messenger and leader of his people, Moses is also shown as the one who was 'brought nigh in communion',[10] who experienced the theophany in the burning bush at the valley of Tuwa and on Mount Sinai, and heard God speak without intermediary, for which privilege he was given the honorary title *Kalīm Allāh*, 'the interlocutor of God'. Moses' experience of the theophany on Mount Sinai is related only once in the Qur'ān.[11] Given the importance that this short passage has for understanding the Islamic perception of Moses, it will be worth quoting it here in full:

> 143 And when Moses came to Our appointed tryst and His Lord had spoken unto him, he said: My Lord! Show me [Thyself] that I may gaze upon Thee. He said: Thou wilt not see Me, but gaze upon the mountain! If it stands still in its place, then thou wilt see Me. And when his Lord revealed [His] glory to the mountain He sent it crashing down. And Moses fell down senseless. And when he woke he said: Glory unto Thee! I turn unto Thee repentant, and I am the first of the [true] believers.
>
> 144 He said: O Moses! I have preferred thee above mankind for My messages and by My speaking [unto thee]. So hold to that which I have given thee, and be among the thankful.
>
> 145 And We wrote for him, upon the tablets, the lesson to be drawn from all things and the explanation of all things, then [bade him]: Hold it fast; and command thy people [saying]: Take the better [course made clear] therein. I shall show thee the abode of evil-livers.

It can clearly be seen here how the Qur'ānic account of this event differs from its biblical counterpart. Verse 145 speaks of the tablets, but that which was inscribed on them is only summarily described. Rather, our attention is focused on Moses' request for the vision of God, which is refused. The Qur'ān does not give any reason for this refusal, unlike the Bible which states that 'no one shall see me and live';[12] but the same is implied in the awesome effect which the manifestation of the divine glory has upon the mountain and Moses. In the Islamic tradition, Moses is, besides Muhammad, the only prophet to have been granted such an intimate encounter with God. Muhammad's night journey and ascension (*miʿrāj*) are mentioned twice in the Qur'ān,[13] but the description is allusive and poetic rather than explicit, for example: 'Then he drew nigh and

10. Qur'ān 19.52.

11. Qur'ān 7.143–45 (although Moses' period of forty days' retreat at Mount Sinai is alluded to earlier in the Qur'ān [2.51]).

12. Exodus 33.20.

13. 17.1 and 53.8–18.

came down, Till he was [distant] two bows' length or even nearer', and 'The eye turned not aside nor yet was overbold. Verily he saw one of the greater revelations of his Lord.'[14] Much more detailed accounts of Muhammad's *mi^crāj*, based upon his own description of the experience, have nevertheless been preserved in the biographies of the Prophet's life (*Sīra Rasūl Allāh*).[15]

Inevitably, the experiences of these two prophets came to be compared. Concerning the *miʿrāj*, the Qur'ān does not state that Muhammad saw God, yet that possibility is not closed as in the case of Moses. Indeed, it is widely held in Sunni tradition that on the night of the *miʿrāj*, when Muhammad had gone beyond the 'lote tree of the uttermost end', he did see God, although there is a difference of opinion as to whether it was a vision of the eyes or heart.[16] The denial of the vision of God to Moses in the Qur'ān therefore provided a scriptural basis for a distinction in rank which Islamic tradition was to make between the two prophets. In Qur'ānic commentaries, we find such comparisons being made as 'God spoke to Muhammad without a veil, whereas He spoke to Moses from behind a veil', and 'God divided hearing His speech and seeing Him between Moses and Muhammad. Moses heard God speak twice and Muhammad saw Him twice';[17] or, more mystically, 'Moses had not, like Muhammad, gone beyond hearing and mentioning to witnessing (*mushāhadat*) ... Muṣṭafā [18] had gone beyond the bounds of listening to the point of union ... Remembrance was effaced in the Remembered, the sun in light itself. It is impossible to speak when immersed in vision.'[19]

Comparisons such as these are not in any way intended to belittle the station of Moses, but simply to increase love and respect among Muslims for Muhammad. Thus, the twelfth-century Persian Sufi exegete Rashīd al-Dīn Maybudī, quoted above, listed all the aspects of Moses' life that are mentioned in the Qur'ān, and said, 'God mentioned all this that the people of the world should know his special relationship, intimacy and proximity [with God], yet, with all this distinction and rank, he did not go beyond the foot of obedience to the Prophet Muhammad.'[20]

14. Qur'ān 53.8–9 and 53.17–18.
15. As, for example, in Muhammad Ibn Isḥāq's account, cited in n. 5 above.
16. Qur'ān 53.12. Numerous traditions on this subject are quoted in Ṭabarī's commentary on the Qur'ān: *Jāmiʿ al-bayān* (ed. M.M. Shākir and A.M. Shākir; Cairo: Dar al-Maʿārif, AH 1374/1955), XXVII, pp. 26–29.
17. *Jāmiʿ al-bayān*, XXVII, p. 27.
18. Muṣṭafā, which literally means 'chosen one', is one of the names given to Muhammad.
19. Rashīd al-Dīn Maybudī, *Kashf al-asrār wa ʿuddat al-abrār* (10 vols.; Tehran: Intishārāt-e Amīr Kabīr, 1951–59), I, p. 53.
20. Maybudī, *Kashf al-asrār*, VII, p. 286.

Moses in Sufi Tradition

For Sufis, Moses has the special position of being the prophet whom they regard, more than any other, as the prototype of the spiritual wayfarer. As Paul Nwyia has observed, the Qur'ānic accounts of Moses inspired Sufi exegetes to 'meditate upon his experience as being the entry into a direct relationship with God, so that later the Sufis would come to regard him as the perfect mystic, called to enter into the mystery of God'.[21]

One of the earliest mystical interpretations of the story of Moses is to be found in the commentary attributed to Jaʿfar al-Ṣādiq (d. 765 CE),[22] who is held by Shīʿite Muslims to be the sixth imam,[23] and revered by Sufis as a great mystic. According to this interpretation, Moses' journey to Midian and thence to Tuwa was a spiritual journey, which culminated in his experience of the theophany of the burning bush. His 'spiritual progress' began when he set out for Midian, for the Qur'ān informs us, 'And when he turned his face to Midian he said: "Peradventure my Lord will guide me in the right road."'[24] This, as the commentary explains, indicates that as Moses turned his face towards Midian, the orientation of his heart was towards God. The orientation of his heart (towards God) was the first condition of his being 'honoured with God's speech'.[25] The second condition was fulfilled when he came to the waters of Midian and prayed, 'My Lord! I am needy of whatever good Thou sendest down for me.'[26] As the commentary relates, this prayer was a manifestation of 'poverty' towards God, that is, his awareness of his own utter neediness.[27] Inner poverty requires the complete emptying of the heart. Thus, when Moses came to the valley of Tuwa, he was commanded, 'Take off your shoes', and this

21. P. Nwyia, *Exégèse coranique et langue mystique* (Beirut: Dar el-Machreq éditeurs, 1970), p. 83.

22. This commentary is included in Abū ʿAbd al-Raḥmān al-Sulamī's compilation of early Sufi exegesis, the *Ḥaqāʾiq al-tafsīr*. Jaʿfar's commentary has been extracted from Sulamī's work and published in P. Nwyia, 'Le Tafsir Mystique attribué à Gaʿfar Ṣādiq', *Mélanges de l'Université de Saint Joseph* 43 (1967), pp. 179–230, and republished in N. Pourjavady (ed.), *Majmūʿa-ye āthār-e Abū ʿAbd al-Raḥmān al-Sulamī* (Tehran: Iran University Press, AH 1369/1990). There remains, however, considerable doubt concerning this attribution. Gerhard Böwering, for example, calls the author of these interpretations 'Pseudo Jaʿfar al-Ṣādiq', and considers that he probably lived in the first half of the tenth rather than the eighth century: G. Böwering, 'The Light Verse: Qurʾānic Text and Sufi Interpretation', *Oriens* 36 (2001), pp. 113–44 (135).

23. The Shīʿa believe that after Muhammad, only 'Ali (the Prophet's nephew and son-in-law) and his descendants were the rightful inheritors of leadership of the Islamic community.

24. Qur'ān 28.22.

25. Qur'ān 7.144. Sulamī, *Ḥaqāʾiq al-tafsīr*, in Nwyia, 'Tafsir Mystique', p. 216, and Pourjavady (ed.), *Majmūʿa*, p. 49.

26. Qur'ān 28.24.

27. Sulamī, *Ḥaqāʾiq al-tafsīr*, in Nwyia, 'Tafsir Mystique', p. 216, and Pourjavady (ed.), *Majmūʿa*, p. 49.

symbolized the command for him to cut off his heart from everything other than God.[28] Finally, the commentary attributed to Jaʿfar al-Ṣādiq explains how Moses' experience of the theophany in the burning bush was only possible through his annihilation (that is, the complete effacement of his consciousness), and his subsisting through the divine presence.[29] The explanation here takes the form of an address made by Moses to God: 'You! You are the One Who is and Who will be eternally, and Moses has no place beside You, nor the audacity to speak, save that You make him subsist through Your Subsistence, and that You attribute him with Your attributes.'[30]

In interpreting Moses' experience of the theophany on Mount Sinai, this same commentator (allegedly Jaʿfar al-Ṣādiq) explained in similar vein that Moses was, at the moment of hearing God speak, absent from himself, that is, annihilated from his own attributes. Yet in the interpretation of Moses' request for the vision of God, the commentary does not really go beyond the theological position that Moses' request was refused simply because it is impossible to see God, or certainly not with the mortal eye. When Moses afterwards repented of his request (v. 143), this is, in Jaʿfar's interpretation, an indication that he was the first to realize this theological truth.[31]

Later Sufi commentators, however, and especially those who emphasized the mystical way of love, sought to excuse Moses for his seemingly outrageous request for the vision of God. How could he have done otherwise? So overcome was he that he could not restrain himself. It was the ecstasy of hearing God speak which compelled him to seek the completion of union through vision. So it is with the mystics, whose thirst only increases when they are given something to drink, and it is said that even when in paradise they are granted the vision of their Lord, we should not imagine that their longing for their Lord becomes one jot less. It is the Sufis' belief that this intense longing for God is initiated by, or is the inevitable response to, God's love for us, which they say is attested to in the words of the Qur'ān, 'He loves them and they love Him.'[32] So, according to one interpretation, when the angels reprimand Moses for the

28. Qur'ān 20.12; Sulamī, *Ḥaqā'iq al-tafsīr*, in Nwyia, 'Tafsir Mystique', p. 209, and Pourjavady (ed.), *Majmūʿa*, p. 42.

29. The state of annihilation from self and the concomitant state of subsisting in or through God (denoted by the terms *fanā'* and *baqa'* respectively), were seen by many Sufis as the highest spiritual attainment in the mystical path.

30. Sulamī, *Ḥaqā'iq al-tafsīr*, in Nwyia, 'Tafsir Mystique', p. 209, and Pourjavady (ed.), *Majmūʿa*, p. 42.

31. Sulamī, *Ḥaqā'iq al-tafsīr*, in Nwyia, 'Tafsir Mystique', p. 197, and Pourjavady (ed.), *Majmūʿa*, p. 30. God's refusal to allow Moses to see God was used on both sides in the theological debate concerning whether or not God could be seen, either in this world or the next. Those who believed that God could not be seen in this world, but that vision of God would be granted to the blessed in the next life, interpreted the 'not' (*lan*) in 'Thou shalt not see Me', as a 'not' of limited duration. Others, such as the Muʿtazilites, who believed that the vision of God was impossible both in this life and the next, interpreted the 'not' (*lan*) as 'never'.

32. Qur'ān 5.54.

audacity of his request, he protests, 'You must forgive me for I did not come to this myself. He asked me first', and this is followed by the explanation, 'It was God who out of love began to reveal this mystery to a handful of earth; no wonder if earth's temerity went beyond its limit!'[33] Another Qur'ānic story of Moses which holds particular interest for Sufis is that of his meeting with Khiḍr. The episode is narrated only once in the Qur'ān,[34] and is not referred to in any other context. Since the story does not appear anywhere in the Bible, it might be useful to summarize it briefly here.

Moses is on a journey, determined to reach the 'place where the two seas (or rivers) meet'. When he eventually arrives at this spot, he finds a person described in the Qur'ān as 'one of Our [God's] servants to whom We have given mercy from Us, and to Whom We have taught knowledge from Our presence (*ʿilm ladunī*)'. This figure is unnamed in the Qur'ān, but Islamic tradition has identified him as 'al-Khaḍir' (the Green Man) or, as he is more popularly known, 'al-Khiḍr' (the Green). Moses begs to be allowed to accompany Khiḍr in order to learn 'guidance' (*rushd*) from him. However, Khiḍr warns him that he will not be able to bear with things of which he has no knowledge or experience. Moses persists in his request and Khiḍr gives him permission, but only on condition that he does not question him about anything he does, unless he himself raises the subject first. Moses' fulfilment of this condition is then put to the test three times, as Khiḍr carries out before his eyes three outrageous and apparently unreasonable actions: first, they embark on a ship which Khiḍr promptly holes, endangering the lives of all those on board; then they meet a young lad whom he kills; and finally, they enter a city where he repairs a wall without taking payment, even though the people there have shown them no hospitality. On witnessing each of these shocking acts, Moses forgets his undertaking, and is unable to restrain himself from expressing his outrage. When he fails the test for the third time, they agree to part, but not until Khiḍr has provided an 'interpretation' for the three acts which Moses could not understand. In each case, he explains to Moses the spiritual benefit that was concealed within these apparently destructive or unbeneficial acts.

Clearly, Sufis saw in Moses and Khiḍr a prefiguring of the traditional relationship between disciple and spiritual master, and a lesson on the correct conduct that should be observed by the disciple towards the master. But the story also seemed to pose a problem: how could a mere 'servant of God' tell Moses, a prophet, that there was knowledge that he did not have? Some scholars found a solution in the tradition that Moses had once imagined that there was no one in the world more knowledgeable than himself; this was God's way of teaching him otherwise. Others even claimed that the Moses named in this story was not Moses the prophet.[35] Sufis, however, saw the story not as a problem but as a challenge to reflect upon the nature of divinely inspired

33. Maybudī, *Kashf al-asrār*, III, p. 732.
34. Qur'ān 18.61–83.
35. In his history, Ṭabarī places the story of Khiḍr outside his chapter on Moses.

knowledge,[36] and the status of 'friendship with God' (*wilāya*) *vis-à-vis* prophethood (*nubuwwa*). Perhaps the best-known response to this challenge is that presented by Ibn ʿArabī (d. 1240) in his *Fuṣūṣ al-ḥikam* (Bezels of Wisdom). He explained that there is no question of Khiḍr being superior in knowledge to Moses; each of these two were perfect in a different kind of knowledge and each respected the other and maintained the required 'divine proprieties'. Moses, out of recognition for Khiḍr's rank, said, 'If I ask you anything more, then do not keep company with me', which made it possible for Khiḍr, who knew that he was obliged to obey the apostle, to terminate their companionship. Khiḍr for his part, out of deference to Moses' prophetic knowledge, said, 'I have knowledge from God that you do not have, just as you have knowledge from God that I do not possess.'[37]

Moses in Other Islamic Literature

So far, we have mainly looked at Moses as he is portrayed in the Qur'ān and *hadīth*, and discussed in conventional and mystical exegesis. But Moses features in many other branches of Islamic literature. We find all the Qur'ānic stories of Moses retold with the addition of many colourful details in the more popular genre of *Qiṣaṣ al-anbiyā*ʾ (Tales of the Prophets). Here we learn, for example, how when still an infant, Moses was sat on Pharaoh's lap and proceeded to tweak his adopted father's beard. Apart from the discomfort which this caused him, Pharaoh immediately had misgivings that this might be the very child who, as his dream had foretold, would bring about his ruin and that of the Egyptians. To allay the fears of her husband, Āsiya arranged a test to demonstrate that Moses did not know what he was doing. Two plates were placed before him, one containing rubies, and the other red-hot coals. It was only due to Gabriel's intervention that the discerning child picked up the live coals rather than the rubies and placed them in his mouth, so burning his tongue and producing the speech impediment for which he came to be known. This story does not appear in the Bible but in the Midrash,[38] and it entered Islam as part of the so-called *Isrāʾīliyyāt*, traditions which were learned from Jewish converts to Islam or early Muslims through their contact with Jews.

Moses also became the protagonist in stories that do not appear to have origin-ated in any scriptural tradition. For example, the now world-famous poet

36. The nature of the knowledge which had been vouchsafed to Khiḍr, *ʿilm ladunī*, became the subject of numerous discussions in philosophy and mysticism. Al-Ghazālī even wrote a treatise entitled, *Epistle concerning ʿilm ladunī* (*Al-risāla al-laduniyya*).

37. Ibn ʿArabī, *Bezels of Wisdom*, p. 260.

38. See, for example, J.Z. Lauterbach, *et al.*, 'Moses', in *Jewish Encyclopedia* (New York and London: Funk & Wagnalls, 1905), IX, pp. 44–59 (47); and L. Ginzberg, *Legends of the Jews* (trans. H. Szold; Philadelphia, PA: Jewish Publication Society of America, 1909–38), II, p. 272, where the infant Moses, rather than tweaking Pharaoh's beard, removes his crown and places it on his own head, a much more ominous sign in the eyes of Pharaoh and his advisers.

and mystic Jalāl al-Dīn Rūmī (d. 1273) included a tale of 'Moses and the Shepherd' in his *Mathnawī*. In this story, Moses took on the role of a strict theologian who expressed his horror at the anthropomorphic devotions of a shepherd.[39] The shepherd, being a simple fellow, expressed his love and devotion for God in the only way he knew: 'O God ... Where art Thou, that I may become thy servant and sew Thy shoes and comb Thy head? That I may wash Thy clothes and kill Thy lice and bring milk to Thee, O worshipful One.' Horrified at hearing these words, Moses accused the shepherd of blasphemy, but then he, in turn, was rebuked by God for having 'parted one of His servants from Him'. God explained that everyone has been given by God a different way of acting and expression, and that God looks at hearts, not tongues. The story is, among other things, intended as a criticism of, and warning to, those who, in order to avoid anthropomorphism, negate all the divine attributes: 'If anyone say of a king, "He is not a weaver," what praise is this? [That person] is surely ignorant.'[40] Elsewhere in Rūmī's *Mathnawī*, Moses, the 'spirit-enkindler', becomes a symbol for reason, while Pharaoh, the 'world-incendiary', symbolizes imagination, which by nature is dependent on sensuality.[41]

Moses in Modern Thought

We turn now from the Moses of Sufi allegory to Moses in modern thought, as exemplified in the Qur'ānic commentaries of two influential but very different writers and thinkers of the twentieth century, ʿAllāmeh Ṭabāṭabāʾī and Sayyid Quṭb.

The Iranian philosopher and jurisprudent Sayyid Muhammad Ḥusayn (ʿAllāmeh) Ṭabāṭabāʾī (1903–81) received a traditional Shīʿite education at Najaf in Iraq. Respected both as a teacher and a spiritual presence in Iran, Ṭabāṭabāʾī attempted in his numerous writings to harmonize his knowledge of theology, philosophy and mysticism with the traditional teachings of the imams. This approach is evident in his voluminous commentary on the Qur'ān, entitled *Al-Mīzān fi tafsīr al-Qurʾān* (The Balance of Judgment in the Exegesis of the Qur'ān), where his discussions of the scripture are always followed by a section on the imams' sayings concerning the subject-matter of the verses. Much of his commentary on the story of Moses is taken up with his attempts to demonstrate Moses' infallibility: the doctrine that prophets were '*maʿṣūm*' (immune from error) was of central importance to the Shīʿa, who extended it to include their imams. Two events in the Qur'ānic account of Moses raise the question of his infallibility: his request for the vision of God (which according to Shīʿite theology is impossible in this life and the next); and his apparently committing a falsehood when he claimed that he would be patient with Khiḍr. Ṭabāṭabāʾī attempted to

39. Jalāl al-Dīn Rūmī, *Mathnawī*, I, pp. 310–13.
40. Jalāl al-Dīn Rūmī, *Mathnawī*, I, p. 309.
41. Jalāl al-Dīn Rūmī, *Mathnawī*, II, pp. 399–400.

solve the problem of Moses' request for the vision of God by using a number of theological and philosophical arguments to demonstrate that the 'vision' here requested could in no way have been a vision of the eyes, but a kind of immediate or necessary knowledge.[42] In response to the second question, he exonerated Moses from any accusation of falsehood by pointing out that he had placed the condition of 'God willing' on his undertaking to Khiḍr.[43]

A very different approach to exegesis of the Qur'ān is that of Ṭabāṭabāʾī's Egyptian contemporary, the Islamic reformist and activist Sayyid Quṭb (1906–66). Unlike Ṭabāṭabāʾī, Quṭb was not a religious scholar, but a talented secular writer who rediscovered Islam after becoming disillusioned with Western values and Western interference in Middle Eastern politics. In his famous commentary *Fī Ẓilāl al-Qurʾān* (In the Shade of the Qur'ān), Quṭb ignored the vast corpus of traditional knowledge about the scripture, interpreting much of the Qur'ān according to his own radical view of the current political and sociological problems facing the Islamic world. This is particularly true of the first thirteen volumes of the commentary, which he revised during ten years of imprisonment, prior to his execution for his association with the Muslim Brotherhood. Typical of Quṭb's commentary is his interpretation of the breaking of the covenant by the children of Israel,[44] in which he stated that all the afflictions which the Jews have suffered throughout history are due to, first, their breaking of the covenant, and secondly, their rejection of Muhammad's message.

Yet, while he repeatedly condemned the children of Israel, Quṭb had nothing but love and reverence for their prophet Moses. In fact, it would be hard to find in Islamic exegetical literature a warmer and more moving account of Moses than in Quṭb's commentary on the theophany of the burning bush. Here, there is no question of comparing Moses' experience with Muhammad's *miʿrāj*. Quṭb's aim was to emphasize the preciousness and awesomeness of the theophany itself. Even the sūra in which it is narrated is described as having 'a special "shade" which arches over the entire sky. An exalted mighty shade, which humbles hearts, stills breaths, and at which faces are lowered. That is the shade which bestowed the manifestation of the Merciful to Moses.'[45]

Quṭb drew many lessons from the stories of Moses which have relevance to what he considered to be the present-day challenge facing Muslims. He examined the conversion of Pharaoh's magicians and observed that they were first of all convinced in their minds; they only gained victory over Pharaoh's threats once belief had conquered their hearts. Similarly, the 'companions of truth' will not gain mastery over the outer world until they rise up inwardly through God.[46] He stressed the tremendous worldly power and might of

42. Sayyid Muḥammad Ḥusayn Ṭabāṭabāʾī, *Al-Mīzān fi tafsīr al-Qurʾān* (Beirut: Mu'assasat al-ʿĀlamī, 1997), VIII, pp. 242–46.
43. Sayyid Muḥammad Ḥusayn Ṭabāṭabāʾī, *Al-Mīzān fi tafsīr al-Qurʾān*, XIII, p. 339.
44. Qur'ān 5.13.
45. Quṭb, *Fī Ẓilāl al-Qurʾān* (Beirut: Dār Iḥyāʾ al-Turāth al-ʿArabī, 1966–67), V, p. 63.
46. Quṭb, *Fī Ẓilāl al-Qurʾān*, V, pp. 87–88.

Pharaoh, and wondered at the contrast between the mighty tyrant and the helpless babe who was in his household – did Quṭb intend us to see a parallel here? When, later, Moses went to oppose the greatest king on earth and the most rebellious, he was entering the 'battle between *faith* and *oppression*'.[47] The juxtaposition of these two words (rather than the more obvious opposites of faith and unbelief) is perhaps significant, because in Quṭb's vision, the Islamic revolution (faith) becomes the 'divine imperative for the liberation of humanity from oppressive rulers'.[48] Overall, Moses appears to be one of Quṭb's heroes in the ongoing struggle to 'expel evil and establish righteousness in the world'.[49]

Conclusion

As Muhammad's closest forebear in prophethood and leadership of a community, Moses has a prominent place in the Qur'ān. But he has also taken on in the Islamic tradition a number of other roles. In the examples looked at in this essay, we have seen him variously portrayed as a foil to highlight Muhammad's perfection; a spiritual wayfarer; a perfected mystic; a lover of God overwhelmed by the longing for union; a disciple on the path of knowledge; a zealous theologian; a symbol of reason; and a hero in the battle between faith and oppression. In fact, the Islamic tradition has accorded more versatility to Moses than to any other prophet. Why should this be so? Perhaps because Moses appears more familiar and accessible than the other prophets. The Qur'ān and *ḥadīth* present Moses as a great prophet, of course; but they also show us his more 'human' side: he is the mischievous child who tweaked Pharaoh's beard, the impulsive youth who killed an Egyptian and then fled in fear; he got lost in the valley of Tuwa; he lost his temper with the Israelites and threw down the tablets; and he failed the three tests of forbearance set by Khiḍr. At the same time, the Qur'ān reveals his most intimate, exalted moments of communing with God. Ultimately, whatever other roles he may perform, it is as '*Kalīm Allāh*', as the prophet and messenger who was given the privilege of hearing God speak, that Moses is revered and cherished in Islam.

47. Quṭb, *Fī Ẓilāl al-Qur'ān*, V, p. 73.

48. Y. Y. Haddad, 'The Koranic Justification for an Islamic Revolution: The View of Sayyid Quṭb', *Middle East Journal* 37.1 (1983), pp. 14–29 (18). See also A.H. Johns, 'Let My People Go! Sayyid Quṭb and the Vocation of Moses', *Islam and Christian-Muslim Relations* 1 (1990), pp. 143–70.

49. Quṭb, *Fī Ẓilāl al-Qur'ān*, II, p. 271, as cited in Haddad, 'Koranic Justification', p. 19.

Moses in Jewish, Christian and Muslim Thought

Norman Solomon, Richard Harries and Tim Winter

Jonathan Gorsky contrasts the normative rabbinic view of Moses with other perceptions of him in the literature of the time such as that of the Samaritans, the pseudepigrapha and Philo. In this literature, Moses' own person has an exalted status which parallels the way in which Christians view Jesus. Even allowing for the variety of rabbinic opinions on Moses, there is a common emphasis on his humility, his status as a fellow human being, and the radical distinction that must always exist between creatures and the divine creator, even when the creature is as important to the divine purpose as Moses. It is the self-abnegation of Moses that makes it possible for him to be one through whom the purpose of God is worked.

John Barton outlines three ways in which Moses has been understood in Christian tradition. First, Moses is a mystic who ascended the mount of contemplation, an interpretation which is particularly pronounced in the literature of the Eastern Orthodox Church from Gregory of Nyssa onwards. Secondly, Moses is the leader of a liberation movement, an emphasis that has been particularly visible in modern liberation theology. Thirdly, there is the ambivalent relationship that Christianity has had with Moses as a lawgiver. It is to be noted that, according to Jonathan Gorsky, the emphasis in Judaism is not on Moses as a lawgiver, for it is God who gives the law, even though it is given to the people of Israel through Moses.

Annabel Keeler, in explicating the Islamic view of Moses, points first of all to his great importance. He is mentioned 502 times in the Qur'ān, far more than the references to Jesus, Noah and even Abraham. In Islam, he is described in a number of ways which parallel the prophet Muhammad while it is often made clear that Muhammad exceeds him in importance. Not surprisingly, Moses' character exhibits some of the main themes of Islamic theology, particularly the fundamental religious and moral injunction that we are to submit ourselves to God. Thus when Pharaoh was drowning in the Red Sea, he said, 'I believe that there is no God save Him in whom the Children of Israel believe, and I am of those who surrender [unto Him].'[1] As in Judaism, there is an emphasis upon

1. See Annabel Keeler's paper, 'Moses from a Muslim Perspective', above.

the otherness of God, so that in the Qur'ān, Moses was denied a vision of God, even though he asked for one and was brought near in communion. Particularly interesting is the way in which Moses is taken up, in different ways, in Sufi traditions. So some Sufi commentators, who emphasize the mystic way of love, try to account for Moses' desire for a vision of God. As one Sufi explained, 'It was God who out of love began to reveal this mystery to a handful of earth; no wonder if earth's temerity went beyond its limit!'[2] In modern times, the Islamic reformist Quṭb saw the struggle between Moses and Pharaoh not so much as one between faith and unbelief as between faith and oppression, that oppression being paralleled by the situation of many Muslims in the modern world.

In these three portraits, at once overlapping and contrasting, there are many particular themes that could be pursued in a more scholarly, detailed way. However, what might be drawn out of them for the interfaith conversation and pilgrimage today?

In their understanding of Moses, both Judaism and Islam bring out the radical otherness of God, the abyss between the uncreated ground of all that exists and creaturely existence. Human beings can only come before this transcendent and holy reality with a sense of awe. Islam makes this particularly prominent in its denial to Moses of a vision of God, at least in this life. Jonathan Gorsky, in his analysis of Judaism, brings it out in his stress on the humility and self-abnegation that characterize a genuine mystic. Traditional Christianity has certainly shared this emphasis. As a modern biblical scholar has written, commenting on Ephesians 3.18–19, the prayer which ends asking that we might grasp 'the breadth and length and height and depth, and to know the love of Christ that surpasses knowledge': '[humanity] must know God or perish; but unless [it] knows him as ultimate mystery, [it] does not know him at all'.[3] At the same time, Christianity has wanted to stress the accessibility of God in Jesus. A proper balance between the ultimate mystery of God, and God's availability to us in the human form of Jesus, has not always been kept. So it may be that Islam and Judaism sometimes have an interrogative role to play in relation to modern Christianity at this point. God is God, one who by definition brings about a radical reappraisal of our creaturely life in relation to its divine origin.

In Judaism, Moses led the people out of Egypt and was the one through whom God gave the law to Israel for a particular purpose. This purpose was to create a community, dwelling in a land, that would faithfully reflect the divine will in its communal living. Similarly, in Islam, the purpose of the revelation to Muhammad, anticipated in Moses, was to bring about a community of people united in their obedient submission to God's revealed will. Christianity shares with both these religions the idea that God wants to bring about true community, and in this case, it is achieved through incorporation into Christ. These ideas of community are worth exploring a little further.

2. See Annabel Keeler's paper, 'Moses from a Muslim Perspective', above.
3. G.B. Caird, *Paul's Letters from Prison* (London: Oxford University Press, 1976), p. 70.

From a Christian point of view, God's purpose is to bring about an inclusive, universal society characterized by profound, mutual care that draws deep on the depth of love within God's own self: a community that has to be built up in this life but which has its consummation beyond space and time in the communion of saints. Because something, somewhere along the line, has gone radically wrong, Jesus came to reconstitute or recreate human society around himself, inviting people to follow him in the way of love. From a Jewish point of view, God's purpose is also to build up a true community, a society that faithfully reflects God's mind and will. However, in the case of Judaism, the emphasis is upon a particular people being summoned to do this. God's purpose in relation to the rest of humanity is left somewhat unclear. The people of Israel know that they have been summoned and given the responsibility to create in their own life a community that is obedient to the divine purpose. From an Islamic point of view, the intention, as in Christianity, is to bring about a universal community, the Umma, which will come about through loving submission to the divine will as revealed to Muhammad.

Although there is a difference in perspective between Christianity and Islam on the one hand and Judaism on the other, all three religions emphasize the facts that the divine purpose is to bring about true community and that true community depends upon a right relationship to the divine. In this, they all reject any understanding of religion as 'a flight of the alone to the alone', not least its modern form of a purely internalized, private spirituality.

A third area for continuing exploration is the modern emphasis in some forms of Christianity and some forms of Islam on the story of Moses as a sign that God wills to liberate people from all forms of oppression and injustice. This theme was emphasized in modern Judaism at the time when Jewish communities in the former Soviet Union and the Middle East felt particularly vulnerable, and the ingathering of Jews to Israel was seen as a new exodus of the oppressed. It is also there in the work of Marc Ellis who applies the ideas of liberation theology to the plight of the Palestinian people.[4]

A final area of exploration could be the Christian insight that human beings are made to reflect the glory of God, a theme which finds its locus in the story of Moses as interpreted especially in the Eastern tradition of Christianity. Gregory of Nyssa, for example, said that Moses 'shone with glory', and suggested that this was because the human soul thirsts for what is beautiful and is never satisfied with purely earthly forms of beauty. We wish 'to enjoy the Beauty not in mirrors and reflections, but face to face'.[5] For Gregory Palamas, the emphasis is on the uncreated light which transfigured Jesus on the mount of transfiguration. This uncreated light which transformed Jesus can also transform human beings. 'The chosen apostles were transformed by the divine

4. M. Ellis, *Towards a Jewish Theology of Liberation* (Maryknoll, NY: Orbis Books, 1987).

5. Gregory of Nyssa, *The Life of Moses* (ed. A.J. Malherbe and E. Ferguson; New York: Paulist Press, 1978), p. 114.

ecstasy on the mountain, contemplating the irresistible outpouring of your light and your unapproachable divinity.'[6] Again, Gregory quotes Macarius: 'Our mixed human nature, which was assumed by the Lord, has taken its seat in the right hand of the divine majesty in the heavens, being full of glory not only [like Moses] in the face, but in the whole body.'[7]

This view is rooted not only in a Christian understanding of the transfiguration of Jesus on the mountain, with Moses on one side and Elijah on the other both prefiguring and pointing to this, but in Paul's exegesis of the Moses story. According to Paul, there is no veil over our face, because we read the Hebrew scriptures with a true hermeneutical key: 'all of us, with unveiled faces, seeing the glory of the Lord as though reflected in a mirror, are being transformed into the same image from one degree of glory to another'.[8] This is all part of the process of theosis or divinization. For according to the theology of the Eastern Church, we are not simply made in the image of God, we are called to grow into this likeness, and that means being increasingly irradiated and ultimately transfigured by the divine glory.

There are parallels to this in both Jewish and Islamic mystical traditions. While Judaism, for example, rejects the notion of divinization, Moses is an archetype for those who have mystical experience of God. The Bible itself records his visions, from the vision at the burning bush to the vision in the cleft of the rock, where he beheld the attributes of God.[9] Maimonides saw Moses as the most gifted of the prophets, greatest in understanding and therefore closeness to God;[10] Kabbalists 'interpret' him as personifying the divine emanations that constitute the 'image of God' and in communion with the divine presence.[11] In Islamic tradition, Moses is depicted as fainting in front of the burning bush. In contrast, Muhammad, when taken up in his ascension to heaven, remains alert and awake.[12] This contrast suggests that an alert openness to the leading of God is prized even more than mystical ecstasy.

6. Gregory Palamas, *The Triads* (trans. N. Gendle; ed. J. Meyendorff; London: SPCK, 1983), p. 81.

7. Palamas, *Triads*, p. 77.

8. 2 Corinthians 3.18.

9. Exodus 3 and 33 respectively.

10. This is a major theme in several of his works, for instance *Mishneh Torah: Yesodei Ha Torah* 7.6.

11. See the discussion of the Sefirot in the section on Kabbala and psychology in Norman Solomon's paper below, 'The Image of God in Humanity from a Jewish Perspective'.

12. 'Notre Prophète – que Dieu lui donne Sa bénédiction et la paix! – était leur imâm et le plus parfait d'entre eux. Voilà pourquoi, quand il fut élevé vers les cieux, qu'il vit ce qui se trouvait là-haut comme Signes et que lui fut révélé ce qui lui fut révélé d'espèces de confidences, il se retrouva le matin, parmi eux, sans que son état ait changé et sans que cela n'apparaisse sur lui, à la différence de Moïse suite à sa perte de conscience (voir Coran, VII, 143) – que Dieu leur donne à tous Sa bénédiction et la paix!' (Y. Michot, 'Textes spirituels d'Ibn Taymiyya. I: L'extinction (fanâ')', *Le Musulman* 11 [1990], pp. 6–9 and 29 [8]).

Finally, there is the question of law. Judaism and Islam are united in regarding law as integral to their religions. To many modern Christians, this seems strange. Nevertheless, historically, Christianity has also viewed law as having a crucial place within God's revealed purpose. In Matthew's Gospel, for example, Jesus does not abrogate the law. He is the new Moses who interprets the law in a definitive way. Thomas Aquinas, who dominates most of the Western Christian tradition, had an architectonic scheme uniting law at all levels: the divine law, natural law, revealed law, positive law and canon law. Furthermore, the long tradition of moral casuistry sought to apply the basic principles of this law in detail to a whole range of particular situations. Although Lutheranism, having the cross as the fulcrum for its theological perspective, has a lesser role for law, within Protestantism Calvinism begins not with a cross but with the mind of God disclosed in the Hebrew scriptures (and united with the New Testament), and the concept of divine law is a very natural part of its understanding of Christianity. This has been carried over into those Protestant sects which have been influenced by Calvinism. Individualistic and pietistic forms of Christianity which totally disregard the role of law in religion are in this respect at least uncharacteristic of the main sweep of Christian history. This said, there would nevertheless be a difference between the application of this law between Christianity and Islam. However influential the Church has been, there has been a tacit acknowledgment of two spheres of authority, with the rendering to Caesar what is Caesar's and a rendering to God what is God's. Even in Byzantine history, where the emperor was regarded as God's representative on earth and where his sacral status was recognized in the liturgy at Hagia Sophia in Constantinople, the law that he used was primarily the old Roman law, which may have been accommodated to natural law in some respects, but which was not seen as explicitly divinely revealed. Islamic and Jewish law, understood as a way of life covering all aspects of religion and the secular world, would be seen more explicitly as an expression of the divine purpose and mercy for humankind. Interestingly, the Jewish word for law, *halakha*, is in Judaeo-Arabic sources translated as the word so basic to Islam, namely *sharīʿa*. In Christianity, however important the concept of law might be in the divine purpose, it would be true to say that Jesus becomes for Christians what Torah, the Jewish religion, is for Jews.

Chapter 3: Jesus

Jesus from a Christian Perspective

Kallistos Ware

Who is Jesus?

'Who do you say that I am?', Jesus asked his disciples as they journeyed to Jerusalem.[1] Nineteen centuries later, Dietrich Bonhoeffer (1906–45), awaiting death in a Nazi prison, asked himself the same question: 'What is bothering me incessantly is the question ... who Christ really is, for us today.'[2]

Who is Jesus? 'You are the Messiah, the Son of the living God', Peter replied to Jesus' question.[3] It is an answer that almost all Christians, today as in the past, would be willing to endorse, even though there are a few biblical critics who doubt whether Jesus believed himself to be the Messiah. Difficulty begins, however, over the interpretation of the phrase 'Son of the living God'. Does this mean that Jesus is a divine person, who pre-existed his human birth from Mary, 'true God from true God', in the words of the creed, coexisting with the Father from all eternity? Or is Jesus 'Son of God' in the sense that he is a human person who came to enjoy an exceptionally close relationship with God, and was specially chosen by God to be God's witness and messenger?

During the two thousand years of Christian history, the person and work of Jesus have been interpreted in many different ways. He has been regarded, more particularly since the nineteenth century, as a charismatic rabbi, a Palestinian peasant, a moral reformer or a political revolutionary,[4] whereas by others, beyond and above all these things, he is still seen as the 'only-begotten' or unique Son of God. Complications arise because, for the Christian believer, Jesus is on the one hand a historical figure, born around 4 BCE and executed by crucifixion around 30 CE, while on the other hand he is alive now, a personal

1. Matthew 16.15.
2. D. Bonhoeffer, *Letters and Papers from Prison* (ed. E. Bethge; London: SCM Press, enlarged edn, 1971), p. 279.
3. Matthew 16.16.
4. Cf. A. Hastings, 'Jesus', in A. Hastings, A. Mason and H. Pyper (eds.), *The Oxford Companion to Christian Thought* (Oxford: Oxford University Press, 2000), pp. 340–43 (341).

saviour with whom we enjoy a direct and continuing relationship in faith, hope and love.

Bewildered by the diversity of images used to describe Jesus, Ephrem the Syrian (c. 306–73) felt in danger of drowning: 'This Jesus has made so many symbols that I have fallen into the sea of them.'[5] Swimming through Ephrem's sea of symbols, let us consider first the New Testament account of Jesus, and then the understanding of this account by the Church during the past two millennia.

Jesus in the New Testament

The central fact concerning Jesus in the New Testament is his resurrection from the dead. Writing not more than twenty-five years after the event, Paul stated: 'I handed on to you as of first importance what I in turn had received: that Christ died for our sins in accordance with the scriptures, and that he was buried, and that he was raised on the third day in accordance with the scriptures.'[6] Without the acceptance of Jesus' resurrection, Paul insisted, the Christian message is rendered meaningless: 'If Christ has not been raised, then our proclamation has been in vain.'[7] At a somewhat later date, all four gospels – written, in the view of most scholars, between thirty-five and seventy years after the death of Jesus – conclude with an account of the resurrection. Their narratives differ in detail, but all agree that the tomb where his body had been laid was found to be empty; and Luke and John in particular make clear that after this, he was once more alive and present among the disciples, in the same body as that in which he had died upon the cross.[8]

As David Ford observes, the resurrection story is 'not about resuscitation', but it is 'a God-sized event'.[9] In the view of the New Testament writers, Jesus has been made alive again by the power of the Holy Spirit,[10] in a way that is totally unprecedented, and that has created the new community of the Church. While Jews and Muslims find it possible to regard Jesus as a prophet, this belief in the resurrection as an event within history is something distinctively Christian, for which no exact parallel can be found in Judaism or Islam.

Looking at the portrayal of Jesus' life prior to the resurrection, we are struck at once by the difference between the three Synoptic Gospels (Matthew,

5. *Hymns on Nisibis* 39.17, quoted in S. Brock, *The Harp of the Spirit: Eighteen Poems of Saint Ephrem* (Studies Supplementary to Sobornost, 4; London: Fellowship of St. Alban and St. Sergius, 2nd edn, 1983), p. 16.

6. 1 Corinthians 15.3–4.

7. 1 Corinthians 15.14.

8. Luke 24.39–40; John 20.27.

9. D.F. Ford, 'Christology', in Hastings, Mason and Pyper (eds.), *Oxford Companion to Christian Thought*, pp. 114–18 (115).

10. Romans 1.4.

Mark and Luke) and the fourth gospel (John). Two of the Synoptic Gospels contain infancy narratives, recounting how Jesus was born from a virgin named Mary, without having any human father.[11] Elsewhere in the New Testament, there is no explicit reference to the virgin birth. Paul, for instance, said only that Jesus was 'born of a woman',[12] underlining the reality of his birth but not its miraculous character. In the Synoptics, Jesus is stated at many points to be the Messiah and the Son of God. Nothing, however, is said about his eternal pre-existence as a divine person.

In the fourth gospel, by contrast, this is precisely the point at which the evangelist commenced: 'In the beginning was the Word [Logos], and the Word was with God, and the Word was God.'[13] The Logos was God's instrument in creation: 'All things came into being through him.'[14] This eternal and divine Logos then became incarnate as Jesus of Nazareth: 'the Word became flesh and lived among us'.[15] Later in the same gospel, Jesus himself affirmed his pre-existence, using the divine title 'I am': 'before Abraham was, I am'.[16] Praying to God the Father, Jesus spoke of his unity with the Father before the creation of the universe: 'So now, Father, glorify me in your own presence with the glory that I had in your presence before the world existed.'[17] All of this leads up to the culminating moment in the gospel as a whole, when Thomas says to the risen Christ, 'My Lord and my God!'[18]

Similar claims are made in Paul's epistles: Jesus is 'the image of the invisible God, the firstborn of all creation; for in him all things in heaven and on earth were created'.[19] For the author of the epistle to the Hebrews, Jesus is 'the reflection of God's glory and the exact imprint of God's very being', through whom God 'created the worlds'.[20] Here, then, Jesus is clearly regarded as a divine person, existing before his human birth and, indeed, before the creation of the world. This is clearly different from the Synoptic standpoint.

In the gospels, Jesus is represented, not as a scribe, nor as an ascetic and a desert-dweller like John the Baptist, but as an itinerant preacher, close to ordinary people. He showed compassion for the poor, the marginalized and social outcasts such as tax-collectors and prostitutes. He liked children, and in his dealings with women – some of whom he numbered among his immediate disciples – he displayed a freedom and openness that was unusual for a Jewish rabbi at that time. It is nowhere suggested that he had a wife, although it is not

11. Matthew 1–2; Luke 1–2.
12. Galatians 4.4.
13. John 1.1.
14. John 1.3.
15. John 1.14.
16. John 8.58.
17. John 17.5.
18. John 20.28.
19. Colossians 1.15–16.
20. Hebrews 1.3 and 1.2.

explicitly said that he was unmarried. He performed exorcisms and miracles of healing, and also nature miracles such as the stilling of the storm at sea.[21]

In his parables, Jesus spoke about the life of countryside and home – about the shepherd, the sower, the woman searching for a lost coin – but there is a relative absence of imperial, civil or military images. A central place is assigned in his teaching to the kingdom of God, which is seen as something in the future, and yet at the same time already present in a hidden manner. Jesus placed strong emphasis upon God's eagerness to forgive sinners, upon his mercy and loving-kindness, but he also gave warnings about judgement and hell-fire. While upholding the Jewish law,[22] he saw love as more important than juridical or ritual correctness.[23] The heart of his preaching is precisely the primacy of love.

Jesus was regarded by others as a prophet, and he himself behaved as one, especially in his use of symbolic actions or 'signs'. Prominent among these 'signs' was his choice of twelve disciples, representing the twelve tribes of Israel; this signified that he had come to found the new Israel. His entry into Jerusalem on a donkey signified that he was the expected Messiah.[24] At his final supper, he established a new 'covenant fellowship', in which the bread signified his body broken for the sake of humankind, and the wine his blood poured out for the salvation of the world.[25] The most important 'sign' of all was his actual death on the cross, conferring forgiveness of sins and new life.

After the death and resurrection of Jesus, the gospel story ends with his ascension into heaven.[26] His disciples were left expecting his imminent return to earth,[27] his 'second coming' in glory. This the Christian Church still awaits.

Paul's claim that Christ died and rose from the dead 'in accordance with the scriptures' draws our attention to a fundamental theme in the New Testament understanding of Jesus.[28] As the long-expected Messiah, Jesus fulfilled the prophecies of the Old Testament. His birth from a virgin was in accordance with Isaiah's prophecy, '"Look, the virgin shall conceive and bear a son, and they shall name him Emmanuel," which means, "God is with us."'[29] Similarly, the fact that he was born in Bethlehem, his subsequent flight into Egypt, and the massacre of the innocents were all seen as fulfilling Old Testament prophecies.[30] Above all, the Old Testament is interpreted in the gospels as foreshadowing his passion and death. Jesus is the suffering servant, prophesied in the book of

21. Mark 4.35–41.
22. Matthew 5.17; Luke 16.17.
23. Matthew 9.13; Mark 12.28–34.
24. Cf. Zechariah 9.9.
25. Mark 14.22–24; cf. 1 Corinthians 11.23–26.
26. Luke 24.50–51.
27. Acts 1.6–11.
28. 1 Corinthians 15.3–4.
29. Matthew 1.23; cf. Isaiah 7.14. In the Hebrew text, the word used is *almah*, meaning simply 'a young woman'; but Matthew follows the Greek version, which employs the word *parthenos*, 'a virgin'.
30. Matthew 2.6, 15 and 18; cf. Micah 5.2, Hosea 11.1 and Jeremiah 3.15.

Isaiah.[31] Among other things, the Old Testament is seen as foretelling the betrayal of Jesus for thirty pieces of silver,[32] the gambling of the soldiers for his garments,[33] his thirst,[34] and the fact that none of his bones was broken.[35] These are but a few examples out of many. For the Christian believer, this fulfilment of prophecy makes clear the continuity of sacred history. The Old Testament and the New form a single unity. Jesus is to be found everywhere in the pages of the Old Testament: the Hebrew scriptures point forward towards him and cannot be properly understood without him. Needless to say, this is very different from the Jewish reading of the Old Testament. Many biblical scholars in the West today tend to play down this appeal to prophecy. But for the New Testament writers themselves and for the early Church, the way in which Jesus fulfilled the prophecies of the old covenant constituted a decisive confirmation of his divine mission.

Throughout the Synoptic Gospels, one thing is abundantly clear. Jesus was a Palestinian Jew, living within a Jewish society. The manner in which he thought and taught, the illustrations that he used in his parables, and his personal behaviour all reflected his upbringing within Judaism. This Jewishness of Jesus has been often neglected by Christians in the past, but it has been rightly re-emphasized during the past thirty years by writers such as Geza Vermes.[36]

From Above or From Below?

How has the Christian Church interpreted this New Testament picture of Jesus? In a celebrated essay, Karl Rahner distinguished two main approaches, which he labelled 'christology from above' and 'christology from below'.[37] Christology from above ('katagogic' Christology) views Jesus as a divine person who has existed eternally, the second member of the Holy Trinity, the Son of God begotten from the Father 'before all the ages', who at a certain point in history underwent a second birth from a human mother, taking into himself all the fullness of our created human nature. The Virgin Mary is in this way *theotokos*, 'God-birthgiver' or 'Mother of God'. Although through his incarnation Jesus has 'humbled' or 'emptied himself',[38] yet despite the self-emptying or *kenosis* he still remains true God.

31. Matthew 8.17; see Isaiah 53.4, and cf. Acts 8.30–33 and 1 Peter 2.24–25.

32. Matthew 27.9–10; see Zechariah 11.12–13, and Jeremiah 32.6–15 and 18.2–3.

33. John 19.23–24; see Psalm 22.18.

34. John 19.28; see Psalm 22.15.

35. John 19.36–37; see Psalm 34.20, Exodus 12.46, Numbers 9.12, and Zechariah 12.10 and 13.6.

36. See in particular his seminal work, originally published in 1973, *Jesus the Jew: A Historian's Reading of the Gospels* (London: SCM Press, 3rd edn, 2001).

37. 'The Two Basic Types of Christology', in K. Rahner, *Theological Investigations*, XIII (trans. D. Bourke; London: Darton, Longman & Todd, 1975), pp. 213–23 (213).

38. Philippians 2.8.

Christology from below ('anagogic' Christology), on the other hand, starts not with Christ's pre-existence but with his human birth. Jesus is a human being, a prophet or a righteous person, who during his earthly life was taken up into a uniquely intimate fellowship with God. So, through his example and teaching, he provides a true disclosure of who God is. Whereas Christology from above appeals primarily, but not exclusively, to the fourth gospel, Christology from below bases itself mainly on the Synoptic Gospels, above all Mark, attaching particular importance to the parables and moral teaching of Jesus. Its exponents usually reject the virgin birth, but accept the miracles of healing, although not the nature miracles. Many of them, but by no means all, reject a literal understanding of the bodily resurrection.

While this distinction between Christology from above and Christology from below is helpful as a general characterization, in practice it needs to be carefully qualified.[39] In Karl Barth's opinion, any sound Christology has to be simultaneously both katagogic and anagogic: 'The New Testament obviously speaks of Jesus Christ in both these ways: the one looking and moving, as it were, from above downwards, the other from below upwards ... Both are necessary. Neither can stand or be understood without the other.'[40] A number of the theologians who have set out 'from below' have in fact ended up with a picture of Jesus not dissimilar from that found in those who work 'from above'. Wolfhart Pannenberg, for instance, began with the evidence of Jesus in history, but through a historical-critical account of the resurrection he ended up by affirming the divinity of Jesus Christ and the doctrine of the Trinity.[41] John A.T. Robinson started from Jesus as 'a man among men', but concluded by describing him as 'God for us', and by asserting an 'essential identity' between Christ and God.[42]

Those who approached Christology 'from below' in early Christianity have usually been categorized as 'adoptionists'. Adoptionism regards Jesus as a human person specially 'adopted' by God, who was raised to divine status either at his baptism or at his resurrection. This is the view often taken by Jewish Christians, such as the second-century Ebionites, who lived mainly beyond the Jordan. They denied Christ's pre-existence and the virgin birth, regarding him as the human child of Joseph and Mary, on whom the Spirit descended at his baptism.[43] The best known of the third-century adoptionists, Paul of Samosata, had a Greek rather than a Jewish background. He was condemned by a council

39. See, for example, the criticisms of N. Lash, 'Up and Down in Christology', in S.W. Sykes and D. Holmes (eds.), *New Studies in Theology 1* (London: Duckworth, 1980), pp. 31–46.

40. *Church Dogmatics* IV/1 (Edinburgh: T&T Clark, 1956), p. 135; cited in Lash, 'Up and Down in Christology', p. 36.

41. See his major work *Jesus: God and Man* (London: SCM Press, 1968).

42. J.A.T. Robinson, *The Human Face of God* (London: SCM Press, 1973).

43. The rather sparse evidence concerning the Ebionites is summarized in A. Grillmeier, *Christ in Christian Tradition* (London and Oxford: Mowbrays, 2nd edn, 1975), I, pp. 76–77.

at Antioch in 268 for asserting, among other things, that Jesus was 'a human being like us, but better in every way'.[44]

Arianism is often considered an example of Christology 'from below', but this is not strictly accurate. Arius of Alexandria (d. 336) was not in fact an adoptionist, for he regarded Christ not as a human person but as a kind of demi-god, who is neither true God nor yet 'a human being like us', but occupies a halfway house between the uncreated and the visible worlds: 'a created being, but not like other created beings', as he put it.[45] Thus Christ existed before his human birth and, indeed, before the creation of the world, although he is not co-eternal with God the Father.

Arianism was condemned at the Council of Nicaea (325), the First Ecumenical Council. Its creed, revised and expanded by the Second Ecumenical Council, at Constantinople (381), constitutes the classic formulation of Christology 'from above'.[46] In the long central paragraph concerning Jesus Christ, there are two sets of affirmations, the first dealing with his relationship to God, the second with his relationship to humankind. At the outset, it is said, 'We believe ... in *one* Lord Jesus Christ': he is not God and a human being coexisting side by side within the same body, but a single and undivided person who is God and human at once. Then, on the Godward side, it is affirmed that Jesus is *kyrios* or Lord (a divine title); he is 'the only-begotten [or unique] Son of God, begotten from the Father before all the ages', that is to say, in eternity; he is 'true God from true God'; he is begotten or born, but not created; he is 'consubstantial' or 'one in essence' (*homoousios*) with the Father (in other words, what the Father is, the Son is also; there is entire equality between them); and he is the Father's agent in creation, 'through whom all things came to be'. In this way, Jesus Christ is proclaimed to be totally and unreservedly one with God the Father.

Next, on the human side, it is said of Christ that 'for us humans (*anthropoi*) and for our salvation he came down from the heavens, and became incarnate from the Holy Spirit and the Virgin Mary, and became human (*eninthropisen*)'. Here, I have deliberately avoided the more familiar translation, 'for us men ... [he] became man'; for in fact the creed uses here the Greek word for a human

44. Fragment S.26, in H. de Riedmatten, *Les Actes du procès de Paul de Samosate* (Fribourg: Editions S. Paul, 1952), p. 153. There are doubts as to how far Paul should in fact be classified as an adoptionist.

45. Letter of Arius to Alexander of Alexandria, in H.G. Opitz (ed.), *Athanasius Werke* (Berlin: De Gruyter, 1934), III/1, pp. 12–13 (12). On Arianism, see R.D. Williams, *Arius: History and Tradition* (London: SCM Press, 2nd edn, 2001); on the Nicene response, see J. Behr, *The Nicene Faith* (Formation of Christian Theology, 2; 2 vols.; Crestwood, NY: St. Vladimir's Seminary Press, 2004).

46. For the full text of the Nicene-Constantinopolitan creed, in both the original (325) and the expanded (381) forms, see J. Pelikan and V. Hotchkiss, *Creeds and Confessions of Faith in the Christian Tradition*, I (New Haven, CT and London: Yale University Press, 2003), pp. 159 and 163.

being, *anthropos*, and not the word for a male, *aner*. Jesus was indeed a male, but that is not what the creed is concerned to assert; it is interested in his basic humanness, not in his maleness. The creed then goes on to assert how this same Christ has died by crucifixion, has risen from the dead and ascended into heaven, and will come again 'to judge the living and the dead'. Christ, as God incarnate, has entered into all the fullness of human life, and not only that, but into all the fullness of human death. Totally and unreservedly one with God, he is also totally and unreservedly one with us humans. He is, in Bonhoeffer's phrase, the 'beyond in the midst'.[47]

This twofold character of the one Christ – entirely God and entirely human – was stated with greater precision by the Fourth Ecumenical Council, assembled at Chalcedon in 451. Applying the distinction between essence (*ousia*) or nature (*physis*), on the one side, and person (*hypostasis*, *prosopon*), on the other, Chalcedon regarded Jesus, in his divine aspect, as different in person from God the Father, but one with the Father in essence. At the incarnation he then took a human nature, without thereby being changed in his divine nature. In this way, stated Chalcedon, he is one person in two natures, 'complete in Godhead and complete in humanness ... truly God and truly human ... one in essence with the Father according to Godhead and one in essence with us according to humanness, like us in everything, except for sin'.[48]

So the creed and the Chalcedonian definition ascribe to Jesus a double solidarity, a twofold identification, with God the Father on the one side, and with us human beings on the other. Yet this does not signify any division within the one Christ. He who underwent a genuine human birth and a genuine human death is not a second subject of attribution alongside the divine Son of God, but is one and the same with him. Moreover, Christ is not half divine and half human. On the contrary, there is in him a double fullness: not 'fifty-fifty', but one hundred per cent divine and one hundred per cent human, yet at the same time one and not two.

Such is the basic paradox asserted in traditional Nicene Christology. If it be asked why Christians were led to advance such bold and baffling claims about Jesus, a clue may be found in the words of the creed already quoted, 'for us humans and *for our salvation*'. In the view of the early Church, if Christ were to be considered as less than fully God or as less than fully human, the scheme of salvation would break down.

Among the various models used by early Christians to describe Christ's redemptive work – ransom, sacrifice, substitution, victory – perhaps the most far-reaching is the notion of salvation through *mutual participation*. Salvation means healing, and this healing is effected more specifically through sharing, through mutual exchange. Like is healed by like: Jesus saves us by becoming

47. Bonhoeffer, *Letters and Papers from Prison*, p. 282.

48. For the key passage in the Chalcedonian definition (in a somewhat different translation), see Grillmeier, *Christ in Christian Tradition*, I, p. 544.

what we are, by sharing totally in our human nature, thereby enabling us to share in what he is. Thus through a reciprocal 'exchange of gifts', he takes our humanness and in return communicates to us his divine life.

This idea of an exchange is already enunciated in the New Testament by Paul: 'though he was rich, yet for your sakes he became poor, so that by his poverty you might become rich'.[49] Elsewhere, Paul varied the metaphor: Christ's descent to our fallen condition makes possible our ascent to the heavenly realm.[50] Irenaeus of Lyons (c. 130 – c. 200) took up this notion, writing: 'In his unbounded love, he became what we are, so as to make us what he is.'[51] Yet more emphatically, the leading opponent of Arianism, Athanasius of Alexandria (c. 296–373), affirmed: 'He became human that we might be made god.'[52] The 'hominization' of God, that is to say, makes possible the 'deification' (*theosis*) of humankind.[53]

This kind of 'participation' soteriology leads us directly to the affirmation of the 'double fullness' in Christ. Unless he is fully divine and fully human, the 'exchange of gifts' is fatally impaired. Only if he is true God can he communicate to us the gift of divine life, and only if he is truly human can we humans receive that gift from and through him. Developing the inner logic of this 'participation' soteriology, we may affirm two complementary principles.

First, *only God can save*. Salvation is a divine act that originates in God, not in any created and inferior intermediary. A prophet or a holy person cannot be the saviour of the world. In the words of Athanasius, 'If Christ also, like us, merely shared in Godhead through participation, and was not himself the essential Godhead and image of the Father, then he would not divinize us, since he would himself require to be divinized.'[54] One who himself requires to be saved cannot be our saviour. If, then, Jesus is indeed to be our saviour, it follows that he must be fully God.

Second, *salvation has to reach the point of human need*. Only if Christ is genuinely human as we are, can we humans share in what he has done for us as God. As Maximos the Confessor (c. 580–662) put it, 'We lay hold of the divine to the same degree as that to which the Logos of God, deliberately emptying himself of his own sublime glory, became truly human.'[55] If, then, Jesus is to be our saviour, he must take up into himself integral human nature. Such are the underlying principles that are presupposed in Nicene Christology. Not all Western theologians today accept their validity. But, in the eyes of the

49. 2 Corinthians 8.9.
50. Philippians 2.5–11.
51. *Against the Heresies* 5, preface.
52. *On the Incarnation* 54.
53. On salvation as *theosis*, 'deification' or 'divinization', see N. Russell, *The Doctrine of Deification in the Greek Patristic Tradition* (Oxford: Oxford University Press, 2004).
54. *On the Synods of Rimini and Seleucia* 51.
55. *On the Lord's Prayer* (*PG* 90.877A).

early Church, the scheme of salvation through sharing would work only if Jesus, as God incarnate, is entirely one both with his Father and with us human beings.

The implications of the second principle, that Christ the saviour has to be genuinely human, need to be explored further. To reflective Christians at the present day, it is obvious that Jesus, whatever else he may be, is an authentic human being such as we are; what many contemporary Christians find much harder to believe is that he is God. In the early centuries of Christianity, on the whole the reverse was true. Adoptionists were in the minority; far more numerous were the docetists. Docetism, from the Greek *dokeo*, 'I seem', is the view that Christ's humanness is only apparent and not real; he seemed to have a human body and soul like ours and he seemed to suffer, but he did not actually do so.

Docetic Christology is found, for example, in second-century Christian Gnostic circles. In the apocryphal *Acts of John*, it is said that Jesus never closed his eyes in sleep, and never left any footprints in the earth when he walked. His outward appearance was constantly changing: as the *Acts of John* expressed it, 'his unity has many faces'.[56] In other Gnostic or semi-Gnostic texts, it is claimed that Jesus did not in fact die on the cross, but his place was taken by Simon of Cyrene or even by Judas Iscariot. This is similar to the view of the crucifixion found in the Qur'ān.

Whereas second-century docetists doubted the full reality of Christ's physical body, a more subtle form of docetism was advanced two centuries later by Apollinarius of Laodicea (c. 310–90). He maintained that, whereas Jesus had a genuinely human body, he did not have a human rational soul, but in his case the place of the soul was taken by the divine Logos. This meant that Christ did not possess feelings, emotions and temptations such as we do; he did not possess a human will, and so he did not have true human freedom. Thus Apollinarius could not accept the full force of the statement in the epistle to the Hebrews (and this is surely one of the most important christological texts in the whole of the New Testament): 'we do not have a high priest who is unable to sympathize with our weaknesses, but we have one who in every respect has been tested as we are, yet without sin'.[57]

Responding to Apollinarius, Gregory of Nazianzus (c. 329–79) appealed to the second of our soteriological principles, asserting: 'What has not been assumed has not been healed.'[58] Salvation has to reach the point of human need; like is saved and healed by like. If, then, Jesus has not assumed the fullness of human nature into himself, our salvation will be incomplete. To deny the existence of Christ's human soul is to deny also the salvation of our souls; the 'exchange of gifts' is rendered impossible.

56. *Acts of John* 91; cf. 88–89 and 93.
57. Hebrews 4.15.
58. *Letter* 101, to Cledonius (*PG* 37.181C).

Such in outline are the reasons that have led Christians to affirm that the eternal Son, 'true God from true God', has become completely human, and that as God-become-human he has suffered, died and risen from the dead. In the perspective of this traditional Christology, when Christians look at Jesus crucified, they see not only a suffering human being but suffering God. The fourth-century Nicene teaching has continued to prevail in the Christian East up to the present. In the West, it was accepted without question by mediaeval scholastic theologians such as Thomas Aquinas (c. 1225–74), and in the sixteenth century by the leading Reformers such as Luther and Calvin. In the Anglican tradition, it is unambiguously reaffirmed in the second of the Thirty-nine Articles of Religion (1562). Marginal figures – for example, Michael Servetus and the Socinians – called into question the Nicene teaching, but they are in no way representative of the Reformation as a whole.

In the nineteenth and twentieth centuries, however, the situation changed drastically in the West as a result of what is often termed 'the quest for the historical Jesus'.[59] The new orientation in Christology came about in consequence of two related factors. First, under the influence of post-Enlightenment philosophy, Christian thinkers in the West doubted whether it was possible any longer to affirm, in a literal way, statements concerning the divine realm such as 'true God from true God' or 'begotten before the ages'. Second, under the influence of the critical study of the Bible, an increasing number of scholars called in question the historicity of the gospels. Discarding what they regarded as 'mythological' elements such as Christ's divine pre-existence, his virgin birth, his bodily resurrection and his ascension into heaven, they sought to present him simply as a human teacher. Other critics went further than this, concluding that in the end we know virtually nothing about his life and teaching. Thus Rudolf Bultmann (1884–1976) maintained that the 'Jesus of history' can no longer be reconstituted; we can only speak about the 'Christ of faith'. Since the 1950s, however, there has been a widespread reaction against such radical scepticism.

What, then, is our present situation? In all major Christian groups – Roman Catholic, Orthodox, Anglican, Protestant – there are fundamentalists who reject wholesale the critical study of the Bible, and who accept without question all that is stated about Jesus in the New Testament. Their attitude towards scripture is similar to that of orthodox Muslims towards the Qur'ān. In their official teaching, however, all major Christian groups today accept that the Bible can and should be studied according to the rigorous criteria of textual, literary and historical criticism. Among Roman Catholics, for example, there has been a renaissance of biblical studies since the Second Vatican Council (1962–65),

59. This is the English title of a celebrated book by Albert Schweitzer, published in 1910 (the German original appeared in 1906), but the phrase is often applied more broadly to the whole movement of New Testament historical criticism from the late eighteenth century onwards.

while even a strongly traditionalist body such as the Orthodox is beginning to give greater attention to scriptural scholarship.[60] At the same time, Protestants, Anglicans, Orthodox and Roman Catholics, while insisting that the Church gives attention to the results of scholarly research concerning the Bible, from whatever source they come, would all of them add that the Church tests these results in the light of its experience and understanding of the faith as a whole.

To say this, however, is at once to admit that the critical-historical study of the New Testament documents does not and cannot provide on its own a conclusive answer to the question 'Who is Jesus?' Beyond the historical evidence, matters of faith and theological principle are also involved. Many scriptural specialists are convinced that the course of critical inquiry since the Enlightenment renders it no longer meaningful to affirm today the traditional Nicene and Chalcedonian statements about Christ. Yet there are others today who, while accepting the use of biblical criticism, still find it possible to affirm that Jesus is 'true God from true God'. Historical research on its own is unable to settle the question.

It is obvious that, in any interfaith dialogue between Jews, Christians and Muslims, 'Christology from above' creates difficulties that do not arise in the same way with 'Christology from below'. The liberal understanding of Jesus, which sees him as no more than a prophet and a moral teacher, can be readily accepted by many Jews – Claude Montefiore (1858–1938) is a notable example – although of course they do not regard him as the Messiah. Muslims are likewise willing to acknowledge Jesus as a prophet (indeed, they also believe in his virgin birth, although they do not consider that this implies pre-existence as the eternal Son of God). Yet, even if an 'anagogic' approach greatly facilitates interfaith dialogue, it has to be recognized that today, as in the past, the overwhelming majority of Christian believers continue to uphold the Nicene view of Jesus. Even a 'neutral' body such as the World Council of Churches states, as its basis of membership, that it is 'a fellowship of Churches which confess the Lord Jesus Christ as God and Saviour'. Adherents of the traditional christological standpoint are by no means opposed to friendly contacts with other religions, but they find it impossible to abandon what is, in their eyes, the distinctive mark of the Christian faith – belief in Jesus as the divine and eternal Son of God.

The Nearness yet Otherness of Jesus

Yes, indeed: Jesus has been interpreted by Christians in different ways over the past twenty centuries. It would, however, be a grave error to imagine that, in

60. For a joint Orthodox-Anglican statement, firmly approving the use of critical biblical study, see K. Ware and C. Davey (eds.), *Anglican-Orthodox Dialogue: The Moscow Statement Agreed by the Anglican-Orthodox Joint Doctrinal Commission 1976* (London: SPCK, 1977), pp. 83–85.

their understanding of Jesus, they are divided into two sharply opposed camps, 'traditionalist' and 'liberal'. Most contemporary Christians, on the contrary, would agree with Barth that our theology of Christ has to be simultaneously 'from above' and 'from below'. Most of them, that is to say, seek to insist, in one way or another, upon both the *nearness* and the *otherness* of Jesus.

The nearness of Jesus: we Christians are agreed in seeing Jesus as not just '*a* human' but '*the* human', the supreme example of what it is to be a human being, the 'second Adam' who shows us in himself the veridical dimensions of our human personhood. He is the mirror in which we see reflected our own authentic face. 'Who am I?' we ask; and the reply is, 'Look at Jesus'. As is said in a Christmas homily attributed to Basil the Great (c. 330–79), the birth of Jesus marks the birthday of the whole human race.[61] Because he is the truest and fullest expression of our humanness, Jesus is immediately close to each one of us. 'Gentle and humble in heart',[62] he carries our burdens and shares our sorrows and our joys. He understands our innermost fears and longings, and through his loving companionship he gives us strength and hope.

The otherness of Jesus: if Jesus is the supreme example of what it is to be a human being, yet he is also for all Christians, or almost all, more than *merely* human. He reveals God to us. He answers, not only the question 'Who am I?', but equally the question 'Who is God?' He is our window into the divine realm, the one who speaks to us with the authority of God's own self: 'Never has anyone spoken like this!'[63] With the two disciples whom Jesus accompanied on the road to Emmaus, we exclaim: 'Do not our hearts burn within us when he speaks to us?'[64]

The nearness of Jesus, his human solidarity with us, is strikingly expressed by the Russian writer Ivan Turgenev (1818–83) in his prose poem *Khristos*. He dreams that he is in a village church together with the peasant congregation. A man comes to stand beside him. 'I did not turn towards him, but immediately I felt that this man was Christ.' When, however, he eventually turns and looks at him, he perceives 'a face like everyone's face. A face like all men's faces ... And the clothes on him like everyone else's.' Turgenev is astonished. 'What sort of a Christ is this then? ... Such an ordinary, ordinary man.' But then he concludes: 'Suddenly I was afraid – and came to my senses. Only then did I realize that it is just such a face – a face like all men's faces – that is the face of Christ.'[65]

The otherness of Christ, his testimony to 'the beyond', is evident in the earliest non-Christian reference to the Christian community, written by someone speaking on the basis of personal contact. Pliny the Younger, Roman governor

61. *On the Nativity of Christ* (*PG* 31.1473A).
62. Matthew 11.29.
63. John 7.46.
64. Cf. Luke 24.32.
65. See S. Hackel, 'Some Russian Writers and the "Russian Christ"', *Eastern Churches Review* 10.1–2 (1978), pp. 43–51 (48).

of the province of Bithynia, in a letter written to the Emperor Trajan around the year 112, recounted how he had been interrogating some local Christians. They told him, so he wrote, that at their meetings it was their practice 'to sing a hymn to Christ as to a god' (*carmen Christo quasi deo dicere*).[66] Here, then, from an independent and, indeed, somewhat hostile witness, there is direct confirmation of what most Christians see as the essence of Christianity: we worship the human being Jesus as God. Even if there are Western Christians who find it problematic to assert, in unqualified terms, that Jesus is God, yet all of them, or almost all, are willing to address their prayers to Jesus, in the firm conviction that these prayers are heard by God.

This nearness yet otherness of Jesus, affirmed in one way or another by almost all who call themselves Christians, means that there is an element of antinomy and paradox in our understanding of his person. The paradox is particularly acute in traditional Nicene Christology: how, it may well be asked, can a single, undivided person think, feel, know and will simultaneously both as God and as a human being? The gospels unfortunately give us little help at this point. Except on rare occasions, such as Jesus' temptation in the garden of Gethsemane,[67] they speak only about his outward words and actions, not about his inner experiences. The evangelists did not share our modern obsession with matters psychological. The dimension of paradox, however, is not limited to Nicene Christology. For all Christians, not just for the 'Nicenes' but for others as well, there is something profoundly puzzling about Jesus. He is, to adapt Paul's phrase, 'unknown, yet well known'.[68] With good reason, confronted by his nearness yet otherness, by the strange combination of his humanness and his divineness, we speak of the *mystery* of Jesus. By 'mystery', in the religious sense of the word, is meant not simply an unsolved problem, a conundrum or enigma, but something that is indeed revealed to our understanding, yet never totally revealed, because it reaches into the depths of God. Let us never underestimate the apophatic dimension of all sound Christology, whether 'from above' or 'from below'. Jesus is to be approached with the full resources of our reasoning brain, but that is never sufficient. He is to be approached also with wonder, awe and wordless prayer. There is a danger in trying to say too much. 'Let all mortal flesh keep silence, and stand with fear and trembling.'[69]

In the presence of this nearness yet otherness, few have expressed more eloquently the feeling of wonder and mystery than the writer with whom we began, the Christian poet Ephrem the Syrian. Often it is the poets who are the best theologians of all. In a series of paradoxes, he spoke of Jesus as 'the Hidden One who revealed himself', 'the Rich One who became poor', 'the Mighty One who put on insecurity'. There is no one else like him:

66. Pliny, *Letters* 10.96.7.
67. Mark 14.32–42.
68. Cf. 2 Corinthians 6.9.
69. Hymn at the Great Entrance in the Liturgy of St. James: see F.E. Brightman, *Liturgies Eastern and Western* (Oxford: Clarendon Press, 1896), I, p. 41.

Whom have we, Lord, like you:
The Great One who became small,
The Wakeful who slept,
The Pure One who was baptized,
The Living One who died,
The King who abased himself to ensure honour for all.
Blessed is your honour![70]

70. *Hymns on the Resurrection* 1.22, in Brock, *Harp of the Spirit*, p. 30; cf. p. 14. See also S. Brock, *The Luminous Eye: The Spiritual World Vision of Saint Ephrem* (Cistercian Studies Series, 124; Kalamazoo, MI: Cistercian Publications, 1992), p. 25.

Jesus from a Jewish Perspective

Sybil Sheridan

More than anything, the issue that divides the Jew from the Christian and the Muslim is the person of Jesus. Much dialogue is concerned with common ideals and aims, while a minority of braver souls may tackle the issues that divide the faiths; but how does one have a dialogue when the subject in hand is of no interest to one party?

While, in one sense, this is a mistaken view (Christianity having shaped Judaism significantly over the period since its inception), whether or not the person of Jesus has had an influence on Judaism is more questionable. Ask the average Jew in the street what they think of Jesus and you will probably get one of three answers: that Jesus did not exist, that Jesus existed but was misguided, or that he existed and was plain evil. While there are many Jews today who do not share these views, and are quite sympathetic to the notion of Jesus as a prophet (though clearly not as Messiah or Son of God), the reality is that Jesus simply has no meaning in their lives. Thus the serious contemplation of the person of Jesus is limited to the realms of academia. Judaism exists – or at least, thinks it exists – without reference to the person of Jesus, and studies that show the opposite are rare and recent.

Jesus in Early Rabbinic Literature

There is still some dispute as to whether or not Jesus is referred to in the Talmud. Censorship over the Christian centuries, and the tendency to obliqueness by the authors when referring to contemporary events, mean that it is sometimes hard to know to whom a passage is referring. For example, in the Babylonian Talmud, *Sanhedrin* 103a, the blessing of Psalm 91.10 that 'no scourge [shall] come near your tent' is interpreted to mean, 'you will not have a son or disciple who publicly burns his food'. Publicly to burn food is understood to mean misapplying learning, or openly practising heresy. While most versions of the Talmud end the interpretation there, some editions contain the additional words '*k'gon Yeshu notsri*' ('for example, Jesus Nazarene'), thus identifying the generalized comment about heretics with the specific person of Jesus.

Another example is the Talmudic material about Ben Stada. *Shabbat* 104b has the statement: '"He who cuts upon his flesh." It is a tradition that Rabbi Eliezer said to the Sages, "Did not Ben Stada bring spells from Egypt in a cut which is upon his flesh?" They said to him, "He was a fool and they do not bring a proof from a fool."' *Sanhedrin* 67a says in connection with catching a heretic, 'The witnesses who were listening outside bring him to the court, and have him stoned', with some manuscripts having the addition, 'This is what they did to the Ben Stada in Lod, and hung him on the eve of Passover.' Is Ben Stada, that is, the son of Stada (sometimes identified as Yeshu ben Stada), the Jesus of the gospels? Both the texts continue in uncensored manuscripts, 'The son of Stada? He is the son of Pandera. Rav Hisda said, "The husband's name was Stada, the lover's was Pandera." But the husband was Pappos the son of Judah. "His mother was called Stada." But his mother's name was Miriam the dresser of hair. As they say in Pumbedita, this one turned away.'

Ben Stada and Ben Pandera are identified as the same person in the Talmud.[1] Their connection to Jesus is to be guessed at by the similarities that connect to his life. What we learn is that Yeshu ben Stada went to Egypt – which may be a statement based on the flight in Matthew 2.13. Egypt was seen as a place of magic and esoteric knowledge and so he returns with spells cut upon his flesh. In several texts, Yeshu is seen as a magician, which may be based on the stories of healing, casting out demons, and miracles from the gospels. Yet the context of the passage in *Shabbat* 104a asks whether or not it is permitted to 'write' on flesh on the sabbath. Ben Stada is brought up as proof of the permissibility of this action, and then dismissed. He was a fool and you cannot derive proof from a fool. The anti-Christian sentiment is evident, but the context is interesting in that it brings a person rather than a text as a proof. This precisely mirrors the sabbath controversies of the gospels, in which Jesus renders himself the proof-text when he plucks corn, and heals on the sabbath.[2]

The two names Ben Stada and Ben Pandera inevitably lead to the question, how can one man have two fathers? This could be one of many references in Jewish literature to the illegitimacy of Jesus – the inevitable Jewish response to Christian claims of the virgin birth. But yet another name is used in the text: Pappos ben Yehuda – a man referred to elsewhere,[3] who was so suspicious of his wife that he locked her up every time he went out. While the dating for Pappos ben Yehuda makes it impossible that he was Jesus' father (he supposedly lived a century after the crucifixion), the reference is made to confirm the suggestion of adultery. The same idea is behind the mention of Ben Stada/Pandera's mother. In Talmudic Judaism, one only used the name of the mother if one had no knowledge of who the father was.

1. R.T. Herford, *Christianity in Talmud and Midrash* (New York: Ktav, 1975), p. 37.
2. Matthew 12.1–8 and Luke 6.1–12.
3. Babylonian Talmud, *Gittin* 90a.

Sanhedrin 67b continues. The mother's name is not Stada. Her name is Miriam; she was a dresser of women's hair. While the Greek for Miriam is Mariam, the Aramaic words for a woman's hairdresser are '*megadla neshaya*'. Magdalen may be the wrong Mary in Jesus' life, but it does seem to suggest that this text is indeed referring to Jesus.[4] The implication of illegitimacy again raises its head, confirmed by the last sentence in the passage: she is called Stada because '*satat da mi-ba'alah*', 'this one turned away from her husband'. This passage, written in Babylonia some three or four hundred years after Jesus' death, appears to show a popular knowledge of the story of his life. The author probably did not know the gospels, however; they were '*sefarim hitsoniim*', books outside the sacred texts.[5]

Perhaps a more sophisticated knowledge of Jesus' life can be found in the Tosefta, a work written in the land of Israel a century or two earlier and therefore closer to the events described. '"For accursed of God is the hanged man" (Deuteronomy 21:23). Twins who resemble each other: one ruled over the whole world, one took to robbery and was crucified on a cross, and everyone who passed to and fro said, "It seems that the King is crucified." Therefore it is said, "Accursed of God is the hanged man."'[6] Here, it seems that the text is commenting on the words on the cross.[7]

Other rabbinic passages seem to associate Jesus with the non-Jewish prophet Bilaam who set out to curse Israel and ended up blessing her. The modern view is sympathetic to Bilaam's character. He seems to offer a universalistic message, and though a non-Jew, clearly acknowledges the power of the Jewish God. The opening words of his famous blessing, 'How fair are your tents, O Jacob, your encampments, O Israel',[8] are among the prayers invoked daily and upon entering the synagogue. But the Talmud sets him up as an arch-enemy who leads the people into idolatry. *Sanhedrin* 106b mentions the following incident:

> A certain heretic asked Rabbi Hanina, 'Have you ever heard how old Bilaam was?' He answered him, 'There is nothing written about it, but from what is written, "Men of blood and deceit shall not live out half their days,"[9] he must have been 33 or 34 years old.' He said, 'You have answered me well. I have seen the chronicle of Bilaam and in it is written, "Bilaam the lame was 33 years old when Pinhas the Robber killed him."'[10]

4. Not all scholars agree: cf. Herford, *Christianity in Talmud and Midrash*, p. 37; and I. Epstein, *The Babylonian Talmud*, *Sanhedrin* 67a (London: Soncino Press, 1935), pp. 456–57 n. 4.
5. Mishnah Sanhedrin 10.1 and Mishnah Yadayim 4.6.
6. Tosefta Sanhedrin 9.7.
7. Matthew 27.37.
8. Numbers 24.5.
9. Psalm 55.23.
10. Babylonian Talmud, *Sanhedrin* 106b.

The association of this and other Bilaam passages with Jesus is partly due to the identification of Pinhas the Robber (in Aramaic, *pinhas lista'a*) with Pontius Pilate. The authoritative person in this exchange is the heretic. He knows the details of Bilaam's life, having read the chronicles of Bilaam (for which we should read, the gospels of Jesus). The passage, however, is uncompromising in its condemnation of the prophet. It continues, 'Mar, the son of Rabina, said to his sons, concerning all these:[11] Do not take scriptural passages to preach against them – except in the case of Bilaam the wicked. Whatever verses you find, use them to preach against him.' Many dispute the connection with Jesus, which is far from clear,[12] but this last sentence is clearly directed towards a specific contemporary opponent rather than an ancient Moabite. Ironically, the one thing this reference shares with Christian texts of the same period is an assertion that Jesus was not a Jew.

We have to conclude that references to Jesus are questionable, scant and not particularly theologically developed. There is a very different mood here, from that of the one well-known heretic of the first century, Elisha ben Abuya, also known as *Aher*, 'the other one'. He was a rabbi who abandoned Judaism for Greek and Roman philosophy. Yet his opinions are quoted and his story told in the Talmud.[13]

The reason may not be that difficult to ascertain, however. Elisha ben Abuya was a very highly regarded rabbi before his apostasy, very much part of the established scholarship that produced the Mishnah. He was not an outsider as was the Galilean and uneducated Jesus. Moreover, Elisha did not seek to influence others and remained respectful of Judaism. One story is told of a walk with his friend and former pupil, Rabbi Meir. He was anxious that the latter did not break the rules concerning travelling a distance on the sabbath, even though he himself happily rode on.[14] Finally, no religious movement sprung up around him. He was never a threat to the established faith, or indeed the government of the period.

We have to conclude that if references to Jesus do appear in early rabbinic literature, they are a response to the already established Church, and not to the person of Jesus. There is the well-known reference in the *tefilla*, the daily prayer which today reads, '*v'la-malshinim*, and for slanderers, let there be no hope; and let all wickedness perish in a moment',[15] yet it is known as *birkat ha-minim*, the 'blessing against heretics'. Its original form referred to *minim* ('heretic') rather than *malshinim* ('slanderer') and was probably directed against

11. This refers to the preceding passage which listed all types of heretics barred from the world to come.

12. L. Ginzberg, 'Some Observations on the Attitude of the Synagogue towards the Apocalyptic-Eschatological Writings', *Journal of Biblical Literature* 41 (1922), pp. 115–36 (121–22 n. 18).

13. Babylonian Talmud, *Ḥagiga* 14b–15b, and *Qiddushin* 49b.

14. Babylonian Talmud, *Ḥagiga* 15b.

15. J.H. Hertz, *The Daily Prayerbook* (London: Soncino, 1948), p. 142.

Nazarenes, Sadducees and others who denied the authority of rabbinic Judaism.[16]

Jesus in the Jewish Middle Ages

The Talmudic references continued to be developed and the stories elaborated upon during the Middle Ages, resulting in a series of texts known collectively as the *Toldot Yeshu*, 'the history of Jesus'. Dating these is difficult, but by the ninth century when they came to the attention of the bishops of Lyon, Agobard and Aub, they seemed to have been in circulation for some time and probably originated several centuries earlier. Over the years, the stories grew, and as persecution of the Jews by Christians reached its ultimate cruelty during the Crusades, so did the absurdities and degradations that were ascribed to Jesus in these texts.

In one version, Jesus is described as an illegitimate boy whose mother was raped by a neighbour and whose husband ran away. This seems to be a reworking of the biblical story of *Shlomit bat Divri*,[17] whose father is identified in the Midrash as the Egyptian slave-driver killed by Moses. In the Midrash, the mother is raped and her husband later leaves her.[18] The parallel is appropriate. The son in the Bible blasphemes in the camp of Israel and is put to death by the community. In the *Toldot*, as the boy Jesus grows, he shows a prodigious cleverness. After some early escapades,

> Yeshu fled to Jerusalem and in the Temple he learnt the 'Ineffable Name'. In order that the brazen dogs, which stood by the gate of the place of sacrifice and barked at all who learned the Name and so made them forget it, in order that they should not make him forget the Name, Yeshu wrote it on a piece of leather and sewed it in the flesh of his thigh. He gathered around him in Bethlehem a group of Young Jews and proclaimed himself the Messiah and Son of God; and as a retort to those who rejected his claims he said that 'they sought their own greatness and were minded to rule Israel'; while to confirm his claims he healed a lame man and a leper by the power of the 'Ineffable Name'. He was brought before Queen Helena, the ruler of Israel, and she found him guilty of acts of sorcery and beguilement. But Yeshu restored a dead man to life, and the queen, in her alarm, began to believe in him.[19]

The sages then set up a rival claimant, one Yehuda Iscarioto who shows the same magical powers and who ultimately betrays Jesus. The sages hang Jesus

16. S.W. Baron, *A Social and Religious History of the Jews* (New York: Columbia Press, 2nd edn, 1958), II, p. 135.
17. Leviticus 24.10–25.
18. Exodus Rabba 1.28.
19. D. Thau, 'The Toledot Yeshu' (unpublished rabbinic dissertation, Leo Baeck College, 1985), p. 4. This is based on several versions as quoted by J. Klausner, *Jesus of Nazareth* (trans. H. Danby; London: Allen & Unwin, 1929).

on a cabbage stalk; he is buried quickly but his body is removed, which gives rise to claims of his resurrection. Then the body is produced, at which point the disciples flee abroad and preach the message of Yeshu to the gentiles.

The style and details of many of the *Toldot* are crass and unpleasant; they were designed for private consumption only. In the public sphere, there were disputations between Jew and Christian. From earliest times, these concentrated less on the life of Jesus, and more on the justification as to why Jews do not accept him as their Messiah. Later mediaeval disputations centred around interpretations of scripture, with Jews justifying their rejection of Jesus on the grounds of the warlike nature of Christianity, and its rejection of Torah law. Manuals known as *Sifrei Nitsahon*, 'books of refutation', were written in order to help in the refutation of Christianity. As time went on, these became increasingly urgent. Public spectacles in the thirteenth century encouraged putting the Jew 'on trial' against an adversary, usually a Jewish convert to Christianity. The focus would be on the Jew defending his refusal to convert.

Disputations served to move the focus away from the person of Jesus to the institution of the Church, which for Jews was the real enemy. Interpretations of Jesus at the time were seen through the Church's teaching of him. But the disputations remain important, not because of their content, but because they set up a pattern that exists to this day. Even so-called 'dialogue' follows elements of the disputation model, and Jewish views of Jesus with very few exceptions remain apologetic in nature.

Jesus in Modern Jewish Thought

As a result of the eighteenth-century European Enlightenment, a new approach became possible. Jews, embracing western European culture, learnt to read in the vernacular. Knowledge of the New Testament became part of their education. The gentler climate for Jews in the world resulted in a more positive response. Thus Jacob Emden (1697–1776), although an opponent of the Enlightenment, was able to write the following about Jesus:

> The Nazarene brought about a double kindness in the world. On the one hand, he strengthened the Torah of Moses majestically ... on the other hand, he did much good for the gentiles ... by doing away with idolatry and removing the images from their midst. He obligated them with the Seven Commandments so that they should not be as the beasts of the field.[20]

But it was Moses Mendelssohn (1729–86), the 'father of the Enlightenment', who defined the changes in perception and set a new standard for dialogue in a changed world.

20. J. Emden, *Lehem Shamayim* (1728; unpublished translation by J. Katsev). Cf. commentary on Mishnah Avot 4.11: 'Every gathering which is for the sake of heaven will in the end be established.'

> As long as those who were powerful still spilled blood on behalf of religion, those who were weak had no alternative but to ... snap their fingers in their pockets, that is, to slander the religion of their opponents behind closed doors. As the mood of persecution has weakened on the one side, so has hatred given way to gratitude on the other; now it is the duty of all good people to consign the old discords to oblivion.[21]

It didn't quite work like that. The old Christian attitudes remained, and Jews in German lands continued to suffer under huge disabilities, even if not outward persecution. Dialogue was still disputative in tone, still a 'loaded dice', according to Walter Jacob, with the desire on the Christian side to convert Jews. Mendelssohn himself was in 'disputation' with the Christian clergy of the time, but through reading the gospels he discovered a new respect for Christianity and for Jesus. Mendelssohn was perhaps the first to show real sympathy with Christianity. Jesus was a Jew, a special person, even a prophet – so long as he spoke out in the tradition of Torah. But, he claimed, Jesus could not abrogate the Torah. God the omniscient would never have given Torah at one time in history and take it away again in another.

Joseph Salvador (1796–1873), in response to the '*Hep Hep*' riots in Germany over proposed citizenship for Jews in 1819, wrote *Jesus-Christ et sa doctrine*, published in 1838. It was the first serious evaluation of Christianity from a Jewish point of view. He tried very hard to be impartial, following the trend among Christian scholars to find 'the historical Jesus', but concluded that the ethical elements in the life of Jesus could be traced to Judaism, while the impurities were of pagan origin. Salvador claimed that Jesus as a historical figure was portrayed most authentically in the Gospel of Matthew, although he dismissed the virgin birth, and suggested that Jesus fled to Egypt in order to escape rumours of illegitimacy – an echo of the *Toldot Yeshu* which was revived at this time, also in response to the riots. He saw the antagonism with Pharisees as authentic and the source of the split between Judaism and Christianity, while suggesting that Jesus' trial was over the question of blasphemy. 'It is certain that the personal plan of the son of Mary failed: he wished through his words to unite the different schools of the Hebrew people. He sought to articulate their hopes in the dogma expressed by him, but neither before, nor after his death was this realised. His struggle with Pharisaism was never crowned with victory.'[22]

Thinkers who in the main followed Salvador took up the same pattern. They were sympathetic to Jesus as a historical figure, and identified him as a Jew promoting Jewish teachings. Where he departed from Jewish teachings, those ideas were pagan foreign influences containing a less impressive message. These scholars continued their scepticism about the virgin birth and resurrection and made a

21. W. Jacob, *Christianity through Jewish Eyes* (Cincinatti, OH: Hebrew Union College Press, 1974), p. 17.

22. Jacob, *Christianity*, p. 29.

distinction between the person of Jesus and what Christianity became. This view is still found today, with writers such as Hyam Maccoby seeing Jesus as an essentially Jewish figure and laying the 'blame' for Christianity on a pagan Paul.[23]

Abraham Geiger (1810–74), one of the founders of Reform Judaism, wrote extensively on Jesus. For him, Jesus was a Jew, a Pharisee 'with Galilean colouration'. The universalistic elements that rose from the pages of the New Testament were either the result of 'pagan' or Pauline influence. Geiger claimed that the words of Jesus would have led to the foundation of a Jewish sect were it not for the catastrophic events surrounding the destruction of the temple. 'We cannot deny him a deep introspective nature, but there is no trace of a decisive stand that promised lasting results ... there was no great work of Reform nor any new thought that left the usual paths.'[24]

Geiger's critical tone is not unusual for his period. Despite his evident scholarship, he was ignored by the Christian academic establishment which refused to take seriously any comments by a Jew.

> It is truly a sad state of affairs with Christianity and its theologians ... Now Jesus has to be something simply extraordinary, he is and remains the focal point of history, and in the end since he didn't do anything, now he has to be made into some kind of God, even if it is a weakened one. Naturally the Judaism of his time must furthermore be portrayed bleakly, so that he rises radiantly above it. The most refined self-deception.[25]

But Geiger did confirm the historicity of Jesus the person. The search for the 'historical Jesus' popular among Christian scholars led many Jews of the period to try and prove his non-existence. In England, half a century later, an altogether different approach was developed by the scholar Claude Montefiore (1858–1938). In the softer climate of English Jewish-Christian relations, Montefiore showed no tendency to apologetics in his writings. He was totally in sympathy with the liberal Christianity of his day, and set about founding a liberal Judaism upon the same principles. His intention was different from those who went before him: it was not to explain Jewish views to Christians that he wrote on the subject, but Christianity to Jews. For that reason, he published his *Synoptic Gospels*,[26] a commentary for Jews to read. In it, he used rabbinic literature to demonstrate Jesus' absolute adherence to rabbinic Judaism.

Jesus, Montefiore claimed, was a hero in the prophetic tradition and therefore should be considered part of Judaism:

> The Liberal Jew at any rate will not be deterred from gaining all the good he can from the Gospels (or from the rest of the New Testament) because there are many

23. H. Maccoby, *The Mythmaker: Paul and the Origins of Christianity* (London: Weidenfeld & Nicholson, 1986).

24. Jacob, *Christianity*, p. 43.

25. Letter from Geiger to Derenbourg, quoted in S. Heschel, *Abraham Geiger and the Jewish Jesus* (Chicago, IL: University of Chicago Press, 1998), p. 196.

26. C.G. Montefiore, *The Synoptic Gospels* (London: Macmillan, 1909).

> things in it which he holds to be erroneous. The Pentateuch also contains things which he holds to be erroneous, it also contains a lower and a higher. So too the Prophets. But he does not therefore reject them. He regards them historically and gratefully accepts and ardently treasures whatever there is in them which is true and good and great ... In the same way, he will, I believe, be glad to study and absorb (even though they are not a portion of his 'Bible') the Gospels and the other books of the New Testament. They too are *sui generis*; they too can add something of value and power, something fresh and distinguished to his total religious store.[27]

Thus Jesus the Jew has much to teach us. Though he said little that was new, the person of Jesus is so attractive that we can learn about Judaism from him. Montefiore's stance was criticized in his time, and only now, nearly a hundred years later, are there Jews tentatively taking up the threads of his argument.[28]

The experience of the Shoah led to a re-evaluation of Christian claims, and the persistence of mediaeval ideas in the secular context of Nazi Germany meant a more cautious approach by some Jewish scholars. Others, notably Leo Baeck and Martin Buber, responded by insisting that dialogue was all the more important.

Leo Baeck (1873–1950) continued to develop the lines of Geiger both in the study of Jesus as a Jew and in creating an apologetic against Christian claims, but he went further. When one rids the gospel of layers of accretion, he claimed, one finds that it is indeed a Jewish document. Not only was Jesus a Jewish man with Jewish hopes (a 'Jew among Jews'); not only 'Jewish history and Jewish reflection cannot ignore him'; the book that reflects his life and teachings is in essence a 'book that can be claimed as part of Jewish literature'.[29] 'We encounter a man with noble features who lived in the land of the Jews in tense and excited times and helped and laboured and suffered and died: a man out of the Jewish people who walked on Jewish paths with Jewish faith and Jewish hopes.'[30] The implications of this thought for Jews are not developed, as with the coming of Paul and the establishment of Christianity, the gospel was removed from the Jewish sphere of influence. Judaism and Christianity, as faiths, are opposed: classical religion versus romantic religion.

27. Montefiore, *Synoptic Gospels*, p. cvi.

28. Even now his approach seems radical. Rabbi Tony Bayfield, writing in 2000, boldly acknowledged the truth of Christianity for Christians ('I believe that many Christians find in the life, death and resurrection of Jesus as described in the New Testament and in the tradition that flows from those events the fullest disclosure of the nature of God and God's will for them. Such faith involves no necessary error or illusion'), yet he does not go as far as Montefiore: it is truth for Christians, not for Jews ('Just as Sinai was the central episode of revelation, the covenantal moment for the Jewish people, so too, from my Jewish perspective, is Calvary for Christians and Christianity') (T. Bayfield, 'Partnership in Covenant', in T. Bayfield, S. Brichto and E.J. Fisher (eds.), *He Kissed Him and They Wept: Towards a Theology of Jewish-Catholic Partnership* [London: SCM Press, 2001], pp. 25–40 [31]).

29. Jacob, *Christianity*, p. 148.

30. L. Baeck, *Judaism and Christianity* (trans. W. Kaufmann; Philadelphia, PA: Jewish Publication Society of America, 1960), p. 100.

Martin Buber (1878–1965) similarly talked of two types of faith, but in his case, two types of Christianity: those of Jesus and Paul. As a Jew, he favoured the former.

> From my youth onwards, I have found in Jesus my great brother. That Christianity has regarded and does regard him as God and Saviour has always appeared to me a fact of the highest importance which, for his sake and my own, I must endeavour to understand ... I am certain, more than ever certain, that a great place belongs to him in Israel's history of faith and that this place cannot be described by any of the usual categories.[31]

Buber saw Jesus in the tradition of rabbinic Judaism, with his Jesus appearing somewhat in the guise of a Hasidic master! 'We Jews know Jesus internally in his Jewish motivations and moods; this path remains closed to the nations who believe in him.'[32] This latter statement caused great controversy among Jews who on the whole would reject such a personal identification with Jesus.

Of contemporary scholars writing on the subject, the most well known are Geza Vermes and David Flusser. Both are academics, whose effect has been largely in an academic sphere. Vermes has been enormously influential on a generation of Christian ministers and theologians in presenting the idea of Jesus as a Jew of his own time, influenced by the religious and political ideas that surrounded him. His influence in Jewish circles, however, has been more moderate. Admired greatly, his work does not impinge on Jewish beliefs. The general view would be that Jesus was a Jew, and nothing more; and so has nothing to teach that cannot be found already written in Jewish texts.[33]

Flusser, an Israeli working in Jerusalem, has had more influence in that most of his students are Jewish. His main contribution has been to place Jesus in his historical and cultural context for Israelis and thus present him as part of Jewish history. This means that the study of the gospels is not only permissible but acceptable. The discovery of the Dead Sea Scrolls opened up the view of first-century Judaism to a picture far broader than portrayed, for example, by Josephus. Thus it has been possible for Flusser to argue that the virgin birth lies strongly within Jewish tradition, and that the notion of incarnation is part of the faith of the period. But while going further than any other in taking the stories relating to Jesus into a Jewish context, he has done this in a secular environment. It is history and philosophy, not theology. So, like Vermes, Flusser has had no impact on Judaism or on the Jews who practise it.[34]

Yet the subject continues to fascinate Jewish religious leaders and academics. The many years of dialogue since the Shoah have established a firm foundation

31. Jacob, *Christianity*, p. 176.
32. Jacob, *Christianity*, p. 176.
33. G. Vermes, *Jesus the Jew* (London: Collins, 1973), and *idem*, *The Religion of Jesus the Jew* (London: SCM Press, 1993).
34. D. Flusser, *Judaism and the Origins of Christianity* (Jerusalem: Magnes Press, 1988), and Flusser with R.S. Notley, *Jesus* (Jerusalem: Magnes Press, 1997).

of encounter, which has resulted in a greater confidence, clarity and willingness to extend boundaries. In recent years, the focus has moved away from the Jewishness of Jesus into areas less often associated with Judaism, but which are nevertheless authentic expressions of the faith. Elliot Wolfson has offered an insight into the incarnation that he has suggested can help Christians as well as Jews to come to terms with the idea.

> In the physical space circumscribed by words of prayer and study, the imaginal body of God assumes incarnate form. This is the intent of the statement attributed to R. Abbahu, '"Seek the Lord while He can be found" (Is. 55:6). Where is He found? In the houses of worship and the houses of study.' The rabbinic notion of incarnation embraces the paradox that God's body is real only to the extent that it is imagined, but it is imagined only to the extent that it is real.
>
> The conception of God's imaginal body evident in different phases of Jewish thought can contribute significantly to Christian reflection on the doctrine of incarnation. Indeed, the Judaic perspective should induce us to alter our views regarding corporeality in general.[35]

Wolfson concludes, 'In the end, the Christological doctrine of incarnation is not, as Paul surmised, a stumbling block particularly to the Jews, but rather to anyone whose religious sensibility has not been properly nourished by the wellspring of poetic imagination.'[36]

Conclusion

Despite the religious leaders, theologians and academics engaging with and adopting the person of Jesus in Jewish tradition, this general trend has made no impact at all on the beliefs and practice of the Jewish faithful. Yet things may change. From the early 1970s, British universities accepted Jews into their divinity faculties as students. A large number of these students subsequently became progressive rabbis and undoubtedly their ministry has been affected by what they studied. Some rabbis, through Jewish-Christian dialogue and personal study, have come to different conclusions about the life and person of Jesus.[37]

35. E.R. Wolfson, 'Judaism and Incarnation: The Imaginal Body of God', in T.S. Frymer-Kensky, *et al.* (eds.), *Christianity in Jewish Terms* (Boulder, CO and Oxford: Westview Press, 2000), pp. 239–54 (253–54).

36. Wolfson, 'Judaism and the Incarnation', p. 254.

37. See, for different examples, S. Brichto, *The Gospel of St. Luke and the Acts of the Apostles* (London: Sinclair-Stevenson, 2000); *idem*, *The Genius of Paul: Paul's Letters* (London: Sinclair-Stevenson, 2001); *idem*, *Apocalypse: A Revolutionary Interpretive Translation of the Writings of St. John* (London: Sinclair-Stevenson, 2004); M. Hilton, *The Christian Effect on Jewish Life* (London: SCM Press, 1994); M. Hilton and G. Marshall, *The Gospels and Rabbinic Judaism: A Study Guide* (New York: Ktav, 1988); S. Sheridan, 'John's Gospel through Jewish Eyes', in J. Romain (ed.), *Renewing the Vision* (London: SCM Press, 1996), pp. 135–45; and M.L. Solomon, 'Christ through Jewish Eyes', in D.J. Goldberg and E. Kessler (eds.), *Aspects of Liberal Judaism* (London: Vallentine Mitchell, 2004), pp. 184–201.

Many initiated and participated in Jewish-Christian text-study groups, which at the start were confined, for courtesy's sake, to the Hebrew Bible. However, increasing confidence has led in recent years to joint New Testament study, though how, if at all, such study will affect either religion will take many years to determine. Though these are small groups and not particularly influential, who knows what may happen in the future? Jewish anti-Christian sentiment was shaped by Christian persecution; in the current climate of mutual tolerance and respect, a very different picture emerges. The Judaism and Christianity of the next centuries may be very different from today.

Jesus from a Muslim Perspective

Basil Mustafa

The names Jesus, the Messiah and Maryam appear in the text of the Qur'ān sixteen, ten and thirty-three times respectively. All are mentioned in the context of the divine order prescribed for guiding and counselling humanity to worship the one, supreme God, the creator. The stories of prophets in the Qur'ān are not independent narratives but a textual depiction of the lives of venerable figures whose conduct represents a spiritual and moral norm for humanity. 'And We gave [Abraham,] Isaac and Jacob, and We guided each of them – and before that We guided Noah and, from among his descendants, David and Solomon and Job and Joseph and Moses and Aaron – and that is how We reward those who are good.'[1]

Muslim thought about Jesus is derived directly from the two sources of Islamic faith, the Qur'ān and *ḥadīth*. These testify that the life of Jesus was strikingly full of miraculous events. For many, a single event, namely that of the virgin birth of Jesus, stands out as the first of the great miracles during his life. However, tracing back his lineage, we can learn that God's grace was bestowed earlier on his noble family, and that his virgin birth was but a culmination of other miraculous events which have been granted to his household.

Jesus' Lineage and Birth

On a few occasions, the Qur'ān starts the narration of the life of Jesus with the mention of his righteous grandmother, traditionally known as Hannah or the wife of Imran. The third chapter of the Qur'ān, named ṣūra 'Āl-ʿImrān', speaks about a woman of devout faith who was expecting to give birth, and she vowed to dedicate that child to God: 'O my Lord: I do dedicate unto Thee what is in my womb for Thy special service.'[2] Hannah named her child Maryam (Mary) and prayed for God's protection for her and her progeny: 'I have

1. Qur'ān 6.84–87.
2. Qur'ān 3.35.

named her Maryam (Mary) and I commend her and her offspring to Thy protection.'[3] God had certainly shown favour to the new-born and accepted her as a devout servant: 'Right graciously did her Lord accept her: He made her grow in piety and to the care of Zakarīyā was she assigned.'[4] Maryam grew up in devotion and service of the Lord. She spent her days praying in the temple. Her uncle Zakarīyā, who was a priest at the sanctuary, often noticed that she had something extraordinary to eat and drink: 'Every time that [Zakarīyā] entered the chamber to see her, he found her supplied with sustenance. He said: "O Maryam, Whence [comes] this to you?" She said, "From Allah: for Allah provides sustenance to whom He pleases without measure."'[5] Ibn Kathīr in his commentary on the above verse narrates that she had plentiful fruits of all kinds throughout the seasons of the year: summer fruits in winter, and winter fruits in summer.[6]

Maryam's spiritual upbringing was to prove vital to her chosen mission. She showed steadfastness on receiving the news from the angel messenger that she was to bear a child. God had decreed the virgin birth of Jesus Christ and announced it to the world twice, in the most spectacular manner: first, privately to his mother Maryam, and second, publicly to the Jewish community when Jesus himself miraculously spoke as a new-born to the Israelites to say, 'I am indeed a servant of God; He has given me Revelation and made me a Prophet and He has made me blessed wherever I may be, and He has enjoined on me prayer and charity as long as I live.'[7]

This event was a divine announcement of the eminence of Jesus. The Qur'ān speaks of the miraculous conception and birth of Jesus; and declares that Jesus is 'eminent in this world and the next, and one of those who are brought into proximity to God'.[8]

The Mission of Jesus

The Qur'ān also makes mention of the mission of Jesus. The purpose of his prophethood was summarized in two aspects. First, he was to be a sign to people: his noble lineage from a family of priests, his wonderful and miraculous birth and his blessed life were to serve as beacons of faith to those who strayed away from the path of God. Second, his mission was to bring solace and salvation, to show mercy and compassion to the ungodly world of the time. Jesus' life has set a true example for those who choose to emulate his unrelenting

3. Qur'ān 3.36.
4. Qur'ān 3.37.
5. Qur'ān 3.37.
6. Ibn Kathīr, *Tafsīr al-Qur'ān al-Karīm* (3 vols.; Beirut: Dār al-Qur'ān, 1981), II, p. 279.
7. Qur'ān 19.30–31.
8. Qur'ān 3.45.

pursuit of devotion to God, moral virtues and selfless living. 'And We wish to appoint [Jesus] as a Sign to people and mercy from Us; and it is a matter which has been decreed.'[9]

The absolute monotheism of Islam is represented in the doctrine of *tawḥīd*, the unity and sovereignty of God, which dominates Islamic belief and practice. Muslims believe that God has created humankind and the universe not in a random or vainglorious manner, but for a divine purpose. This purpose is that humans may worship God, and fulfil their ethical vocation of doing good deeds and avoiding shameful ones as part of their submission to God. 'I have only created Jinn and mankind, that they may serve Me.'[10]

The world which God created is one that fits this moral vocation of humans.[11] It is one in which they are free and effective, and where the realization of goodness, truth and beauty is actually possible. Human beings stand among the noblest of all God's creatures, because they are the only creatures on earth who are so equipped with intellectual and spiritual faculties to undertake that responsibility. 'We honoured the progeny of Adam: provided them with transport on land and sea; gave them for sustenance things good and pure; and conferred on them special favours [spiritual faculties] above a great part of your creation.'[12] Islam teaches that people are born pure and innocent, and remain so until they choose to infringe the practice of their faith by misdeeds. When people become forgetful and rebellious, God sends messengers with fresh revelations to remind them.

Islam's articles of faith were not proclaimed as a new religion, for all the messengers of God had preached the same message of submission to the creator. To Muslims, therefore, Jesus was a messenger of God to the people of Israel. The miraculous conception and virgin birth of Jesus, as well as his other miracles, served to prove his prophethood, to illustrate the dignity that was accorded to him by God, and to support those who believed in him. The Qur'ān asserts in many ways that Jesus is God's messenger, and makes it clear that he is the promised Messiah foretold in the Torah. The Qur'ān refutes in unequivocal terms the doctrine of Jesus as the son of God and the doctrine of Jesus as the incarnation of God in any sense or form.

> And they say, 'The Merciful has betaken a son. You have indeed come up with something terrible. Whereby almost the heavens are torn, and the earth is split asunder and the mountains fall in ruins.[13]
>
> And we did not send any Messenger in the past without inspiring in him, 'Surely there is no god but I; so worship Me.' And they say, 'The Merciful has chosen a son

9. Qur'ān 17.21.
10. Qur'ān 51.56.
11. I.R. Al-Faruqi, *Islam* (Maryland: International Graphics, 1984), p. 7.
12. Qur'ān 17.70.
13. Qur'ān 19.88.

> Glory be to Him! They are only slaves who have been honoured. They do not speak before he has spoken, and what they do is by His command.[14]

The doctrine of Jesus as a messenger of God is an integral part of the Islamic faith. Jesus represents one of the rings in that chain of prophets that relate humanity to its creator. The chain must remain connected, unbroken and unblemished for a Muslim's faith to remain sublime.

Muslims have always maintained that Jesus and his mother Mary were human beings, even though their lives were shrouded with many miraculous events, the most magnificent of which was the virgin birth of Jesus. The Qur'ānic description of Jesus as a 'Spirit from Him' is understood in the light of the original creation when God fashioned humanity and breathed into it of God's spirit.[15] 'When I have fashioned him (in due proportion) and breathed into him of My spirit, fall ye down in prostration unto him.'[16]

According to Abū ʿUthmān al-Jāḥiẓ, who lived in the ninth century CE, the birth of Adam and Eve was more unique than that of Jesus, for they had neither father nor mother.[17]

Jesus the Ascetic Prophet

It is fascinating to trace the deep spiritual connections which exist between Jesus and Muhammad through the texts of *ḥadīth* and other narratives. These traditions serve to illuminate the character of Jesus as an ascetic prophet. His code of behaviour, acts of daily worship and moral teachings were described and reaffirmed as a continuation of the guidance which the prophets before him had brought.

The most authentic collection of *ḥadīth* is that of al-Bukhārī. The following *ḥadīth*, which relates the messages of Jesus and Muhammad, is narrated in the book of 'Traditions of Prophets' in al-Bukhārī's collection:

> It has been transmitted by ʿUbāda ibn al-Ṣāmit, may God be pleased with him, that the prophet Mohammad, may God bless him and grant him peace, said, 'Whoever bears witness that there is no god except God, alone without any partner; and that Mohammad is His slave and His messenger; and that Jesus is the slave of God and His messenger and His word which he bestowed on Mary and a spirit from Him;

14. Qur'ān 21.25–27.
15. Qur'ān 4.171: 'O People of the Scripture! Do not exaggerate in your religion nor utter aught concerning Allah save the truth. The Messiah, Jesus son of Mary, was only a messenger of Allah, and His word which He conveyed unto Mary, and a spirit from Him. So believe in Allah and His messengers, and say not "Three" – Cease! (It is) better for you! – Allah is only One Allah. Far is it removed from His Transcendent Majesty that He should have a son. His is all that is in the heavens and all that is in the earth. And Allah is sufficient as Defender.'
16. Qur'ān 15.29.
17. J. Robson, *Christ in Islam* (Lampeter: Llanerch Publishers, 1995), p. 8.

> and that the Garden is true and the Fire is true, then God will make him enter the Garden, however few his good actions may have been.[18]

It was also narrated on the authority of Abū Mūsā al-Ashʿarī, that the prophet Muhammad said, 'If anyone believes in Jesus son of Mary and then believes in me, then he will have a double reward.'[19]

The meaning of the above tradition is affirmed in the Qur'ān, which states with reference to the people of the book, 'O ye who believe, Be conscious of God and believe in His apostle [i.e. Muhammad] and He will bestow on you a double portion of his mercy.'[20]

In another *ḥadīth*, Abū Hurayra reported: 'I heard God's messenger as saying, "I am most akin to the son of Mary among the whole of mankind and the prophets are of different mothers, but of one religion, and no prophet was raised between me and [Jesus the Christ]."'[21]

In the classical Islamic literature written on asceticism between the eighth and twelfth centuries CE, Jesus appeared as a model figure of conduct and good manners. The character of Jesus as depicted in the narrations attributed to him has been a source of inspiration to many who have been in pursuit of an ascetic lifestyle in Muslim societies. It has been suggested that many of the ascetic passages may have come through Christian channels, and have been accepted in good faith by Muslims.[22] However, these are likely to have been expressed or changed in a way as to bring them into line with Muslim piety and moral conduct. The main sources of the earliest narrations are found in two major collections of ascetic literature: *The Book of Asceticism and Tender Mercies* by Ibn al-Mubārak (d. AH 181/797), and *The Book of Asceticism,* by Ibn Ḥanbal (d. AH 241/855).[23] Narrations of later centuries are found in al-Thaʿlabī's (d. AH fifth/eleventh century) *Stories of the Prophets* and in al-Ghazālī's (d. AH 505/1111) *The Revival of the Religious Sciences*.[24] The authenticity of these passages has always been an issue of concern to scholars. I have therefore selected a few which have parallels in the primary textual sources of Islam.

1. Some people said to Jesus, 'Direct us to some work by which we shall enter paradise.' He said, 'Never say anything.' They said, 'We are not able to do that.' So he said, 'Then never say anything but what is good.'[25]

18. M.M. Khan (trans.), *Sahih Al-Bukhari* (9 vols.; Beirut: Dar Al-Arabia, 1985), IV, no. 644.
19. Khan, *Sahih Al-Bukhari*, IV, no. 655.
20. Qur'ān 57.28.
21. Khan, *Sahih Al-Bukhari*, IV, no. 651.
22. Robson, *Christ in Islam*, p. 14.
23. T. Khalidi (ed. and trans.), *The Muslim Jesus: Sayings and Stories in Islamic Literature* (Cambridge, MA and London: Harvard University Press, 2001), p. 32.
24. Khalidi, *Muslim Jesus*, p. 42.
25. Robson, *Christ in Islam*, p. 44.

We can find a specific reference to the wisdom and virtue of silence in the saying of the prophet Muhammad: 'Let him who believes in Allah and the Last Day either speak good or keep silent.'[26]

2. Jesus said, 'Make yourselves lovable to God by hating the disobedient, and come near to God by keeping away from them, and seek God's favour by being displeased with them.' They said, 'O spirit of God, with whom, then, shall we associate?' He said, 'Associate with him the sight of whom reminds you of God, whose words increase your words, and whose works make you desire the next world.'[27]

The meanings contained in this passage greatly resemble that of the Qur'ānic verse: 'And keep thy soul content with those who call on their Lord morning and evening, seeking His face; and let not thine eyes pass beyond them, seeking the pomp and glitter of this life; nor obey any whose heart we have permitted to neglect the remembrance of Us.'[28]

3. Jesus said, 'Seek a great amount of what fire cannot consume.' Someone said, 'And what is that?' He said, 'Kindness.'[29]

The theme of human kindness is frequently emphasized in the textual sources of Islam. It is mentioned in the context of kindness to parents, children, neighbours, relations and elders, as well as animals. The prophet Muhammad commanded that: 'the Compassionate One has mercy on these who are merciful. If you show mercy to those who are on the earth, He Who is in the heaven will show mercy to you.'[30]

4. Jesus said, 'The world is a place of transition, full of examples; be pilgrims therein, and take warning by the traces of those that have gone before.'[31]

The prophet Muhammad gave similar advice to his companion ʿAbdullāh ibn ʿUmar when he said to him: 'Be in the world as though you were a stranger or a wayfarer.'[32]

26. Khan, *Sahih Al-Bukhari*, VIII, no. 47.
27. Robson, *Christ in Islam*, p. 43.
28. Qur'ān 18.28.
29. Robson, *Christ in Islam*, p. 46.
30. A. Hasan (trans.), *Sunan Abu Dawud* (3 vols.; New Delhi: Al-Madina Publications, 1985), III, p. 1375.
31. Robson, *Christ in Islam*, p. 62.
32. Khan, *Sahih Al-Bukhari*, VIII, no. 425.

5. Jesus said, 'If a man send away a beggar empty from his house, the angels will not visit that house for seven nights.'[33]

The same meaning is echoed in the Qur'ānic verse: 'And they feed, for the love of God, the indigent, the orphan, and the captive.'[34]

6. Jesus struck the ground with his hand and took up some of it and spread it out, and behold, he had gold in one of his hands and clay in the other. Then he said to his companions, 'Which of them is sweeter to your hearts?' They said, 'The gold.' He said, 'They are both alike to me.'[35]

The End of Jesus' Life

Yusuf Ali, in his translation of the meanings of the Qur'ān, comments that the end of the life of Jesus on earth is as much involved in mystery as his birth.[36] The Qur'ānic teaching is that Jesus was neither crucified nor killed, notwithstanding certain apparent circumstances, which produced that illusion in the mind of his enemies.

> They said (in boast), 'We killed Christ Jesus the son of Mary, the Apostle of God,' but they killed him not, nor crucified him, but so it was made to appear to them, and those who differ therein are full of doubts, with not (certain) knowledge but only conjecture to follow, for of a surety they killed him not. Nay, God raised him up unto Himself; and God is Exalted in Power, Wise.[37]

The Qur'ānic term '*rafaʿa*' used in the above verses, which denotes elevation, means that instead of being disgraced by his enemies, Jesus ascended into heaven as a mark of the exaltation attributed to him, all accomplished to vindicate the purity and innocence of the apostle from the false charges levied against him.

The issue remains whether or not Jesus suffered a physical death prior to his ascension even though he was not killed. The Qur'ān refers twice to the end of Jesus' life on earth with the reflexive of the fifth form of the verb '*wafā*' ('*tawaffā*'), which literally means 'taken away completely'.

> Behold! Allah said: 'O Jesus! I will take thee [*mutawaffika*] and raise thee to Myself and clear thee (of the falsehoods) of those who blaspheme; I will make those who

33. Robson, *Christ in Islam*, p. 62.
34. Qur'ān 76.8.
35. Robson, *Christ in Islam*, p. 77.
36. A.Y. Ali, *Meaning of the Holy Qur'an: Text and Translation* (Brentwood, MD: Amana Corporation, 1991), p. 236.
37. Qur'ān 4.157–58.

> follow thee superior to those who reject faith, to the Day of Resurrection: Then shall ye all return unto me, and I will judge between you of the matters wherein ye dispute.'[38]
>
> Nothing did I tell them beyond what You ordered me to say: 'Worship God who is my Sustainer as well as your Sustainer.' And I bore witness to what they did as long as I dwelt in their midst; But since you took me [*tawaffaytanī*], You alone have been their keeper: For You are witness unto everything.[39]

This verb is used elsewhere in the Qur'ān in two contexts: death and sleep. 'It is God that takes the souls (of men) at death and those that die not (He takes) during their sleep. Those on whom He Has passed the decree of death, He keeps back (from returning to life), but the rest He sends (to their bodies) for a term appointed.'[40]

Muslim commentators on the Qur'ān have used both meanings of the verb to explain the end of Jesus' stay on earth. Ibn Kathīr explained in his commentary on the Qur'ān that a majority of commentators expressed the view that it was a state of unconsciousness similar to sleep into which Jesus went prior to his being raised to heaven.[41] Al-Ṭabarī in his own commentary, *Jāmiʿ al-bayān*, elaborately mentioned the two opinions, but then concluded with the view that Jesus' stay on earth was terminated by a state of unconsciousness (sleep) prior to his ascension. He also expounded his view by quoting the prophetic tradition affirming Jesus' return and eventual death and burial, and argued that a physical death is conceivable only once for a human being.[42] Since then, a consensus of scholarly opinion has converged in favour of what was made to appear as death in this case.

The return of Jesus to this world towards the day of resurrection is a theme found in the prophetic tradition. On his last mission to this world, Jesus will lead the believers to victory against the Antichrist (*Dajjāl*) and his followers. He will then establish a just rule on earth in accordance with the teachings of Islam, and will affirm the words of God stated in the Qur'ān. People will live in peace and prosperity during that time.

Conclusion

Certainly, the picture which many Muslims have of Jesus is derived from the two primary sources of religious knowledge, the Qur'ān and *ḥadīth*. The discourse about Jesus in public circles, however, has been largely influenced by the Christian doctrine of Jesus as the Son of God, the redeemer, and the

38. Qur'ān 3.55.
39. Qur'ān 5.117.
40. Qur'ān 39.42.
41. Ibn Kathīr, *Tafsīr*, II, p. 286.
42. M. al-Ṭabarī, *Jāmiʿ al-bayān ʿan taʾwīl al-Qur'ān* (10 vols.; Beirut: Dar al-Fikr, 1978), III, pp. 202–204.

Muslim rejection of it. A wider and more informed account of his life and his teachings, based on Islamic textual sources, is invaluable to all faith communities. Despite the significant doctrinal differences between Islam and Christianity about the person of Jesus, there are, as this paper has shown, definitive spiritual and moral values in relation to him that are shared between the two faiths.

Jesus in Christian, Jewish and Muslim Thought

Norman Solomon, Richard Harries and Tim Winter

Bishop Kallistos distinguishes two main approaches to the person of Jesus: Christology from above and Christology from below. Christology from above, that is to say, traditional Christology as formulated in the historic creeds of the Church in the first centuries, claims that Jesus is truly God and truly human. At the incarnation, the eternal Son of God took human form. While remaining fully divine, he took to himself a human body and soul. The dynamic behind this paradoxical position is soteriological. If we are to be saved, only God's own self can save us. But if we are to be saved, it is as human beings, so it is necessary for God to become one with us. This general understanding of Christian salvation perhaps has particular force against the background of a belief that God calls us to participate in his own life. So as Irenaeus wrote, 'in his unbounded love, he became what we are, so as to make us what he is'. Athanasius made the point even more clearly: 'he became human that we might be made god'.[1]

Christology from below also has its antecedent in the early Church. Various groups believed that Jesus was a human being who through divine grace had been raised into a special relationship with God and so reveals God in a unique way. But the approach from below is the one we are familiar with today through critical biblical scholarship which looks at Jesus in his setting, seeking to understand him in human terms. This does not inevitably lead to a liberal Christology. Indeed in Roman Catholicism today, as well as in a vast amount of Anglican and Protestant scholarship, all the tools of biblical scholarship are used to locate and understand Jesus in his context, while it is argued that there is a legitimate development from what is seen there to the later, exalted christological formulations in the New Testament and the early Church. Nevertheless, those who affirm the legitimacy of this development will have a prior faith which gives credence to it. As Bishop Kallistos suggests, 'the critical-historical study of the New Testament documents does not and cannot provide on its own a conclusive answer to the question "Who is Jesus?" Beyond the historical evidence, matters of faith and theological principle are also involved.'

1. For quotations, see Kallistos Ware's paper, 'Jesus from a Christian Perspective', above.

According to Sybil Sheridan, it is difficult to know if Jesus is referred to in the Talmud at all, because of censorship at a time when Christianity was a dominant, intolerant religion and a Talmudic tendency to obliqueness when referring to contemporary events: certainly the references, such as they are, are very obscure. Even if we include the earlier Tosefta, 'references to Jesus are questionable, scant, and not particularly theologically developed'.[2] Insofar as they do appear in early rabbinic literature, they are a response to the already-established Church and not to the person of Jesus. By the ninth century, stories about Jesus were put together in texts known as *Toldot Yeshu*. These, for private consumption only, are 'crass and unpleasant'. In the public sphere in the Middle Ages, there were disputations, when Jews were placed in a defensive position, having to give reasons why they did not accept the Christian claims about Jesus. These disputations have had the unfortunate effect of setting up a pattern that has lasted until today, for even in dialogue, Jewish views of Jesus with very few exceptions 'remain apologetic in nature'.

A major change took place at the Enlightenment when Moses Mendelssohn, perhaps for the first time, showed real sympathy for Christianity and maintained that Jesus was a special person, even a prophet, albeit one who did not abrogate the Torah. Joseph Salvador wrote a life of Jesus, trying to be impartial, and, like Christian scholars, sought to find an actual historical Jesus. He concluded that the ethical elements in the life of Jesus were derived from Judaism but that pagan 'impurities' had been added on. For Abraham Geiger, similarly, Jesus was a Jew 'with Galilean colouration', but he was disappointed that Christian academics failed to take seriously both his enormous scholarship and also Judaism itself. As Geiger put it, 'naturally the Judaism of his time must furthermore be portrayed bleakly, so that he rises radiantly above it. The most refined self-deception.' Claude Montefiore took a rather different route, seeking to explain Christianity to Jews, especially by his influential commentary on the gospels in which he sought to demonstrate the absolute adherence of Jesus to rabbinic Judaism. Considering Jesus an outstanding prophet, he argued that he should be seen as an authentic part of Judaism. Both Leo Baeck and Martin Buber, highly significant figures of great learning, continued the tradition of seeing Jesus in fully Jewish terms, and contrasted him with later non-Jewish developments, especially those attributed to Paul. More recently, Geza Vermes and David Flusser have continued this emphasis on Jesus the Jew, the former being highly influential in Christian circles but not Jewish ones, and the latter having some influence among Jewish students in Jerusalem. All this more positive, modern emphasis, however, 'has made no impact at all on the beliefs and practice of the Jewish faithful'. But, Sybil Sheridan concludes, 'who knows what may happen in the future?'

Unlike early Judaism, Islam has much to say about Jesus. His birth is prepared for in the Qur'ān by his righteous grandmother, and even more by his devout

2. For quotations, see Sybil Sheridan's paper, 'Jesus from a Jewish Perspective', above.

mother, Maryam, or Mary. He was miraculously conceived and born of a virgin mother. His birth and life were marked by miracles. Indeed, as soon as he was born, he announced to the people of Israel that he was a servant of God and a prophet who had been given a revelation. This revelation, however, was the same as that of all the prophets – a message which culminates in Muhammad – namely, that God is one, that we human beings are to submit to God, and that, because we go astray, God sends messengers that we might learn the truth and once again submit in loving obedience to the creator. Within this scheme, Jesus has a special place as the supreme messenger prior to the coming of Muhammad. Any idea of incarnation or of Jesus being the Son of God is strongly denied.

In the *ḥadīth*, the early traditions associated with Muhammad, Jesus is depicted as a holy person, an ascetic prophet from whose good example much has been and can be learnt. While the chain of prophecy culminates in Muhammad, for Islam, all prophets are regarded as equal. In the Qur'ān, Jesus is exalted straight to heaven and is not crucified, even though some people thought they had killed him. Furthermore, he will return again towards the day of judgment to lead believers to victory against the Antichrist and his followers. He will establish a just rule in accordance with the teaching of the Qur'ān, and life will be characterized by peace and prosperity.

If we begin with a Christology from below, Judaism, Christianity and Islam might appear to have much in common. But there are a number of difficulties. For while most Jewish and Christian scholars will take for granted the use of critical scholarship to establish, so far as is possible, the outlines of the life and teaching of Jesus, and indeed can reach at least some agreed conclusions, Islamic scholars have been reluctant to use these methods in relation to the Qur'ān. The emphasis in Islam would be on the overriding purpose and providence of God, and not so much the human instruments of that purpose. So while there are some aspects of the Qur'ānic view of Jesus that Jewish and Christian scholars can integrate into their own picture, some cannot be so easily accommodated. For a number of scholars, it will be the miraculous elements that prove a particular difficulty. For others, it is the Qur'ānic view of the crucifixion – that it did not happen – which is, literally, a crux. Some Christian scholars have argued that the Qur'ān is susceptible of being interpreted in a way which allows for Jesus actually being crucified. On this view, the enemies of Jesus who thought they had crucified him were wrong not because Jesus was not crucified, which he was, but because it was all along God's intention that Jesus should meet his death in this way – his death therefore was due to God, and not to the plotters.[3] Clearly this question of whether or not Jesus was crucified is crucial for Christians because it is this fact, they believe, which gives substance to the claim that God shares our anguish to the full.

3. G. Parrinder, *Jesus in the Qur'an* (London: Sheldon Press, 1976), pp. 105–21.

When it comes to the faith claims of Christianity and Islam, clearly there is a major difference, though again, some Christian scholars have sought to show that the abyss is not as great as has traditionally been thought. For example, the concept of 'messenger' or 'prophet' of God, according to some, can at least be pushed in a more Christian direction, with God sharing in something of the experience of God's prophets. On this view, Jesus is a prophet who allowed God to share the pain of rejection to the full (few Muslim theologians, however, have viewed the idea of a suffering God as coherent).

This raises the question of how different religions interpret their own past, in particular how Jews and Christians understand the Hebrew scriptures. For most of Christian history, it has been fundamental to Christian belief that these scriptures prefigure and foretell the coming of Jesus as the crucified Messiah. The New Testament sees in Jesus the fulfilment of certain scriptural passages, which it often quotes. Later, the argument from prophecy was seen as one of the main evidences for the truth of Christianity. This approach has never been regarded as convincing by Jews, not least because the coming of Jesus failed to bring in the messianic age. After his death, life continued with much the same mixture of good and evil as before, whereas for Jewish belief, the Messiah will usher in a radically changed world. Today, both Christian and Jewish scholars seek to understand passages of scripture in their own context and many Christians, too, are wary of using them as predictions of Christ. Obviously a major difference for the three religions is their evaluation of the Christian claim that God raised Jesus from the dead. This makes it possible for Christians, using all the tools of modern biblical scholarship (that is, starting with a Christology from below, Jesus in his actual historical context), nevertheless to continue to affirm that Jesus is not only human but God. Wolfhart Pannenberg, in *Jesus: God and Man* for example, believes that the implicit claims in the ministry and teaching of Jesus about a unique status were 'retroactively validated' by the resurrection. He makes this claim using a particular philosophy of history. For him, the claim that Jesus is God and human is a doxological statement, that is, one which opens out into praise, not an assertion on the basis of which other assertions can be made.[4] Whether or not the resurrection of Jesus can carry the weight of such doctrinal affirmations, it is clearly crucial to Christian faith. Except for a very few unrepresentative Jews, such as Pinchas Lapide, the claimed resurrection of Jesus is of no interest to Jews. For Muslims on the other hand, while the resurrection is not recorded in the Qur'ān, the divine validation of Jesus is proclaimed when God takes Jesus to God's self – particularly if we take the traditional interpretation that God outwitted those who plotted Jesus' death, thereby averting the crucifixion. Muslims would see the 'death' of Jesus in the context of the economy of deliverance of prophets by God, an approach in which definite historical facts are hard to verify, and in any case not the overriding consideration. However, crucifixion need not necessarily pose a problem for Islam, which has its own martyrological tradition.

4. W. Pannenberg, *Jesus: God and Man* (London: SCM Press, 1968).

The value of this kind of approach should not be seen in terms of trying to convert the dialogue partner, but rather in terms of trying to help her or him understand what might be involved in another religion's fundamental beliefs. A similar exercise has taken place recently among the Jewish scholars who contributed to the volume *Christianity in Jewish Terms*.[5] This book of essays takes concepts like incarnation and shows that it is possible to understand them in Jewish terms. Whether or not this turns out to be acceptable to either Jews or Christians is a further matter. The point is that an idea which has previously been thought to have no resonances at all with historic Judaism might at least be able to be understood in a way which is faithful to Jewish beliefs and terminology.

Christianity and Islam are at least agreed in taking the person of Jesus seriously. Jesus is vital for both faiths. The Qur'ān does not speak about Jesus in any way *but* respectfully. Just the opposite is true of Judaism. As Sybil Sheridan wrote, 'how does one have a dialogue when the subject in hand is of no interest to one party?' Here, however, we need to make some distinctions. A figure can be of no interest to a dialogue partner in the sense that the figure has no place in what constitutes the religion. In this sense, it is certainly true that Jesus is of no interest to Judaism. In a similar way, Muhammad is of no significance in framing Christianity's view of salvation. He came a long time after the formation of the New Testament and therefore has no role in the canonical scriptures or early tradition. That said, a figure can become of interest if they are of importance to the dialogue partner. Muhammad is of great interest to Christians, we might say, because he is fundamental to Islam, to which Christians wish to relate. Here we come back to the basic imaginative sympathy without which no dialogue of any kind is possible. There is a yet further sense, however, in which a figure who is of no significance for the formative basis of the religion might become of importance. This is because of the desire to have a consistent world-view in which significant religious figures have a place. Islam is different from Judaism and Christianity here because Jesus has a canonical place within Islam; he is accounted for, as it were, in a way which is not open to question in Islamic terms. Christianity, while it might have no place for Muhammad in its formative writings, might, however, want to make a positive place for him in its understanding of the workings of God with humanity as a whole.

Historically, Judaism has been in a somewhat different position, in that it has not had a developed theology for God's truth outside the specific revelation of the Torah to the Jewish people. There has been the Noahide covenant, according to which humanity as a whole is capable of recognizing right from wrong – but how far this allows a revelation of God to humanity outside Judaism is a controversial issue. In the past, Christianity had similar difficulty in affirming truth in non-Christian religions. But today, most Christians, like Liberal and

5. T.S. Frymer-Kensky, *et al.* (eds.), *Christianity in Jewish Terms* (Boulder, CO and Oxford: Westview Press, 2000).

Reform Jews, seek to make theological space in one way or another – but that points to the later chapter on pluralism. The point here is that though Jesus may be insignificant for Jewish life and practice, he might become of significance first because he is of significance to dialogue partners, in this case Christians and Muslims, and secondly, because in trying to fathom God's way with the world outside Judaism, it might be thought, as it was by Leo Baeck, Martin Buber and a good number of other distinguished Jewish scholars, that Jesus has a special place in carrying the insights of Judaism to the wider world.

Chapter 4: Muhammad

Muhammad from a Muslim Perspective

Tim Winter

Islam is a broad church, divided as well as united by readings of the life of its founder. The twentieth century saw the Prophet reinvented in multiple and sometimes improbable ways: as a pacifist (by Hasan Askari), a radical socialist (Muṣṭafā al-Sibāʿī), a Third Worldist, anticolonial hero (Ali Shariati), an Arab nationalist (Michel Aflaq), a Nietzschean or at least a Bergsonian superman (Allama Iqbal), an eco-warrior (Fazlun Khalid), a feminist (Fatima Mernissi), an arch-conservative (King Fahd), a scientist (Maurice Bucaille), a postmodern foe of metanarratives (Farid Esack), and a proto-democrat (Muhammad Asad). The list could be extended, but the diversity must answer finally to an authority – not to a hierarchy, which for better or worse has been largely absent from Islam – but to historians, and, more complicatedly, to patterns of devotion to the Prophet which are recurrent enough in Islamic history cautiously to be described as normative. Before moving on to my own reflections, I propose to indicate these patterns by offering some quotations. Such patterns are often the least familiar aspect of Islam to outsiders, not least because they evince an emotional warmth which is sometimes believed to be foreign to the 'sandy soil' of this religion.

The Prophet as Intercessor

At the eschaton, the Prophet shall appear not as a stern judge but as a merciful intercessor; and this orthodox teaching predictably triggered a rich devotional literature. Here is a poem, in rhyming couplets, by ʿAbd al-Raḥmān Jāmī (d. 1492). He pulls out all the organ-stops of Persian panegyric, but his sincerity is nonetheless clear.

> Bestow your generous attention, O seal of the prophets; for greatly bereaved is the world since your demise, O Messenger of God.
>
> You who are indeed last of the messengers and their seal.
>
> How can you ignore us when drowned in wretchedness and ill of fortune are we?
>
> Through your evergreen freshness, O dearest one, grace now this world, and from your restful sleep awake, to fill us with guiding light.

Lift now your countenance from within your Yemeni cloak, for your blessed face is the very life and light of day.

Turn for us the darkness of our sorrowful night into blessed light of day, and crown for us our day with successful accomplishments.

O Messenger, grant refuge and help for the needy and console the hearts of those filled with love for you.

Sinners are we, drowned in the sea of our iniquity. Yet great is the thirst of our endeavour to follow your way.

In spite of our many heinous sins, may God grant you to intercede for us, for otherwise we are lost.

May you arrive on the plain of reckoning, while we, encircled by our sins, look on as you bend your head in prayer, calling out: 'Forgive my people, God, forgive them!'[1]

The Prophet as Personal Guide

Most theologians accept that the Prophet now lives in the state known as *barzakh*, an 'isthmus' between this world and the next. In Muslim piety, it is common to find the belief that the Prophet can appear to spiritual seekers in order to provide consolation and guidance. Here is a modern example from a diary made during a forty-day solitary retreat:

As I pray, all at once an image is before my eyes, sharp and clear: I see Muhammad (peace be upon him) sitting in a white Arabian gown. I see slender, fine hands, powerful, with a slightly tanned skin-color, and similar feet, bare but for brown leather sandals. I see no face or head; it's as if I'm too close to see it ...

I ask him to show me his heart, to teach me the way of the heart, the way of poverty. He opens his garment to show his chest, and his heart is like a gleaming, reflecting mirror, like an indescribably powerful silvery-white sun that burns up and destroys everything in its cool fire. It seems unbearable and at the same time irresistible. It turns every superfluous thing to ashes, burns everything empty and clean. I stay there for a long time, right in front of this glittering, all-penetrating light source, secure in his strong arms, kept safe.[2]

The Prophet as Moral Exemplar

From al-Ghazālī (d. 1111):

The Messenger of God (upon him be peace) was the mildest of men, but also the bravest and most just of men. He was the most generous of men, so that never did a gold or silver coin spend the night in his house. If something remained at the end of the day, because he had not found someone to give it to, and night descended,

1. Abbreviated from the paraphrase of Muhammad Zakariyya Kandhlawi, *Virtues of Salaat Alan Nabi* (Johannesburg: Waterval Islamic Institute, 1983), pp. 197–202.

2. M. Özelsel, *Forty Days: The Diary of a Traditional Solitary Sufi Retreat* (Brattleboro, VT: Threshold Books, 1996), pp. 84–85.

he would go out, and not return home until he had given it to someone in need. From what God gave him ... he would take only the simplest and easiest foods: dates and barley, giving anything else away for God's sake. Never did he refuse a gift for which he was asked. He used to mend his own sandals, and patch his own clothes, and serve his family, and help them to cut meat. He was the shyest of men, so that his gaze would never remain long in the face of another person. He would accept the invitation of a freeman or a slave, and accept a gift, even if it were no more than a gulp of milk, or the thigh of a rabbit, and offer something in return. He never consumed anything given as charity. He was not too proud to reply to a slave-girl, or a pauper in rags. He would become angered for his Lord, never for himself; he would cause truth and justice to prevail even if this led to difficulties for himself or for his companions. He kept a sheep, from which he would draw milk for his family. He would walk among the fields of his companions.

He never despised any pauper for his poverty or illness; neither did he hold any king in awe simply because he was a king. He would call rich and poor to God, without distinction.[3]

The Prophet as Prototype of the Mystic

Jalāl al-Dīn Rūmī is said to be the most widely read poet in America;[4] but since the New Age 'versions' into which he is translated are often reluctant to challenge America's generalized dislike of Islam, the founder has for the most part been excluded. And yet in the original, he is there triumphantly, not as some prudent nod to doctors of the law, but as Rūmī's ideal, the 'astrolabe of God', the model of the spiritual wayfarer and of the perfected saint. 'This is my beloved,' Rūmī insisted, 'this my physician, this my tutor, this my cure.' His life provides a series of icons the contemplation of which transforms the observer; he is the 'philosopher's stone' which transmutes leaden hearts into gold.

Several long *ḥadīths* recount the story of the Prophet's ascension into heaven from Jerusalem, recalling how even Gabriel could not accompany him into the ultimate presence of God. This most mystical moment in his career was used by Rūmī as an archetype of the Sufi's flight:

When Muḥammad passed the Lote-tree and Gabriel's observation post, station and limit,
He said to Gabriel: 'Come, fly after me!' He replied: 'Go! Go! I am not your match.'
Again he said: 'Come, O burner of veils! I have still not reached my zenith.'
He replied: 'O my sweet glory! If I fly beyond this limit, my wings will burn.'[5]

3. Summarized from Abū Ḥāmid al-Ghazālī, *Ihyā' ʿUlūm al-Dīn* (Cairo: Muṣṭafā al-Ḥalabī, AH 1347/1929), II, pp. 315–20.
4. *Christian Science Monitor*, 25 November 1997.
5. W.C. Chittick, *The Sufi Path of Love: The Spiritual Teachings of Rumi* (Albany, NY: State University of New York Press, 1983), p. 222.

Gabriel, for Rūmī, represented the intellect, which, according to this oldest trope of mysticism, could not attain to God. Only the Burāq, the Prophet's fabulous steed, which is Love itself, could make the final journey beyond the mysterious lote tree. The God known in this way is a God of justice, sometimes implacable, as well as a God of mercy. The Prophet, therefore, who is his 'viceregent' (*khalīfa*) and whose temper must mirror his plenitude, must actualize on earth the divine names of Rigour (*jalāl*) as well as those of Beauty (*jamāl*). Hence: God forgives, and the Prophet forgives. God judges, and so does God's Prophet. He is 'God's scales on earth on which good and evil are judged'.[6] He is like Noah's ark: some will not be saved, and must perish. The Qur'ān in his hand is like the rod of Moses, which is guidance for the believers, directing them to the Promised Land; but which is also a serpent which consumes those guilty of pride and unbelief.

Hence the Prophet, like Moses, has enemies, who represent types of human distraction, egotism and a demonic scuttling away from the light. But even as he administers justice, he is entirely detached. For he is 'like the moon, and his companions are the stars, and the heavenly bodies are not obstructed in their journey by the barking of dogs'.[7]

As the perfect human being, the Prophet manifests God's rigour. But while Rūmī accepted this as proof of his theomorphic nature, his Prophet is primarily the treasurer of God's mercy; while God is wrathful, he has also told his Prophet that 'My Mercy outstrips My wrath.' 'Muhammad has come "as a mercy to the worlds" (Qur'an, 21:107), and from the Ocean of Absolute Certainty he grants pearls to the inhabitants of this world, peace to the fishes.'[8]

Further Reflections

Secular preoccupations have led Western commentators far from the themes dear to Rūmī and to most adherents of traditional forms of Islam. Such commentators appear indifferent to Muslim devotionalism, and are uninterested in exploring the spirituality of the Prophet. Instead, the preoccupation has been with *eros* and *thanatos*, Freud's twin concerns of humanity, responsible equally for our greatnesses and our debilities; and Christian and secular assessments of the Prophet have sometimes harboured negative judgements on both counts.[9]

6. Chittick, *Sufi Path of Love*, p. 64.
7. A. Schimmel, *The Triumphal Sun: A Study of the Works of Jalāloddin Rumi* (Albany, NY: State University of New York Press, 1993), p. 284.
8. Schimmel, *Triumphal Sun*, p. 283.
9. For instance, S. Khalaf, 'Protestant Images of Islam: Disparaging Stereotypes Reconfirmed', *Islam and Christian-Muslim Relations* 8 (1997), pp. 211–29.

Eros

The Prophet's sexuality, which for many Sufis formed the basis for an elaborate and explicitly erotic symbolism of union with God, can be understood as a divinely ordained sign against a Christianity which by his time had routinely associated sexual activity with original sin, and virginity with angelic detachment. The Prophet had lived as an ascetic, fasting the arduous twenty-four-hour 'Fast of David' which he forbade his followers. We are told that his house was windowless, with a low ceiling, and that a piece of sackcloth served for a door.[10] Yet our information about his worship in the small hours comes mainly from his young wife ʿĀ'isha, who has preserved for us many of his prayers.[11] We are far, here, from the devotions of the desert fathers, struggling alone in their cells.

For mediaeval Europeans confident that virginity was a proleptic anticipation of the life of the blessed, such a conjugation of sanctity and sexuality could only be a blasphemy. The Prophet was false precisely because he encouraged his people to live in a 'garden of nature'; his law was a *lex venerea*, whence the tradition of worshipping on Friday – the day of Venus.[12] Mediaeval polemic of this kind, however, seems to have been largely dispelled by radically new attitudes to sexuality which have overtaken the Christian world. The argument now is not about the compatibility of sexual plenitude with spirituality: the Islamic view here is now not terribly difficult for Christians. Instead, the argument hinges on the question of the moral status of polygamy. Here I do not propose to do much more than recall my conversation with a Bosnian minister of culture, who told me how his government was under intense pressure from Muslim women's groups to legalize polygamy, a move impossible because of opposition by international monitors. In Bosnia, the recent conflict had ensured that women substantially outnumbered men. 'It is better,' the minister opined, 'to have half a husband than to be forever on the shelf.'[13]

10. Nūr al-Dīn al-Samhūdī, *Wafā' al-wafā' bi-akhbār dār al-Muṣṭafā* (Cairo: Maṭbaʿat al-Ādāb, AH 1326/1908), I, pp. 383–84.

11. Including the famous prayer 'O God, place light in my heart ...' narrated by Bukhārī; for a translation of these *ḥadīths*, see *Mishkat Al-Masabih* (trans. J. Robson; Lahore: Sh. Muhammad Ashraf, 1970), I, pp. 247–49. For the arguments over ʿĀ'isha's age, see R. Maqsood, *Hazrat A'ishah: A Study of Her Age at the Time of Her Marriage* (Birmingham: Islamic Publication Centre International, n.d.).

12. N. Daniel, *Islam and the West* (Edinburgh: Edinburgh University Press, 1960), p. 145.

13. Faced with the breakdown of normative Western marriage and relationship codes, a small number of contemporary thinkers are turning to this primordial institution for possible guidance. Philip Kilbride, professor of anthropology at Bryn Mawr, aroused much interest with his book *Plural Marriage for Our Times: A Reinvented Option* (New York: Bergin and Garvey, 1994). Audrey Chapman has written a more popular study entitled *Man-Sharing: Dilemma or Choice* (New York: HarperCollins, 1991); see also A. Blake, *Women Can Win the Marriage Lottery: Share Your Man with Another Wife* (Orange County, CA: Orange County University Press, 1996).

It is often pointed out that Islam, like the polygamous Hebrew religion which preceded it, emerged in the context of tribal warfare in which polygamy provided the best available mechanism for the social reintegration of widows. The Prophet was acting normally for an Arab ruler. All but one of his wives were widows, and most of his wives were, by the standards of the time, well advanced in years.

Such is the temper of modern apologetic; but traditional Muslims would be impatient with this observation, which appears to miss the point when set beside the fact that by these marriages, these women became apostles and initiates, entitled 'Mothers of the Believers', astoundingly privileged to share their lives with 'the Best of Creation'.

Thanatos

Hamlet ponders 'whether 'tis nobler in the mind to suffer the slings and arrows of outrageous fortune, or to take arms against a sea of troubles, and by opposing, end them'. Here, some Christian verdicts have also been negative, moved by the nobility of victimhood. Kenneth Cragg is typical as he laments what he sees as the Prophet's option 'for community, for resistance, for external victory, for pacification and rule'.[14]

Muslims, whose founder succeeds Christ and views him with reverence, are unsure why Cragg cannot regard the two men as images of differing but divinely guided responses to radically unlike situations. It is evident that Christians are christologically obliged to profess the superiority of Jesus, but an awareness of context should serve at least to reduce the categoric quality of the comparison, a reduction to which some recent theological turns are surely hospitable. Could it be that just as arguments over the Prophet's sexuality have become muted in the past fifty years, parallel arguments over the Prophet's political life are being likewise eroded? By no means all Christians share Cragg's belief that passive, suffering witness is the only morally authentic response to the injustices of the world. There is a growing willingness today to reassess the practical consequences of rendering unto Caesar that which he is likely to abuse.[15]

We may ask ourselves whether the twentieth-century fruits of the path of accommodation, of 'awaiting the day of the Lord', did not interrogate and even make impossible the Pauline focus on the one who commanded to 'resist not him that is evil', instead of the Jewish Messiah who drove out moneychangers with a whip of cord, that 'other Jesus' who sought to 'turn the world upside down'.[16] Much New Testament scholarship now purports to have unearthed activist, even Zealot strands to Jesus' teaching, which had been carefully muted or excised by gospel-writers fearful of Roman inquisition. Such a view disturbs any 'two kingdoms' theology, and is utterly devastating to anaemic Victorian

14. A.K. Cragg, *Call of the Minaret* (Oxford: Oxford University Press, 1956), p. 93.
15. See Keith Ward's paper on this point, 'Muhammad from a Christian Perspective'.
16. Matthew 5.39 (RV) and Acts 17.6.

Christs of the Holman Hunt variety. Could it facilitate a Christian appreciation of another cleanser of temples?

Even without such a re-Judaizing of Jesus, modern Christians are making such a turn: 'I will want to show that the Christian Bible and the gospel of Jesus Christ our Lord is subversive of all injustice and evil, oppression and exploitation, and that ... he is the liberator God of the Exodus who leads his people out of every kind of bondage.'[17] The exodus theme seems conspicuous, rather than the cross: a discreet redistribution of stress which, in the case of the Latin American liberationists, has led to some of the most serious tensions within the modern Catholic Church. Could these be, as Shabbir Akhtar has argued, the birthpangs of a new possibility in Christianity, which must render intriguing its spectacular anticipation in Islam?[18] The *hijra* stands already as the sign of liberation, not only from the world (as in Rūmī) but from the tyrants who abuse it. Indeed, one of the commonest Muslim claims about the Bible is that it foretells a new Moses: 'I will raise up for them a prophet like you from among their own people; I will put my words in the mouth of the prophet, who shall speak to them everything that I command.'[19] It is a new exodus prophet who is foretold, who will bear a literally inspired scripture.

'If Moses was the liberator of the enslaved Israelites, Muhammad was the liberator of the whole of mankind, through liberation of the weak among them', claims an Indian Muslim who describes his work as 'liberation theology'.[20] The exodus event so lamented by Cragg is a true and not an illusory, profane liberation; like the earlier emigration, it leads not to the desert but ultimately to Jerusalem and the construction of a place of God's glory.

The Third Temple, with its blue and gold splendour offering to the three religions of Jerusalem something of the heavenly blessing brought down by the Prophet's ascension, stands at the centre of a new Third Empire. Mehmed the Conqueror made this explicit when in 1453 he claimed the mantle of the Byzantine rulers. The Third Empire, however, was in this sense Solomonic: it acknowledged the possibility of prophetic kingship and sacred sexuality: it was hence a manifestation of the finest dimensions of the Old Testament. Islam thus becomes the glorious triumph of Judaism: of its monotheism, its law, its martial prowess and its tender sexuality. Unlike Paul's Christianity, which seems to consummate Judaism by negating it, Islam's overtaking of the Hebrew message is also its universalization.

17. D.M. Tutu, *The Rainbow People of God: South Africa's Victory over Apartheid* (London: Doubleday, 1994), p. 56.

18. S. Akhtar, *The Final Imperative: An Islamic Theology of Liberation* (London: Bellew, 1992). For some rich Christian resources on 'turning the world upside down', see A. Bradstock and C.C. Rowland (eds.), *Radical Christian Writings: A Reader* (Oxford: Blackwell, 2002).

19. Deuteronomy 18.18. For the Muslim exegesis, see for instance the popular account of F. Siddiqui, *The Bible's Last Prophet* (Alexandria, VA: Al-Saadawi, 1995), pp. 12–21.

20. A.A. Engineer, *Islam and Liberation Theology: Essays on Liberative Elements in Islam* (Delhi: Sterling, 1990), p. 23.

The Third Empire formed the subject of a remarkable meditation by Henryk Ibsen. In his play *Emperor and Galilean*, the Norwegian sage wrestled with the common nineteenth-century problem of how to replace Christianity with a faith that would acknowledge the flesh and the need to challenge social injustice. The play concerns Julian the Apostate, who seeks to return the world to the harmony between body and spirit which prevailed before war was declared between the two. The Roman gods, he opines, were open-minded and cultivated. They valued the 'sweet lust of the flesh', and also heroism and willpower. Such had been the First Empire; the Second, inaugurated by Constantine and Helena, is an austere inversion, a world of denial, lived 'on the pillars where saints stand on one leg', as the faltering emperor tells Basil of Caesarea.[21]

Julian's choice is hence shown as spiritually and morally acute. He reinstates the ancient cults, and seeks a universal reconciliation. However, Ibsen (who had himself flirted with Wagnerian dreams of self-realization through an adversion to pagan identities) made it clear that Julian's attempt to recreate the First Empire must be frustrated. 'The old beauty is no longer beautiful', the emperor concedes to Basil, but 'the new truth is no longer true.' He becomes a pedant-tyrant, deluded by his own sense of destiny, and loses a titanic battle against the Persians. His heart almost breaks as he admits his failure to Maximus, his pagan counsellor:

> JULIAN: Say it then! Who shall conquer? The emperor or the Galilean?
> MAXIMUS: Both emperor and Galilean shall go down ... If in our time or hundreds of years hence, I know not; but it shall happen when the right man comes ... O thou fool, who hast drawn thy sword against the future, – against that third empire, – where the two-sided shall reign.
> JULIAN: The Third Empire? Messiah? Not the kingdom of the Jewish people but of the spirit, and the Messiah of the kingdom of the world.
> MAXIMUS: Logos in Pan – Pan in Logos.[22]

Julian cannot be that man; he is vanquished by his delusions. For like Peer Gynt, indeed like most of Ibsen's antiheroes, he is an 'idealist', while what the world awaits is a 'realist'. This opposition has nothing to do with the philosophical tussle which uses the same terms. For Ibsen, the words implied a tension between purely ethical strategies. Bernard Shaw, debating Ibsen, noted that according to the idealist, 'Realism means egotism; and egotism means depravity.'[23] But the opposite is the case. Idealism is a covert 'realization of

21. H. Ibsen, *The Emperor and the Galilean* (trans. C. Ray; London: Tinsley, 1876), p. 55. The play is historically quite credible: cf. G. Bowersock, *Julian the Apostate* (London: Duckworth, 1978).

22. *Emperor and Galilean*, pp. 252–53. Cf. the Portuguese writer Teixiera de Pascoaes: 'In every human being, at heart, two gods must be incarnate: ... Jesus and Pan' ('Unamuno's Yoismo and Its Relation to Traditional Spanish Individualism', in R. Martínez-López [ed.], *Unamuno Centennial Studies* [Austin, TX: University of Texas Press, 1966], pp. 10–26 [13]).

23. G.B. Shaw, *The Quintessence of Ibsenism* (London: Walter Scott, 1891), p. 101.

oneself', self as ego; it is egotism of the type that leads Peer Gynt to accept a slatternly woman riding on a pig as a princess, simply because he needs a princess. 'Idealism' is nothing but a 'romantic fancy'; hence, with hindsight, we would class Hitler as an idealist, and his Third Reich as a disastrous inversion of the Third Kingdom which, as with the ill-fated Julian, comes to grief on an eastern battlefield.

For Ibsen, our humanity is unearthed by a 'realist' rediscovery of *livsglaede*, joy of life, which is repressed by our inertness in the face of sinful structures, and by our hesitations over sex. Pastor Rosmer, the failed hero of *Rosmersholm*, abandons his family's political conservatism in favour of social activism, and discovers a sexual nature that his conventional wife will not arouse. For Shaw, this country parson gropes towards self-realization by losing his Christianity, and through the awareness that he must act for the consummation of his physical nature and for the ennoblement of society. 'He looks at the world,' Shaw noted, 'with some dim prevision of the Third Empire.'[24]

Shaw acknowledged the influence of Ibsen on his own work, and this is nowhere more conspicuous than in his opposition of 'idealism' to 'realism'. Pacifism, or militarism, and sexual repression were for him the most manifest representations of idealism, most of his early plays functioning as pegs on which to hang this dialectic. Shaw was aware, of course, of the inadequacy of his own Fabian freethinking response. How to achieve sexual liberation without arriving at libertinism was a question few in his circle really resolved. However, his most ambitious play, as important to him as *Emperor and Galilean* had been to Ibsen, was conceived as a vehicle for his superman. As Hesketh Pearson recorded:

> For many years [this was 1913], Shaw had been meditating a play on a prophet. The militant saint was a type more congenial to his nature than any other, a type he thoroughly sympathised with and could therefore portray with unfailing insight. In all history the one person who exactly answered his requirements, who would have made the perfect Shavian hero, was Mahomet.[25]

In his diary, Shaw himself wrote: 'I had long desired to dramatise the life of Mahomet. But the possibility of a protest from the Turkish Ambassador – or the fear of it – causing the Lord Chamberlain to refuse to license such a play, deterred me.' And so, as Pearson recorded, he wrote *Saint Joan* instead.

Shaw, like Ibsen, professed to love God but not Christianity. He described it as 'a growing thing which was finally suppressed by the crucifixion',[26] which preached 'an insane vengeance bought off by a trumpery expiation'.[27] Its

24. Shaw, *Quintessence of Ibsenism*, p. 101.
25. H. Pearson, *Bernard Shaw* (London: Collins, 1942), p. 375.
26. M. Holroyd, *Bernard Shaw* (London: Chatto & Windus, abridged edn, 1997), p. 411.
27. Cited in G. Whitehead, *Bernard Shaw Explained: A Critical Exposition of the Shavian Religion* (London: Watts, 1925), p. 12.

ideology of non-resistance was a charter for tyrants, and usually defeated even its own purpose of establishing a space for religion. 'Social salvation must come before individual righteousness is possible.'[28] Hence Joan of Arc, or the outline of 'Mahomet' dimly visible between the lines of the play, is a 'born leader', whose voices heard from God are genuine (the only supernatural stage-direction in Shaw which is not the prelude to the exposure of some humbug); she is a 'protesting prophet, subverter, active agent of the Life Force',[29] who is condemned by 'idealists' (the Church), who opposes convention but upholds the sanctity of the political virtues, because, as Shaw passionately believed, 'government is impossible without religion'.[30]

The Islamic resonances are obvious enough. We are not surprised to learn that *Saint Joan* was composed while Shaw was copy-editing T.E. Lawrence's *Seven Pillars of Wisdom*, with its tales of Arabian derring-do.[31] No doubt the two friends discussed the Prophet together, although it seems that Lawrence had abandoned his project of writing Muhammad's biography by the time of his death, which occurred shortly afterwards.

Such early twentieth-century convergences between the Muslim Prophet and European post-Christian ideals had much to do with romanticism. There is an Enlightenment notion of the 'noble savage' at work here, which is not wholly alien to the Muslim case. The mediaevals condemned the Prophet's 'garden of nature'; thinkers alienated from doctrines of original sin found his naturalism (a better word than 'realism') strangely compelling. During his ascension, Gabriel offers the Prophet a cup of wine, and a cup of milk. He chooses the latter, and the angel exclaims: 'You have been guided to nature.'[32] For in taking nourishment directly from the natural world, rather than at one remove via a process of fermentation and corruption, the Prophet seems to confirm the fully theophanic nature of the world, and our ability to be reconciled to God by being reconciled to it. The incident is probably intended as a refutation of sacramentalism. Its corollary, of immense contemporary import, is that 'to be at peace with the earth one must be at peace with Heaven'.[33]

28. Whitehead, *Bernard Shaw Explained*, p. 59.
29. Holroyd, *Bernard Shaw*, p. 522.
30. Whitehead, *Bernard Shaw Explained*, p. 43.
31. Holroyd, *Bernard Shaw*, pp. 525–26.
32. Muslim, Īmān, 272.
33. S.H. Nasr, *Man and Nature: The Spiritual Crisis of Modern Man* (London: Unwin Paperbacks, 1976), p. 14.

Muhammad from a Christian Perspective

Keith Ward

In this chapter, I aim to show that, although many traditional Christian assessments of Muhammad have been negative, since the nineteenth century there have been notable attempts to state a more positive view. I will look at the work of Bishop Kenneth Cragg as a leading example of such attempts. He shows how Muhammad can be seen by Christians as a true prophet, a person inspired by God, and how Christians can see the Qur'ān as divine revelation, while not accepting that it is inerrant. Cragg draws a contrast between Jesus as the expression of self-giving love, and Muhammad as a statesman and warrior, concerned for social justice. I will suggest that the contrast is not absolute, and that their lives and teachings can be seen as complementary revelations of divine will. Even though this will not resolve some basic differences between Christianity and Islam, it is important for Christians to appreciate the ideal of complete devotion to God that Muhammad represents for Muslims.

Negative Christian Assessments of the Prophet

The history of Christian assessments of Muhammad is, I regret to say, largely one of calumny and misrepresentation. The reasons for this are not far to seek. The Qur'ān forbids Muslims to speak of a 'Son of God', or to say that 'God is (one of) three'. Since these themes are central to Christian belief, it has seemed to many Christians that the revelation to Muhammad must have been false, and therefore that the Prophet must have been deluded, if not actually wilfully opposed to Christian belief.

In consequence, there has not been much effort to attempt a positive appreciation of the Prophet, which catches something of Muslim reverence for him, or of the ideal of human life that he represents for Muslims. The general approach has rather been one of depicting him as a heretic, with a false and inadequate understanding of God. In mediaeval times, he was named by some Christians as 'Mahound', the devil or the spirit of darkness. His possession of a number of wives has been depicted as sexual licence (even though King Solomon had a thousand wives, and escapes censure on that score). His successful military skill has been depicted as warlike aggressiveness (even though the Christian crusaders were applauded while they massacred the Eastern Orthodox Christians in Constantinople). And his richly poetic descriptions of paradise have been depicted as promises of endless sexual orgies with young virgins (even though sex is never mentioned in the Qur'ānic passages which speak of communion with the beautiful angelic messengers of God).

In mitigation, it might be said that exaggerated and (to modern ears) unsavoury accounts of this sort were propagated by some Muslims themselves, eager to stress Muhammad's prowess as a warrior and sexual hero, and to develop a rather materialistic notion of paradise. In this, they were perhaps mostly concerned to validate their own addiction to military and sexual exploits, and their own rather materialist orientation. Nevertheless, they did portray the Prophet in a way which they saw as positive, but which was perceived by Christians (who in any case felt themselves under threat from Muslim military successes) as morally dubious. This provided ample ammunition for Christian critics, but I suppose one must say that Islam, like Christianity, sometimes needs to be defended from its erstwhile defenders. Certainly Christians were more than ready to see a negative side to Muhammad. They developed and exaggerated those aspects of tradition about Muhammad that stressed military prowess and patriarchal dominance.

Correspondingly, they underplayed or overlooked the equally strong elements of tradition that spoke of Muhammad's tolerance, democratic and non-hierarchical attitudes, and uncompromising adherence to monotheism.

Thus one of the greatest of all Christian poets, Dante Alighieri, placed Muhammad in the inferno, torn to pieces by pigs. Luther took Muhammad and the pope to be the two arch-enemies of Christ. Voltaire wrote a vitriolic attack on the Prophet in his play *Mahomet*, written in 1742. But it is too embarrassing to continue with records of such attempts to demonize Muhammad. They exist, and Christians must repent and ask forgiveness for their own stupidity and spitefulness.

Christian Views of Muhammad as a Prophet

It should be recorded that there have also been attempts to arrive at a more sympathetic and positive assessment of the Prophet, and among the British, the poet Carlyle was one of the first who, in a lecture on heroes and hero-worship, delivered in 1840, tried to see him as a genuine hero among the prophets.[1] Especially in the last century, Christian writers have tried to do justice to Muhammad as a messenger of God who devoted his life to obedience to God and to accepting his difficult vocation as a prophet. There have been many books written by Christian authors that attempt a more sympathetic portrayal

1. T. Carlyle, *On Heroes, Hero-Worship, and the Heroic in History* (ed. M.K. Goldberg; Berkeley and Los Angeles, CA and Oxford: University of California Press, 1993), pp. 37–66.

of the Prophet, though it is probably impossible for a Christian to see Muhammad quite as a Muslim would see him, for reasons I will try to make clear. A sensitive and positive evaluation is quite possible, however, and among recent Christian writers it is perhaps Kenneth Cragg who has given the matter most serious attention.

Cragg was Anglican bishop of Jerusalem, and is one of the foremost Christian commentators on Islam, with a formidable knowledge of his subject and a real desire to further understanding and friendship between Islam and Christianity. In a number of books, but most particularly in *Muhammad and the Christian*,[2] he writes primarily for Christians in a way that has undoubtedly increased immeasurably Christian understanding of and admiration for Islam.

From the outset, he accepts Muhammad as a true prophet of the unity, sovereignty, demand and judgement of God. He accepts Muhammad as one who lived in full and conscious obedience to God, and thus as one who realized the ideal of the Muslim life, as, indeed, 'the first of Muslims', of those who submit to God, in primacy and honour. The first major difficulty that arises for Christians is that the Qur'ān often seems specifically to contradict the New Testament, which is the written basis of Christian faith, most clearly by denying the crucifixion of Jesus, which is the very heart of Christian devotion. Accordingly, it is not possible for Christians to accept the inerrancy of the Qur'ān, and in that respect they are not able to accept the Muslim estimate of Muhammad as the vehicle of the actual words of God. It is possible, Cragg insists, to accept something as a revelation even when it is not inerrant, and very many Christians accept the Bible in this way. But few, if any, Muslims would be able to agree on this point.

There is a fundamental question here about the nature of divine revelation. Christians have usually said that the Bible is inspired by God, and they have usually thought it inerrant. But it is clear that the Bible was written by many different people at very different periods of history, and that it contains many varying points of view, from the pessimism of the book Ecclesiastes to the easy optimism of some of the psalms. So the idea of inspiration has always been a complex one in Christian theology, and only rarely has it been held that there is anything like dictation of actual words by God, as direct author. Thus it is quite possible for Christians to interpret inspiration in a rather broad sense, which does not entail inerrancy, especially on matters of obscure or otherwise unknown fact.

Such a course is not usually available to Muslims, for whom Muhammad is simply the mouthpiece of the Qur'ān, which he heard and recited as heard. The meaning of the Qur'ānic verses may be wholly obscure, and not amenable to any interpretation one can think of. But they are still revealed directly by God, and are not subject to revision. So there is almost bound to be a difference between Christians and Muslims on just what sort of a prophet Muhammad was.

2. A.K. Cragg, *Muhammad and the Christian* (Oxford: Oneworld, 1999).

Christians can see him as truly inspired by God, as called to proclaim a strict monotheistic faith, and as chosen by God for that purpose. In seeing him thus, they can place him on the same level as all the prophets of Israel and the apostles of the early Christian Church. It may even be possible to place him, from an authentically Christian viewpoint, on the same level as Jesus, insofar as prophethood is concerned (remembering that, for Christians, Jesus is 'more than a prophet'[3]). In other words, a Christian can see Muhammad as inspired in just the same sense as Jewish and Christian prophets, and thus accord him the highest honour as a true prophet. Nevertheless, they would in this still fall short of the Muslim perception that Muhammad was uniquely chosen to utter the definitive and unquestionable words of God's own self.

Christians are not agreed among themselves on the precise nature of revelation, on the extent to which it takes verbal, propositional form. But it would be broadly accepted that it is the person of Jesus that is the central focus of revelation, that it is in his person that one discerns the visible image of the invisible God.[4] Muslims do not usually see either Jesus or Muhammad in that way. Humans are not, for Islam, created in the image of God, and Muhammad, while usually being seen as a perfect human being, is not seen as an image or expression of the divine, which remains wholly other. Muhammad is the perfect messenger, the one who submits truly and fully, but not one who shows what God is (some Muslim groups, like the Ismailis, do in fact see Muhammad rather in that way, but they are considered heterodox).

So the Christian perception of Muhammad as a prophet can never quite agree with the Muslim perception. For the Christian, Muhammad can be seen as a God-inspired man, with an authentic divine message that is, however, not without restricted views naturally arising from his time and place. For the Muslim, Muhammad is the perfectly transparent, but always wholly and solely human, vehicle of the very words of God, who never lies or dissembles. It is quite possible for Christians to give Muhammad the highest honour as a prophet, and to see in him a specific human ideal. But the difference in perception that remains is due to a difference in the understanding of what revelation is, and how it is given and received. If that point is fully grasped, there would be less temptation to try to denigrate either Jesus or Muhammad. It might be possible to see both as embodying different sorts of divine revelation, or at least as being taken to encapsulate different understandings of divine revelation. They would remain distinctively themselves, not different types of the same thing. But it could be understood how both could become the originative sources of divine revelation, in different ways, for the communities which live by their teachings.

3. Luke 7.26.
4. Cf. Colossians 1.15.

Jesus and Muhammad

The basic difference in the understanding of revelation leads to another set of differences about the human vehicle of revelation. Muhammad was a successful statesman and warrior, whose teachings led to the uniting of many Arabian tribes, and their cohesion into a powerful moral and military force. Jesus, Christians affirm, died as a criminal, and his followers remained for many years as an oppressed or marginal minority, without any political role. Muslims are often unable to see any virtue in the rather passive attitude of Jesus in the face of opposition to him. Correspondingly, Christians sometimes see Muhammad's unhesitating use of force to overcome opposition as a weakness rather than a strength. This leads, even in Cragg's exposition, to making a marked contrast between the self-giving love of Jesus and the alliance with armed struggle that Muhammad enjoined on his followers.

Cragg rightly takes the crucifixion of Jesus to be central to Christian revelation. It shows, more than anything else, the length and depth of the self-giving love that is prepared to suffer to the utmost to reconcile humanity to God. The Qur'ān, however, denies that Jesus was crucified at all. He was directly raised to the presence of God, his mission having failed, and it only seemed to the Jews that they crucified him. One reason for this denial could be that a Muslim cannot see how God's servant could suffer defeat. But the denial of Jesus' crucifixion points to what, from a Christian point of view, must seem to be a certain lacuna in Muhammad's proclamation of the divine message. As Cragg puts it, 'For the Christian, the pattern of Muhammad's *Sirah* (his life) will always be in conflict with the power and perspective of the cross.'[5] Muhammad was clearly a fighter and a political leader. A large part of his attraction for Muslims is that he is seen as the ideal prophet, husband, preacher, leader, ruler, administrator and man. He could not be ideal if he was not fully involved in the social and economic life of his people. A life would be seen as less than ideal if it seemed to involve some sort of flight from social involvement and responsibility. The ideal person must be married, and must be a successful leader, in a political sense.

When Christians take Jesus as their ideal, as they do, they are seeing things rather differently. Jesus was almost certainly not married, he was anything but a successful political figure, and he is represented as recommending non-violence and as accepting an unjust death without seeking to remedy the oppression of the Jewish people at that time. In consequence, Christians see suffering love as a crucial element of divine self-revelation, and are very wary of seeing violence of any sort as part of the divine message. The contrast is often, however, over-stressed, by Christians and Muslims alike. Pacifism has always been a minority view among Christians, and the doctrine of the just war can be virtually identical with a Muslim interpretation of *jihad*. There are ascetics,

5. Cragg, *Muhammad and the Christian*, p. 53.

monks and nuns among Christians, but again they have always been in a minority, thought to have a special vocation that is not part of normal Christian discipleship. Christians do not see Jesus as the totally ascetic figure depicted in some Muslim accounts. He was, after all, regarded by some as a 'glutton and a drunkard'.[6]

On the Muslim side, Muhammad has rarely, if ever, been seen as one who was determined to expand Islam by the sword, and as primarily concerned to establish a Muslim empire. As a devotee of a compassionate and merciful God, these were primary virtues of the Prophet also. He is seen as one who was concerned to eliminate injustice and oppression in the name of God. That does sometimes involve the use of force, and he was certainly committed to using force to oppose injustice and to defend Muslims when they were threatened or betrayed. In this, he was following in the way of the great prophets and kings of Israel like Samson and David, who liberated their people from oppression by force on many occasions. The important thing is to use force minimally and effectively, to seek both justice and mercy, not to impose religion on others. Cragg says, 'any appreciation of Muhammad *in situ* must resolutely retain the contrasted meaning of the love that suffers as the Christ ... an abiding and irreducible disparity persists'.[7] I am not sure that 'disparity' is the right word here, though a disparity has certainly existed between many specific Muslim and Christian communities on the issue. It might be preferable to say that Christians stress suffering love as a great value, while Muslims stress the compassionate exercise of justice under God as their distinctive insight. The two are not, however, incompatible. Christians ought, after all, to have a sense of social responsibility, and Muslims ought to practise patience and endurance for the sake of their loyalty to God.

A Positive Christian Assessment of the Prophet

Cragg says, 'Muhammad emerges ... as assuming far too readily and practising far too freely the sanction of power'.[8] What he has in mind is that there are well-known difficulties for Muslim and Christian alike about incidents in early Muslim history, such as the massacre of the Bani Qurayzah, when tradition reports that seven hundred captured men were beheaded with the consent of the Prophet, and their wives and children taken into slavery. Such reports are not directly taken from the Qur'ān, and they are contested and variously interpreted in Islam. But one can see the difficulty that very severe and what some might see as callous judgements have seemed to many to have the sanction of the Prophet.

6. Matthew 11.19.
7. Cragg, *Muhammad and the Christian*, p. 51.
8. Cragg, *Muhammad and the Christian*, p. 3.

In this situation, it is fair to point out that the Bible itself records many similar incidents that are apparently ratified by God, and that Muhammad subsequently practised great restraint and mercy in dealing with defeated enemies. There are problems that still remain pressing and severe about what to do with the Qur'ānic injunctions to holy war and severe punishment. But it is just as true that there are problems about what to do with the New Testament injunctions to turn the other cheek and not resist evil at all. Both Christianity and Islam have not got very clear guidelines about how peoples and governments should behave now, in the light of the personal actions of their founding teachers. A great deal of sensitive interpretation is needed to apply ancient examples and precepts in a world which is very different than either a desert of nomadic tribes or an outpost of a brutal military dictatorship. Past precedents perhaps constitute guidelines for the present rather than unbreakable rules to be applied however much circumstances have changed. Christians see Muhammad's call to *jihad* as very worrying when employed as a rallying call by terrorist groups that call themselves Islamic. But that does not mean that there is no place for the use of force in the conduct of human affairs. And it is hardly plausible to think of Muhammad as a terrorist, or that he did not care for innocent human lives.

Perhaps at this point, even Cragg's sincere endeavour to understand oversimplifies by contrasting sharply the Christian stress on grace and love, sin and redemption, with the Muslim stress on Islamic *jihad* and acceptance of political power. As he himself says, 'All prophetic religion is necessarily combative, committed to *jihad*.' What Jesus said to a small group of politically powerless disciples under military occupation might be very different to what a disciple might feel it right to do when in a position of political power. And what Muhammad (or God speaking through him) said to a group of tribespeople, with a real chance of taking power and making their violent and divided society more unified and just, might be very different to what a wise and benevolent ruler of a stable Muslim country might do to non-Muslim but otherwise peaceful minorities within that country.

Perhaps at this point, an idea of complementarity might be preferable to an insistence on incompatibility. It might be that the humane conduct of the warrior and political leader who was the Prophet of God can be treasured along with the self-sacrificial and forgiving love of Jesus who was chosen to be the leader of the people of the new covenant. One might see some signs of a convergence of this sort in the Sufi (but not only Sufi) devotion to the Prophet which takes him to be a proper focus of devotion, though only as reflecting the glory of God and always pointing beyond himself to that glory. The ideal wisdom of the man of affairs is unlikely to be totally different in kind from the wisdom of one whose destiny was to accept his own death in obedience to the divine will to deliver his people from pride and self-will. Might these not be two forms of divinely given wisdom?

I do not wish to press this point too much. It is not for me to say what Muslims might think of it, though as a Christian I would have little difficulty with seeing Muhammad as a vehicle of divine revelation, both in his teaching of divine sovereignty and judgement, and in his life of faithful obedience.

Nevertheless, incompatibilities do remain. Either Jesus was crucified, and that is an important fact about human destiny, or he was not. Either Muhammad recited God's final revelation, fulfilling, correcting or abrogating all that had gone before it, or he did not. We have to admit a genuine and irreducible difference of belief at this point. But we can also say that such differences are honestly different assessments of the facts as they appear to us, and their resolution must be left in the hands of God, who alone knows the whole truth. Those differences do not entail that the Muslim has faith and the Christian is an infidel, or vice versa. They do not entail that anyone should disparage either Muhammad or Jesus. Proper reverence can be given to both, even though it is not to be expected that the precise assessment of each, or even the account of each life which seems most likely, will be the same.

A contemporary Christian assessment of Muhammad can, I suggest, honour him as a true prophet and as a wise, courageous and compassionate leader, an ideal for those who seek to guide and rule society. Christian loyalty to the self-renouncing love seen in Jesus will remain the fundamental guide for Christian living and Christians will revere and worship Jesus as the one who, they believe, embodies the image of God in human form. But it might actually expand Christian wisdom to embrace also, to respect and revere, the ideal of the fully socially engaged Prophet who submits every detail of life to the divine will, and calls all men and women to affirm that there is no god but God, and that there is none who can be compared to God. A proper Christian appreciation of Muhammad may deepen the understanding Christians have of their own faith and, as long as people can accept genuine, conscientious differences in matters of faith, encourage friendship and understanding between Christians and Muslims. In the modern world, that is no longer just a possibility. It has become – and is this not by divine decree? – a necessity.

Muhammad from a Jewish Perspective

Norman Solomon

The simple answer to the question, 'What is the Jewish view of Muhammad?' is 'There is no Jewish view.' The question rests on an assumption that is demonstrably wrong, namely, that Muhammad figures in some way in Jewish theology.

For chronological reasons, it is obvious that neither the Bible nor the Talmud, the literary foundations of Judaism, contains any reference to Muhammad. The rise of Islam, indeed, marks the close of the Talmudic period in Judaism. Muslim apologists, especially Jewish converts to Islam such as Samu'al (Samuel) ben Judah ibn Abbas (ibn Yaḥyā al-Maghribī; c. 1125–75), have sometimes read 'prophecies' of Muhammad into the Bible, just as Christians have claimed the foretelling of Jesus in the Hebrew scriptures, but the claims do not bear serious scrutiny.

There are, of course, later *reactions* to Muhammad and to Islam, but these are not part of constitutive Jewish theology. They do not constitute a formal position, nor are they binding on any Jew. But they possess some historical interest, and in that vein I shall review some of the more notable ones, including the 'classical' position of Halevi and Maimonides on the significance of Islam, the acknowledgment by Netanel ibn Fayyumi of the limited authenticity of Muhammad's prophecy, and some influential modern scholarship and views.

Pre-modern Jewish Reactions

Presumably the Jews of Arabia in Muhammad's own time formed some opinion of him. He had at least one Jewish wife, and some Jews were among his earliest followers. During his period in Medina following the *hijra*, Jews were numbered as allies of one of the eight clans who supported him. However, many were neutral or opposed him, and several instances are recorded of Muhammad and his followers fighting against them and punishing them; those who survived such treatment may well have regarded him as deluded, a violent and treacherous adventurer. But this is no more than speculation; information about this early period comes to us mainly from the Qur'ān itself and other Muslim sources, and there is no direct evidence as to what Jews thought.

However, the period immediately following the death of the Prophet and prior to the establishment of Abbasid imperial authority offers some glimpses into Jewish reactions. An apocalyptic tract called the *Nistarot of Rabbi Shim'on bar Yohai*, published by Adolf Jellinek in the 1860s, contains the following:

> When he[1] beheld the kingdom of Ishmael come he began to say, 'Is not what the wicked kingdom of Esau has done to us sufficient, that the kingdom of Ishmael comes too?' The angel Metatron at once answered him, 'Fear not, O son of man! The Holy one, blessed be He, brings the kingdom of Ishmael only to save you from this wicked one (Rome). He will send a prophet to them and conquer the Land [of Israel] ...'
>
> And the second king who arises from Ishmael will love [the people of] Israel and conquer all the kingdoms. And he will come to Jerusalem and he will repair its breaches and the breaches of the Temple and hew out Mount Moriah and build there a place to bow down at the *'even ha-shetiya* (foundation stone).[2]

The *Nistarot*, though redacted later, was composed in the wake of the Muslim conquest of Mesopotamia, which itself followed the Persian wars against Rome. 'Esau' is Rome, or Christendom, and 'Ishmael' the Muslims; *Nistarot* places the Muslim conquests in an eschatological context, and implies that Muhammad had a positive role to play in the messianic process.

Pirqei d'Rabbi Eliezer, like the *Nistarot* a Hebrew pseudepigraphic composition, originated in early eighth-century Palestine just prior to the fall of the Umayyad dynasty, but before the rise of the Abbasids. Like the *Nistarot*, it places the rise of Islam, hence the career of the Prophet, in an apocalyptic context, though negatively; it looks forward to the downfall of the Umayyad caliphate as an omen of the end of the (Jewish) exile.

In the same period, in Persia, Abū ʿĪsā (Isaac ben Jacob of Isfahan) proclaimed himself a prophet and herald of the Messiah. He led a revolt against the Muslims, and was killed when the rebellion was ultimately suppressed. However, his followers did not believe that he was dead but rather that he had entered a cave and disappeared; the 'Īsāwīya or Isfahanian sect continued for some centuries. Abū ʿĪsā apparently taught that five prophets, among them Jesus and Muhammad, preceded the coming of the true Messiah and that he himself was the final harbinger; however, the missions of Jesus and Muhammad were restricted to their respective communities. The Isawiyan notion of the 'hidden

1. That is, the second-century sage Shim'on bar Yoḥai, in a vision of the future.

2. A. Jellinek, *Bet Ha-Midrash* 3.78–79. The six volumes of *Bet Ha-Midrash* were published in Vienna between 1853 and 1878; I have translated from the 1938 Jerusalem reissue of Bamberger and Wehrmann. There is a similar citation in G.D. Newby, 'Jewish-Muslim Relations 632–750 CE', in B.H. Hary, J.L. Hayes and F. Astren (eds.), *Judaism and Islam: Boundaries, Communication and Interaction* (Festschrift W.M. Brinner; Leiden: E.J. Brill, 2000), pp. 83–96 (84), though as Newby cites vol. IV, this is possibly from the *Prayer of Shim'on ben Yohai*, a fuller version of the *Nistarot*.

prophet' is remarkably close to the Shīʿite concept of *ghayba*, or 'occultation', of the imams.[3]

It is difficult to assess the impact of these heterodox ideas on mainstream Judaism. Several Jewish philosophers in Muslim lands, not least Judah Halevi and Moses Maimonides, looked on Islam and Christianity as stages in the messianic process, the former for spreading belief in the pure unity of God, the latter for spreading knowledge of the scriptures.[4] But they did not, as a corollary, assign a significant personal position to either Jesus or Muhammad.

So far as the mainstream Jewish community is concerned, there is little overt reference to Muhammad in pre-modern Jewish writing, even though there are numerous discussions of Islamic theology as well as polemics against Islam. But in contrast with Jewish polemics against Christianity, in which the person and nature of Jesus are openly addressed, and where there is a well-attested if marginal *Toldot Yeshu* tradition,[5] the person of Muhammad scarcely features in Jewish polemics against Islam.

The late Hava Lazarus-Yafeh suggested three reasons for this apparent reticence.[6] Jews were reluctant to offend the oppressor; Jews were forbidden, under some versions of the Pact of Umar, to study the Qur'ān; and Jews were forbidden by *halakha* (Jewish law) to teach Torah to Muslims.[7] The second and third reasons are hardly convincing since several Jews were familiar with the Qur'ān, as Lazarus-Yafeh herself documented, and Maimonides' ruling that Jews ought not to teach Torah to Muslims cannot be assumed as the norm. The first reason is more plausible, given Islamic sensitivity to insults to the Prophet; any such perceived insult might easily have led to wholesale slaughter or forcible conversion of Jewish communities. Commenting on the degrading status of the Jews he came across in Egypt in 1833–35, Edward William Lane wrote:

> At present, they are less oppressed: but still they scarcely ever dare to utter a word of abuse when reviled or beaten unjustly by the meanest Arab or Turk: for many a Jew has been put to death upon a false or malicious accusation of uttering disrespectful words against the Kur-án or the Prophet.[8]

3. On Abū ʿĪsā and his followers, see I. Friedlander, 'Jewish-Arabic Studies', *Jewish Quarterly Review* 1 (1910–11), pp. 183–215; 2 (1911–12), pp. 481–517; and 3 (1912–13), pp. 235–300; and Newby, 'Jewish-Muslim Relations'. Friedlander (pp. 482–83) compares docetism, occultation, *ghayba* and *rajʿa*.

4. This thought is developed in my essay in this volume, 'Pluralism from a Jewish Perspective', and in Sybil Sheridan's article, 'Jesus from a Jewish Perspective', above.

5. See W. Horbury, *Jews and Christians in Contact and Controversy* (Edinburgh: T&T Clark, 1998).

6. H. Lazarus-Yafeh, *Intertwined Worlds* (Princeton, NJ: Princeton University Press, 1992), pp. 7–8.

7. Cf. Maimonides, *Responsa* (ed. J. Blau; Jerusalem: Mekitse Nirdamim, 1986), no. 149, I, pp. 284–85.

8. E.W. Lane, *An Account of the Manners and Customs of the Modern Egyptian* (ed. E.S. Poole; London: John Murray, 5th edn, 1871), II, p. 305.

But there is in addition to Lazarus-Yafeh's suggestions an obvious theological reason, namely, that the person of Muhammad is of significance to Muslims only in so far as it affects his status as Prophet and exemplar, whereas Jesus is regarded by Christians as not merely a prophet but as a unique incarnation of God. Jews certainly address the question of the authenticity of Muhammad's prophecy, but there is no call to address any claim of divine status, Davidic descent, virgin birth or other such claims as are made for Jesus.

The *majālis*, or open debating sessions, that took place typically in the court of a caliph or emir in early Islamic times might have provided a forum in which Jews could safely express their views on Muhammad, as they certainly did on aspects of Muslim belief. Unfortunately, the literary reports of these meetings are notoriously unreliable, and it is likely that Jews remained prudently circumspect despite the promise of open debate.[9]

There are reports that Anan ben David, the eighth-century founder of Karaism,[10] acknowledged the prophetic missions of Jesus and Muhammad, but Leon Nemoy among others thinks these reports are without foundation.[11] Another notable Karaite, Jacob al-Kirkisānī (tenth century), wrote a tract *Kitāb fi Ifsād Nubuwwat Muḥammad* in refutation of Muhammad's claim to prophecy.

Several Rabbanites likewise openly rejected the prophetic claims made for any text other than the Bible. Such refutations are indeed a cornerstone of rabbinic apologetic in the Islamic world, and underlie the emphasis on the uniqueness and permanence of Moses' prophecy which constitutes a central theme of Jewish religious philosophy from Sa'adia to Maimonides.

But of interest in the *person* of Muhammad there is scarcely a trace. Jews surely had their thoughts, and perhaps in private conversation referred to the Prophet of Islam as *ha-mushagga*, 'the crazy man', as Maimonides at least once referred to him,[12] no doubt alluding to Hosea 9.7; but on the whole they kept their thoughts to themselves.

Netanel ibn Fayyumi

One Rabbanite Jew who is known to have acknowledged Muhammad's claim to prophecy is the Yemenite Jewish communal leader and philosopher Netanel

9. Several studies of these meetings are collected in H. Lazarus-Yafeh, M.R. Cohen, S. Somekh and S.H. Griffith (eds.), *The Majlis* (Wiesbaden: Harrassowitz Verlag, 1999).

10. A major schism within mediaeval Jewry, especially in the Near East, centred on the teaching ascribed to Anan ben David, who rejected rabbinic interpretation of scripture. His followers were known as Karaites ('scripturalists'); those Jews who continued to follow rabbinic teaching were called 'Rabbanites'.

11. See Nemoy's article on Anan in *Encyclopedia Judaica*.

12. *Mishneh Torah: Hilkhot Melakhim*, in a censored passage near the end.

ibn Fayyumi, who in his *Bustān al-ʿuqūl* ('The Garden of Intellects'),[13] written in 1164,[14] asserted the authenticity of the prophecy of Muhammad as revealed in the Qur'ān, and at least the possibility that there were additional authentic revelations (he did not mention Christianity).

The *Bustān* indicates a strong degree of Muslim-Jewish tension. In chapter 6, for instance, Netanel referred to 'what they assert because of the power they exercise over us, because of our weakness in their eyes, and because our succor has been cut off', and declared, 'The nations do revile us, treat us contemptuously and turn their hands against us, so that we stand among them in speechless terror as the sheep before the shearer'; he amplified the theme of Jewish suffering under Muslim rule to the extent of citing swathes of Hebrew laments by Solomon ibn Gabirol and Judah Halevi.[15]

Clearly, the book targeted a Jewish public. It was written in Judaeo-Arabic in Hebrew characters, the bulk of its content was devoted to the exposition of Judaism, and it presupposed in its readers ready familiarity with the Hebrew text of scripture, with Midrashic thought, and with the *mitzvot* (divine commandments). On the philosophical level, it was an attempt at a synthesis of the contemporary culture – in this case the world-view represented by the *Rasā'il Ikhwān al-Ṣafā* – with Judaism; yet an apologetic intent is rarely far from the surface.

Netanel maintained that Muhammad was an authentic prophet.[16] The outflow of the divine wisdom through the universal intellect and the universal soul, he suggested, expresses itself 'in an individual man whose spirit is free from the impurity of nature and is disciplined in the noblest science and the purest works ... [a] prophet'.[17]

> Know then ... nothing prevents God from sending into His world whomsoever He wishes, since the world of holiness sends forth emanations unceasingly ... Even before the revelation of the Law he sent prophets to the nations ... and again after its revelation nothing prevented Him from sending to them whom He wishes so that the world might not remain without religion ... Mohammed was a prophet to them but not to those who preceded (sc. were prior to) them in the knowledge of God.[18]

13. Natanaël Ibn al-Fayyumi, *The Bustan al-Ukul* (ed. and trans. D. Levine; New York: Columbia University Press, 1908; repr. 1966), p. x. Page references to the Judaeo-Arabic and English sections of this work are given in accordance with the following illustration: Ar. p. 45; Eng. p. 72.

14. So R. Kiener, 'Jewish Isma'ilism in Twelfth Century Yemen: R. Nethanel ben Al-Fayyumi', *Jewish Quarterly Review* 74 (1984), pp. 257–58.

15. Ibn al-Fayyumi, *Bustan al-Ukul*, Eng. p. 105.

16. S. Pines, 'Nathanael ibn Al-Fayyumi et la Théologie Ismaélienne', *Revue de l'Histoire Juive en Egypte* 1 (1947), pp. 5–22. This is well developed by C. Sirat, *A History of Jewish Philosophy in the Middle Ages* (Cambridge: Cambridge University Press and Editions de la Maison des Sciences de L'homme, 1985), pp. 88–93 and 424, and in the French version, which has some different references: *La Philosophie Juive Mediévale en Terre d'Islam* (no place given: Presses du CNRS, 1988), pp. 74–79 and 248.

17. Ibn al-Fayyumi, *Bustan al-Ukul*, Eng. p. 95.

18. Ibn al-Fayyumi, *Bustan al-Ukul*, Eng. pp. 103–105. For Netanel, as for most mediaevals, 'older' equals 'better'.

God 'sends a prophet to every people according to their language',[19] and 'permitted to every people something He forbade to others';[20] the specific commands of Torah and Qur'ān differ because the people to whom they are addressed are at different stages of spiritual development.

Rabbi Yosef Kafiḥ, the modern editor and translator (into Hebrew) of Netanel's work, seeking to defend Netanel from criticism by Jews who may have been surprised by Netanel's endorsement of the Prophet of Islam, contends that Netanel was writing with tongue in cheek, arming his brethren with a way of acknowledging Muhammad when necessary in confrontation with Muslims, yet at the same time restricting the validity of Muhammad's message to the Arab people.[21] But this is a misunderstanding. Netanel presented the reader with a fully integrated system of thought which allows a measure of religious pluralism. The statement about Muhammad is in no way detached from the rest of his thought, as a mere *ad hoc* or *ad hominem* argument; it is a key statement within an extensively elaborated philosophical system which carries the social implication of respect for the heirs of the prophets, these heirs being the 'imams, administrators, the learned and the wise'.[22] That Netanel was aware of similar views deriving from Abū ʿĪsā seems improbable.

Netanel's work was virtually unknown beyond his native Yemen until modern times, so had little influence on later Jewish thought.

Modern Views

Modern Jewish interest in Islam and its Prophet arose in the West in a secular academic context more than a theological one. Bernard Lewis has written:

> In the development of Islamic studies in European and, later, American universities, Jews ... play an altogether disproportionate role ... not only in the advancement of scholarship but also in the enrichment of the Western view of Oriental religion, literature, and history, by the substitution of knowledge and understanding for prejudice and ignorance.[23]

Martin Kramer and others have analysed the ideological dilemmas that led Jews such as the poet Heine to a sometimes romantic view of Islam, and led more sober scholars to the rejection of the 'Orientalist' ideology of 'difference and supremacy'.[24]

19. Ibn al-Fayyumi, *Bustan al-Ukul*, Eng. p. 109; cf. Qur'ān 5.48 and 14.4.
20. Ibn al-Fayyumi, *Bustan al-Ukul*, Eng. p. 107.
21. Y. Kafiḥ, *Gan ha-Sekhalim* (Jerusalem: Halikhot Am Israel, 2nd edn, AM 5744/1984), pp. 10–11.
22. Ibn al-Fayyumi, *Bustan al-Ukul*, Eng. p. 51; Ar. p. 31.
23. B. Lewis, *Islam in History: Ideas, People, and Events in the Middle East* (Chicago, IL: Open Court, rev. edn, 1993), pp. 142–44.
24. M. Kramer (ed.), *The Jewish Discovery of Islam* (Tel Aviv: Tel Aviv University, 1999), p. viii.

Among the early scholars, Abraham Geiger (1810–74) was not only a radical religious reformer but one of the major architects of the scientific, that is to say historical, study of Judaism. His doctoral dissertation for the University of Bonn, published in Bonn in 1833 when he was rabbi at Wiesbaden, bore the title *Was hat Mohammed aus dem Judenthume aufgenommen?* (What did Muhammad take from Judaism?) It is the work of a young man, and contains several errors which he subsequently corrected (though many remain), but for all its faults and its *tendenz* it was a pioneering study and inspired generations of Jewish scholars to take Islam seriously. From the title, one might imagine that the thesis is about Muhammad personally; some of it is, though Geiger used later Islamic sources rather uncritically as evidence of the Prophet's activity.

Other Jewish scholars who distinguished themselves in Islamic studies include Geiger's French contemporary Salomon Munk (1803–67); Moritz Steinschneider (1816–1907), the 'father of modern Jewish bibliography' and teacher of the Hungarian Ignaz Goldziher (1850–1921), one of the founders of modern Islamic scholarship; Geiger's own errant disciple Daniel Chwolson (1819–1911); and, more recently, Shlomo Dov Goitein (1900–85) and Georges Vajda (1908–81). All of these contributed to a better understanding of the history of Islam, some of them with special attention to the period of its formation and hence the life of the Prophet, though their focus was history rather than theology; numerous contemporary scholars follow in their footsteps.

Modern Jewish theologians, with greater freedom of expression than their mediaeval forebears, have given renewed attention to the relationship between Judaism and Islam, though many of them continue, with modifications, in the line of Judah Halevi and Maimonides, who allotted to Islam an eschatological function, at the same time denying its specific truth-claims.

The early twentieth-century philosopher Franz Rosenzweig (1886–1929) was an ardent admirer of Halevi. When serving in the German army in the Balkans in 1917, Rosenzweig received orders to deliver a lecture to officers on Muhammad and Islam.[25] The text of the lecture does not survive, but in his later works Rosenzweig tried hard to place Judaism in relation to Christianity and Islam. For instance,

> While Mohammed took over the concepts of revelation externally, he necessarily remained attached to heathendom in the basic concept of creation. For he did not recognize the interconnection which ties revelation to creation.
>
> Thus it could not dawn on him that the concepts of creation – God world man – need an inner conversion to transform themselves into sources of power for revelation ... These recondite prophecies did not turn into emerging revelations. Their sealed eyes did not open radiantly ... It was a belief in revelation derived directly from paganism, with God's will as it were, without the design of his providence, in 'purely natural' causation.[26]

25. Letter to his parents, dated 17 February 1917, cited in English translation in N.H. Glatzer, *Franz Rosenzweig: His Life and Times* (New York: Schocken Books, 1953), p. 48.
26. F. Rosenzweig, *The Star of Redemption* (trans. W. Hallo; Notre Dame, IN and London: University of Notre Dame Press, 1970), p. 117.

What Rosenzweig seems to be saying, obscurely, is that Muhammad failed to grasp the concept of God working constantly and redemptively in and with the world, but rather conceived of God's greatness as an arbitrary freedom; in creating the world, God engaged in a 'creative caprice', but really had no need of a world in which to perform the work of redemption. Again: 'Can there be a more thorough renunciation of the concept that God himself 'descends', himself gives himself, surrenders himself to man? He sits enthroned in his heaven of heavens and presents to man – a book.'[27]

Rosenzweig was, in a sense, writing about Muhammad, presenting him personally as the creator of a clearly defined religion, and presuming to point out his 'error'. This is entirely unsatisfactory: it fits neither the traditional Muslim understanding of the Prophet as merely the vehicle of revelation, nor the historical perspective through which the dynamic and diversity of Islamic thought may be grasped. Rosenzweig's theology led him to stereotype not only Islam, but Christianity and Judaism too.

Most contemporary Jewish thinkers would reject Rosenzweig's simplistic characterization of the three faiths. They would recognize the vast range of thought that exists within each of the faiths, and the considerable overlap between them. But a modern theologian would tend also to take a softer line on doctrinal definition and to be more open to the notion that absolute religious truth cannot be captured in language, and that the great faiths, including those from further East, may all have something of value to contribute to human understanding of the infinite. God cannot be tied to one person, to one scripture, or within the bounds of an exclusive tradition.

Conclusion

Such considerations influence our attitude towards Islam, rather than specifically towards the Prophet. It remains true that the answer to the question, 'What is the Jewish view of Muhammad?' is 'There is no Jewish view', since the question rests on the erroneous assumption that Muhammad figures *as a person* in Jewish theology. He doesn't, but like Jesus he has become a figure of increasing *historical* interest to Jews. At the same time, Islam itself is increasingly seen not as a rival or usurper with a competing claim to exclusive truth, but as another manifestation of the infinite self-revelation of God.

27. Rosenzweig, *Star*, p. 166.

Muhammad in Muslim, Christian and Jewish Thought

Norman Solomon, Richard Harries and Tim Winter

In Islam, Muhammad is the last of prophets, from whose proclamation of the Qur'ān Islam is derived. The revelation of God which Muhammad brought is the same as that mediated through previous prophets, but before him, all communities had knowingly or unwittingly corrupted revelation for their own purposes. Muhammad, therefore, is regarded as the seal of the prophets; after him, there can be no further prophet or revelation because now the pure and uncorrupted revelation exists in the world. Muhammad himself is not regarded as superhuman. Nevertheless, he is the first living commentary on the meaning of the Qur'ān in the practice of life.

Tim Winter explores some of the warmer, more devotional understandings of Muhammad within Islam. Although, particularly in the twentieth century, Muhammad has been understood in multiple ways, ways which reveal the agendas of the writers, Winter suggests that there are 'patterns of devotion to the Prophet which are recurrent enough in Islamic history cautiously to be described as normative'.[1] Among these patterns is the view that the Prophet shall appear at the end-time not as a stern judge but as a merciful intercessor. He is also thought of and appealed to as a personal guide, providing consultation and direction to spiritual seekers. He is a moral exemplar, exhibiting the qualities we most admire in other human beings. And he is the prototype of the mystic: Rūmī, the most widely read poet in America, looked to him as the supreme mystic and understood Muhammad's ascension into heaven from Jerusalem as an archetype of the Sufi's flight into closeness with God.

Winter then considers the different approaches to *eros* in the two religions. Traditionally, Christianity has had a more negative attitude to sexuality than Islam. This is frankly acknowledged today and most Christians now would regard sexual instinct as part of the creation about which God said, 'It is good.'[2] Ibsen and Shaw, whom Winter discusses, were clearly wrestling with their own negative and therefore, as many would regard it today, unhealthy, inherited Protestant attitudes to sexuality.

1. Quotation from Tim Winter's paper, 'Muhammad from a Muslim Perspective', above.
2. Cf. Genesis 1.

Finally, Winter explores aspects of the contrast which Cragg finds, and which Keith Ward wishes to qualify, in the two religions' respective understandings of suffering and power, and therefore the image which both religions have of their founders in these respects.

Ward points out that, historically, Christianity has been almost entirely negative about Muhammad, but that today there is a re-evaluation by many scholars. He focuses particularly on the work of Kenneth Cragg who affirms, unequivocally, that Muhammad is a genuine prophet of God. Nevertheless, there are differences between the two religions in the approach to Muhammad's person because of different understandings of revelation. For Muslims, revelation is contained in the words of the Qur'ān, recited by the Prophet. Christians cannot easily assent to this high view of Qur'ānic revelation, if only because it seems in tension with some basic Christian assertions. So they are bound to see Muhammad as a prophet who lived within a particular historical and cultural setting, with all its inevitable limitations. However much Christians honour Muhammad, they will never quite see him as Muslims do. Nevertheless it would be a crucial advance in Christian thinking to honour the Prophet rather than to denigrate him.

In addition, there is, according to Cragg, a crucial contrast between the figure of Christ and the person of Muhammad, shown in the willingness of Jesus to undergo suffering and death, which brought about human redemption. By contrast, for Cragg, Muhammad, at least in the second stage of his public role, was the ruler of a community and someone who countenanced the use of force to defend and expand the political society in which the new revelation was set. Ward questions whether the contrast drawn by Cragg should be stated in quite such stark terms.

Norman Solomon stresses that Muhammad is not a figure in Jewish theology. There have, however, been reactions to the Prophet by various Jewish thinkers down the ages, though even in such cases the main emphasis has been on Islam within a Jewish perspective, for example as helping to prepare the way of the Messiah, rather than on the figure of Muhammad himself. When Jewish writers have discussed him, it has been in consistently negative terms, with the very interesting exception of Netanel ibn Fayyumi who wrote in 1164,

> Nothing prevents God from sending into His world whomsoever He wishes ... Even before the revelation of the Law he sent prophets to the nations ... and again after its revelation nothing prevented Him from sending to them whom He wishes so that the world might not remain without religion ... Mohammed was a prophet to them but not to those who preceded them in the knowledge of God.[3]

Unfortunately, as Norman Solomon points out, Netanel's work was virtually unknown outside his native Yemen and therefore had little influence on later Jewish thought. This insistence that Muhammad is not a figure in Jewish

3. See Norman Solomon's paper, 'Muhammad from a Jewish Perspective', above.

theology raises the question of how far it is possible for a religious tradition to develop. Religious traditions constantly face new facts and issues. For example, in recent decades, the Christian Churches have had to grapple with the moral legitimacy of artificial means of contraception, the ordination of women, gay partnerships and so on; and all religions are now conscious of being set in a world of competing religious claims which have to be faced and taken seriously. The Roman Catholic Church, with its belief in a magisterium, or authoritative teaching office, has been in a stronger position than other Churches for grappling with these issues in at least one respect. When it has come to a mind, it has been able to communicate its teaching as a clear and definite part of a Christian world-view. So, for example, the Second Vatican Council took a much more positive attitude to the role of other religions within the providence of God than the Church had ever taken before, and this was set forth as definite Church teaching. While Judaism does not have a body that can issue definitive theological statements, neither does it have a rigidly defined theology. To say, as Norman Solomon does, that Muhammad does not figure in Jewish theology, is not to say that Muhammad cannot be addressed from the point of view of Jewish theology. He is rather saying that Jewish theology can be constituted without reference to Muhammad, and that it does not have a fixed theological position on Muhammad; an individual Jewish thinker is free to take her or his own position, theological or otherwise, on Muhammad, as on Jesus, or Buddha, or any other figure she or he might regard as significant. Norman Solomon himself ends on a positive note, allowing theological space for other religions, though of course there are other Jews who do not accept this.[4]

Two questions can be raised from these considerations of Muhammad. The first stems from Tim Winter's treatment of devotional images for the Prophet: what controls the rich strain of devotional images? Within Christianity, there has been a similar development in devotion to the Virgin Mary, most of it very intense and some of it beautiful. From the perspective of the Churches of the Reformation it is only those aspects of this tradition which can be anchored in and justified by the Christian scriptures that can be regarded as legitimate. In contrast to this, a no less rich series of devotional images has been applied to Christ, but these have been regarded as legitimate because the process of looking at him in this way is not only seen in the New Testament but can be seen there to be part of a developing tradition which becomes essentially open-ended as far as what might be allowed in terms of exaltation. Islam, given its scripturalist instincts, has often wrestled with this; but the majority of scholars are clearly comfortable with the devotional themes which Winter outlines, and find scriptural foundations for them.[5]

4. See the comments on the chief rabbi's book, *The Dignity of Difference*, in the commentary later in this book, 'Pluralism in Jewish, Christian and Muslim Thought'.

5. For this rich literature, see A. Schimmel, *And Muhammad is His Messenger: The Veneration of the Prophet in Islamic Piety* (Chapel Hill, NC: University of North Carolina Press, 1985).

A second, more significant, issue concerns the Muslim and Christian evaluations of suffering and power. Both Christianity and Islam, as well as Judaism, believe that God is the uncreated source of all that exists, who has the power not only to bring the universe into existence and moment by moment sustain it in being, but also to bring it to its desired consummation. In addition, for Christianity, 'though [Christ Jesus] was in the form of God, he did not regard equality with God as something to be exploited, but emptied himself, taking the form of a slave, being born in human likeness. And being found in human form, he humbled himself and became obedient to the point of death – even death on a cross.'[6]

That said, it seems that Ward and Winter are quite right to suggest that the contrast between the Christian and Muslim ideal is not so stark or incompatible as might at first sight appear. For the fact is that although Jesus suffered on the cross as a powerless figure, in the fourth century Christians had to exercise power, as they have done in many countries since then, and have had to develop the concept of the godly ruler, indeed, a ruler who has had to wield force in the exercise of his – or occasionally, her – duties. From this has come the long tradition of Christian thinking on the morality of warfare, as well as much discussion on issues of justice, both criminal and social. In short, on the whole (the obvious exception being pacifists), the example of Jesus, as one who suffered rather than inflicted suffering on others, has been seen first of all as the way in which God has brought about human redemption and secondly as a moral example which might be followed in private life and personal relationships but which has not been necessarily regarded as a model for politicians to follow in guiding the fortunes of a state. So it may be that the role model of Muhammad as the divinely guided leader, concerned with the implementation of divine justice in all aspects of life, and willing to use proportionate force for this purpose when it was strictly necessary, can be seen as in some way complementary to that of a suffering Jesus. At least, that is how it might be seen from a Christian perspective, particularly one rooted in the ideas of liberation theology. What is perhaps not so clear is how the image of a suffering Jesus might fit as a legitimate role model into Islamic thought.

Kenneth Cragg set up the contrast between Jesus and Muhammad in a particular way. It is not, however, how some others, including most Muslims, would want to posit the contrast in the first place. It has been suggested, for example, that the real contrast between Muhammad and Jesus is between someone who is involved in the ordinary business of living and someone who withdrew from the world of work, economics and politics. But again, this is to set up a polarity in terms which modern Christians would be unwilling to recognize. For them, such a contrast might have been true in the fourth century, when Christian monasticism, and in particular retreat into the desert by hermits, was making much headway, and may have had some force in the great

6. Philippians 2.5–8.

periods of mediaeval monasticism, but it would not be true either of the present day or, properly understood, of the ministry of Jesus himself. What we can say, from a straightforward factual point of view, is that Muhammad was the leader and guide of a community. Jesus was not such a leader and guide. He gathered round himself a small group of friends whom he charged to proclaim the good news of the breaking into this life of the divine rule, the kingdom of God, summoning people to live under that rule, but he did not legislate in detail for what might be involved in living such a life and certainly did not apply it on a large scale to society as a whole. Furthermore, it is not always easy to see from the New Testament whether the age to come is primarily of this world, or whether it shades into a world which moves beyond space and time as we know them. So historically, Muhammad and Jesus had different roles or different vocations, and there is no need to set up a tension between them from that point of view.

When it comes to suffering, it is not just Jesus who suffered. The suffering of Muhammad is a common theme of Sunnī Muslim devotional literature: his extreme poverty and hunger, the illness and death of all but one of his children, and the waywardness of his people. Moreover, there is a very strong tradition of martyrdom, particularly in Shīʿite Islam, which takes dramatic form in Iran on certain festivals. This goes back to al-Ḥusayn, the third Shīʿa imam, whom Shīʿites regard as having been wrongfully deposed and killed. Similarly, Jesus neither looked for suffering for its own sake, nor avoided it when it became inevitable. He would rather not have died, as we know from the prayer recorded in the garden of Gethsemane, 'Father, ... remove this cup from me', referring to the cup of suffering.[7] Nevertheless, Jesus knew that if he carried his message to Jerusalem, mounting opposition would end in his rejection and death. This he saw and accepted: 'yet, not what I want, but what you want'.[8] This attitude characterized the most notable of Christian martyrs during the first two and a half centuries of the Church's existence, even though some local Roman rulers thought that the Christians they encountered were too eager to gain a martyr's crown.

7. Mark 14.36a.
8. Mark 14.36b.

PART II:

Resources for the Modern World

Chapter 5: The Image of God in Humanity

The Image of God in Humanity from a Jewish Perspective

Norman Solomon

Genesis 1.27 relates that God 'created man in his own image' (RSV). What does this mean, and how has it been interpreted by Jews throughout the ages? What model does it offer for human conduct, and what are its implications for how all members of the human family should relate to one another? This essay attempts to answer such questions. The Hebrew term *adam*, often translated 'man', is generic, and Genesis 1.27 ('male and female he created them') makes clear that both sexes are made in God's image. So it would be better to translate Genesis 1.27 gender-neutrally, as the New Revised Standard Version, 'God created *humankind* in his image'.

The idea that humans are made in the divine image has made people think deeply about what human beings are, about what distinguishes them from other animals. It leads them to enquire, 'What does it mean to say that the human reflects the divine?' 'What is it to be human?'

Did the original redactor of Genesis imagine God in a human form, modelling humans quite literally in the same basic shape as God's self? Probably not. The rabbis who received the text, and who defined subsequent Judaism, certainly rejected such an anthropomorphic conception of God. They did not take the verse in a literal sense with reference to bodily shape, but interpreted it as indicating some distinctive quality that humans, but not animals, share with the divine.

Rashi (1040–1105), a traditional Jewish commentator, inferred that humans are said to be like God because they are able 'to understand and to discern'.[1] Nahmanides (1194–1270) stressed the duality of human nature, for while the body is like the earth from which it was formed, the soul is like the 'higher beings' who reflect the divine; as a much earlier rabbinic source expressed it, 'The soul of man comes from heaven; his body from earth'.[2] Straight after Adam and Eve were created, they were blessed with the words, 'and have dominion over the fish of the sea and over the birds of the air, and over every living thing

1. This Hebrew liturgical idiom, a felicitous combination of two biblical words, occurs in the second blessing preceding the morning reading of the *shema*.

2. *Sifré* Deuteronomy 306.

that moves upon the earth'.[3] The blessing is a consequence of being made in the divine image. Because they resemble the creator God, men and women have a responsibility towards all creation, just as a ruler has towards his or her subjects; they must 'govern' justly, not exploiting animals even for food. According to Genesis, the first people were vegetarians; meat-eating was a concession to human weakness after the Flood, not the ideal human state.[4]

These three qualities of language-based intelligence, spirituality and moral responsibility define the 'image of God' as reflected in men and women. Elements of all three qualities occur lower in the evolutionary scale (the 'order of creation'), as has been demonstrated in modern studies of animal behaviour, with regard to altruistic behaviour as well as intelligence. But nowhere are they developed to a level comparable with that which characterizes humans.

Rabbinic Concepts

Jewish understanding of the divine aspect of the human personality was further developed by the rabbis in the period of the Talmud.[5]

The Hebrew scriptures tend to view the human being as an indivisible whole; mostly, words translated as 'soul' have no metaphysical connotation. The rabbis, however, consistently assumed the dual nature of body and soul. Sometimes, they seem to be saying that body and soul relate to one another as a partnership. But on the whole, it is the soul, rather than the body or the combination of body and soul, which is seen as reflecting the divine image; body and soul may even be in conflict.

> Just as the Holy One, Blessed be He, fills the whole world, so the soul [*neshama*] fills the body; just as the Holy One, Blessed be He, sees yet is not seen, so the soul sees yet is not seen; just as the Holy One, Blessed be He, sustains the whole world, so the soul sustains the body; just as the Holy One, Blessed be He, is pure, so is the soul pure; just as the Holy One, Blessed be He, dwells in the innermost chambers, so does the soul dwell in the innermost chambers. Let the one who has these five things give praise to the One who has these five things![6]

The pre-existence of the soul is occasionally indicated,[7] and the process of ensoulment described:

3. Genesis 1.28.
4. Genesis 1.29 and 9.2.
5. Both Talmudim emerged through discussion of the Mishnah, completed early in the third century. The 'Palestinian' Talmud was completed in Galilee around 450 CE, the more definitive Babylonian Talmud around 600 CE in what is now Iraq.
6. Babylonian Talmud, *Berakhot* 10a.
7. Babylonian Talmud, *Ḥagiga* 12b; *Avoda Zara* 5a.

> There are three partners in [the generation of] a person, the Holy One, blessed be He, his father, and his mother. His father generates the seed of whiteness, out of which [are formed] bones, sinews, nails, the [soft matter of the] brain in his head, and the white of the eye. His mother generates the red seed, out of which [are formed] skin, flesh and hair, and the dark part of the eye. The Holy One, blessed be He, puts in him *ruaḥ* and *neshama*[8] and facial appearance, and the seeing of the eye, the hearing of the ear, the speech of the mouth, the movement of the legs, and discernment and understanding. When his time comes to depart from the world the Holy One, blessed be He, takes His portion, and leaves before his mother and father their portion.[9]

The idea that *ruaḥ* and *neshama*, constituents of the soul, are injected into the embryo by God suggests that they exist independently of the body. Even so, facial appearance (i.e. character), speech, movement and understanding manifest qualities of the soul; since they come from God, they are the vehicle of the divine image.

Modern science regards character, speech, movement and understanding as biologically and socially formed and directed, rather than as originating and functioning independently of the body. However, this difference as to origin does not obscure the fact that these are the qualities that distinguish the human individual, and it is among them that the divine image must be sought.

But what does it mean to say that a set of qualities constitutes the 'divine image' in people? This is certainly a very strange way to talk, far from the way people would talk about such qualities in ordinary, let alone scientific, conversation. By talking in this way, religious people express the conviction that the qualities in question are (a) the most significant qualities that people have and (b) qualities which possess a significance beyond the life of the individual who exhibits them.

Individuality and Individual Worth

The Mishnah (early third century CE) carries a graphic description of how the court should impress on witnesses in capital cases the seriousness of their testimony:

> How do they impress on witnesses in capital cases the gravity of their testimony ... [They say:] Be aware that capital cases are unlike property matters. In property matters, the defendant [if his plea fails] pays money and [his sin] is forgiven; in capital cases, his life and the life of his [unborn] descendants till the end of time depend on [the outcome] ... Adam was created alone to teach that whoever destroys one life, scripture accounts it as if he had destroyed a whole world; and whoever preserves one life, scripture accounts it as if he had preserved a whole world ... [It teaches also] the greatness of the Holy One, blessed be he, for when a man mints several coins in one press they are all alike, yet the king of kings of kings, the Holy One, blessed be he, minted everyone in the form of the first Adam, and no-one is identical with another.[10]

8. These two words, meaning 'wind' and 'breath', carry respectively the ideas of 'spirit' and 'soul'.
9. Babylonian Talmud, *Nidda* 31a. Cf. *Sanhedrin* 91b.
10. Mishnah, *Sanhedrin* 4.5. It is unknown whether the procedure outlined in the Mishnah is historical or idealized.

This text affirms not only the intrinsic value of each human life, but also the richness of human diversity. The reference to Adam, who was 'made in the image of God', establishes the context and the rationale. Humans matter because they are made in this image. Someone who takes the life of another, even of a potential but unborn other, somehow (to use another rabbinic phrase) 'diminishes the image [of God]'.[11]

Imitatio Dei

Abraham J. Heschel (1907–72), seeking a broad cultural context for the Hebrew notion of humanity in the image of God, observed: 'In ancient Egypt it was said: The king does what Osiris does. Man must become like the god as much as possible, it is suggested in Plato's Theaetetus.'[12]

To 'become like God' would no doubt have been regarded by the rabbis of the Talmud as a blasphemous expression. There can be no apotheosis of the human, and no assimilation of the human to the divine. However, scripture does require people to 'walk in [God's] ways', and talk of 'the way in which the Lord your God commanded you to walk':[13] 'Said Rabbi Ḥama bar Ḥanina: How can a person walk after God? Is it not written "For the Lord your God is a consuming fire" [Deuteronomy 4.24]? But follow God's attributes. As He clothes the naked ... as He visits the sick ... comforts the bereaved ... buries the dead ... so should you.'[14] Clearly, Ḥama bar Ḥanina did not advocate emulating other characteristics attributed to God in scripture, such as God's anger, 'jealousy' and vengeance. 'Imitating God' (*imitatio Dei*) consists in emulating God's love and compassion, so far as this is possible for humans.

The line separating the human from the divine becomes blurred in later Jewish mysticism. Maimonides had to reconcile the Aristotelian notion of the soul as 'form' of the body, hence perishable, with the Jewish (in reality, Platonic) idea of the soul as a separate, independent entity that could survive the body's destruction. He concluded that there were two souls. One, like that of animals, perished with the body; the other, the seat of our intelligence, had been imparted to us by God as the distinctive human form, in God's image.[15] Ḥasdai Crescas (1340–1410) and other critics of Maimonides proposed 'love' rather than 'intelligence' as the characteristic human virtue.[16]

11. Babylonian Talmud, *Yevamot* 63b, where the context is a reproach of a man who fails in his duty to procreate. Cf. Genesis Rabba 34.14, cited below.

12. A.J. Heschel, *The Prophets* (2 vols.; New York and London: Harper Torchbooks, 1971), pp. 101–102.

13. Deuteronomy 28.9 and 13.5.

14. Babylonian Talmud, *Sota* 14a.

15. Maimonides, *Mishneh Torah: Yesodey ha-Torah* 4.9.

16. H. Tirosh-Rothschild, 'Jewish Philosophy on the Eve of Modernity', in D.H. Frank and O. Leaman (eds.), *History of Jewish Philosophy* (History of World Philosophies, 2;

It was not a great jump for the mystics to turn the idea of a soul 'from God' into that of a soul which was *part* of God, to whom it would return. Many of the later mystics referred to the soul as *ḥeleq E. mi-ma'al*, taking advantage of the vagueness of the Hebrew preposition, which would allow the phrase to be translated 'a portion *of* God above' as well as, more properly, 'a portion *from* God above'.[17] Moshe Idel has argued that some mystics went beyond this, approaching the concept of *unio mystica*, absorption of the soul into the divine being; he has suggested that Plotinus' concept of mystical union may be traced through Numenius to Akiva and to Philo.[18]

Kabbala and Psychology

Maimonides adopted the apophatic approach to God developed, though he was unaware of this, by the Christian Pseudo-Dionysius on the basis of earlier Hellenistic thought: nothing can positively be stated of God; attributes can only be denied. This *via negativa*, with its extreme rejection of anthropomorphism, was resisted by Kabbalists in thirteenth-century Spain, since it seemed to contradict both scripture and the rabbinic tradition. On the other hand, the plain anthropomorphic understanding of scripture was implausible. The Kabbalistic solution lay in the development of the doctrine of the Ten Sefirot, or emanations, through which God created the world. The following triadic scheme is a typical list and arrangement of the sefirot, each triad generating the next; the pairs are masculine (left) and feminine (right).

Table 1. *The Ten Sefirot*

First triad:	*keter* (crown)	
	ḥokhma (knowledge)	*bina* (understanding)
Second triad:	*ḥesed* (love, compassion)	*din* (law, justice)
	tiferet (beauty)	
Third triad:	*netzaḥ* (eternity)	*hod* (glory)
	yesod (foundation)	
Summation:	*malkhut* (royalty)	

Andover and New York: Routledge, 1997), pp. 499–573 (500–502).

17. The expression *ḥeleq E. mi-ma'al* was certainly used in the sixteenth century, for instance by Maharal of Prague, *Derush al ha-Torah* 10a, and is frequently used by Isaiah Horovitz (?1565–1630); it may have been used earlier.

18. M. Idel, *Kabbala: New Perspectives* (New Haven, CT and London: Yale University Press, 1988), p. 39.

In this list, the first triad corresponds to *thought*, the second to *soul*, the third to *material*. The *sefirot* collectively comprise *Adam Qadmon* (the First Adam, or Primal Man), in whose image human beings are made. Thus:

keter (crown)	head
ḥokhma (knowledge)	brain
bina	heart
ḥesed (compassion)	right arm
din	left arm
tiferet	chest
netzaḥ (eternity)	right leg
hod	left leg
yesod	genitals
malkhut	complete body

This strange theosophy enabled Kabbalists to have the best of both worlds. On the one hand, God-in-God's-self, the *Ein Sof* or Infinite, could not be spoken of, and was totally beyond anthropomorphism. On the other hand, the idea of humans made 'in the image of God' was given firm expression.

Whereas the rabbis of Talmud interpreted 'image of God' in terms of ethical discernment and action, the Kabbalists added to this the concept of a harmony of spiritual constitution between the human and the divine.

Recent Jewish movements of renewal, including forms of neo-hasidism, frequently interpret the *sefirot* in psychological terms. Through this, they popularize Kabbala as a key to personal self-understanding.

Recognizing God in Others

Since all people, according to the Bible, are descended from one couple, they must all share in the same divine image. The recognition of the 'image of God' in the other demands that she or he be treated with respect, that his or her life be valued as sharing in the divine being: 'Rabbi Akiva explained: "Whoever sheds blood, scripture accounts it as if he had diminished the image [of God], for 'God made people in his image'."'[19]

Akiva was speaking in the context of murder; Eleazar ben Azariah applied the same reasoning to a man who failed to raise a family, that is, to increase the divine likeness in the world. From the two, we learn that the recognition of the divine in our fellow human being ought both to prevent us from harming him or her and also to seek positively to 'increase their being', that is, promote their welfare.

19. Genesis Rabba 34.14. Similar statements are attributed to both Akiva and Eleazar ben Azariah in Tosefta, *Yevamot* 5.5.

The Lithuanian-born French Jewish philosopher Emmanuel Lévinas (1905/6–95) likewise grounded ethics in recognition of the Other; he accused Western philosophy of the suppression of the Other (any idea, person or race that does not fit the dominant patterns of thought) by the Same (being, essence, unity of spirit).[20]

Lévinas sought to connect philosophy and religion within the ethical dimension and to address the question of what it meant to be human in a century dominated by conflict, persecution and Holocaust. The central concept of his most influential work, *Difficile Liberté* (1963), is the encounter between human beings, the way in which the Other can become depersonalized; existence, centred in relationship with the Other, must be understood in its ethical as well as its existential dimension. Lévinas went beyond Martin Buber's philosophy of relationship in propounding and developing the concept of the unique 'face' by which each individual is defined in the 'epiphany' of being addressed by the Other. 'The vision of the face is not an experience, but a moving out of oneself, a contact with another being';[21] he contrasted this with the modern Western emphasis on fulfilment through richness of personal experience. He applied this concept to the politics of the Middle East, arguing that if the state of Israel was to exist, this could only be in mutual recognition with the Arab world, in the affirmation by each side of existence for its neighbour.

Conclusion

Genesis' bold statement that 'God created humankind in his image' has lost none of its power to stimulate thought about what being human means and about what demands it makes. Concern for nature (Bible), moral responsibility (Talmud), intellectual endeavour (Maimonides), love (Crescas), spirituality (Kabbala) and self-understanding (neo-hasidism) all derive from this powerful notion.

Most important is the notion that *all people*, irrespective of race or gender, are in the same image. The recognition of the divine image in the Face of the Other (*pace* Lévinas) is the call to mutual respect and to partnership in creating a better world.

Has God made humanity in God's image, or has humanity made God in *its*? It makes no difference, since the concept of God is always interpreted in terms of the highest ideals that humans can conceive, and it is these we are summoned to accomplish when we hear that we are made 'in the image of God'.

20. English versions of the major works in which he argues these matters include: *Totality and Infinity: An Essay on Exteriority* (trans. A. Lingis; Pittsburgh, PA: Duquesne University Press, 1969); and *Otherwise Than Being, or, Beyond Essence* (trans. A. Lingis; The Hague and London: Nijhoff, 1981).

21. E. Lévinas, *Difficult Liberty: Essays on Judaism* (trans. S. Hand; London: Athlone Press, 1990), p. 10.

The Image of God in Humanity from a Christian Perspective

Alison Salvesen

> Do not allow a woman to come into your cell and do not read apocryphal literature. Do not get involved in discussion about the image. Although this is not heresy, there is too much ignorance and liking for dispute between the two parties in this matter. It is impossible for a creature to understand the truth of it.[1]
>
> We do not deny that all humans[2] are according to the image of God. But as to the way in which they are according to the image, we do not concern ourselves unduly ... To believe is to acknowledge the Scripture and not deny it, but doubt rejects grace. Therefore there is something in humanity that is according to the image, but it is God who knows what manner it takes.[3]

Bible-reading communities have long accepted the notion that humanity is created in God's image, but have often wrestled with the question of where exactly that resemblance lies, since God is without form.[4] There has been no full agreement on its meaning and implications from the time of the New Testament to the present day. Furthermore, it is not easy to draw a sharp distinction between Jewish and Christian understandings of the idea, since Christians drew heavily upon Hellenistic Jewish interpretations and were aware of rabbinic thought on the matter. But there are also characteristic Christian interpretations which take a christological or trinitarian line. This paper will look at the original Hebrew text and its Greek translation in the pre-Christian period and the formative period of Judaism and Christianity; New Testament interpretations; how patristic writers explained the nature of the

1. B. Ward (ed.), *Apophthegmata Patrum: The Sayings of the Desert Fathers* (Kalamazoo, MI: Cistercian Publications; Oxford: A.R. Mowbray, rev. edn, 1984), p. 25.

2. The ancient writers used the non-gender-specific words for humanity *ʾadam* (Hebrew) and *anthrōpos* (Greek) alongside the gender-specific terms for a man, *ʾiš* (Hebrew) and *anēr* (Greek).

3. Epiphanius of Salamis (c. 315–403 CE), *Ancoratus* 55, in G. Dindorf (ed.), *Epiphanii Episcopi Constantiae Opera* (Leipzig: T.O. Weigel, 1859), I, pp. 149–50.

4. For the latest discussion of the subject, see W.R. Garr, *In His Own Image and Likeness: Humanity, Divinity and Monotheism* (Leiden: E.J. Brill, 2003).

image of God in humanity; and finally modern approaches to the problem, including the issue of gender.

The Scriptural Background

The central text, Genesis 1.26, is startlingly concrete in both Hebrew and Greek because of the terms it uses: 'Let us make humankind in our image [Hebrew *ṣelem*; Greek *eikōn*], according to our likeness [Heb. *d^emut*; Gr. *homoiōsis*].'[5]

Two other passages in Genesis use similar terminology to that of 1.26–27:

> When God created humankind, he made them in the likeness of God ... Adam ... became the father of a son in his likeness, according to his image, and named him Seth.[6]
>
> Whoever sheds the blood of a human, by a human shall that person's blood be shed; for in his own image God made humankind.[7]

Modern scholarship has identified all three of these passages as part of the Priestly History (P) in Genesis. This is a document dating perhaps from the sixth century BCE and originally separate from the account in chapters 2–4 by the writer known as the Yahwist (J). However, for earlier Christians and Jews, the first few chapters of Genesis were all part of the single history of creation revealed by God to Moses.

Both *ṣelem* and *eikōn* are commonly used of statues and likenesses made by humans, and the sense of *d^emut* and *homoiōsis* is almost as strong. Apart from the passages mentioned, *ṣelem* occurs twelve times in the Hebrew Bible, mostly in the sense of a statue or graphic representation. The word *d^emut* occurs twenty-five times (two of which are disputed readings), and though it is usually more abstract than *ṣelem*, it generally refers to the resemblance of one thing to another. In fact, the equivalent terms are found paired on a bilingual Aramaic-Assyrian statue of a governor found in Syria and dated to the eleventh century BCE, and they appear to be synonymous.[8] The biblical text therefore appears to suggest that humans bear a physical resemblance to God, the corollary being that the almighty, eternal and invisible Deity must be like humans in some way. This is an idea that believers would find ludicrous and irreverent. Attempts to

5. Writers in antiquity also discussed how the plural verb ('Let *us* make') should be interpreted, but they tended to treat it separately from the question of the image.

6. Genesis 5.1 and 3.

7. Genesis 9.6.

8. A.R. Millard and P. Bordreuil, 'A Statue from Syria with Assyrian and Aramaic Inscriptions', *Biblical Archaeologist* (Summer 1982), pp. 135–40. The original publication placed it in the ninth century BCE, but this date has since been revised. *Dmwtʾ* ('image') and *ṣlmʾ* ('statue') are used several times to describe the monument in the Aramaic text written on it.

understand the Hebrew prepositions *b*– ('in') and *k*– ('like, according to') in other ways, in an attempt to tone down the expression, are not particularly convincing.[9] For instance, it has also been suggested by biblical scholars that *b*- here indicates identity. This would mean that humankind *was* the image of God, not just in God's image, making the task of the interpreter even harder.

Two modern scholars, James Barr and Moshe Weinfeld, suggest that a dispute existed between two schools of thought on the issue, represented by the Priestly writer (P) of Genesis and by Deutero-Isaiah.[10] Barr believes that P was implicitly attacking Deutero-Isaiah's stand on the impossibility of representing God, since if God is like nothing at all on earth, no relationship is possible between creator and creature. P is thus closer to Ezekiel and the theophanies he described. Weinfeld argues the opposite, that Deutero-Isaiah was attacking the theology concerning God's image and other aspects of creation that is expressed in P.[11]

Elsewhere in the Hebrew Bible, Psalm 8.4–8 expresses thoughts on creation in different language. Here, the Lord makes humanity (*ʾenoš, ben ʾadam*) 'a little lower than the *ʾelohim*'. Though *ʾelohim* very often means 'God', here the word is usually understood as angels or divine beings. God crowns humans with glory and honour, and makes them rule over the works of God's hands. Though this gives humans a highly exalted status, it does not raise quite the same difficulties concerning anthropomorphism, since there is no reference to God's image. In fact, the passage in the psalms was often used by early interpreters to explain Genesis 1.26–27 in terms of humankind's dominion over the earth as a parallel to God's kingship in the heavens.

Pre-Christian Interpretations

The first direct references to Genesis 1.26–27 are found in Jewish writings of the Second Temple period. The main text is Sirach (Ecclesiasticus) 17.3: 'he endowed them with strength like his own, and made them in his own image [*eikōn*]'. Though the writer did not explain precisely what this image entails, he did speak of God giving humans mastery over animals, along with the physical senses, intelligence, speech, knowledge and recognition of God's glory. 2 *Enoch* 65.2 takes a similar line. The *Testament of Naphtali* declares that the

9. See P.A. Bird, 'Sexual Differentiation and Divine Image in the Genesis Creation Texts', in K.E. Børresen (ed.), *The Image of God: Gender Models in Judaeo-Christian Tradition* (Minneapolis, MN: Fortress Press, 1995), pp. 5–28.

10. Isaiah 40–55; for example, Isaiah 40.18, 'To whom then will you liken God, or what likeness compare with him?'

11. J. Barr, 'The Image of God in the Book of Genesis: A Study of Terminology', *Bulletin of the John Rylands Library* 51 (1968), pp. 11–26, and M. Weinfeld, 'The Creator God in Gen. 1 and in Deutero-Isaiah [Hebrew]', *Tarbiz* 37 (1967–68), pp. 105–32 (English summary pp. I–II).

Lord knows people's every thought and inclination because he created everyone after his own image: this implies an affinity at the level of the mind.[12] But Wisdom of Solomon 2.23–24 interprets the image of God's own nature as the incorruptibility and immortality with which humanity was originally endowed. Such books were influential if not exactly authoritative in Christianity, and some of these themes were taken up at a later date.

The other important influence on early Christian interpretation was the Greek Jewish writer, Philo of Alexandria (c. 40 CE). In an allegorical interpretation of Genesis 2.1–3.19, he argued that God first made God's image, the Logos, and then created humanity 'after the image', i.e. resembling the Logos rather than God's own self. The resemblance in each case is at the level of mind, *nous*, which in the Deity governs the universe and in humans controls the rest of the body. Philo argued that the human of Genesis 1.26–27 is not a physical being but an incorporeal and incorruptible one, whereas Genesis 2.7 describes the creation of a mortal endowed with senses.

New Testament Interpretations

All these interpretations mentioned above form the background of the New Testament and early Christian understandings of the theme. As for the gospels, surprisingly, Jesus is only once reported as referring directly to the image of God. According to Matthew 22.15–21, Jesus was asked if Jews should pay taxes to the occupying Romans. In reply, he asked whose head was represented on the coinage. When they answered, 'The emperor's', he gave the famous retort, 'Render therefore to Caesar the things that are Caesar's, and to God the things that are God's' (RSV). This suggests that humans are stamped with God's image as a coin is stamped with that of the ruler, and that they therefore belong to God. The image is thus a symbol of ownership, and the interpretation attributed to Jesus may be unique in this respect.

Elsewhere in the New Testament, the image of God can refer to the God-given worth and dignity of humankind: 'with [the tongue] we bless the Lord and Father, and with it we curse those who are made in the likeness of God'; 'for a man ought not to have his head veiled, since he is the image and reflection of God; but woman is the reflection of man'.[13] In the second passage, the genderless term 'human' found in the Hebrew and Greek Bibles was made gender-specific ('man') by Paul, and the human creation stories of Genesis 1 and 2 were harmonized. This places woman at one remove from the divine image,

12. *Testament of Naphtali* 2.5. The *Testaments of the Twelve Patriarchs*, of which the *Testament of Naphtali* forms part, are generally agreed to be a Christian composition based on much older Jewish documents. In fact, a fragment of the *Testament of Naphtali* was found among the Dead Sea Scrolls.

13. James 3.9 and 1 Corinthians 11.7.

but tellingly, the interpretation here is not one that Paul repeated elsewhere.[14] His thinking on the image was dominated by a quite different approach, as follows.

By far the commonest line of interpretation in the New Testament is christological, but has obvious points of similarity with Philo's exposition:

> For those whom he foreknew he also predestined to be conformed to the image of his Son, in order that he might be the firstborn within a large family.[15]
>
> Just as we have borne the image of the man of dust, we will also bear the image of the man of heaven.[16]
>
> And all of us, with unveiled faces, seeing the glory of the Lord as though reflected in a mirror, are being transformed into the same image from one degree of glory to another.[17]
>
> ... Christ, who is the image of God.[18]
>
> [Christ], though he was in the form of God, did not regard equality with God as something to be exploited.[19]
>
> [Christ] is the image of the invisible God, the first-born of all creation.[20]
>
> [You] have clothed yourselves with the new self, which is being renewed in knowledge according to the image of its creator. In that renewal there is no longer Greek and Jew, circumcised and uncircumcised, barbarian, Scythian, slave and free.[21]
>
> [Christ] is the reflection of God's glory and the exact imprint of God's very being.[22]

Thus the incarnate Christ, the second Adam, is the only true 'image of God', but Christians can come to resemble him through imitating him in their ethical behaviour. In both Philo and the New Testament, the understanding of Christ as the true image of God bolsters the belief in a Logos who is intermediary between God and humanity. It also rescues exegetes from having to explain in what way ordinary humankind resembles God when the human condition is so far removed from the holiness of a transcendent God.

Interpretation of the Image in Patristic Writers

Identification of the Logos both with the image of God and with Christ led Irenaeus in the second century CE to see humanity as created in the image not

14. See L. Fatum, 'Image of God and Glory of Man: Women in the Pauline Congregations', and A. Hultgård, 'God and the Image of Women in Early Jewish Religion', in Børresen (ed.), *Image of God*, pp. 50–133 and 29–49 respectively.
15. Romans 8.29.
16. 1 Corinthians 15.49.
17. 2 Corinthians 3.18.
18. 2 Corinthians 4.4.
19. Philippians 2.6.
20. Colossians 1.15.
21. Colossians 3.10–11; cf. Philippians 3.21.
22. Hebrews 1.3.

of God but of the Human-God Christ, by whose mediation people can become the image of God as well. This view is also found in the Alexandrian writers Clement of Alexandria, Didymus and Athanasius.

The use of the terms *eikōn* and *homoiōsis* in Greek philosophy should be noted as a strong influence on Christian understanding of Genesis 1.26–27. Plato had used *eikōn* for an image suggesting a tangible reality, a visible reflection of the invisible, and *homoiōsis* as a technical term for the process of assimilation to God by the practice of a virtuous and contemplative life. But Christian writers were equally influenced by the biblical text. Genesis 5.3 gives the possibility of conferring image through begetting, with obvious implications for exploring the nature of Christ as Son and image of God. Furthermore, the Hebrew reads, 'in our image, according to our likeness', with *ṣelem* and *dᵉmut* modifying each other, but the Greek translation adds the conjunction, 'according to our image *and* likeness'. This led to the widespread idea that the divine *image* was conferred on all humanity regardless, but the *likeness* was something separate, achieved by the individual insofar as he or she strives for perfection.

So while the view that Christ is the only true image of God was accepted throughout Christianity, it never obscured the belief that God had also endowed humanity with God's image in some way, nor did it remove the desire to explain the meaning of that resemblance. A great variety of possibilities was suggested concerning the nature of humanity's resemblance to God. Some are surprisingly prosaic, and favour the view that humans were created *upright*, unlike animals: the Greek Bible's use of the term 'fourfooted' for the beasts in Genesis 1.24 facilitates the contrast with the bipedal first humans.

More exegetes followed the interpretation of Sirach/Ecclesiasticus, *Testament of Naphtali* and *2 Enoch*, that intelligence, the senses, and speech are involved, marking off the human race from the beasts which they are to rule. More spiritually, the second-century writer Tatian argued that the resemblance is in the human possession of a soul (*pneuma*), since God does not have flesh and even beasts demonstrate some understanding and knowledge. Augustine of Hippo, one of the most influential exegetes, summed up the image of God in humanity as soul/mind (*mens*), and this is the source of human power over animals, for instance in hunting.[23]

Some early Latin writers such as Tertullian and Hilary of Poitiers stressed the moral aspects of human nature, especially free will, since the latter also explained how people are free to reject God and thus to tarnish the divine image within them.

One very common and uniquely Christian view is that the divine image in humanity is trinitarian, with mind, reason and spirit (*nous*, *logos* and *pneuma*) reflecting the triune God. This was a doctrine developed especially in Augustine's writings, and followed by Thomas Aquinas. It not only provides

23. See J.E. Sullivan, *The Image of God: The Doctrine of St Augustine and its Influence* (Dubuque, IN: Priory Press, 1963), pp. 44–45.

a non-anthropomorphic understanding of God, but also makes of Genesis 1.26–27 a proof-text for the existence of the Three in One because of the plural verb 'let us make' which is often explained by Christian writers as God the Father addressing the Son and Spirit.

Others ignored a direct resemblance on the physical or spiritual level, perhaps in order to avoid any possibility of anthropomorphism. Instead, they concentrated on the analogy of human power on earth, chiefly in lordship over the animals, with God's power over the whole creation. This interpretation is based on a possible understanding of the Hebrew grammar of Genesis 1.26, 'let us make humankind in our image and according to our likeness, *and* they shall rule over …', which can legitimately be taken as '*that* they may rule over', aided by the order of events in vv. 26, 27, 28 and 30. Psalm 8 was also taken to support this line of thinking, as was demonstrated earlier. Altogether, it was a popular theme, found first in Irenaeus in the second century CE, and then especially among authors from the Syrian region. Controversy over the definition of the image of God in humanity came to a head in the late fourth century, when two extreme positions could be found. A misunderstanding of Origen's comments on the image of God,[24] coupled with a strong doctrine of original sin, led some to believe that the divine image was not only defaced at the Fall but even lost in humanity. In contrast, some (known as the Anthropomorphites) supposed that God possessed a body resembling that of humans.

A few interpreters wearied of attempts to define or locate the image of God in humans since it provoked so much controversy and chose instead a reverent agnosticism exemplified in the quotations given at the beginning of this essay. Epiphanius and the desert fathers drew a parallel between the mystery of the eucharistic bread being Christ's body and the wine his blood, and the mystery of humans being in God's image even though they are formed from the earth.[25] Both are realities, even though they are incomprehensible to mortals.

As for those who did attempt to find in what way humans resemble God, we can summarize their respective positions roughly as follows:[26]

24. See the fragments of his *Commentary on Genesis* 1.13, and *On First Principles* 3.6.1.

25. Epiphanius, *Ancoratus* 57, in Dindorf (ed.), *Epiphanii Episcopi Constantiae Opera*, p. 151; Ward, *Apophthegmata Patrum*, p. 53. For a different interpretation, see the saying of Abba Isidore, 'in obeying the truth, man surpasses everything else, for he is the image and likeness of God' (Ward, *Apophthegmata Patrum*, pp. 97–98).

26. Epiphanius provided a list of some of the ideas held in his own day (end of the fourth century CE) concerning the location of the image in humans: the human appearance, the soul, the mind, virtue, the body or baptism (*Ancoratus* 55, in Dindorf [ed.], *Epiphanii Episcopi Constantiae Opera*, p. 149)! See J.F. Dechow, *Dogma and Mysticism in Early Christianity: Epiphanius of Cyprus and the Legacy of Origen* (Patristic Monograph Series, 13; Macon, GA: Mercer University Press, 1988), pp. 302–15.

1. An inner quality such as the soul or mind: the trinitarian reflection falls within this category.
2. An outward form, usually the posture.
3. An exalted position on earth analogous to that of God in heaven.
4. The dominant view, however, is that Christ alone is the true image, and that only through him can humans come to resemble the divine.

Modern Approaches

Perhaps somewhat surprisingly, modern Christian theology and biblical scholarship have tended to repeat these traditional themes rather than produce any radically new observations on humanity's fashioning in the image of God.[27] However, there is currently a greater emphasis on the relational aspect found earlier in Augustine: being in the image of the triune God means that humans can relate to God and to each other in a meaningful way, just as the persons of the Trinity relate to each other. Though this capacity for relationship has been marred by the Fall, it is restored in Christ, the truest image of God.

The most important trend in modern thinking on the theme of the *imago Dei* has been the feminist re-examination of the essentially patriarchal biblical texts and their interpretation by male exegetes of the past.[28] To the present (female) writer, at least, the wording of Genesis 1.27b with its use of the non-gendered *ʾadam*, 'human', suggests either that woman as well as man is made in God's image, or that the image exists in humanity collectively rather than in individuals. However, while certain interpreters from Paul to Karl Barth have taken it that the divine image is more 'dilute' in women, with profound implications for their position in Church and society, others argue for equality, either in the original divine plan of Genesis, or through the redemption of humanity by Christ.[29] Basil of Caesarea (d. 379) stated explicitly that 'woman possesses, like man, the privilege of being created in God's image. Equally honourable in their two natures, sharing equal virtuousness, they are equal in reward and like in condemnation.'[30] Adopting similar arguments to those of the

27. See G.A. Jónsson, *The Image of God: Genesis 1.26–28 in a Century of Old Testament Research* (Coniectanea Biblica, Old Testament, 26; Stockholm: Almqvist & Wiksell International, 1988), and C. Crowder, 'Humanity', in A. Hastings, A. Mason and H. Pyper (eds.), *The Oxford Companion to Christian Thought* (Oxford: Oxford University Press, 2000), pp. 311–14.

28. See the important volume of essays edited by Børresen, *Image of God*, several of which are cited in this essay, and G.P. Luttikhuizen, *The Creation of Man and Woman: Interpretations of the Biblical Narrative in Jewish and Christian Tradition* (Leiden: E.J. Brill, 2000). Rather surprisingly, John Calvin emerges as a defender of the full, spiritual equality of women in terms of the image of God, and even opens the door to a greater temporal equality: J.D. Douglass, 'The Image of God in Women in Luther and Calvin', in Børresen (ed.), *Image of God*, pp. 236–66.

29. See K.E. Børresen, 'God's Image, Man's Image? Patristic Interpretation of Gen. 1,27 and 1 Cor. 11,7', in Børresen (ed.), *Image of God*, pp. 187–209.

30. *De creatione hominis sermo* 1.18.

patristic writers, some feminist scholars believe that the Bible can be understood in a way that supports the idea that women bear the image as fully as men. Others are convinced that the texts are irredeemably androcentric, and reject any attempts to reconcile scripture with egalitarian views on gender.[31] All this is obviously part of a broader debate on the relevance of scripture and Christian tradition to gender issues. In the end, one is tempted to conclude with Epiphanius that the presence of the image of God in humanity is a matter of confession, but beyond definition.

31. R.R. Ruether, 'Christian Tradition and Feminist Hermeneutics', in Børresen (ed.), *Image of God*, pp. 267–91 (287).

The Image of God in Humanity from a Muslim Perspective

Yahya Michot

It is recorded in the two most rigorously authenticated collections of Prophetic traditions (al-Bukhārī [d. 870] and Muslim [d. 875]), on the authority of the Messenger's companion Abū Hurayra (d. c. 678), that the Prophet (peace be upon him) said: 'God created Adam in His form' (*khalaqa Allāh Ādam ʿalā ṣūrati-hi*). This *ḥadīth* also circulated in another version, the authenticity of which is, however, often questioned: 'The son of Adam was created in the form of the Merciful' (*fa'inna bna Ādam khuliqa ʿalā ṣūrat al-raḥmān*).[1] For the great theologian and man of letters Ibn Quṭayba (d. 889), it should be understood in reference to the Bible, Genesis 1.26: 'Let us make humankind in our image.'

Statements attributed to the Prophet would thus seem to prove that a visible image of God can indeed be found in humanity. And if such a proof was not considered clear enough, a confirmation could be drawn from another *ḥadīth*, which is as famous as the first one and according to which the Prophet said, 'I have seen my Lord in the most beautiful form.' Or, in another version: 'My Lord came to me, last night, in the most beautiful form.' Or, in yet another version, transmitted with many variants: 'I have seen my Lord in my sleep, in the form of a young man with long hair, in some greenery, with golden sandals, and, on his face, a golden veil.' Or: '... in the form of a young man with abundant hair, beardless, with green clothes'. Or, even: 'The Lord was seen similar to a young bridegroom when He took off His veil.'[2]

1. On this *ḥadīth*, see D. Gimaret, *Dieu à l'image de l'homme: Les anthropomorphismes de la* sunna *et leur interprétation par les théologiens* (Paris: Cerf, 1997), pp. 123–36. The first part of this paper follows closely Gimaret's analysis. See also Ibn al-Jawzī (d. 1201), *Kitāb akhbār al-ṣifāt*, M.L. Swarts (ed. and trans.), *A Medieval Critique of Anthropomorphism* (Leiden: E.J. Brill, 2002), pp. 170–76.

2. On this *ḥadīth* and its various versions, see Gimaret, *Dieu*, pp. 154–64; Ibn al-Jawzī, *Akhbār*, in Swarts (ed. and trans.), *Critique*, pp. 176–84; and H. Ritter, *The Ocean of the Soul: Man, the World and God in the Stories of Farīd al-Dīn ʿAṭṭār* (trans. J. O'Kane with editorial assistance of B. Radtke; Leiden: E.J. Brill, 2003), pp. 459–61.

If God could be represented on religious mosaics by a Muslim, God would then most probably not be depicted as an almighty, bearded, aged *pantokrator* but, rather, as a handsome and somewhat effeminate young man.[3] One also understands why a French specialist of classical Islamic theology, Daniel Gimaret, published some years ago a book entitled *God in the Image of Man: The Anthropomorphisms of the* Sunna *and their Interpretation by the Theologians*. The purpose of the following paper is to examine some of the classical Islamic approaches to this 'image' supposedly shared by God and humanity. The spiritual views of the great Damascene Shaykh al-Islām Ibn Taymiyya (d. 1328) will be contrasted with the positions of various theologians and Sufi masters.

'Nothing is Like Him'

One would search in vain for the kind of Islamic mosaics just imagined. The *ḥadīths* relating to the creation of Adam in a divine form as well as to the vision of God, by the Prophet, as a most beautiful young man, were indeed 'duly' dealt with by Muslim theologians, so that they were purified from all assimilation of the transcendent God to God's creatures. The Qur'ān is categorical: 'Nothing is as His likeness' (*ka-mithli-hi*);[4] and it would have been unimaginable that the Prophet said anything contradicting this fundamental of the religion.

Concerning the creation of Adam, the most frequent tendency among classical Muslim theologians was to deny that the 'His' of 'in His form' refers to God. In fact, it should then be written 'his', without a capital letter, as the form alluded to is Adam's own form, or the form of another man, but in no way God's form. In the first case, the *ḥadīth* would mean for example that God created Adam in paradise with the form that he later carried on having on earth; or that God created him with his form of complete, adult man, not as an embryo, a child or an adolescent; or that God created him in his totality, without forgetting any detail, etc. In the second interpretation, the Prophet was effectively referring to somebody specific, known to his audience, when he said, 'God created Adam in his form', i.e. the form of that particular person about whom he was speaking when he uttered this saying. For some, the name of that person could even have been *al-Raḥmān*. Hence the second version of the *ḥadīth*: 'The son of Adam was created in the form of *al-Raḥmān*.'

When theologians accept that 'His' refers to God, they nevertheless do everything they can to understand it in such a way that it cannot provide any ground for establishing a similarity of form between God and humanity. For

3. Cf. the link made by H. Corbin between the image of God as seen by the Prophet and the *Christus juvenis* of early Christian iconography: H. Corbin, *Alone with the Alone: Creative Imagination in the Sufism of Ibn ʿArabī* (trans. R. Manheim; Princeton, NJ: Princeton University Press, 1998), pp. 380–81.

4. Qur'ān 42.11.

Ḥanbalīs, who generally consider that 'His' necessarily refers to God, one must accept this 'form' (*ṣūra*) of God in its reality, without raising questions about its modalities (*bi-lā kayfa*). God has a form just as God has an essence (*dhāt*) and it is obvious that God's form is different from all other forms. For Ashʿarīs like Ibn Fūrak (d. 1015), it is not likely that 'His' refers to God but it is explicable anyway. The *ḥadīth* can mean that God created Adam *ʿalā ṣifati-hi*, i.e. with the same qualities as God: intelligence, speech, knowledge, life, will, sight and hearing.[5] Or it can mean that the Adamic form may also be understood, in some sense, as divine, i.e. coming from God. Things can indeed be attributed to God in many ways. What, for example, do we understand when we hear the Kaʿba referred to as 'the House of God' (*bayt Allāh*)? Similar explanations can also be proposed for 'the form of the Merciful' (*ṣūrat al-raḥmān*).

As for the *ḥadīth* of the vision of God as a handsome ephebe by the Prophet, the classical theologians' interpretations are once again characterized by a desire to deny that God has a visible form (*ṣūra*), especially a human one. Insistence was put on the fact that this vision was probably a dream, as confirmed in some versions of the tradition. Now a dream is produced by imagination, and an imagined form does not necessarily correspond to reality. To see God in a dream can thus not be a proof that God has this or that form, nor even that God has any one form rather than any other. On the other hand, if we accept that this vision was not a dream but a true vision, the rules of Arabic grammar allow us to understand the words 'in the most beautiful form' (*fī aḥsan ṣūra*) used by the Prophet as referring to himself, not to God. He could then have meant: 'When I saw my Lord, I was in the most beautiful form.' In other words, when God manifested Himself to the Prophet, He made him more beautiful. And even if this 'most beautiful form' really is referring to God, it can still be interpreted in several ways that will protect God's transcendence from any assimilationism. 'Form' (*ṣūra*) could in this case mean 'attribute' (*ṣifa*) and the Prophet could have seen God with His best attributes *vis-à-vis* him, with His attribute of beneficence to him, or with His attributes of majesty, splendour, highness, etc. Finally, the most explicitly anthropomorphic versions of this *ḥadīth* are generally considered invented and inauthentic, as they are not found in any of the six main collections of traditions, nor in Ibn Ḥanbal's *Musnad*. Some theologians were, however, ready to address the hermeneutic problem to which these versions give rise. Once again, Arabic grammar allowed them to argue that it could in fact be the Prophet, not God, who is alluded to, the 'young

5. The philosopher Averroes (d. 1198) seems to have had a similar understanding of the *ḥadīth* of Adam's creation: 'Among the attributes (*ṣifa*) that are in the Creator there are attributes whose existence we demonstrated by means of the attributes that belong here to the noblest of the creatures, i.e. man. [This is how], for example, we established the existence, for Him, of knowledge, life, power, will, speech, etc., and this is what is meant by the words of the [Prophet] (pbuh!), "God created Adam in His form"' (Averroes, *al-Kashf ʿan manāhij al-adilla*, quoted by Ibn Taymiyya, *Dar' taʿāruḍ al-ʿaql wa l-naql* [ed. M.R. Sālim; 11 vols.; Riyāḍ: Dār al-kunūz al-adabiyya, AH 1399/1979], X, p. 245).

man with a lot of hair, beardless, with green clothes' being a symbolic image of the spiritual states in which he was while seeing God. Or, if this vision was a true one and took place during, possibly, the Prophet's nocturnal ascension to heaven (*miʿrāj*), these surprising descriptions could mean that the Prophet was not distracted by all the beauties of paradise that were then manifested to him, and never saw anything else but his Lord.[6]

The technical *maestri*, the scholastic virtuosity displayed by Muslim classical theologians in their interpretations of the *ḥadīths* concerning the form in which Adam was created and the form in which God was seen by the Prophet, are impressive. In their sometimes quite astonishing and varying exegeses, the most interesting aspect remains their unanimous effort to free God's transcendence from all kind of anthropomorphism. On the one hand, God has no human form of any kind. On the other hand, as far as we humans are concerned, one of God's most beautiful names in the Qur'ān is *al-muṣawwir*, 'the former', 'the giver of forms'.[7] In the Qur'ān, it is also said, and repeated, that 'He formed you and made your forms beautiful.'[8] It would, however, be totally wrong to think that this form of ours, this beautiful form given to us by God, is God's visible form, and that God created us in God's image. As Ibn Taymiyya put it, in reference to Genesis 1.26–27:

> *We will create a human in Our form, who will resemble Us* ... If this is in the Torah, or something like this, [it means] at the utmost that God is creating somebody who resembles Him in some respect ... It will also be said that two existents do not [exist] but [with], between them, a value (*qadr*) in which they are associates (*mushtarak*) and a distinctive value. They indeed inevitably must be associates in the fact that they are both existent, both stable (*thābit*) [beings], both effective (*ḥāsil*) [things], and that each of them both has a reality (*ḥaqīqa*) which is its essence, its self (*nafs*), and its quiddity (*māhiyya*). If, furthermore, the two existents were differing patently, like whiteness and blackness, they would inevitably have to be associates in that which is named the 'existence', the 'reality', etc. and – even – in things that are more peculiar than that, for example the fact that each of them is a colour, an accident, subsisting by something else, and so forth. Despite that, both would be different. As, between each pair of existents, there is something gathering and something separating, it is well known that God, exalted is He, nothing is like Him (*ka-mithli-hi*) neither as far as His essence is concerned, nor as for His attributes, nor as for His actions. It is thus neither permitted to affirm of Him any of the peculiarities of the created [things], nor to make Him be in their likeness, nor to affirm

6. For Ibn Taymiyya, the *ḥadīth* 'I have seen my Lord in this or that form' did not refer to the ascension (*miʿrāj*) of the Prophet, which took place during his Meccan period, but to a vision, during sleep, later on, in Medina: 'Although the vision of the prophets is revelation, it was not a vision in wakeful state, during the night of the ascension' (Ibn Taymiyya, *Majmūʿ al-fatāwā* [ed. ʿA. R. b. M. Ibn Qāsim; 37 vols.; Rabat: Maktabat al-maʿārif, AH 1401/1981], III, p. 387).
7. See Qur'ān 59.24.
8. Qur'ān 40.64 and 44.3; see also 95.4–6.

> of anything among the existents [anything] like any of His attributes, nor any resemblance [to Him] in any of His peculiarities, praised is He and greatly exalted far above what the unjust ones say![9]

A Loving Servanthood

'Form', 'image' and 'similarity' do not seem very appropriate terms to approach the special relationship between humans and the Most High in Islam. Terms like 'signs' (*āyāt*) and 'covenant' (*mīthāq*) may in fact offer a far more useful path to follow.

God says in the Qur'ān: 'We will show them Our signs on the horizons and within themselves.'[10] Instead of presenting humanity as some kind of privileged image of God, the Qur'ān draws our attention to the fact that the whole creation, the universe as well as ourselves, and this microcosm as well as the macrocosm, are full of signs that can be traced back to God. And, of course, all these signs tell us something about God's own self, God's names, God's attributes (knowledge, omnipotence, wisdom, mercy, etc.) and God's acts. From this point of view, they complement these other *āyāt* that the verses of the Qur'ān constitute. God is the *bāṭin*, the 'secret', and the *ghayb*, the 'hidden', the 'unknown', in His essence. Through the creation and the revelation, God nevertheless also becomes the *ẓāhir*, the 'manifest'. There is a discontinuity of reality between the creator and us. Our relation is neither one of equality or similarity, nor one of sharing and intimacy. So do we know that, just like God's other creatures, we receive from God, as attributes, things that are *with regard to us* like those attributes with regard to God. From God's signs (*āya*), the created ones as well as the scriptural ones, those which we discover in ourselves as well as around us, we are, however, convinced of the existence, not only of some kind of correspondence, or correlation (*munāsaba*), between God and us, but of a very ancient bond destined to deepen evermore. According to the Qur'ān, before even the creation of Adam, the whole of humankind was raised briefly from inexistence in order to answer God's question: 'Am I not your Lord?'[11] They answered affirmatively and it is this covenant of divine sovereignty which provides the best introduction to the Islamic understanding of humans' relations with God. The Most High is the creator of everything – evil as well as good, including our most secret thoughts – our omnipotent Lord (*rabb*) Whose decree none of His creatures is able to escape. We are God's slaves, totally subjugated (*ʿabd* in the sense of *muʿabbad*) to God's creative will,

9. Ibn Taymiyya, *Dar'*, trans. in Y. Michot, 'A Mamlūk Theologian's Commentary on Avicenna's *Risāla Aḍḥawiyya*: Being a Translation of a Part of the *Dar' al-Taʿāruḍ* of Ibn Taymiyya, with Introduction, Annotation, and Appendices', Part 2, *Journal of Islamic Studies* 14 (2003), pp. 323–77 (370–71).

10. Qur'ān 41.53.

11. Qur'ān 7.173.

decision, and power. He is the God (*ilāh*) of the worlds, Who loves and commands good, hates and forbids evil, and sends prophets to guide people by making His ethical imperative known to all. We are invited to be God's obeying servants (*ʿabd* in the sense of *ʿābid*), who serve and worship Him by following the guidance of His Prophet and implementing the message he conveyed. He is the only one Who has the right to be feared, invoked for help, trusted, loved and divinized (*ma'lūh*) by human hearts. At the end of the day, we fear nobody but Him and trust nobody but Him, obey nobody but Him, love nobody but Him and have no other god than Him – and all this, thanks to His grace upon us and His mercy. For Ibn Taymiyya and several other classical scholars, this is the Muslim way, the way of Muhammad (peace be upon him), and it interests them far more than any philosophico-theological exploration of God's essence or any putative similarity of form or image with God.[12]

God's Handwriting

One could argue that many Muslim mystics did not follow the theologians in their sometimes extreme caution about the traditions concerning the form in which Adam was created and the form in which God was seen by the Prophet. Rather they used them to have the sons of Adam benefit from various kinds of particular association with God or, even, apotheosis. Three examples will suffice to illustrate this: al-Ghazālī (d. 1111), Ibn ʿArabī (d. 1240) and Rūzbehān Baqlī (d. 1209).[13]

Asked about the meaning of the *ḥadīth* of Adam's creation, the Persian Abū Ḥāmid al-Ghazālī started by drawing the attention to the equivocality of the word *ṣūra*, which cannot only designate a 'form perceptible through the senses' (*ṣūra maḥsūsa*) but an 'arrangement of ideas (*tartīb al-maʿānī*) that are not perceptible through the senses', as when we say, 'the form of a question is such and such'. In this tradition, *ṣūra* has also the meaning of an 'ideal form' (*ṣūra maʿnawiyya*) and 'refers to the essence, the attributes and the acts':

> The true nature of the essence of the spirit is that it is a substance subsisting by itself, which is neither an accident, nor a body, nor a substance occupying space (*mutaḥayyiz*), which does not indwell in a location (*makān*) and a position (*jiha*), which is neither joined to the body and to the world nor disjoined [from them], which is neither entering into the bodies of the world and the [human] body nor

12. On Ibn Taymiyya's theology of lordship/Godhead and spirituality of servanthood/worship, see Y. Michot, 'Textes spirituels d'Ibn Taymiyya', 1–16, *Le Musulman* (1990–98); and *idem*, 'Pages spirituelles d'Ibn Taymiyya', 1–21, *Action* (1999–2002). Both series can be read online at www.muslimphilosophy.com/it/default.htm.

13. On the *ḥadīth* of the Prophet's vision of God in Sufism (and Shīʿism), see Corbin, *Alone*, pp. 272–83; and A. Schimmel, *Mystical Dimensions of Islam* (Chapel Hill, NC: University of North Carolina Press, 1975), pp. 289–93.

> exterior [to them]. Now, all this is also the case with the true nature of the essence of God Most High. As for the attributes, [the spirit] was created living, knowing, powerful, willing, hearing, seeing, speaking; and so is also God Most High. As for the acts, ... someone who examines the acts of God Most High and how He makes plants and animals appear on the earth by putting the heavens and the planets in motion – and this by the fact that the angels obey Him in putting the heavens in motion – knows that the Adamic [being]'s administration (*taṣarruf*) of his microcosm – I mean his body – resembles the Creator's administration of the macrocosm.[14]

In his widely acclaimed spiritual *summa* entitled *The Revival of the Religious Sciences*, al-Ghazālī was logically led to criticize vehemently those who would be tempted by a materialist reading of the *ḥadīth* of Adam's creation:

> *God created Adam in His form*. If, by these words of [the Prophet], God bless him and give him peace, you understand the outer form which is perceptible by the eye, be an absolute assimilationist (*mushabbih*) just as it is said: "Be a pure Jew! Otherwise, do not play with the Torah!" If, thereby, you understand the inner form which is perceived by insight (*baṣīra*), not by the eyes, be a pure proclaimer of God's exemption from all similarity with His creatures (*munazzih*) and a virile proclaimer of His holiness (*muqaddis*)! Cover quickly the way! You will be in the sacred valley of Ṭuwā. Listen, with the secret part of your heart, to what will be revealed to you! Perhaps you will find some guidance at the fire and perhaps you will be called, from the pavilion of the Throne, with the [words] with which Moses was called: "I am your Lord!"[15]

In *The Niche for Lights*, al-Ghazālī's interpretation of the *ḥadīth* of Adam's creation reached a summit of allegorizing exegesis:

> But let us climb once more to the presence of lordship (*ḥaḍrat al-rubūbiyya*). We say: If there is, in this presence, something through which the differentiated sciences are engraved upon substances receptive to it, the similitude of this thing is 'the Pen' [of

14. Abū Ḥāmid al-Ghazālī, *al-Ajwibat al-Ghazāliyya fī l-masā'il al-ukhrawiyya (al-Maḍnūn al-ṣaghīr)*, in M.M. Abū l-ʿAlā' (ed.), *al-Quṣūr al-ʿawālī min rasā'il al-imām al-Ghazālī* (Cairo: Maktabat al-Jandī, AH 1390/1970), II, pp. 181–82 with some corrections. Complete Italian translation of these pages is in *Scritti scelti di al-Ghazālī* (ed. L. Veccia Vaglieri and R. Rubinacci; Turin: Unione Tipografico-Editrice Torinese, 1970), pp. 637–38. According to Ibn Taymiyya, al-Ghazālī considered that 'the meaning of the words of [the Prophet] "He created Adam in His form" is that man is neither a body nor corporal, and that he has no connection with this body except by managing (*tadbīr*) [it] and administering (*taṣarruf*) [it]. The relation of Adam's essence to this body is like the relation of the creator to the world, in that none of these [human essences] indwells in this body, even if it is existing in it' (Ibn Taymiyya, *Bayān talbīs al-Jahmiyya fī ta'sīs bidaʿi-him al-kalāmiyya* [ed. M. b. ʿA. R. bin Qāsim; 2 vols.; n.p.: Mu'assasa Qurṭuba, AH 1392/1972), I, p. 615. On Ibn Taymiyya's critique of al-Ghazālī's spiritualist interpretation of this *ḥadīth*, see also his *Bughyat al-murtād* (ed. M. b. S. al-Duwaysh; n.p.: Maktabat al-ʿulūm wa l-ḥikam, AH 1408/1988), pp. 277–79.

15. al-Ghazālī, *Iḥyā' ʿulūm al-dīn* (4 vols.; Cairo: ʿĪsā l-Bābī l-Ḥalabī, AH 1377/1957), IV, p. 245. Complete Italian translation of these pages is in Veccia Vaglieri and Rubinacci (eds.), *Scritti*, pp. 507–508. The last few lines paraphrase Qur'ān 20.10–12.

God] (*qalam*; Q. 68.1; 96.4). If some of these receptive substances are prior in receiving, so that they transfer these sciences to others, their similitude is 'the preserved tablet' (Q. 85.22) and 'the unrolled parchment' [of God] (Q. 52.3). If there is something above the engraver of the sciences that controls it, then its similitude is 'the hand' [of God] (Q. 23.88). If this Presence – which comprises the hand, the tablet, the pen, and the book – has a regular hierarchy, then the similitude of this hierarchy is 'the form' (*ṣūra*). And if the human form is found to have a hierarchy that takes this shape, then the human form is 'in the form of the All-Merciful'. There is a difference between saying 'in the form of the All-Merciful' and 'in the form of God', because the divine mercy is that to which the Divine Presence gives form through the [human] form. God showed beneficence to Adam. He gave him an abridged form that brings together every sort of thing found in the cosmos. It is as if Adam is everything in the cosmos, or an abridged transcription of the world. The form of Adam – I mean this form – is written in God's handwriting. It is a divine handwriting that is not written with letters, since God's handwriting is incomparable with writing and letters, just as His speech is incomparable with sounds and letters, His pen with wood and reed, and His hand with flesh and bone.[16]

Just as a person's handwriting reveals in some way their personality, al-Ghazālī confirmed in his *Maḍnūn* that humanity is in fact an image (*mithāl*) of God:

There is no likeness (*mithl*) of God, Praised and Most High is He, for He said, Most High is He: 'Nothing is as His likeness (*ka-mithli-hi*)' (Q. 42.11). [God] has however an image (*mithāl*).[17] The [following] words of the Prophet, blessing and peace be upon him, are an allusion to this image: 'God created Adam in His form.' [God], Most High and Holy is He, is existing, subsisting by Himself, living, hearing, seeing, knowing, speaking, and so is also man. If man was not qualified by these attributes, he would not know God, Praised and Most High is He. This is why the Prophet said, blessing and peace be upon him: 'Whoever knows himself knows his Lord.'[18] All that for which man does not find an image from himself, it is difficult for him to pronounce it to be true and to affirm it.

A few lines further, however, al-Ghazālī eventually reaffirmed the unknowable nature of God: 'Man's knowledge does not comprehend the most particular qualification of God Most High because in the originated [beings], in the creatures, there is no image, no model (*unmūdhaj*) of that particular qualification.'[19]

16. al-Ghazālī, *The Niche of Lights (Mishkāt al-Anwār)* (ed. and trans. D. Buchman; Provo, UT: Brigham Young University Press, 1998), p. 31.

17. 'If it is said that there is a likeness (*mithl*) of the Prophet and no likeness of God Most High, we say that [to say so] is ignoring the difference between "likeness" and "image" (*mithāl*). An image is not tantamount to a likeness. A likeness is tantamount to being equivalent in all the attributes whereas, in an image, there is no need of an equivalence' (al-Ghazālī, *al-Maḍnūn bi-hi ʿalā ghayr ahli-hi*, in Abū l-ʿAlā' (ed.), *al-Quṣūr al-ʿawālī*, II, p. 129).

18. On this inauthentic *ḥadīth*, see A. Altmann, *Studies in Religious Philosophy and Mysticism* (Ithaca, NY: Cornell University Press, 1969), pp. 1–40.

19. al-Ghazālī, *al-Maḍnūn bi-hi ʿalā ghayr ahli-hi*, in Abū l-ʿAlā' (ed.), *al-Quṣūr al-ʿawālī*, II, p. 135.

For the Andalusian Ibn ʿArabī, W.C. Chittick explains, the most fundamental determinant of human existence was the fact that it manifests the divine form, as God created Adam in God's own form. He was thus created in the form of 'Allāh', the 'all-comprehensive name' that implicitly includes all the divine names, the latter being, after all, 'nothing but designations for the possible modalities of *wujūd*'s manifestation and nonmanifestation'.[20] In the *ḥadīth* of Adam's creation, Ibn ʿArabī did not see a danger of anthropomorphic reduction of God but, rather, grounds for a theomorphic exaltation of the Perfect Man. According to Ibn Taymiyya, 'those speaking of absolute unicity and unification', i.e. Ibn ʿArabī and his disciples, said that:

> Man is the likeness (*mithl*) of God and that the meaning of His words 'Nothing is as His likeness (*ka-mithli-hi*)' (Q. 42.11) is that nothing is like man, who is the likeness of God.[21]
>
> They took over from the philosophers the latter's saying that man is the microcosm ... and added to this that God is the macrocosm, on the basis of their heterodox principle concerning the unicity of existence, and that God is the very existence of the creatures. Among the loci of manifestation, man is the caliph encompassing the names and the attributes.[22]

Rūzbehān Baqlī of Shīrāz not only accepted the two *ḥadīths* of Adam's creation and the Prophet's vision of God as authentic and referring to God but understood them in relation to another famous saying of the Prophet: 'God is beautiful and He loves beauty.'[23] Adam, the heavenly *Anthrōpos*, hence becomes 'God Himself as putting on the garment of existence (*libās-e hastī*) and assuming the human qualifications'.[24] There is no incarnation in this process but a theophany the secret of which is divine love and which is the form itself taken by this love.[25] 'This beauty which God loves is His own beauty, which He shows

20. W.C. Chittick, *Imaginal Worlds: Ibn al-ʿArabī and the Problem of Religious Diversity* (Albany, NY: State University of New York Press, 1994), p. 32. 'Since human beings comprehend *all* names, each human individual reflects every divine attribute to some degree. But during the course of a human life the divine names manifest themselves in all sorts of intensities, combinations, and interrelationships. The result may or may not be a harmonious and balanced personality. In the last analysis the mode in which the names display their properties determines human destinies in this world and the next. From the human point of view, this mode of display is completely unpredictable. As a result, the human situation stands in stark contrast with that of all other creatures, which are created within known and fixed stations (*maqām maʿlūm*)' (p. 32).

21. Ibn Taymiyya, *Dar'*, in Michot, 'Mamlūk Theologian's Commentary', p. 370.

22. Ibn Taymiyya, *Majmūʿ al-fatāwā*, XXXV, p. 44.

23. See H. Corbin, *En Islam iranien: Aspects spirituels et philosophiques. III: Les fidèles d'amour. Shīʿisme et soufisme* (Paris: Nouvelle Revue Française – Gallimard, 1972), pp. 83–146.

24. Rūzbehān, translated in Corbin, *Islam*, pp. 83–84.

25. 'The Divine anthropo*morphosis* is in the human form, not in the materiality of the "flesh". It is because they confuse the two (Christians in order to profess incarnation, jurists (*foqahā'*) in order to condemn it), that one is led to confuse human *Eros* with carnal sexuality' (Corbin, *Islam*, p. 85).

to Himself in Adam's form.'[26] Consequently, every beauty in this world, especially human beauty, participates in divine beauty. Beauty is the manifestation of the divine. Man is an *imago Dei*. The ladder toward the love of the Merciful can then be defined as love of beauty and Platonic gazing at it, especially human beauty. The lovely beardless ephebe can then also be regarded as the true witness (*shāhid*) of divine beauty. In some Sufi circles, remarks A. Schimmel,[27] 'metaphorical love' and looking at youth (*shāhidbāzī*) 'developed into a highly refined spiritual art, but could also degenerate into a more or less crude homosexuality'.

'I Become His Ear'

Far away from al-Ghazālī, Ibn ʿArabī, Rūzbehān and their like, at the other end of the wide spectrum of Islamic spirituality, Ibn Taymiyya proposed a sober and voluntaristic mysticism which does not ignore the very special relationship obviously existing between humanity and God but prefers to envisage it in terms of humble love and active worship (*ʿibāda*). When meditated on in the light of the Qur'ān and of the paradigmatic experience of the Prophet, God's signs and the pre-eternal covenant simultaneously lead the believer to surrender to God's creative will and obedience to God's revealed law. Real love, indeed, does not mean pretending to assimilate oneself to the Beloved by knowing or contemplating Him,[28] to become one and identical with Him through ecstasy,

26. Corbin, *Islam*, p. 89. See also Ritter, *Ocean*, pp. 448–519.

27. A. Schimmel, *As through a Veil: Mystical Poetry in Islam* (New York: Columbia University Press, 1982), pp. 67–68, and *Dimensions*, pp. 289–92. 'As for someone gazing at the beardless youths (*murd*) with the opinion that he is gazing at the divine beauty (*al-jamāl al-ilāhī*) and setting this as a way for him [to draw nearer] to God – just as groups of those claiming to [possess] knowledge do it – what he says of such [supposed contemplation of divine beauty] is of a more serious infidelity than what the idol-worshippers say and than the infidelity of the people of Loth. Such [individuals] are among the worse free-thinking (*zindīq*) renegades who, according to the consensus of the entire community, must be killed. The idol-worshippers said: "We do not worship them but in order that they may bring us nearer to God" (Q. 39.3) whereas these consider God as existing in the idols themselves and as inhering (*ḥāll*) in them. By [God's] appearing (*ẓuhūr*) and manifestation (*tajallī*) in the creatures, they do not mean that the latter furnish evidence for (*dāll ʿalā*) Him and are signs for them. They rather mean that He, praised is He, appears in them and manifests Himself in them. They assimilate this to the appearing of the water in the glass, of the cream in the milk, of the oil (*zayt*) in the olive, of the oil (*duhn*) in the sesame [seed], and similar [processes] that imply the inhering (*ḥulūl*) of His essence itself in His creatures or His being one (*ittiḥād*) with them in all of the creatures, similarly to what the Nazarenes said, in a restrictive way, about the Messiah. They consider the beardless youths as loci of apparition for the [divine] beauty and use this most serious [form of] associationism as a way to declare licit the abominations or, even, to declare licit every forbidden thing' (Ibn Taymiyya, *Majmūʿ al-fatāwā*, XXI, p. 255).

28. On Ibn Taymiyya's critique of the conception of philosophy as a process of assimilation (*tashabbuh*) to the divine, see his *Dar'*, in Michot, 'Mamlūk Theologian's Commentary', pp. 339–70.

possession or incarnation,[29] or to extinguish oneself in Him, but, rather, to put one's will in conformity with His will: that is to say, on the one hand, to accept His decree in the creation and, on the other hand, to love what He loves, to hate what He hates, and to behave accordingly, in unconditional obedience to His commanding of good and prohibition of evil, beyond a natural order that, without revelation, would somehow remain vain and incomplete. It is in this situation of active concord and harmony between their own volitions and God's will, as revealed to the Prophet Muhammad (peace be upon him), that the believers, because they become the friends, or the saints, of God (*walī Allāh*), can effectively be said to start offering, through their behaviour, a living image of some of the divine attributes and names. *Tawḥīd*, the realization of God's oneness and of God's exclusive reality and importance as Lord of the worlds and God of the hearts, then also becomes a *tawḥīd al-ṣifāt*, a process in which qualities and attributes of the Most High appear through those of His servants. And as this theophanic *praxis mystica* could not be achieved without God's guidance and grace, God could indeed be regarded, then, as having in some way created His friends in His image. At this point, one cannot help but remember the most famous tradition of the supererogatory acts (*ḥadīth al-nawāfil*), in which God says:

> Whoever treats a friend of Mine as an enemy, on him I declare war. My servant draws near to Me by means of nothing dearer to Me than that which I have imposed as a duty on him. And My servant continues drawing nearer to Me through supererogatory acts until I love him; and when I love him, I become his ear with which he hears, his eye with which he sees, his hand with which he grasps, and his foot with which he walks. And if he asks Me [for something], I give it to him. If indeed he seeks My help, I help him. I have never hesitated to do anything as I hesitate [to take] the soul of the believer: he hates death and, Me, I hate to harm him.[30]

When the Prophet Muhammad (peace be upon him) is considered the Perfect Man (*al-insān al-kāmil*), it is from this point of view. It is not because he substantially possessed any supernatural or divine nature but because he became, in his everyday life and in his prophetic leadership of his community, a kind of living Qur'ān, offering a perfect realization and implementation of the Qur'ānic ethics. He was divinely elected (*muṣṭafā*) to such an honour, and

29. In his great refutation of Christianity, Ibn Taymiyya attacked the claim that Genesis 1.26–27 is one of the scriptural proofs of Trinity and compared these verses to the *ḥadīth* of God's creation of Adam 'in His form' (*al-Jawāb al-ṣaḥīḥ li-man baddala dīn al-Masīḥ* [ed. ʿA. b. H. bin Nāsir, ʿA. ʿA. b. Ī al-ʿAskar and H. b. M. al-Ḥamdān; 7 vols.; Riyāḍ: Dār al-ʿāṣima li-l-nashr wa l-tawzīʿ, AH 1419/1999], III, pp. 440–49).

30. See W.A. Graham, *Divine Word and Prophetic Word in Early Islam: A Reconsideration of the Sources, with Special Reference to the Divine Saying or* Ḥadīth Qudsī (The Hague and Paris: Mouton, 1977), pp. 173–74 (I have changed some elements of Graham's translation). See also the Taymiyyan texts translated in Michot 'Textes' 1, 6–7 and 15–16, and 'Pages' 8–11.

nobody can expect or claim to share it with him. Every Muslim is, however, invited to follow him in his humble and loving worship of the Lord God, Islam being essentially an *imitatio Muhammadi* (peace be upon him), between the unacceptable extremes of a-scriptural naturalism and innovation.

For al-Ghazālī, Adam's spiritual form, which corresponds to the form of the Merciful, was not only an abridged transcription, a summarized image of the whole world, but it made him some 'divine handwriting' and an 'image' of God. Al-Ghazālī was a philosophizing esotericist who paved the way for Ibn ʿArabī's excesses. For the Andalusian Shaykh al-Akbar, we can become, ontologically speaking, the most perfect image of God and our life generally reflects some particular combination of the divine names. We are, however, unconscious of that fact because we are distracted by the importance we give to our humanity. Our first goal should therefore be, in some way, to eliminate mentally our human individuality and efface our own selves, to become no-thing, just loci for an unstained manifestation of God. Ibn ʿArabī was a theosophist and a gnostic. In Rūzbehān's potentially ambiguous contemplative Sufism, every beautiful being and handsome human face participates in, and is the witness to, God's beautiful essence. It should therefore be contemplated and loved as such, as an *imago Dei*. Rūzbehān was an aesthete.

In a Taymiyyan perspective, images, forms and faces can cause drunkenness and spiritual inebriety as dangerously as music, alcohol or other intoxicants.[31] God's *āyāt* on the other hand, the verses of the Qur'ān as well as God's signs in the world and in ourselves, especially the pure model of the Prophet, offer a clear guidance for worshipping God and for simultaneously becoming, while developing a humanist action – in the noblest sense of the word – channels for a theophany. In some way, it could then be suggested that God would indeed have created, not only Adam but us, *ʿalā ṣūrati-Hi*, i.e. according to God's wise vision of a creation and creatures that would only find their fulfilment by following the path of the last Messenger sent by God 'as a mercy for the worlds'.

31. See Y. Michot, *Musique et danse selon Ibn Taymiyya. Le* Livre du *Samāʿ* et de la danse *(Kitāb al-samāʿ wa l-raqṣ). Traduction de l'arabe, présentation, notes et lexique* (Paris: Vrin, 1991); *idem*, *Ibn Taymiyya. Le haschich et l'extase. Textes traduits de l'arabe, présentés et annotés* (Beirut and Paris: Albouraq, 2001); *idem*, 'Textes' 5; and *idem*, 'Pages' 18–19.

The Image of God in Humanity, in Jewish, Christian and Muslim Thought

Norman Solomon, Richard Harries and Tim Winter

One of the issues that has concerned the Abrahamic Group, which has been applicable to every discussion, has been the nature of religious language. We deal with this in the current section not because it is applicable only here but because it is particularly appropriate. In what way can human words and concepts be said to convey truth about the divine? The greatest scholars of each of our traditions are agreed that when humans speak about God, the words used cannot be taken in a straightforward sense. Some scholars say that language about God is metaphorical. That is, terms do not apply to God in their primary sense (as when the Bible says that God 'rides on the clouds'). They are literally false, but suggestive of something true which is not explicitly stated. In the case of God, it may not even be stateable. The extreme case of this view is that we do not know what is meant by saying, for example, 'God is compassionate'. We must deny that God is compassionate in the way that humans are, and affirm that we cannot understand God at all, so that in a sense it is equally true that 'God is not compassionate'. But we must speak of God in words given in revelation, and what they convey to us is important for our life and devotion, even if it does not objectively describe God.

Most scholars who think language about God is metaphorical take the less extreme view that it is important to say that God is not less than compassionate, and that metaphors do say something true about God, though what the words mean is indirect, elusive and impossible to translate into literal language.

An alternative, and more usual, view is that most terms used of God are not metaphorical, but analogical. That is, they are literally true of God, but not in the sense in which we usually understand them. Examples would be, 'God is wise' or 'God is good'. These are not metaphors, because what they say is true of God. Yet we must not understand wisdom as it is in human beings. God is wise in a way appropriate to the divine nature, which we cannot comprehend. So we can truly say, 'God is wise', but we must not think that we comprehend what that means for God, except in some very general sense – as that God is not stupid or does nothing irrationally. As Yahya Michot writes, 'So do we know that, just like God's other creatures, we receive from God, as attributes, things that are *with regard to us* like those attributes with regard to God',[1] indicating a use of analogy also familiar to the Christian tradition.

There is thus general agreement that we cannot fully comprehend God. There is agreement that we must speak of God in some way if we are to worship God. But God ultimately remains a mystery, hidden in the dazzling cloud of divine glory. As we worship God in words given in revelation, we accept that our ability to understand and interpret them is weak and inadequate, and that our reflections about God, though important, must be qualified by the confession of the divine mystery.

Even more fundamental is the point made by Norman Solomon at the end of his paper when he asks, 'Has God made humanity in God's image, or has humanity made God in *its*?'[2] From one point of view, all our ideas of the divine are human constructs. We create a God whom we most want or most fear. But all three essays are written from another standpoint, namely that whatever the limitations of our human perspectives, shaped as they are by psychological and sociological factors, this language is the vehicle of God's disclosure to us of God's purpose. Alison Salvesen also raises a fundamental question at the end of her paper about the essentially patriarchal biblical texts and their interpretation by male exegetes of the past. While some feminist scholars believe that the Bible can be understood in a way that supports the idea that women bear the image as fully as men, 'others are convinced that the texts are irredeemably androcentric, and reject any attempts to reconcile scripture with egalitarian views on gender.'[3] It has been suggested, however, that the tradition, including male interpreters within it, can be read in a much more inclusive way than this suggests, and the names of Basil of Caesarea, Gregory of Nazianzus and Bernard are suggested as examples. Furthermore, much more biblical scholarship has suggested that the divine image referred to in the opening chapter of the book of Genesis is gender-inclusive because the text says, 'male and female he created them'.[4] In short, the image is not individual rationality but male and female in relationship. There is further discussion of this issue in the section of this book on gender.

It is clear from these essays that each religion has a particular emphasis. For Islam, it is safeguarding the transcendence of God. Yet this stress on the utter otherness of God, the radical divide between the uncreated creator of all things and the created universe, is also present in Judaism, and we can wonder how far within Islam this stress is a reaction to popular rather than more thoughtful

1. See Yahya Michot's paper, 'The Image of God in Humanity from a Muslim Perspective', above (Michot's emphasis).
2. See Norman Solomon's paper, 'The Image of God in Humanity from a Jewish Perspective', above (Solomon's emphasis).
3. See Alison Salvesen's paper, 'The Image of God in Humanity from a Christian Perspective', above.
4. Genesis 1.27.

expressions of Christianity. John of Damascus stressed that what God is, in God's self, is totally unknowable and incomprehensible. Yet, in the terms of Orthodox Christianity, we can know something of God through God's energies. Within the mystical Kabbala tradition of Judaism, which brings God and humanity very close together, it was still recognized that God in God's self, the *Ein Sof* or infinite, could not be spoken of and was totally beyond anthropomorphism. So all three traditions are acutely aware of the limitations of human language. Within Christianity and much of Judaism (for instance, Maimonides), this has given rise to the apophatic way, the *via negativa*, in which every statement about God needs to be denied as much as it is affirmed.

Within Christianity, the emphasis is on Christ himself being the prime image of God. He 'is the reflection of God's glory and the exact imprint of God's very being'.[5] This is just one of a number of quotations which make this point, and represents a perspective very similar to that of Philo, for whom the Logos is the image of God; human beings are in that image only in so far as they reflect that Logos.

For Judaism, the main point is that human beings are capable of exercising choice and acting with responsibility. We have the capacity to walk the ethical path. In Lévinas, this means that the prime duty is not so much to seek union with or assimilation to the divine as to see the image of God in the other. The unique 'face' by which each individual is defined becomes an 'epiphany' through being addressed by the other.

When it comes to a more precise understanding of what is meant by the image, Judaism would point to 'language-based intelligence, spirituality and moral responsibility', though some Jewish writers would put our capacity to love more to the fore. Christianity's understanding is not essentially different from this; although, drawing on Augustine, there might be more emphasis upon our capacity to enter into relationships. Both religions also draw on Psalm 8, which describes human dominion over, or stewardship of, other parts of the created order. Islam is more at ease in thinking of human beings, like all aspects of the created world, as one of the signs of God, 'the giver of forms'. Everything in creation points in some way to God the creator and so do we human beings, but not in such a way as to suggest equality or similarity. At the other extreme are some followers of a minority of mystical traditions, particularly Kabbala, who suggest that we are not just from God, but part of God. This extreme, however, would not be accepted by the mainstream of any of the three religions. That extreme was made possible by a more dualistic interpretation of religion which came into Christianity and Judaism in the third century as a result of the influence of Platonism and neo-Platonism. On this more dualistic understanding, the emphasis can be upon a soul capable of totally independent existence from the body, a spiritual essence with a very particular relationship to the divine. This is in contrast to the more biblical view of human beings as

5. Hebrews 1.3.

a unity of body, mind and spirit, an understanding of human beings as embodied selves or psychosomatic unities. On this understanding, the image of God in humanity does not reside in one part of us, but involves attributes or characteristics of the whole, unified person.

The last aspect to be considered is that of spiritual growth. For Judaism, as Norman Solomon puts it, 'there can be no apotheosis of the human, and no assimilation of the human to the divine'.[6] However, scripture does talk of walking in God's ways.[7] This, following Rabbi Ḥama bar Ḥanina, means following God's attributes. 'As He clothes the naked ... as He visits the sick ... comforts the bereaved ... buries the dead ... so should you.'

In Islam, again, there is deep suspicion of any idea of assimilation of the human and the divine. Michot looks to Ibn Taymiyya, for whom there is indeed a special relationship between humanity and God but this is in terms of humble love and active worship.

> Real love, indeed, does not mean pretending to assimilate oneself to the Beloved by knowing or contemplating Him, to become one and identical with Him through ecstasy, possession or incarnation, or to extinguish oneself in Him, but, rather, to put one's will in conformity with His will: that is to say, on the one hand, to accept His decree in the creation and, on the other hand, to love what He loves, to hate what He hates, and to behave accordingly, in unconditional obedience to His commanding of good and prohibition of evil.[8]

It is in this way that one becomes a friend of God and on the road to becoming a living image of some of the divine attributes and names. In this way, God becomes specially close. In one tradition, God says, 'And My servant continues drawing nearer to Me through supererogatory acts until I love him; and when I love him, I become his ear with which he hears, his eye with which he sees, his hands with which he grasps, and his foot with which he walks.'

Ibn Taymiyya has been differently evaluated by Muslims both in the fourteenth century when he lived, and today. Most Muslims have viewed his approach as excessively austere. This difference of interpretation indicates a wider, more general point, namely that there are as crucial, potentially divisive, discussions within each religion as there are between the religions. If Judaism and Islam are religions of scripture and obedience, or participation in the *work* of God, Christianity might be described as a religion of participation in the *being* of God. For Genesis 1.26, which, as translated, uses both the words 'image' and 'likeness', has been interpreted, particularly in the Orthodox Church, in a way which distinguishes between the two. All human beings are made in the image

6 For quotations, see Norman Solomon's paper, 'The Image of God in Humanity from a Jewish Perspective', above.

7 For example, Deuteronomy 28.9.

8 For quotations, see Yahya Michot's paper, 'The Image of God in Humanity from a Muslim Perspective', above.

of God but we are called to grow into God's likeness. The Orthodox have not hesitated to call this process 'theosis' or divinization. This process of transformation and transfiguration comes about through association with the image of God's own self, the revealed Word, Jesus, through whom the image of glory is restored in those in whom otherwise it would only be reflected fitfully. This kind of language may seem strange to some Jews and Muslims but both Judaism and Islam have counterparts to the concept of participation in the being of God. In Judaism, this is particularly emphasized in the Kabbalistic tradition, already referred to, and, in Islam, in many voices within the important and highly influential Sufi movement. It is also indicated in the Prophet's commandment to 'acquire the qualities of God'. Conversely, it is not just Jews who would emphasize obedience but many Christians and all Muslims. Within Christianity, Protestantism in particular is associated with an ethic of obedience. Furthermore, the balance between an emphasis on God's urgent transcendence and the sense in which God may be said to dwell within God's creation or within human beings has been and continues to be a matter of lively debate within all three religions. If we take proper account of the metaphorical use of religious language, it is doubtful whether the Christian emphasis upon participation in the life of God through Christ is in fact saying anything fundamentally different from, say, the statement attributed to God by the Prophet Muhammad in one tradition that 'I become his ear with which he hears, his eye with which he sees'.

Judaism, Christianity and Islam are not monolithic. They each contain a variety of approaches – doctrinal, prophetic, ethical and mystical – as well as particular schools of interpretation. Given this variety, it would be possible to stress either the similarities or the dissimilarities between the three religions. On the other hand, we might make a judgement about what constitutes the mainstream of each religion, while using the other approaches within it to illuminate and complement that mainstream rather than replace it. If it is argued that defining what is the mainstream involves a personal judgement, this is of course true: but this does not mean that the judgement is purely subjective, relative or unrelated to reality. On the contrary, the fact that these three essays each set forth a mainstream from within the writers' own religions which is recognized by others (debate about Ibn Taymiyya notwithstanding), suggest that this exercise is not arbitrary but rational and capable of being persuasive.

Chapter 6: Pluralism

Pluralism from a Jewish Perspective[1]

Norman Solomon

The construction of a Jewish theology of religious pluralism, relating to the trilateral dialogue of Jew, Christian and Muslim, starts with an easy task but progresses to a hard one. The easy one is to affirm some of the values and doctrines to be found within Christianity and Islam, and to create a 'theological space' in which these other faiths may be allowed a positive role in the divine plan. This is a well-rehearsed theme in Jewish tradition, expounded within even the most conservative circles.

But when this little mountain has been climbed, a big one looms behind it. The traditional assumption, undisputed in pre-modern times, was that Judaism constituted the only fully authentic expression of divine revelation, the comprehensive and absolute truth. Acknowledgment of the value and truth contained in other faiths was at best patronizing, tied to the assumption that one day, all would come to realize the superior truth of Torah. Ancient texts, and this goes for both Bible and Talmud,[2] do not make for a 'dialogue of equals'.

I will take the soft option first, and describe traditional ways of 'making theological space' for Christianity and Islam. After that, I shall explore the possibility that the dialogue might somehow become a dialogue of equals. Can a Jew, consistently with Jewish tradition, engage in religious dialogue with a Christian or a Muslim without needing, to some extent, to negate Christianity or Islam?

Traditional Ways of Making Space for the Other

The Hebrew scriptures are contemptuously dismissive of the religious cults of the surrounding peoples and especially of the previous inhabitants of the land

1. This essay is based on a paper on trilateral dialogue read at the Theological University, Kampen, Netherlands, on 13 November 2000, for OJEC (the Dutch Council of Christians and Jews).

2. On the limits of tolerance in the earliest formative period of rabbinic Judaism and Christianity, see G.N. Stanton and G.G. Stroumsa (eds.), *Tolerance and Intolerance in Early Judaism and Christianity* (Cambridge: Cambridge University Press, 1998).

of Israel: 'Break down their altars, smash their pillars, burn their sacred poles with fire, and hew down the idols of their gods, and thus blot out their name from their places.'[3] This attitude to 'idol worship' has never changed. It continues to challenge Jews, Christians and Muslims in their relationship with Hindus and others who direct their worship through images; indeed, Jews and Muslims are uncomfortable even with Christian use of images and icons in worship.

Nevertheless, by late biblical times, Israelites realized that there were other people in the world who worshipped the one, unseen God. Such people formed the category of *yir'ei Hashem* (God-fearers);[4] perhaps it is to them that the verse 'From the rising of the sun to its setting the name of the Lord is to be praised' refers.[5]

By the third century CE, when the sages were defining Judaism and classifying the *mitzvot* (commandments), they accorded the status of *ger toshav* ('resident alien')[6] to individuals who, while not identifying themselves with the Jewish people by commitment to the Sinai covenant, abandoned idolatry. This recognition was formalized as the Noahide covenant, consisting of seven commandments (*sheva mitzvot*): 'The children of Noah were given seven commandments: Laws [i.e. to establish courts of justice], [and the prohibitions of] Idolatry, Blasphemy, Sexual Immorality, Bloodshed, Theft, and the Limb from a Living Animal [certain types of cruelty to animals?].'[7] Tosefta, our earliest source for this 'code', interpreted each of these 'commandments' in some detail, and the discussion was taken still further in the Talmud and other rabbinic writings,[8] where serious attempts were made to anchor the whole system in scripture, particularly Genesis 9.[9]

Some scholars regard the Seven Commandments as a summary of natural law.[10] David Novak has argued that they constitute a 'theological-juridical

3. Deuteronomy 12.3.

4. Cf. Psalm 115.11.

5. Psalm 113.3.

6. Cf. Leviticus 25.

7. Tosefta *Avoda Zara* 9.4. Some scholars have claimed to discover a hint of the *sheva mitzvot* in Acts 15.29; this is far-fetched and anachronistic. The Tosefta is an early rabbinic supplement to and commentary on the Mishnah, perhaps originating in the mid- to late third century.

8. Babylonian Talmud, *Sanhedrin* 55b onwards.

9. D. Novak, *The Image of the Non-Jew in Judaism* (New York and Toronto: Edward Mellen Press, 1983), pp. 3–51, and D. Novak, *Jewish-Christian Dialogue* (New York: Oxford University Press, 1989), pp. 26–41.

10. See, for instance, Novak's interesting discussion (*Image of the Non-Jew*, p. 231) of Samuel Atlas's suggestion that the distinction between the Noahide law of robbery and the Jewish law of robbery was the rabbis' way of making a conceptual distinction between natural and covenantal law. N. Rakover, 'The "Law" and the Noahides', in B. Jackson (ed.), *Jewish Law Association Studies 4* (Atlanta, GA: Scholars Press, 1990), pp. 169–80, explores the differences between Noahide and Jewish law, and finds it helpful to understand Noahide law as 'a sort of natural human law' (p. 172).

theory rather than a functioning body of laws administered by Jews for gentiles actually living under their suzerainty at any time in history'; they are presented by the rabbis as 'pre-Sinaitic law perpetually binding on gentiles', and their precise formulation reflects 'a period in Jewish history when the line of demarcation between Jews and gentiles was fully drawn, and when Jews were required to determine those moral standards which were inherently right'.[11] This would have happened when the split between Judaism and Christianity was forcing strong lines of demarcation to be drawn.

Modern writers often state that the Seven Commandments include 'belief in God'; this is careless representation of either the prohibition of idolatry or that of blasphemy. None of the extant early versions of the *sheva mitzvot* expressly demands belief in God. Why is this? Most probably because the rabbis were far more concerned with rejecting idolatry than with formulating definitions of God. An explicit demand for belief in God would have required some understanding, some definition, of God, and this was precisely the area into which the rabbis did not wish to enter. They asked only that the worship of idols cease and the worship of God be taken seriously and treated with respect; there was to be no emphasis on the substantive content or definition of belief in God. Precise descriptions of the nature of God did not matter, holiness of life did. In conformity with this view, the third-century Palestinian Rabbi Yoḥanan declared that whoever denies idolatry is called *yehudi* (a Jew).[12] The rejection of idolatry, and the respect for God-talk and worship, are the foundation of Noahide law as conceived by the rabbis. Maimonides held that a gentile ought to adopt the Noahide laws not merely because they are rational but through acceptance of the fact that God had commanded them in scripture.[13] He did not doubt that the human intellect, used with integrity, would lead one to belief in the authenticity of the biblical text and tradition; moral virtue would lead to correct belief.

On 26 October 1773, the philosopher Moses Mendelssohn initiated a correspondence on this theme with Rabbi Jacob Emden of Altona (1697–1776):

> And to me these matters are difficult ... that all the inhabitants of the earth from the rising to the setting of the sun are doomed, except us ... unless they believe in the Torah which was given to us an inheritance to the congregation of Jacob alone, especially concerning a matter not at all explicit in the Torah ... what will those nations do upon whom the light of the Torah has not shone at all?[14]

Mendelssohn, rather than Maimonides and Emden, has become the model for subsequent Jewish thinking, and contemporary writers such as Rabbi David

11. Novak, *Image of the Non-Jew*, p. 34.
12. Babylonian Talmud, *Megilla* 13a.
13. Maimonides, *Mishneh Torah Hilkhot Melakhim* 8.11. For a full discussion, see Novak, *Image of the Non-Jew*, pp. 275–318.
14. Moses Mendelssohn, *Gesammelte Schriften* (ed. F. Bamberger and L. Strauss; Berlin: Akademie-Verlag, 1932), XVI, pp. 178–80. I have used Novak's translation in his *Image of the Non-Jew*, p. 370, to which reference should be made.

Hartman have readily adopted the covenant with Noah as the 'theological space' within which to accommodate people of other faiths notwithstanding their rejection of scripture or rabbinic interpretation.[15]

Attempts have been made to implement the Noahide concept on a practical level. The Kabbalist rabbi Elia Benamozegh of Leghorn (1823–1900), for instance, persuaded a Catholic would-be convert to Judaism, Aimé Pallière, to adopt Noahism rather than full-blown Judaism. In the late twentieth century, a number of Southern Baptists and others in the USA converted to a form of Noahism with some measure of Jewish encouragement; an organization of 'B'nai Noah' with some thousands of followers is based at Athens, Tennessee, where its Emmanuel Study Center publishes a bimonthly journal, *The Gap*.

Closer to the mainstream of Jewish religious activity is the impetus which the concept of the *sheva mitzvot* gives to Jews to accept moral responsibility in society in general, for it demands that support and encouragement be given to 'the nations' to uphold at least this standard. A notable instance of this was a series of public addresses and interventions by the hasidic leader Menahem Mendel Schneersohn (the 'Lubavitcher Rebbe') of New York (1902–94), in which he expounded the Noahide laws in relation to the needs of contemporary society.

The early second-century rabbis Joshua and Gamaliel II debated whether unconverted gentiles 'have a portion in the world to come'; subsequent Jewish tradition has endorsed Joshua's view that 'the righteous of all nations have a share in the world to come'.[16] This doctrine is a rabbinic assertion of the ability of every human being, even *unconverted*, to find favour in the eyes of God; Judaism does not have an equivalent to '*extra ecclesiam non est salus*' (there is no salvation outside the Church).[17]

The reports of this debate between Joshua and Gamaliel do not use the term 'saved', but the relatively cumbersome expression 'have a portion in the world to come'. Quite possibly this reflects a rejection of the perceived Christian presupposition that people are somehow 'condemned' until 'saved' by a special act of cosmic redemption which must be believed in to be efficacious.

Paul wrote: 'There is no longer Jew or Greek, there is no longer slave or free, there is no longer male and female; for all of you are one in Christ Jesus.'[18] Scholars differ radically in their interpretations of Paul's words. Still, the context of 'faith versus law' in which the remark is set means that it is and was popularly understood as meaning that faith, or belief (whether or not that means propositional belief), in Christ Jesus was that which saved, not deeds.

15. D. Hartman, *Conflicting Visions: Spiritual Possibilities of Modern Israel* (New York: Schocken Books, 1990).

16. Babylonian Talmud, *Sanhedrin* 13.

17. Augustine, *De Bapt.* iv, c, xcii, 24. Cf. Cyprian's earlier '*habere non potest Deum patrem qui ecclesiam non habet matrem*' in *De Cath. Eccl. Unitate* vi.

18. Galatians 3.28.

Belief, according to Paul, is the criterion of God's favour, and it is the line of demarcation between the issue of Abraham and other people.

A rabbinic variant runs: 'I call to witness heaven and earth, that whether *goy* [i.e. gentile] or Jew, whether man or woman, whether manservant or maidservant, it is entirely according to the deeds of the individual that the heavenly spirit rests upon him.'[19] The rabbis countered Paul (whether or not they were directly aware of his words) with the statement that 'all is in accordance with the deeds of the individual', a view firmly in accord with the prophet Ezekiel's stress on the concept of individual responsibility.[20]

Historical Development, praeparatio evangelica

Another way to accommodate Christianity and Islam within Jewish theology, to find 'theological space' for them, is hinted at by Sa'adia Gaon (c. 882–942),[21] and more fully developed by Judah Halevi (c. 1075–1141) and Moses Maimonides (1135/8–1204). Islam and Christianity are in error, but can be accommodated as part of the divine design to bring the nations gradually to God. The other monotheistic religions, said Halevi, 'serve to introduce and pave the way for the expected Messiah, who is the fruition, and they will all become his fruit'.[22]

Maimonides rejected the truth-claims of Christianity and Islam on the basis that they fail to meet the criterion of consistency with the Torah of Moses. Despite this, he assigned to both Christianity and Islam a role in the process of world redemption:

> The teachings of him of Nazareth [Jesus] and of the man of Ishmael [Muhammad] who arose after him help to bring all mankind to perfection, so that they may serve God with one consent. For insofar as the whole world is full of talk of the Messiah, of words of Holy Writ and of the Commandments – these words have spread to the ends of the earth, even if many deny their binding character at the present time. When the Messiah comes all will return from their errors.[23]

Several mediaeval Jewish thinkers were familiar with Christian and Muslim texts, and offered comment, whether by way of defence or instruction. Sometimes this

19. The version I have translated is that in *Yalkut Shimoni* on Judges 5. See also Tosefta *Berakhot* 7.18; Jerusalem Talmud, *Berakhot* 9.2; and Babylonian Talmud, *Menahot* 43b.

20. Ezekiel 18.

21. Sa'adia ben Joseph, *Kitāb fi'l-Amānāt wa'l-I'tiqādāt* (Arabic), book 2, chapter 5. Rosenblatt's translation has been republished as S. Gaon, *The Book of Beliefs and Opinions* (trans. S. Rosenblatt; New Haven, CT and London: Yale University Press, 1989). Sa'adia was of course highly critical of christological doctrine, but this did not blind him to the positive aspects of Christianity.

22. J. Halevi, *The Kuzari* (trans. H. Hirschfeld; New York: Schocken Books, 2nd edn, 1964), p. 227.

23. Maimonides, *Mishneh Torah: Melakhim* 11.

is found in the context of the forced 'disputations' which elicited from Jews much keen apologetic.[24] The Provençal rabbi Menahem ha-Meiri (d. c. 1315) coined the expression *umot hagedurot bedarkei hadatot* ('nations bound by the ways of religion') to avoid identification of Christians in his own time with pagan idolaters, and used this category to justify what was probably already a customary relaxation of certain rabbinic laws.[25] This enabled a positive evaluation if not of the doctrines, at least of the way of life, of Christians.

The acknowledgment that some truth may be found in other religions is as far as most were prepared to go in the 'age of faith', when religions rested on their absolute truth-claims. The acknowledgment is common to Judaism, Christianity and Islam. It seems to have arisen first in Christianity, when Christians attempted to explain their relationship with Judaism. Since Christianity sought to 'prove' itself by claiming to 'fulfil' the Hebrew scriptures, it developed a hermeneutic of those scriptures as *praeparatio evangelica*, 'prepar-ation for the good news'. That is, the Israelites and the Jews who succeeded them were 'on the way', but had not completed the journey. Muhammad, the 'seal of the prophets', accomplished the same sort of 'completion' for Islam, leaving Judaism and Christianity as steps on the way to full Islam. It is hardly surprising to find that mediaeval Jewish thinkers adopted the same condescending attitude towards Christianity and Islam.

Authentic, but Culture-bound, Prophecy

Was it not possible to move beyond 'condescension' to an acknowledgment that authenticity might be found in the 'Other'? This is hardly what the Spanish Jewish poet and philosopher Solomon ibn Gabirol (c. 1020–58) had in mind when he penned the lines:

> Thy glory is not diminished by those worshipping others beside thee,
> For they all but aim to come to Thee.[26]

24. See H. Maccoby (ed. and trans.), *Judaism on Trial: Jewish–Christian Disputations in the Middle Ages* (London: Associated University Presses, 1982; republished Oxford: Littman Library, 1992); S. Krauss, *A Handbook to the History of Christian-Jewish Controversy from the Earliest Times to 1789* (ed. W. Horbury; Tübingen: Mohr, 1996); and D. Lasker, *Jewish Philosophical Polemics against Christianity in the Middle Ages* (New York: Ktav and Anti-Defamation League of B'nai B'rith, 1977).

25. Meiri's views are expressed in his Talmudic commentaries, especially that on *Avoda Zara*. For an English language account and discussion, see J. Katz, *Exclusiveness and Tolerance* (Oxford: Oxford University Press, 1961), pp. 114–28.

26. Solomon Ibn Gabirol, *Keter Malkhut* 8, translated by Israel Zangwill in I. Zangwill, *Selected Religious Poems of Solomon Ibn Gabirol* (Philadelphia, PA: Jewish Publication Society of America, 1923), pp. 85–86.

For he continued:

> And all of them imagine they have attained their desire, but they have laboured in vain. Only thy servants are discerning, and walk in the right way.

The further step was, however, taken by an admirer of Ibn Gabirol, the Jewish neo-Platonist Netanel ibn Fayyumi (d. c. 1164), leader of the Jews of Yemen, who adopted into a Jewish context ideas current among the Arabic neo-Platonist group known as the *Ikhwān al-Ṣafā*. Netanel asserted the authenticity of the prophecy of Muhammad, as revealed in the Qur'ān, and at least the possibility that there are additional authentic revelations (he did not mention Christianity).

Here are the steps by which Netanel established his contention that the prophecy of Muhammad is authentic:

> The first creation of God was the Universal Intellect ... its exuberant joy and happiness caused an overflow, and thus there emanated from it the Universal Soul.
>
> Through the necessity of His wisdom ... He mercifully vouchsafed unto mortals a revelation from the holy world – the world of the Universal Soul – which originated from the overflow of its holy cause, the Universal Intellect – which in turn goes back to its originator – may He be exalted! This ... expressed itself in an individual man whose spirit is free from the impurity of nature and is disciplined in the noblest science and the purest works ... [a] prophet.
>
> Know then ... nothing prevents God from sending into His world whomsoever He wishes, since the world of holiness sends forth emanations unceasingly ... Even before the revelation of the Law he sent prophets to the nations ... and again after its revelation nothing prevented Him from sending to them whom He wishes so that the world might not remain without religion.
>
> ... Mohammed was a prophet to them but not to those who preceded (sc. were prior to) them in the knowledge of God.[27]
>
> ... He permitted to every people something He forbade to others.
> He sends a prophet to every people according to their language.[28]

Netanel interpreted revelation in a 'naturalistic' fashion. It is a universal phenomenon, of which Muhammad is a specific instance. He paralleled his philosophical arguments with a skilful use of Jewish Midrashic material.

Netanel's position differed radically from the *praeparatio* stance of Maimonides and others. Maimonides, for all his acknowledgment of the purity of Islamic monotheism and the historic function of Islam in preparing for the Messiah, crudely referred to Muhammad as *ha-meshugga* ('the crazy one').

27. Netanel assumed that older equals better.

28. Ibn al-Fayyumi, *The Bustan al-Ukul* (ed. and trans. D. Levine; New York: Columbia University Press, 1908; repr. 1966), pp. 2 and 94–109. The best edition of the Judaeo-Arabic text, with a Hebrew translation and notes, is Y. Kafiḥ's second version, *Bustan el-Uqul: Gan ha-Sekhalim* (Jerusalem: Halikhot Am Israel, AM 5744/1984). For the last sentence of the quotation, cf. Qur'ān 14.4.

Netanel was neither casual nor tongue-in-cheek in his assessment of Muhammad; his affirmation of Muhammad's prophetic authenticity is not an *ad hoc* or *ad hominem* argument, but a key statement within an extensively elaborated philosophical system which carries the social implication of respect for the heirs of the prophets, these heirs being the 'imams, administrators, the learned and the wise'.[29]

Netanel, unsurprisingly for a man of his time, maintained the absolute superiority of the revelation through Moses; superior because the Israelites were on a sufficiently high spiritual plane to receive it. What is nevertheless remarkable is his acceptance of plural revelations and of the culture-boundedness of revelation. In this, he is far more a philosopher for our time than is the celebrated Maimonides.

Away from Religious Absolutism and Essentialism

In 1973, the Viennese-born Reform rabbi and philosopher Ignaz Maybaum (1897–1976), by then long-resident in England, published a volume entitled *Trialogue between Jew, Christian and Muslim*.[30] Maybaum, building on the work of his mentor Franz Rosenzweig, saw the tasks of Judaism, Christianity and Islam as complementary. Christianity, in his view, developed the spiritual aspect of religion, Islam its political dimension; Judaism alone maintained the essential balance to correct the excesses of the other two. The characteristic forms taken by Christianity and Islam were not arbitrary, but fitted them for their historic missions in the process of world redemption.

This simplistic account of the characters of the three religions is grossly misleading; each has occurred in a wide range of forms, spiritual, authoritarian, both or neither. Judaism, for instance, manifests itself both in extreme otherworldly guise, as among the twelfth-century Hasidei Ashkenaz, and in authoritarian guise, as among some of the contemporary Orthodox. Maybaum knew this full well, so dismissed such manifestations of Judaism as 'not really Jewish', but intrusions of Christianity and Islam respectively; in his view, only Liberal Judaism was truly Jewish. It is unclear what he thought about the numerous forms of Christianity and Islam that did not correspond to his stereotypes. This stereotyping of religions, as that of such concepts as 'Hebrew thought' and 'Greek thought', must be categorically rejected. It is closely akin to the 'essentialism' which, through racial or ethnic stereotyping, has wrought such grave damage in our societies. The historical reality is that there is not one 'ideal' Judaism (or Christianity or Islam), but a rich and varied tradition comprising many Judaisms.

29. Ibn al-Fayyumi, *Bustan al-Ukul*, Eng. p. 51; Ar. p. 31.

30. I. Maybaum, *Trialogue between Jew, Christian and Muslim* (London: Routledge and Kegan Paul, 1973).

Moreover, the Rosenzweig-Maybaum line does not escape the triumphalism and condescension inherent in the mediaeval theologies. This is perhaps most obvious when one considers Rosenzweig's oft-cited argument that Christians need Jesus as 'Son of God' to bring them 'to the Father', whereas Jews do not need Jesus because they are already 'with the Father'.[31] Why, after two thousand years of Christianity, should a difference remain, and Christians, many of whom come from families devoted to Christianity for centuries, find it necessary to convert to their religion with the aid of an approachable mediator, whereas Jews, even totally secular ones, are thought to have an easy familiarity with God from birth?

Rosenzweig's remark was probably apt at the time it was made; Jewish apologetics demanded such a rebuttal of persistent Christian attempts to belittle Judaism and convert Jews to Christianity. Moreover, this was an age of essentialism, when Harnack and Baeck could respectively dogmatize about exactly what a 'true' Christian or Jew was,[32] selectively ignoring the realities of their respective communities. Rosenzweig was following Judah Halevi, whose poetry he loved and translated; Halevi maintained that the Jewish race as such had a distinctive spiritual quality. Such a doctrine may have passed in the eleventh century (Halevi himself had 'transposed' it from the Muslim philosopher Al-Qāsim's self-understanding as a Shīʿite), but is surely no longer acceptable at a time when the world is learning to reject racism.

Conclusion

The attempt to reformulate our religious traditions in terms of Enlightenment and postmodern understanding and to demonstrate their relevance to the contemporary situation is a common enterprise, not specific to any one faith group. It is in the light of this insight that I offer a theology of religious pluralism which maintains continuity with earlier strands in Jewish teaching but does not make extravagant claims of truth or superiority on behalf of Judaism.

The underlying principles are as follows:

1. It is impossible, historically, to establish a single, 'ideal' or 'authentic' form of any religion. Traditions within each of the three religions are too diverse to permit this.
2. This diversity is not a fault, but a sign of the spiritual creativity of each faith, of its continuous 'dialogue with God'.
3. The diverse forms are expressions of faith occasioned by the diversity of human personalities and cultures.

31. F. Rosenzweig, *The Star of Redemption* (trans. W. Hallo; Notre Dame, IN and London: University of Notre Dame Press, 1970): see pp. 350 and 396, and Maybaum's comments in *Trialogue*, p. 86.

32. Adolf von Harnack's original lectures *Das Wesen des Christentums* were given in Berlin in 1899–1900 and Leo Baeck's response, *Das Wesen des Judentums* (The Essence of Judaism), was published in 1905.

Do these assumptions relativize religious faith unduly? Certainly, they demand that we abandon the absolutist claims of our predecessors. This demand does not arise primarily from within interfaith dialogue itself, but from the critical impact of modernity, not least of historical studies, on all traditional expressions of religion.

Diverse forms of expression of faith arise through the diversity of human personalities and cultures, but each individual is rooted in a particular time, place and community. I, as an individual, find myself within a particular community and derive my sense of identity, my forms of expression, my strength, from that location. There is nothing 'relative' about this; I am quite unambiguously located in a particular time, place and community. I cannot 'negotiate' my location; it is an objective fact. (This is not to deny that there might be circumstances in which I would decide to move.) I recognize that you, too, are unambiguously located in a time, place and community. When we both accept this situation, we can engage in dialogue without threatening or feeling threatened. In the dialogue:

1. There is mutual recognition that we are in different 'places', without any one of those places being specially privileged. The beginning of dialogue is simply to disclose to ourselves and to each other what these places are. We must discover ourselves as individuals, not as representatives of religious establishments.
2. There will be openness to the diversity within each tradition.
3. There will be discussion of relationships, including frank acknowledgment of past hurts, with the aim of fostering mutual trust.
4. There will be recognition of common problems arising from the confrontation with modernity. This will include not only the theological issues about God, revelation, redemption and the like, but also social and political issues. When the problems are seen as shared, we can explore them together, drawing critically on the resources of all our traditions.

What I have outlined is a truly creative dialogue. There is, of course, a need for dialogue at less creative levels. There is dialogue among representatives of religious establishments; this can produce guidelines for better relationships. There is dialogue among unreformed fundamentalists; this is certainly better than harangue or violence directed at one another. Individuals who take part in either can move on to something better, for no one remains unchanged in dialogue.

Paul van Buren has spoken of Jews and Christians 'travelling together'.[33] This metaphor, which may be extended to include Muslims, aptly describes the adventure of religious pluralism. Whether or not Jews, Christians and Muslims can extend this form of dialogue to Hindus and others who worship through images is a matter which they might profitably pursue together.

33. P.M. van Buren, *A Theology of the Jewish-Christian Reality* (3 vols.; Lanham, MD: University Press of America, 1995).

Pluralism from a Christian Perspective

Keith Ward

John Hick, in his book *An Interpretation of Religion*, defines pluralism as the view that 'the great post-axial faiths constitute different ways of experiencing, conceiving and living in relation to an ultimate divine Reality which transcends all our varied visions of it'.[1]

Do Christians accept pluralism as so defined, and is there anything in the Christian faith that might lead them to do so? In this paper, I shall survey some main Christian attitudes to pluralism, beginning with its rejection by some conservative evangelical Christians. I shall expound the main orthodox view, often now known as inclusivism, and show that this is a form of pluralism. I shall then outline two other forms of pluralism (hard pluralism and soft pluralism), held by many liberal Christians.

Exclusivism

It is clear that some Christians reject pluralism completely. The 'post-axial faiths' are those that originated or came into their present form after about 200 BCE. This would include rabbinic Judaism, Christianity and Islam. Hinduism and Buddhism might be questionable cases, but it could be argued that they attained their present form only after that time, or at least not earlier than the so-called Axial Age (800 – 200 BCE). For some Christians, Hinduism and Buddhism are heathen faiths, Islam is a heresy at best, and Judaism is a superseded form of religion. The truth is contained in the New Testament and in the life and teaching of Jesus. That provides the only authentic way of relating to God, and it truly tells us what God is and what God desires of us. There have probably always been, and always will be, Christians who take that view. They often think their view is confirmed by the saying ascribed to Jesus in the Gospel of John, 'I am the way, and the truth, and the life. No one comes to the Father except through me.'[2]

1. J.H. Hick, *An Interpretation of Religion* (London: Macmillan, 1989), p. 236.
2. John 14.6.

Another frequently quoted text is, 'there is no other name under heaven given among mortals by which we must be saved'.[3] Some Christians interpret this to mean that only Jesus can save people from their sins and assure them of eternal life with God. So anyone who does not believe in Jesus and go to him for salvation cannot live with God, but will be excluded from the divine presence for ever. This attitude has justly been called 'exclusivism' by Alan Race.[4] It excludes everyone but Christians (and Christians of the right sort) from eternal life with God.

The fact is, however, that the Bible does not actually support such a view. Suppose it is true that only Jesus can give eternal life. It does not follow that those to whom he gives it must have heard of him and must explicitly profess belief in his sacrifice on the cross for them. God can give eternal life to whomsoever God wills. If God chooses to give eternal life through Jesus, God can do that on any conditions God wills. Just as I can be saved from death by someone I do not know, and even without knowing that I have been saved, so it is possible for people to be saved through Jesus without knowing that they have been – that is, until they actually arrive in God's presence, when presumably they will find out!

So even though there are Christians who believe that only those who profess faith in Jesus can be saved, even the most literalist Christian is not logically compelled to believe that. Moreover, there are very good reasons to doubt that this is a satisfactory Christian attitude, even if one looks for the most conservative and orthodox view one can find.

Inclusivism

The statement, attributed to Jesus, that 'no one comes to the Father except through me' comes from the Gospel of John, and it has to be interpreted in the context of that book. The Gospel begins with a statement of astonishing universalism. Jesus is identified with 'the Word', which was in the beginning with God, and which was God. This Word is also described as the light of the world, 'the true light, which enlightens everyone'.[5] Anyone reading that passage can see that the universal Word or Wisdom of God is that which gives life to all men and women, and gives to all of them such light of wisdom as they have. Wisdom itself became embodied in Jesus in its fullest form, so that what had illuminated all creation from beyond, as it were, became embodied as a part of creation, in one finite place and time.

The natural reading is that there is a universal Wisdom of God, the pattern and origin of all things, in which all humans, and indeed all created things, participate to some extent, receiving its light in ways they can appropriate. That

3. Acts 4.12.
4. A. Race, *Christians and Religious Pluralism* (London: SCM Press, 1983).
5. John 1.9.

light, so often dimly or faintly perceived, takes finite form in order to be clearly visible as it truly is. In other words, Jesus is not an utterly new revelation of God, unlike anything ever seen before or since, and solitary in its presentation of truth. Jesus is the full embodiment of a truth dimly perceived by all since the beginning of history. He is the fulfilment and corrective of universal revelation. So when, in chapter 14, Jesus says that no one comes to God except through him, this should be taken, in the overall context of John's Gospel, to mean that no one comes to God except by the Wisdom and Light of God, known to some extent by all in various ways, but now fully presented as it truly is in the person of Jesus. Jesus fully expresses the only way to God, which is the Word and Wisdom of God – and which is, as such, available in some way to all men and women.

This perspective, that Jesus presents in a full and final way what is partly seen throughout history by those who are attentive to the call of conscience, is a natural part of Christian faith. It leads to the view that all humans can gain something of the light of God, and so can know something true, and something important to their ultimate well-being and their salvation, about God. But for the fulfilment of their partial visions, they would do well to turn to Jesus, whom indeed they might naturally recognize as such a fulfilment, the completer, but not the sole source, of divine revelation.

Alan Race called this view 'inclusivist', because it includes all human beings in the class of those to whom salvation – eternal life with God – is offered. No one is excluded just because they have not heard of Jesus, or because they are not Christian.

That view is much more compatible with the central Christian teaching that the God revealed in Jesus is a God of universal love, and it is the most widely held Christian position. It has been officially ratified by the Roman Catholic Church at the Second Vatican Council, and it is embraced by the Eastern Orthodox and by most mainstream Protestant Churches. It is pluralist, by John Hick's definition. Indeed, it is even wider than that, for it implies that it is not only the great world religions that are ways of experiencing an ultimate divine reality, but that all humans, religious or not, are open to the experience of the Holy Spirit, perhaps working invisibly in the human heart. As the Second Vatican Council put it: 'since all men are in fact called to one and the same destiny, which is divine, we must hold that the Holy Spirit offers to all the possibility of being made partners, in a way known to God, in the paschal mystery'.[6] Such a pluralist view is implicit in Christian recognition that the Israelite religion of the Old Testament is a genuine revelation of God, even though it is supplemented and, in some ways, modified, in the New Testament. The

6. Pastoral Constitution on the Church in the Modern World, *Gaudium et Spes*, 7 December 1965, para. 22, in A. Flannery (ed.), *Vatican Council II: The Conciliar and Post Conciliar Documents* (Northport, NY: Costello Publishing Co.; Dublin: Dominican Publications, rev. edn, 1996), p. 924.

messianic expectation of the Old Testament, for example, is generally conceded not to be quite what Christians proclaim as the messiahship of Jesus. So Christians seem committed to the view that there can be genuine revelations that do not contain the fullness of truth.

In addition, there are explicit statements in the New Testament that strongly imply a pluralist view. For example, the first letter of Paul to Timothy says: '[God our Saviour] desires everyone to be saved and to come to the knowledge of the truth.'[7] But if God desires all to be saved, then God must make possible the fulfilment of that desire. It does not follow that all will be saved, but it does follow that all have a real possibility of salvation. Now since it is plain that most humans have not heard of Jesus, there must be the possibility of salvation outside of the Christian faith. And since one can hardly be saved without some knowledge of divine truth, such knowledge must exist outside Christian faith. The obvious place to look for it is in the religious traditions of various societies, since that is where humans seek knowledge of a transcendent reality. On such an understanding, expressed in many other places in the New Testament, both knowledge of truth and salvation are possible outside Christian faith. Orthodox Christianity is committed to pluralism in this sense.

This form of inclusivist pluralism accepts that there are many paths to God, which are capable of leading to eternal life. But it also asserts that the Christian way shows most adequately what God is, and therefore constitutes the most adequate way to salvation. It follows that anyone who comes to recognize that fact ought to become a Christian, and that Christianity has a mission to make this truth known throughout the world, and to hope that the whole world will become Christian in God's own time.

Hard and Soft Pluralism

To some Christians, this seems unrealistic and even patronising. John Hick interprets pluralism in a stronger form than this. Although the view just expressed accords entirely with his definition, Hick holds that Christian faith is just one way to God among others, and that it cannot be considered the fulfilment of other ways, or as superior to them in insight or salvific efficacy. So Christians should not try to convert members of other faiths, and should not hope that all the world will become Christian. The Christian religion will rightly remain one among others, part of a rich diversity of faiths, one among many and not first among equals.

His view might be called 'hard pluralism', in distinction from what I call 'soft pluralism', and it affirms that different religious traditions are equally valid ways of approach to God or to ultimate salvation or liberation.

One of the main reasons Hick provides for arguing that one set of religious truths cannot be preferred to another is that there is no epistemic justification

7. 1 Timothy 2.4.

for doing so. Believers who have been brought up as Jews, for example, often claim to experience God, and perhaps their claims are justified. They are often justified in accepting the truth of Judaism on the basis of their experiences, or of acceptance of what they believe to be a reliable tradition of revelation. The same is true of Muslims and Christians. Unless one is to make an arbitrary exemption of one's own religion, it therefore seems that one must accept that all these believers are justified in believing different things. Christians may think that the fact of Jesus' resurrection gives them a justification for their beliefs that no other religion has. But it seems to most dispassionate observers that the resurrection cannot be established on the basis of historical evidence alone. Historians are familiar with the evidence, and it does not convince all of them, even if they are sympathetic to Christian faith. So belief in the resurrection seems to be a matter of faith rather than of universally accepted evidence. It would not be irrational for a Muslim to look at the evidence and doubt it, but to be convinced by the beauty and power of the Qur'ān that Muhammad is the seal of the prophets. It seems that a Muslim is as justified in believing that as a Christian is in believing that Jesus was crucified and rose from the dead. Even though they are in conflict, both views – and many other religious views too – seem equally justified.

This leads John Hick to the conclusion that, since all these positions are equally justified, we cannot claim that one is more true than the others. I think we should accept that a Muslim or Jew has good reasons for accepting their own revelation, and that these reasons are not much better or worse than the reasons Christians have for accepting Christ. As a matter of fact, all of them tend to appeal ultimately to the inward testimony of the heart to divinely revealed truth. Many religious traditions are roughly equally justifiable. Their adherents are equally justified in accepting them, and there is no neutral position from which one can tell just who is more justified than anyone else.

This does mean that any claims to absolute epistemic certainty in religion must be renounced. We are epistemically certain of something when, and only when, no rational person in possession of all the facts and relevant arguments could deny it. Examples would be that a table is in front of me now, or that animals exist on earth. Whatever justification we have for such beliefs holds for all people everywhere, and nothing could justify the denial of such beliefs.

There is no religious belief that is epistemically certain in this sense. Rational people, knowing all the facts and arguments, can and do disagree about the resurrection, the Qur'ān and the Torah. They disagree about the existence of God and revelation. So, while believers can be subjectively certain about their religious beliefs (they do not in fact doubt them, and are absolutely committed to them in practice), they should not claim to be epistemically certain.

This in turn means that we should never hold that members of other faiths are irrational, immoral or deluded just on the grounds that they have different religious beliefs from us. In justice, we must accept that they have a right to hold religious beliefs that seem true to them, as long as they do not result in clear social harm. We must also expect religious disagreements to exist, and it becomes unrealistic to think that one day everyone on earth will come to religious agreement. This means that religious diversity should be accepted, and that the sort of inclusive pluralism that hopes to convert everyone to Christianity must be modified. It will have to be accepted that Christian beliefs are not so certainly true that we can expect all reasonable people to agree with them in time. It will have to be accepted that many different varieties of religion will continue to exist. And so it will then be reasonable to accept that the vocation of Christianity is simply to witness to the understanding of God it receives from Christ and his Church, and hope that this will contribute to the knowledge and love of God that exists in the world. But it will renounce any campaign to convert members of other faiths to its own point of view.

That is quite a change from many traditional Christian attitudes. It does not mean the end of missionary activity. But it means that such activity will take the form of service to others and witness to the divine love revealed in Jesus, rather than a campaign to get everyone to become members of one Christian Church.

This view might be called 'soft pluralism', since it accepts that various religions are just about equally justifiable, and that it is not necessary or perhaps even desirable to convert everyone to one religious tradition.

Justification and Truth

But justification is different from truth. I can admit that others are justified in holding their beliefs, but at the same time assert that their beliefs are false.

A simple example would be the belief that the earth is the centre of the universe. Human beings who lived thousands of years ago could have been perfectly justified in thinking that the earth was the centre of the universe. On the information available to them, that was a reasonable belief to hold. However, anyone who holds that belief today is irrational, for we have overwhelming evidence that Earth is a small planet in a small solar system in a small galaxy. We can confidently say that ancient humans were justified in thinking that Earth was central to the universe, but also that they were totally mistaken.

So in matters of religious faith, people could be justified in their beliefs, even though those beliefs are false. It does not follow that, because many religious views are more or less equally justified, they are also more or less equally true. The belief that many religious views are equally true could be termed 'hard pluralism', since it is about what is objectively the case, not just about what humans can know to be the case. But there are very good reasons for rejecting such hard pluralism.

On the most simple level, one cannot say that all religious views have equal truth. Islam asserts that Jesus was not crucified, and Christianity asserts that he was. These views cannot be equally true. To this, Hick might say that this truth is not of fundamental importance. Both Islam and Christianity worship one God and look for eternal life with God, and that is the important thing. But what he is then doing is distinguishing unimportant from important truths, and claiming that the important truths are shared. He would no longer be claiming that apparently different beliefs could both be true.

Many truths are shared between different faiths. That is exactly what makes the 'soft pluralist' view plausible. What makes many traditions sharers of truth is that they do agree that there is a supreme reality, that its main attributes are those of compassion, wisdom and bliss, and that the way to union with it is a way of overcoming egoism and of prayer or meditation and moral commitment. But if there is a religion that denies these things, one cannot include it in the soft pluralist community. For instance, a religion that denies any supreme reality, any 'ultimate divine reality', in Hick's phrase, cannot in this respect be as true as one that affirms such a reality.

A crucial case is Buddhism, which, at least in some forms, denies any actually existing supreme substantial reality. In order to include it in his list of acceptable faiths, Hick has to make it sound more like theism, and this he does by, not implausibly, saying that many Buddhists do regard the '*Dharmakaya*', or Buddha essence, as something very like a state of wisdom, compassion and bliss, which is not just the state of some human mind. I agree with him about this. But what one is doing is saying that some Buddhist ideas are remarkably similar to some Semitic ideas about God. Again, one is defending pluralism by finding some important common ground, underneath what are taken to be only apparent linguistic differences. However, one can find hardline Buddhists who would deny there is any such thing as a *Dharmakaya*. Their view can hardly be taken as just as true as the view that there is an all-perfect God.

In the case of the three main Semitic faiths, there is no problem in asserting that they have a common doctrine of God. In mediaeval times, philosophers of Judaism, Christianity and Islam largely agreed in their formulations of what this God was like. So there is no difficulty in saying that all these faiths possess important truths about God, and about ultimate human destiny – resurrection, judgement and, hopefully, paradise. This view is not pluralistic in the sense that there really are incompatible statements, all of which are true in some Pickwickian sense. It is pluralistic in saying that different religious traditions all possess important truths about God and human destiny, precisely insofar as they agree with one another.

This is an important point, which constitutes a very strong argument against anyone who says that only Christianity possesses such truths, or that only in Christianity can one find that ultimate friendship with God which is salvation. But it goes no way at all to showing that incompatible systems are equally true.

Hard Pluralism and Non-realism

Hick's response to this criticism is that the ultimately Real is completely unknowable, and that particular historical or factual disagreements are both not able to be settled and also unimportant to true religious faith. So diverse views of the Real – the personal view of theism and the impersonal view of much Indian or Buddhist religion, for instance – are phenomenal ways in which the Real appears to various human minds. None of them is wholly correct. Divergent accounts are symbolic, metaphorical and partial expressions of an ultimately inexpressible reality. Such accounts make common reference to one transcendent reality. They offer effective means to human salvation. And they contain revisable and limited accounts of transcendent reality.

On such a view, Christian beliefs would be a set of images or symbols for transcendent reality, the historical accuracy of which is not important, that stand for a reality that is unlike anything we can imagine. This is what I call hard pluralism.

The greatest difficulty with it is that it seems virtually to set aside the question of truth altogether. If a Christian asks whether Jesus was crucified, or rose from death, or even existed, the answer seems to be that it does not really matter. If a Christian asks whether God is a triune reality or whether God is a personal and perfect creator, the answer is probably not, but it may be helpful to think of the ultimately Real in that way. If a Christian asks why we should use this set of symbols for God, the answer is, it seems, that we can use them if we find them helpful in living a better life.

Different religions can easily live together in this way, even interchanging their own symbols without any theoretical difficulty. But they will then have become in effect non-realist sets of symbols for living well, and there is not much reason why they should continue to exist as separate traditions at all.

In the end, religions become purely human constructs, and there is no longer any place for claiming that our own religious beliefs are true, even if not wholly accurate in every detail. So hard pluralism can only be embraced by those who are prepared to adopt a mostly non-realist, non-truth-claiming view of religious beliefs. It is important to realize that modern Christianity includes those who have such an approach to religious belief, but it is a relatively small minority.

The Person-relative Nature of Justification

Most Christians will want to claim that their beliefs are objectively true (true whether anyone believes them or not). But they will have various degrees of certainty about their beliefs. I have suggested that no one can reasonably claim epistemic certainty in religion, and this leads to epistemic pluralism, the view that many religious beliefs are more or less equally justifiable. I have also suggested that this does not entail hard pluralism. But it does leave a problem of how we can speak of objective truths when conflicting human claims to know what is objectively true are equally justified.

One possible conclusion from this situation is that there is no way of telling what beliefs are true. However, when it comes to religion, we either have to pray and worship or not, and so we must either act on the belief that there is a God who commands us to pray, or that there is not. The so-called agnostic position that we can refuse to decide the issue ignores the fact that if we do not pray, we are acting on the belief that there is no such God. On some very important matters, including that of religion, there is no escape from the necessity of accepting one view, even if we accept that many views seem equally justified.

A more plausible conclusion is therefore that justification is not a neutrally assessable thing, but is person-relative. That is, what seems justifiable to one person does not seem justifiable to another. It is not that different views seem equally justifiable to everyone. Rather, to some people some arguments seem stronger, some beliefs more obviously true, or more certain, than they do to other people. A Christian who accepts epistemic pluralism will thus say that Muslims or Jews are (or, at any rate, may well be) just as justified as Christians in accepting their revelation, and indeed that atheists may be just as justified in accepting atheism. But they will add that, as a matter of fact, only one of these views is true. The only possible exception to this is if the view that is true has not yet been formulated by anyone, so that the truth, though it is out there, is unknown.

Can we live with the thought that many different beliefs are roughly equally justifiable, though only one of them is true? Yes, if we accept the person-relative nature of justification. What seems justifiable to me does not seem so to you. All of us are quite familiar with this situation. When we have a discussion about any religious, moral, political or historical matter, we will typically come across different perspectives, different emphases and different conclusions from the same evidence. Human judgements differ, and that is part of the interest of human life – that we do not all see things in the same way.

So epistemic pluralism is not really the view that a number of different religious beliefs seem equally justifiable to all concerned. It is rather the view that to different people, different religious beliefs seem equally justifiable. This is a subtle but important difference. It may be a puzzle why the claim that Jesus was crucified seems justifiable to a Christian but not to a Muslim, when the evidence is available to both. But there will be thousands of factors at work in each case – background information, cultural training, basic evaluations, historical and biographical influences, and psychological dispositions – that cumulatively build up a framework within which particular truth-claims are assessed. There is indeed no neutral position, and we cannot escape the initial perspective that we have on such matters. That does not mean it is all totally subjective, as though it was just a matter of personal taste or preference. But it does mean that assessments of very basic, strongly evaluative and existentially far-reaching claims will be made from an involved personal viewpoint. Our claims will be about what is objective, but they will be made from a personal and inculturated viewpoint, and what we must do is try to make that viewpoint as wide and unprejudiced and informed as possible.

The Diversity of Religions

Given that this is so, can we affirm this situation as a positive virtue, and say that it is a positively good thing that beliefs and evaluations differ? This is a step religious believers have found it very hard to take, since they often think that their truth is so important that everyone ought to believe it. The inclusivist view, accepting epistemic pluralism, will certainly tolerate difference, but will find it hard to think it is actually good. Is there anything in Christianity that might lead one to affirm epistemic pluralism as a good thing?

To begin with, freedom of conscience has always been seen to be an entailment of Christian faith. One must do what one believes to be right. So one should believe what seems, after due reflection, to be true. And it may be good to search for truth oneself rather than passively to accept it from others, to follow conscience rather than simply blindly to obey.

In addition, love of neighbour is a primary Christian virtue. Love entails respect for the opinions of others, and for the conscientious decisions they make. So at the least, Christianity enjoins freedom of belief and religious practice whenever that does not harm others. The sixteenth-century Protestant Reformation claimed this as a fundamental right, and at the Second Vatican Council, freedom of religion was affirmed by the Roman Catholic Church.[8] So it is part of orthodox Christianity, even though it has not always been secured in practice.

This does not yet show that diversity is a good thing. Some Christians go much further. The German theologian Friedrich Schleiermacher (1768–1834), sometimes called the 'father of liberal Protestantism', asserted that it is a positively good thing that there are many forms of religious faith. The main reason he gave is that religious faith is not, he held, a matter of accepting doctrinal truths on authority. The authority of the Church had been called in question by the Protestant Reformers. The authority of the Bible was being questioned by the new disciplines of historical and literary criticism, which tended to stress the Bible's internal diversity and the legendary or exaggerated nature of many biblical accounts. Schleiermacher proposed that faith is based on personal experience; it is a matter of realizing one's absolute dependence upon an infinite reality, as apprehended in and through specific finite forms. Religion is, he said, 'the sensibility and taste for the infinite'.[9] The symbols and images of religion were seen as forms under which the infinite reality of God was apprehended and mediated. But that reality remained always beyond human apprehension or imagination.

There are deep strands of thought in all religion that stress the inconceivability of God, and the metaphorical or symbolic nature of all human speech about

8. Declaration on Religious Liberty, *Dignitatis Humanae*, 7 December 1965, in Flannery (ed.), *Vatican Council II*, pp. 799–812.

9. F.D.E. Schleiermacher, *On Religion: Speeches to its Cultured Despisers* (ed. and trans. R. Crouter; Cambridge: Cambridge University Press, 2nd edn, 1996), p. 23.

God. In Christianity, Jesus is seen as the image of the invisible God. So it becomes natural to see finite forms of the natural world as images variously expressing God. Jesus himself can be seen as a sort of living metaphor for God, and for Schleiermacher it was Jesus' intense and continuous sense of God that made him the founder of the Christian Church. The Christian Churches seek to re-evoke the sort of experience of God which Jesus realized, and take him to be both the human image of divine love (the 'Son of God' in a metaphorical sense), and the person through whom God places the divine Spirit in the hearts of men and women, liberating them from egoism for a new life in unity with God (it is in this sense that Jesus is the saviour of the world).

Jesus remains central for this liberal Christian view. But emphasis is placed on the fact of the divine infinity, on the weakness and limitedness of human understanding, and on the symbolic and metaphorical nature of much speech about God. In the light of these things, we might expect God to be much greater than any of the thoughts we have about God. So perhaps one religious tradition, however profound, cannot contain all that there is to be known about God, especially if there are great differences in human temperament and circumstance which mean that humans see God from many diverse viewpoints, each of which has its own peculiar limitations. In addition, Protestants are keenly aware that dominant faiths tend to become over-dogmatic and repressive, so that their encounter with different and critical views is helpful to their own self-understanding.

Finally, where much language about God is symbolic, it may enrich faith to have access to a wider range of symbols for the divine, which other religious traditions may provide. Thus, while liberal Christians may hold that the Christian faith contains central truths that are definitive – the embodiment of the divine in Jesus, the suffering of God, Jesus' victory over death, and the liberation of the world through that victory – they may also think that, given the diversity and limitations of human understanding, it is good that many religious traditions exist, being explorations of the infinity of God from many diverse human standpoints.

Not all liberal Christians agree with Schleiermacher, of course, but liberal forms of Christianity exist in most of the major Christian denominations, and are a well-established part of Christian faith. Liberal Christians stress the need for critical assessment of all religious authorities, the symbolic nature of most religious language, the primary importance of personal experience, and the need for religion continually to revise its understandings to ensure the greatest possible human and cosmic fulfilment. These strands are, I have suggested, all present in Christian tradition, but they have only been fully stressed since the eighteenth-century European movement of thought known as the Enlightenment – which itself, it would be claimed, has a largely Christian basis, even though it reacted against many traditional interpretations of Christianity.

Conclusion

In conclusion, I have held that, while some Christians reject pluralism, orthodox Christianity is committed to pluralism, to the view that many religions share important truths about God, and relate their adherents to God in ways that can lead to salvation. The orthodox position is usually inclusivist, believing that Christ corrects and completes other views. But it may well be epistemically pluralist, holding that many different religious views can properly be considered justifiable by their adherents.

Liberal Christianity can go further, and accept epistemic pluralism as a positive good, holding that many religions have distinctive understandings of God, often expressed in symbol and metaphor, which it is a positive benefit to share, and which each may seek to reflect appropriately in their own tradition. This I have called soft pluralism. The human grasp of truth is tentative and weak, and we would do well to learn from those who differ from us, if we are to understand the fullness of God's revelation to the world, and even if we are to understand our own tradition more deeply.

Hard metaphysical pluralism, the view that many religions are more or less equally true, is a view held by some Christians, though it requires a degree of non-realism about truth that is not acceptable to most believers.

Overall, then, there are four main views on pluralism that Christians tend to hold. The exclusivist view rejects pluralism. This view tends to be the preserve of conservative evangelical Protestants, often called fundamentalists. The inclusivist view is a form of pluralism that maintains the superior adequacy of Christian truth-claims. It is the view most widely held by Catholic, Orthodox and mainline Protestant Churches. Soft pluralism is more positive about the diversity of religious faiths, finding in such diversity a witness to the immensity and richness of God, and the limitations of human understanding of the divine. It is characteristic of what is often called liberal Christianity, which is found as one strand of thought throughout most Christian Churches. The hard pluralist view is affirmed by more radical believers, and tends to be associated with a rejection of the notion of an ultimate objective truth in religion, or at least one that can ever be knowable.

I have tried to describe these positions rather than argue positively for one. But since the central Christian affirmation is that God loves all creatures with an unconquerable love, it seems that, however many Christians take the exclusivist position, some form of pluralism is the natural and reasonable consequence of Christian belief.

Pluralism from a Muslim Perspective[1]

Tim Winter

'Tonight Beshr will be your guest.'

This conviction entered Beshr's sister's mind. She swept and watered her house, and waited expectantly for Beshr to arrive. Suddenly Beshr came like one distraught.

'Sister, I am going up to the roof,' he announced.

He planted his foot on the stairs and climbed several steps, then remained standing like that till the next day. When dawn broke, he descended. He went off to pray in the mosque.

'What was the reason you stood all night?' asked his sister when he returned.

'The thought entered my mind,' Beshr replied, 'that in Baghdad there are so many people whose names are Beshr – one a Jew, one a Christian, one a Magian. My name too is Beshr, and I have attained the great felicity of being a Muslim. What, I asked myself, did the others do to be excluded, and what did I do to attain such felicity? Bewildered by this thought, I remained rooted to the spot.'[2]

Beshr, the Sufi saint, was not alone in his perplexity. To thoughtful inhabitants of the religiously diverse societies of mediaeval Islam, the divine justice seemed to be made painfully obscure by the presence of hosts of sincere unbelievers, who, despite their virtues, were, on the popular understanding, destined for the flames of hell. As in the Christian context, this scandal of particularity has perpetually raised difficult questions about the transparency of God's action in the world, as well as exposing religion to the secular charge of inspiring a lethal intolerance. This chapter will outline a few of the ways in which classical Sunni theology (*kalām*) sought to reconcile the assurance of God's justice and desire for human conviviality, with the revealed fact of God's special grace towards the community of Islam. What have the Muslim divines had to say about the otherworldly prospects for idolators, Jews and Christians, given the

1. An extended version of this paper has been published as 'The Last Trump Card: Islam and the Supersession of Other Faiths', *Studies in Interreligious Dialogue* 9 (1999), pp. 133–55.

2. A.J. Arberry (trans.), *Muslim Saints and Mystics: Episodes from the Tadhkirat al-auliya' ('Memorial of the Saints') by Farid al-Din Attar* (London: Routledge and Kegan Paul, 1966), pp. 82–83.

Qur'ān's simultaneous insistence on the providence of God towards earlier communities, and its own apparently triumphalist tenor?

A History of Salvation

Muslim theologians have almost invariably read their revelation as a frankly supersessionist event, proclaiming the abrogation (*naskh*) of prior religion by the Prophet's faith. Rooted in an original context of polemic against entrenched Arab idolatry, and later, following the exodus to Medina, against local representatives of Judaism and Christianity, the Qur'ān and *ḥadīth* seem not merely to *describe* all of these faiths, but to *argue* against them.

In the cases of Judaism and Christianity, the Qur'ān throughout adopts the view that both were founded by authentic spokesmen of God,[3] and were hence at their points of origin perfect vehicles of grace and salvation. It also repeatedly signals that God's guidance to humanity was not exhausted by the biblical line of prophecy, by recalling the exemplary lives of non-Hebraic messengers.[4] It announces that 'for every people there has been a guide', and that 'We have raised in every nation a messenger proclaiming, Serve God, and shun false gods.'[5]

This understanding of an expansive divine strategy for human 'salvation', or, more precisely, what the less dramatic Qur'ānic soteriology which lacks a doctrine of original sin understands as 'harvesting' or 'success' (*falāḥ*), is the beginning point for the Muslim discussion, and has clear implications. The Qur'ānic perspective, affirmed and elaborated in classical exegesis, appears to be that there is no scandal either of particularity or of multiple religions; there is, in reality, a single religion (*al-dīn*), of which the various present-day faiths may be considered the remnants and offshoots.[6] And because the grace mediated by the word made Book operates non-redemptively, and because scriptures have been 'sent down' before, the new divine initiative is not construed as absolute or categoric in its displacement of what preceded, inasmuch as no new type of relationship between humanity and God is proposed. For Islam, then, pre-Qur'ānic history is not mere prehistory. Humanity did not have to wait for Muhammad in order to gain the opportunity of complete 'success'.

3. For example, Qur'ān 2.136.
4. Such as Hūd and Ṣāliḥ; see Qur'ān 7.65–79.
5. Qur'ān 13.7 and 16.36.
6. The ability of this system to incorporate Far Eastern sages in the register of prophets is demonstrated in, for instance, O. Bakar (ed.), *Islam and Confucianism: A Civilizational Dialogue* (Kuala Lumpur: University of Malaya Press, 1997); and I. Yusuf, 'Parameters for Presenting Islam to the Buddhists Today', in R. Wu (ed.), *Readings in Cross-Cultural Da'wah* (Singapore: Muslim Converts Association of Singapore, 2001), pp. 137–64 (151).

The Other in Scripture

It is this conviction of God's generous filling of history and of the map of the world with signs pointing back to God that permits the Qur'ān's frequently noted advocacy of mutual esteem, which requires Muslims to tell the people of the Book that 'we believe in that which was revealed unto us and was revealed unto you; our God and your God is One.'[7] There are Qur'ānic passages in this vein which seem to verge on an out-and-out pluralism. 5.44–48, in particular, the appearance of which may be predicted whenever Muslims take part in the *ballo in maschera* of so many interfaith encounters, is certainly quite remarkable for a pre-modern religious document, eulogizing the scriptures given to the Jewish prophets and Jesus as 'full of guidance and light', and enjoining the Prophet Muhammad to act as arbiter among the 'people of the Book', until the Judgement brings a definitive unveiling and explanation of all religious differences.

Realistically interpreted, such passages have two obvious objectives: first, to affirm the Judaeo-Christian line of prophecy in order to proclaim Muhammad's triumphant succession to it, and secondly, to make of his religion a 'guardian' over the surviving advocates of the earlier versions of faith. This proclamation drives Islam's historical self-understanding as a protector of Jews, Christians, Hindus and others who are *ahl al-dhimma*, 'protected communities' accorded a covenant of religious inviolability by the custodians of the later and universal revelation.[8] It is well known that the majority of historical Muslim communities have tolerated their minorities, following the Prophet's warning that 'whoever harms a member of a *dhimma* community shall have me as his adversary on the Day of Judgement'.[9] This attitude stems from the Qur'ānic advocacy of a paternalistic supervisory duty, relics of which survived even into the twentieth century. Not unrepresentative are the remarks of the last Turkish governor of Mount Athos in 1912, conversing with a French journalist as he awaited arrest by the conquering Greek armies:

> Look around you. Look at these thousands of monks; visit their monasteries, question them yourself. Of what, in reality, can they complain? Have we touched their rules? Have we violated their property? Have we forbidden their pilgrimages? Have we altered even a tittle of their secular constitution? ... What race, I ask you, what conqueror could have treated these people with greater humanity, greater moderation, greater religious tolerance? Under our law they have remained no less free, indeed freer, than under the Byzantine Emperors ... And they have not had to

7. Qur'ān 29.46.

8. The prevalent school of Islamic law in India, the Ḥanafī, regarded Hindus as *ahl al-dhimma*; see Y. Friedmann, 'Islamic Thought in Relation to the Indian Context', in R.M. Eaton (ed.), *India's Islamic Traditions 711–1750* (New Delhi: Oxford University Press, 2003), pp. 50–63 (52).

9. Aḥmad ibn Ḥanbal, *Musnad*, cited in Ibn Ḥajar al-ʿAsqalānī, *Iṭrāf al-Musnid al-Muʿtalī bi-aṭrāf al-Musnad al-Ḥanbalī* (Beirut and Damascus: Dār al-Fikr, AH 1414/1993), no. 12440.

> endure under our domination a hundredth part of the vexations that you have imposed on your monks in France ... *Allez, Monsieur!* They will regret us. Greeks, Russians, Serbs, Rumanians, Bulgars, all those monks hate each other like poison. They are bound together only by their common loathing of Islam. When we are no longer there, they will tear each other to pieces.[10]

The capacity of Islamic society for this kind of indulgent presiding over non-Muslim communities can be taken as evidence of the sincerity of the claim that earlier dispensations have been superseded far less radically by Islam than, for instance, Judaism was superseded by Christianity, on the classical Christian view. But the accommodation of Jews and Christians in mediaeval Muslim cities cannot safely be read as a sign that the tradition expected similar arrangements to prevail in paradise. The logic of the *dhimma* rules was neither that of a pluralist soteriology nor of a modern secular impartiality based in universal concepts of human rights and a thoroughgoing religious indifferentism. Sumptuary and other laws, mostly dating from the time of the early caliphs, did impose significant disabilities on Christians, Jews and others, and the historical legal practice of Islam furnishes not an interrogation, but a confirmation of the judgement that Christian and Jewish versions of faith are no longer complete, although they are rooted ultimately in revelation and hence merit some form of accommodation.

This evidence is supplied by a number of scriptural passages which moderate and recontextualize the eirenic proof-texts cited by Muslim pluralists, developing a critique of Judaism and Christianity formulated against the backdrop of the Qur'ān's vindications of the prophethood of Muhammad. Let me deal firstly with those concerning the Jews. Rabbinic Judaism of the type practised by the Jews of Medina is censured for attaching halakhic complications to the religion of the prophets. Sometimes this is coupled to jeremiads against the 'stiff-necked' chosen people; so that elements of the law are read as divine punishment for Israel's disobedience.[11] The most drastic censure comes in a famously obscure passage where 'the Jews' are reproached for believing that one ʿUzayr is 'the Son of God', which would render their error equivalent to

10. J.J. Norwich, R. Sitwell and A. Costa, *Mount Athos* (London: Hutchinson, 1966), p. 84.

11. The Qur'ānic charge (4.160) is strongly reminiscent of the pseudo-Targum of Jonathan: 'When they rebelled against My word and refused to accept My prophets, I put them far away and handed them over to their enemies. They went after their own foolish inclinations and adopted decrees that were not good and laws by which they could not live.' This is an attempt to explain the notoriously difficult Ezekiel 20.25: 'I gave them statutes that were not good and ordinances by which they could not live.' The rabbinical interpretation is that God's legislation was not in fact bad, but that as a punishment God permitted the Israelites to follow their own fallible desires; this would seem also to be the Muslim view (J.D. Levenson, *The Death and Resurrection of the Beloved Son: The Transformation of Child Sacrifice in Judaism and Christianity* [New Haven, CT and London: Yale University Press, 1993], pp. 5–6).

that of the Christians.[12] The identification of 'Uzayr was, however, deeply problematic for the tradition. Some identified him with Ezra, condemned by some for 'falsifying' the Torah;[13] but it has recently been suggested that the reference is to the prophet Enoch, who in some Near Eastern Jewish traditions had been identified with Metatron, in which case the Qur'ānic critique is here paralleling that of Karaite and some rabbinical polemic against the apparent compromise of strict monotheism entailed by the veneration or worship of this creator-angel.[14] If this identification is correct, the inference is that the Qur'ān is here to be read as taking one Jewish side against another, thereby denouncing a local aberration rather than indicting the religion as a whole.

Overall therefore, despite the existence of a clear Qur'ānic reproach to some Jews, the Qur'ān does not appear to offer a categoric denunciation of Judaism, but only points out a number of errors in its later evolution which justify its supersession by Islam. The Qur'ān's explicit denial of Jewish responsibility for the crucifixion of Christ ensured that anti-Semitism after the European fashion never took firm root in Islamic soil;[15] indeed, the mediaeval Mediterranean world could witness what Samuel Goitein famously described as a 'fructuous symbiosis' between Judaism and Islam.[16]

Traditional Islam's claim to supersede Christianity is of greater complexity. Again, it becomes necessary to distinguish between a local and a general polemic, recognizing (against much Muslim reflection) the purely ephemeral character of some Islamic scriptural criticisms of regional sectaries, and the abiding import of passages which bear on doctrines held by the Chalcedonian Churches. In the latter category we find, most irreducibly, an argument against the attribution of divine status to Jesus, as in the following passage from the Qur'ān:

> O people of the Book, do not commit an excess in your religion, and do not say anything but the truth in respect of God. The Messiah, Jesus son of Mary, was only a messenger of God and His word, which He conveyed unto Mary, and a spirit from Him. So believe in God and [all] His messengers, and say not: 'Three!'[17]

12. Qur'ān 9.30.

13. H. Lazarus-Yafeh, *Intertwined Worlds: Medieval Islam and Bible Criticism* (Princeton, NJ: Princeton University Press, 1992), pp. 50–74.

14. G.D. Newby, *History of the Jews of Arabia* (Columbia, SC: University of South Carolina Press, 1988), pp. 60–61.

15. Qur'ān 4.157: 'They did not kill him, and they did not crucify him; but something was made to appear to them' (*shubbiha lahum* – this phrase has been variously understood and translated; but the exoneration is clear).

16. S. Goitein, *Jews and Arabs: Their Contacts through the Ages* (New York: Schocken Books, 1955), p. 130: 'Never has Judaism encountered such a close and fructuous symbiosis as that with the medieval civilization of Arab Islam.'

17. Qur'ān 4.171.

As in its treatment of Judaism, but more sharply, the Muslim revelation deploys arguments against a historically evolved Christianity in order to justify the latest divine intervention. Given that Islam explicitly disclaims categoric novelty, its very legitimacy would be questioned were it not to point out deteriorations in its precursors. Hence, for instance, the frequent insistence that original revelations have not been reliably conserved in the biblical text.[18] Hence also, and most strikingly, the Qur'ānic rejection of the crucifixion, a denial perhaps more rhetorical than historiographic in intention. In the Muslim exegesis, Christianity erroneously asserted both uniqueness and divinity for its prophet,[19] and adopted the cross as the sign for this. The cross signals a *sui generis* intersection of heaven and earth, and hence contests the Qur'ān's insistence that an infinitely generous Lord must have actualized multiple perfect interventions. To negate the doctrine, the symbol itself seems to have been erased.

As the Ishmaelite aspect of Semitic revelation,[20] Islam is explicitly universal in its ambitions. A *ḥadīth* records that 'while earlier prophets were sent only to their own nations, I am sent to all humankind'.[21] The Muslims thus become the eschatological community, the last who shall be first. Strategically appropriating Matthew's parable of the vineyard,[22] a *ḥadīth* makes the claim that

> the likeness of the Muslims to the Jews and Christians is that of a man who hired a company of men to work until nightfall. But they worked only until the middle of the day, saying: 'We have no need of your wage.' So he hired others, saying, 'Complete the remainder of this day, and you shall receive the [full] sum which I set forth.' And they worked until, when it was the time of the afternoon prayer, they said, '[Only] that which we have worked shall be yours.' So he hired a further group, who laboured until the day was done and the sun set, and they received the full wage of the other two groups.[23]

The conclusion must hence be drawn that the founding documents of Islam intend an abrogationist salvation history; as Jane McAuliffe concludes from

18. For instance, Bukhārī, Faḍā'il al-Qur'ān, 3.

19. Islam has an Ebionite reading of the life and message of Christ, and some have even posited a historical link: 'There is no doubt about the indirect dependence of Muhammad on Jewish Christianity. The result of this is a paradox with a truly world-historical dimension; while Jewish Christianity disappeared in the Christian church, by contrast it was preserved in Islam, where it has found a place to our day in some of its directing impulses' (Hans-Joachim Schoeps, cited in P.-A. Bernheim, *James, Brother of Jesus* [London: SCM Press, 1997], p. 269). Bernheim's thesis that the apostolic church was led by James in Jerusalem and continued to practise a form of the *halakha*, rejecting Paul's incarnationism, may well suggest the possibility of a linear influence on Islam to the secular historian (although the proof is entirely lacking), but to the Muslim theologian it supplies confirmation of Qur'ānic Christology.

20. See my paper in this volume, 'Abraham from a Muslim Perspective'.

21. Bukhārī, Tayammum, 1.

22. Matthew 20.1–16.

23. Bukhārī, Mawāqīt, 17.

her own, far more exhaustive survey of the Qur'ānic data, 'In no way, then, does biblical Christianity remain a fully valid "way of salvation" after the advent of Muḥammad.'[24] Honestly interpreted, the texts assume that while other communities are to be tolerated, God's new covenant is emphatically with the people of Islam, as upholders of the final Abrahamic restoration. The Muslim conscience, initially nurtured on this scriptural vision of Islam's place in universal history, was in the generations after the Prophet's death shaped also by the spectacle of the religion's success. It was assumed that the absorption of the great patriarchal cities of Antioch, Alexandria and others into the Muslim world could never have been allowed by a God who did not regard Christianity as obsolete, and the fact of Muslim ascendency was often cited by those who argued against what was taken to be a remnant Christianity. Most impressively of all, Islam now presided over Jerusalem itself, a hegemony contested by the Crusaders, and today by Zionism, but nonetheless, for the great bulk of Muslim history, a tangible and almost sacramental argument for supersession. Muslims could claim the Dome of the Rock, built on the site of Solomon's monumental sanctuary, as the Third Temple, the 'house of prayer for all nations' prophesied by Mark.[25] Whereas Mecca demonstrates Islam's restoration of the Abrahamic narrative, Jerusalem appears as the sign of Islam's affirmation of the Mosaic sub-plot within that narrative and its incorporation within the new religion's ambitious claim to embrace the entire world. These claims are exquisitely symbolized by the Dome's universal architectural character, which links, as does the realm of Islam, East and West: 'The Dome of the Rock is, in fact, the *Sposalizio* or *Nuptials* of the East and West; and nowhere else in the world, not even in St Mark's in Venice, are Orient and Occident indissoluble and one. It is the most sacred and holy building I have ever seen.'[26]

Mediaeval Interpretations

Working with the scriptures, and informed by this triumphalist reading of history, the jurists and *kalām* theologians of mediaeval Islam maintained a consensual view that the earlier versions of faith had now been rendered invalid (*bāṭil*). One representative figure, the thirteenth-century Syrian jurist al-Nawawī, insisted that 'someone who does not believe that whoever follows

24. J. McAuliffe, *Qur'ānic Christians: An Analysis of Classical and Modern Exegesis* (Cambridge: Cambridge University Press, 1991), p. 290.

25. For Islam's understanding of the Rock as the Temple, see A. Elad, 'Why did 'Abd al-Malik Build the Dome of the Rock? A Re-Examination of the Muslim Sources', in J. Raby and J. Johns (eds.), *Bayt al-Maqdis: Abd al-Malik's Jerusalem* (Oxford: Oxford University Press, 1992), pp. 33–58 (49).

26. S. Sitwell, *Arabesque and Honeycomb* (London: R. Hale, 1957), p. 134.

another religion besides Islam is an unbeliever, or doubts that such a person is an unbeliever, or considers their sect to be valid, is himself an unbeliever, even if he manifests Islam and believes in it.'[27]

This straightforward image of the trumping of earlier religions by Islam does not, however, logically require the eternal damnation of all who adhere to them. The theodicy of particularism is resolved by the view that damnation is entailed by wilful rejection, not by ignorance. Given Islam's lack of a doctrine of original sin and its consequent assurance that, in the words of a *ḥadīth*, 'every child is born according to the primordial human disposition [*fiṭra*]',[28] a disposition which when maintained is enough to bring success, Islam assumes that all human beings are innocent until proven otherwise, that sanctity is our natural condition even after the Fall, and that heaven is hence the normative destination for post-Adamic humanity.[29] Guided by this anthropology, most early Muslim theologians regarded the intellect as an autonomous source of moral knowledge, and affirmed the capacity of human minds to reflect upon the general revelation in nature so as to know God and the universals of moral law even in the absence of a specific revelation.[30] Indeed, adherents of the Māturīdī branch of mainstream Sunnī theology held that the unreached are obligated (*mukallaf*) in this respect, and that God will judge them for their response to God even though God has not willed that they should have a detailed revealed law.[31] Because they are 'in the same category as the Muslims, but are excused their ignorance of [Islamic] prophecy and the rulings of the *Sharīʿa*',[32] they may be classed as a functional religious community, for whom heaven or hell are meaningful futures.

The other orthodox school, the Ashʿarite, developed a 'high' view of revelation which denied that the unreached might be under an obligation to know God and the moral law. Nonetheless, most Ashʿarites held that they were still *able* to do so. Individuals who infer the unity and justice of God but are ignorant of revealed law 'have the status of Muslims', and can achieve success in the next world. Those who die in a condition of unbelief (*kufr*) because of a failure to make this deduction may expect neither reward nor punishment, although God may admit them to paradise 'through His sheer grace, not as a reward', just as God does for children who die before maturity.[33]

27. Yaḥyā al-Nawawī, *Rawḍat al-Ṭālibīn* (Beirut: Dār al-Fikr, AH 1412/1991), X, p. 70, cited in N. Keller, *Tariqa Notes* (n.p., 1996), p. 25.

28. Muslim, Qadar, 25.

29. Since Adam's penitent 'turning' was accepted (Qur'ān 2.37).

30. Abu'l-Muʿīn al-Nasafī, *Tabṣirat al-adilla fī uṣūl al-iʿtiqād* (ed. C. Salama; Damascus: al-Maʿhad al-ʿIlmī al-Faransī li'l-dirāsāt al-ʿarabīya fī Dimashq, 1990), p. 473.

31. K. Reinhart, *Before Revelation: The Boundaries of Muslim Moral Thought* (Albany, NY: State University of New York Press, 1995), pp. 45, 48 and 59.

32. ʿAbd al-Qāhir al-Baghdādī, *Uṣūl al-dīn* (Istanbul: Madrasat al-ilāhīyāt bi-dār al-funūn al-Turkīya, 1928), p. 262.

33. Baghdādī, *Uṣūl al-dīn*, p. 263.

For Sunnī theologians of either persuasion, the problem nonetheless persisted of how to define the point at which a new revealed religion could be said to have been communicated. Islamic theology never supplied a clear criterion here, although a range of opinions was ventured. One influential view was that of al-Ghazālī, who despite his broadly Ashʿarite pessimism on natural knowledge, made clear his belief that pre-Qur'ānic communities could still experience *falāḥ* even if they chose to reject Islam, when the new revelation has been inadequately conveyed to them. Ghazālī's importance justifies an extended quotation:

> God's grace encompasses many of the earlier communities, even though most shall be exposed to Hellfire, either lightly – even for a moment, or a while – or for an extended period, so that the term 'cohort of the Fire' may be applied to them.[34] More than this, I hold that most of the Christians of Byzantium and the Turks of this day are, God willing, included in grace. By these I mean the inhabitants of the remoter places of the Byzantine and the Turkish lands, whom the call [to Islam] has not reached. These people are in three categories:
>
> [The first] category are those who never once heard the name of Muḥammad (may God bless him and grant him peace), and who are therefore excused.
>
> [The second] category are those who heard his name and knew his attributes, and the miracles that appeared through him. These are people who live adjacent to the lands of Islam, and who associate with the Muslims. It is they who are the unbelievers ...
>
> There exists a third category between these two degrees. These are people who have been reached by the name of Muḥammad (may God bless him and grant him peace), but who have not heard of his attributes and his nature. Instead, they had heard since childhood that a deceiving liar by the name of Muḥammad claimed prophecy, rather as our own children hear that a liar called al-Muqannaʿ[35] claimed that God had sent him, and deceitfully claimed prophecy. In my view, these [of the third category] are included in the first. For although they had heard his name, they heard of attributes which were the opposite of those he in reality possessed. And this would not arouse any motivation to search.[36]

The teaching of Ghazālī unambiguously holds out the prospect of a 'wider hope'. While the blessing of membership of the community of Muhammad confers maximal opportunities for sound belief and holiness of life, theologians may readily accept that God's grace extends beyond the frontiers of Islam insofar as present-day forms of pre-Muslim belief adhered to by communities unaware of the teachings of Islam authentically conserve monotheistic ideas and the principle of the divine justice. In the case of such communities, the concept

34. Ghazālī was alluding to a well-known *hadīth* which describes how God commands Adam to bring out the 'cohort of the Fire' (*baʿth al-nār*), who include nine hundred and ninety-nine out of every thousand souls (Bukhārī, Riqāq, 46).

35. Al-Muqannaʿ (d. 783 CE) claimed to be an incarnation of God, and raised a bloody revolt in central Asia; a regional folk memory of his foul deeds had presumably persisted until Ghazālī's time.

36. Abū Ḥāmid al-Ghazālī, *Fayṣal al-tafriqa bayn al-Islām wa'l-zandaqa* (ed. Sulaymān Dunyā; Cairo: ʿĪsā al-Bābī al-Ḥalabī, AH 1381/1961), p. 206.

of supersession appears to be little more than theoretical. While theologians should study such religious forms in an attempt to identify genuine survivals of their founders' teachings, and may well conclude that some have survived more authentically than others, they are not in a position to assume that the existence of Islam permits judgements as to the fate of their individual adherents. A prudent agnosticism will here seem indispensable to those who hold that only God knows the criterion for assessing the quality of a person's response to the religious options available in his or her cultural setting.

Conclusion

What kind of soteriology do these discussions produce? It is clear that the theological understanding sketched in the foregoing paragraphs cannot be labelled 'pluralist'. Neither, however, is it 'inclusivist' in the sense intended by many contemporary Christian thinkers. Given Islam's assurance of multiple and equivalently saving interventions in history, there is no need to engage in the patronizing exercise of regarding non-Muslims as 'anonymous Muslims', if we take the term 'Muslim' in the denominational sense. Their submission to God, to the extent that they practice it, is derived not ontologically, that is, 'anonymously' from the work of Muhammad, but epistemologically, from natural theology and from remnant teachings handed down from the founders of their own religions, whose detailed instructions are abrogated or have been mislaid, but whose general teachings of the unity and justice of God may be remembered sufficiently to trigger or to reinforce the inference of God's existence and qualities from the natural order. They are not Muslims; but they are, as the theologians put it, adjudged to be in the same category. The *kalām* has hence never needed to develop intricate theories of prevenient grace or postmortem conversion. Optimism about the powers of natural reason, and the insistence on a cyclical process of propositional revelation the details of which are modulated in each prophetic episode, instead of a single personal revelation which tends to divide history and also geography into categorically different parts, renders the question of the *falāḥ* of the Other a comparatively simple one. Such is the verdict of the *kalām*. Only a fifth of humanity is entirely right; but the God who directs history is still merciful, for entire rightness is not a condition of salvation.

In theologies of the divine action, however, no question seems to find a watertight answer; and no doubt this is as it should be. After all, the transcendent God has the right to veil the divine purposes, even from saints of the rank of Beshr, who would no doubt have taught that it is a poor sort of wisdom that seeks to abolish perplexity altogether.

Pluralism in Jewish, Christian and Muslim Thought

Norman Solomon, Richard Harries and Tim Winter

Historically, Judaism and Islam have found it easier than Christianity to make at least some theological space for the other two religions. In Judaism, this has been made possible first of all by the concept of the Noahide covenant, which originated in the third century CE. This laid upon non-Jews the observance of seven moral imperatives including respect for religion even if not explicit belief in God. Thus, according to the early second-century rabbi Joshua, 'The righteous of all nations have a share in the world to come.' The other way in which historically Judaism has allowed for religious and moral insights in Christianity and Islam is through the idea, associated especially with Maimonides, that the spread of these two religions has helped to prepare the world for the coming of the Messiah. Going beyond any of these views was the twelfth-century Yemenite thinker Netanel Ibn Fayyumi, already referred to in the discussion on Muhammad, who argued from a neo-Platonist position for a series of revelations: 'He sends a prophet to every people according to their language.'[1]

A revealing and dramatic example of a recent similar view, and its reception, is the way in which Britain's chief rabbi was prevailed upon to rewrite certain sections of his book *The Dignity of Difference* to accommodate criticisms from some Orthodox rabbis.[2] Where at first he had written that God reveals truth to Jews, Christians and Muslims, he toned this down in the second edition to the more nuanced, traditional view rooted in the concept of the Noahide covenant, which, while it avoids saying that God reveals truth to non-Jews, does allow for the possibility of them living a righteous life and even establishing a relationship with God in their own terms.

In addition to Maimonides and Netanel, Norman Solomon discusses various nineteenth-century Jewish thinkers, finding them unsatisfactory before setting forth his own position. Solomon argues that all religions include a variety of

1. Quotation from Norman Solomon's paper, 'Pluralism from a Jewish Perspective', above.
2. See R.D. Harries, review of J. Sacks, *The Dignity of Difference*, *Scottish Journal of Theology* 57 (2004), pp. 109–15; cf. J. Gorsky, 'Beyond Inclusivism: Richard Harries, Jonathan Sacks and *The Dignity of Difference*', *Scottish Journal of Theology* 57 (2004), pp. 366–76.

different approaches – prophetic, mystical, legal and so on – as well as a variety of traditions, for example within Judaism, orthodox, reform and liberal; within Christianity, Catholic and Protestant; within Islam, Sunnī and Shīʿa: and that this diversity should be regarded as a sign of spiritual creativity rather than a fault. This could be so, but the question still arises as to whether or not there is a family likeness between the approaches and different traditions within any one religion which can distinguish that religion from another religion, which also has a variety of approaches and traditions. Or, to put it another way, if the approaches and traditions within any one religion are so disparate, can one talk of Judaism, Christianity or Islam at all? It may be, as was suggested at the end of the previous section, that despite the real variety, which certainly needs to be acknowledged, there is a still a commonality which enables one to speak of a particular religion and therefore allow for the possibility of dialogue between religions as well as within them.

Norman Solomon's starting point for inter-religious dialogue is the mutual recognition that we are in different 'places', without any one of those places being specially privileged. The beginning of dialogue is to disclose ourselves to each other and what those places are. We do this as individuals, not as representatives of religious establishments. The discussion that ensues will include acknowledgment of past hurts and a recognition of common problems in the modern world.

This starting-point for dialogue, which at one stroke does away with any sense of spiritual or theological superiority in relation to the other religions, does, however, raise the question of truth. It reflects the postmodernist assumption, which we may find it hard to resist, that there is no bird's-eye view from which we can evaluate the relative truths of different religions. We are embedded in our language, culture and religious tradition, and it is from within that that we have to relate to other religious traditions. There is no vantage-point from which we can survey them all. It would be unfortunate, however, if an acceptance of this starting-point led to an abandonment of the very concept of truth. That it need not is one of the themes of the next essay by Keith Ward.

Ward first of all discusses what he terms soft pluralism, the view that many different religions, and especially the Abrahamic faiths, are genuine responses to the same God, while any one faith can affirm that it is the most adequate of them all. Ward suggests that this is not only compatible with orthodox Christianity but is integral to it, as, for example, we can see from the prologue of John's Gospel, where the Word, before it became flesh, is the light which enlightens everyone.[3] This was the position adopted by the Second Vatican Council and is the one held by most major Protestant denominations today.

In contrast to this, Ward outlines a hard pluralism such as that held by John Hick, for whom all religions are equally valid approaches to God. Ward finds

3. John 1.9.

this position untenable for the simple fact that there are fundamental disagreements between religions, as well as truth in common. For example, many Buddhists would deny that there is an ultimate reality in any sense corresponding to the Jewish, Christian and Muslim understanding of God.

As Norman Solomon suggests, it may not be possible to set out a universally accepted justification of the truth of any one religion compared with the others. Nevertheless, believers within any one religion have reasons for believing their particular religion to be true. Ward accepts this 'epistemic pluralism' but only on the condition that there is a truth, one truth, to be found in the end. He suggests that this approach is compatible with Christianity for a number of reasons: first, because of the importance of respect for the conscientious decisions of other people. Secondly, following Schleiermacher, religious truths are primarily to be seen as symbols and metaphors of a reality that lies beyond all of them. Then there are the further facts that religions, particularly in the modern West, have quite rightly adapted to changing situations and, desiring the good of other people in society as a whole, have taken on board or developed insights which were not fully formed in the early stages of the religion. There is also the necessity of having a critical stance towards all religious authorities and religious traditions. So, a liberal Christian view, which Ward puts forward, places emphasis

> on the fact of the divine infinity, on the weakness and limitedness of human understanding, and on the symbolic and metaphorical nature of much speech about God. In the light of these things, we might expect God to be much greater than any of the thoughts we have about God. So perhaps one religious tradition, however profound, cannot contain all that there is to be known about God, especially if there are great differences in human temperament and circumstance which mean that humans see God from many diverse viewpoints, each of which has its own peculiar limitations.[4]

While many might find this position attractive and while it still holds firm to the concept of a truth to be grasped, others who believe that there is only one fully authentic divine revelation, whether Jews, Christians or Muslims, will find this too tentative. Certainly there are Christians who would say that a decisive choice has to be made for or against Jesus Christ, and Muslims who would say that a decisive choice has to be made to embrace the Qur'ānic disclosure of the divine purpose. Tim Winter's approach is closer to this while at the same time making the maximum space for other religions in accordance with traditional Islamic theology.

Winter points to the respect for the people of the book, Jews and Christians, in the Qur'ān, and the way that Islamic powers have offered them protection. So, from one point of view, Judaism and Christianity are part of the divine revelation which finds its consummation in the final disclosure of the Qur'ān

4. See Keith Ward's paper, 'Pluralism from a Christian Perspective', above.

to the prophet Muhammad. Nevertheless, despite this positive evaluation of these religions, their errors are pointed out by Muslim thinkers and there is a clear conviction that they have been abrogated by the final disclosure. For Muslims, this has been borne out by the historical success of their faith, which has taken hold in what were once Christian lands, an achievement symbolized in the Dome of the Rock, the beautiful mosque in Jerusalem. Muslims can designate the sanctuary in which this mosque stands 'the Third Temple', a title which is itself significant, as it is erected on the site of the Jewish temple.

This does not, however, necessarily mean that Jews who remain Jews, and Christians who remain Christians, lose the hope of ultimate salvation. According to the Māturīdī branch of mainstream Sunnī theology, the unreached are obligated by the universal moral law, which they have a capacity to grasp, and God will judge them for their response even though God has not willed that they should have a detailed revealed law. In a similar way, most Ashʿarites held that individuals who infer the unity and justice of God but are ignorant of revealed law 'have the status of Muslims' and can achieve success in the next world. It is Ghazālī who developed this thought in most detail. According to him, there are three categories of people: those who have had no contact with Islam and therefore cannot be judged by its standards; those who do know Islam, but have not responded to it (these are unbelievers); then there is a third category of people, who have been reached by the name of Muhammad but who have been given a false account of him. In short, they have not rejected true Islam but only a distorted version of it and they will therefore be judged in the same category as those people who never heard of Islam in the first place.

Building on these thinkers, Tim Winter then suggests that categories like 'pluralist' or 'inclusivist' cannot really apply to Islam. Rather, Islam suggests that in addition to the divine revelation there is a knowledge of God's unity and the moral law which can be grasped through the use of human intuition. Those who respond to this are not Muslim, 'but they are, as the theologians put it, adjudged to be in the same category'. In short, 'only a fifth of humanity is entirely right; but the God who directs history is still merciful, for entire rightness is not a condition of salvation'. Questions still remain but, Tim Winter suggests, 'the transcendent God has the right to veil the divine purposes ... it is a poor sort of wisdom that seeks to abolish perplexity altogether'.[5] Muslim thinkers claim that they get the balance right between God's severity and God's mercy within an overall conviction that the departed remain in God's hands.

5. For quotations, see Tim Winter's paper, 'Pluralism from a Muslim Perspective', above.

Chapter 7: Gender

Gender from a Jewish Perspective

Sybil Sheridan

Of the three Abrahamic faiths, Judaism can often appear to be the most problematic concerning the issue of gender. The tradition and religious organization are unashamedly patriarchal, and until recently women had no public voice, were excluded from the mystical tradition, and rarely had the education that could have given them access to the rich literary traditions upon which the faith is based. As for homosexuality, it was never an 'issue' and was simply condemned.

However, the situation changed greatly in the twentieth century. First-wave feminism gave rise to the demand for religious education for women, and that education provided women with a voice and the confidence to research and critique long-held beliefs. Second-wave feminism offered the possibility of changing structures and entering the domain of men. In this paper, we will see how that research has changed how Judaism is viewed, how the Jewish God is viewed, and how those structures have altered to include and involve religious women in both the non-Orthodox and Orthodox worlds. The issue of gay and lesbian Jews has come to the fore much more recently, but it appears to be following a similar pattern: exclusion, education, and the demand for change.

Women in Jewish Commandments

'For three violations women die in childbirth; for failing to attend to the laws of *nidda* [menstrual purity], of *ḥalla* [putting aside a piece of dough from the loaf], and of *hadlakat ha-ner* [lighting the sabbath candles].'[1] This passage from the Mishnah has become the focal text relating to women in Judaism. The three *mitzvot* (commandments) mentioned, are the only ones regarded as primarily the responsibility of women.

The passage, however, while it may appear to be about women, is in fact about men. The law of *ḥalla* derives from Numbers 15.19–21, which demands

1. Mishnah Shabbat 2.6.

that when eating the produce of the land of Israel, a portion should be set aside as *t'ruma* (a free-will offering to God). Thus any person making bread, the baker as well as the housewife, male as well as female, was bound by that law. The laws of *nidda* go back to the Torah where, in the book of Leviticus, a woman is charged to separate herself from her husband and touch no one during her menstrual period.[2] Afterwards, she must immerse herself in flowing water – a *miqveh* or stream – before resuming her normal life. The purpose, in the context of the Torah, was clearly one of ritual purity. No man, having touched a menstruating woman, could participate in temple or tabernacle worship. Thus the law was there for the sake of the men, not for the women. The *mitzvah* of *hadlakat ha-ner* does not come from the Torah. It is cited in the Mishnah,[3] and relates to the lighting of a lamp in the home shortly before sundown on the eve of the sabbath to ensure that there would be light there once the sabbath had started. This also, originally, was not exclusively the women's role. The passage thus effectively demonstrates the androcentric nature of rabbinic Judaism, where women are only discussed in relation to male society. Put in crude terms, women are only really 'there' when it is a matter of sex or cooking.

Two further textual examples demonstrate the exclusion of women from the cultural and spiritual life of the community. 'Whereby do women earn merit? By making their children go to the synagogue to learn Scripture and their husbands to the *bet ha-midrash* [study house] to learn *mishnah*, and waiting for their husbands till they return from the *bet ha-midrash*.'[4] The woman's role here is the archetypal enabler rather than participant in the action. 'All positive commandments that are to be performed at a specific time, men are obligated to fulfil them and women are exempt; but all positive commandments that are not to be performed at a specific time, it is the same for both men and women – they are both obligated to fulfil them.'[5] While the exemption may originally have been meant as a kindness, enabling women to attend to the needs of suckling babies and children, the fact that the time-bound positive commandments included the obligations to study and to perform certain religious rituals in effect meant that women had no place in the synagogue at all.

But nature abhors a vacuum. While it may appear to men that the women did 'nothing' while they were away at the *bet ha-midrash*, the chances are that women were following their own religious path. The problem is that whatever rituals they followed were transmitted orally and therefore have been lost, with only the occasional hint appearing in the texts.[6] The three commandments in

2. Leviticus 15.19–33.
3. Mishnah Shabbat 2.1.
4. Babylonian Talmud, *Berakhot* 17a.
5. Mishnah Qiddushin 1.7.
6. For example, Mishnah Sota 6.1, and other references to witchcraft. Further discussion on this subject can be found in S. Sheridan, 'Discovering Hannah', in S. Sheridan and S. Rothschild (eds.), *Taking up the Timbrel* (London: SCM Press, 2000), pp. 24–30.

our first Mishnah text, however, became the supreme example of women's spirituality. Talked of under the acronym ḤaNaH (*ḥalla*, *nidda* and *hadlakat ha-ner*), they recall the biblical Hannah, who is invoked by men as the supreme example of how to pray.[7] Ironically, therefore, Jewish men emulate a woman in prayer while excluding women from the obligation to pray publicly.

Thus we have it: Judaism as a supremely gendered faith, defined and practised by men, and written down for future generations, with women possibly defining and practising their own version: separate, but not necessarily equal.

The Jewish Image of God

The image of God reflects this masculine dominance of the faith. While God is indeed without form and thus genderless, the Hebrew language is gendered and so it is impossible to describe God without the use of masculine or feminine imagery. In fact, both are employed. God is a mighty warrior in Exodus 15, a 'man of war'.[8] God is also like a mother who cares for her child.[9] God is a king who rules all the earth,[10] but God is also merciful (*El Raḥum,* from the Hebrew word for womb which undeniably feminizes God).[11] Wisdom literature gives us *Ḥokhma* (wisdom) as a hypostatized companion and counterpart to the divine: 'The Lord created me at the beginning of his work, the first of his acts of long ago. Ages ago I was set up, at the first, before the beginning of the earth. When there were no depths I was brought forth, when there were no springs abounding with water. Before the mountains had been shaped, before the hills, I was brought forth.'[12]

Rabbinic Judaism introduces us to the *Shekhina*, the divine and definitely female presence of God. She is the most accessible part of God, the part, according to some legends, who joined Israel in exile and thus became separated from the Godhead only to be reunited at Israel's return, and the coming of the Messiah.[13] The mediaeval mystical tradition took this further, calling this aspect of God (with clear reference to Christian mariology) the *Matronit*. Kabbalistic Judaism described *unio mystica* in sexual terms, yet in a faith which abhorred homosexuality this required one or other partner of the union to appear as female. God was so described in the language already mentioned, but equally the male worshipper could play the female role, subsumed into the generic nation Israel (nations always being feminine in Hebrew). This is what happens

7. 1 Samuel 1.10–17; Babylonian Talmud, *Berakhot* 31a.
8. Exodus 15.3.
9. Isaiah 66.13.
10. Psalm 47.8.
11. Exodus 34.6.
12. Proverbs 8.22–25; see also Wisdom of Solomon 7.24.
13. Babylonian Talmud, *Megilla* 29a. See also H. Freeman, 'Chochmah and Wholeness', in S. Sheridan (ed.), *Hear Our Voice* (London: SCM Press, 1994), pp. 179–89.

in the Song of Songs, used for centuries for mystical meditation and seen as an allegory of God's love for Israel and Israel's love for God. Here, the worshipper becomes the woman of the song, visualizing, describing and seeking the ever-elusive lover that is God:

> My beloved thrust his hand into the opening, and my inmost being yearned for him. I arose to open to my beloved, and my hands dripped with myrrh, my fingers with liquid myrrh, upon the handles of the bolt. I opened to my beloved, but my beloved had turned and was gone. My soul failed me when he spoke. I sought him, but did not find him; I called him, but he gave no answer.[14]

Thus Judaism abounds in female imagery but there seems to be no place for the female. Unlike Christianity and Islam, where women have achieved greatness and great holiness through their religious devotion, in Judaism that was quite simply impossible.

Elements of Independent Spirituality

That is not to say that women have no access to the divine. For many, even today, the supreme spiritual moment comes in the *miqveh* when, having immersed in the waters, they address God in blessing. The laws of *taharat ha-mishpaḥa* (family purity) that surround the *miqveh* ceremony accord women quite some power within the matrimonial relationship. It is the woman who by immersing herself enables the man's return to the conjugal bed. Moreover, the twelve days or so of separation during and after menstruation are days when her husband cannot even touch her. It gives the woman space to be herself, and it forces the man to relate to his wife in ways other than the purely sexual. So it is that currently, many feminists are reclaiming *miqveh* and seeing it not as a misogynist tool to emphasize women's uncleanness, but as a physical expression of a woman's femininity and independence.

Another expression of her independence can be seen in the Jewish woman's prayer life. Absolved and ultimately excluded from statutory prayer, women gain an immense freedom to extemporize and innovate. Modern research is revealing a vast and possibly ancient wealth of literature of Jewish women's prayer down the ages.[15] Fanny Neuda, for example, an Austrian rabbi's wife, published a collection of her own prayers in the late nineteenth century that went through at least twenty-five editions.[16] They include such contemporary

14. Song of Songs 5.4–6.

15. Cf. for example, C. Weissler, 'The Traditional Piety of Ashkenazic Women', in A. Green (ed.), *Jewish Spirituality from the Sixteenth Century Revival to the Present* (Los Angeles, CA: Crossroads Press, 1987), pp. 245–75; N. Beth Cardin, *Out of the Depths I Call to You: A Book of Prayers for the Married Jewish Woman* (Northvale, NJ: Jacob Aaronson, 1992); and M. Klein, *A Time to be Born* (Philadelphia, PA: Jewish Publication Society, 2000).

16. F. Neuda, *Stunden der Andacht*, first published in Prague by Wolf Pascheles in 1879.

invocations as prayers on behalf of a son conscripted into the army, prayers on adopting a child, and prayers for a woman in an unhappy marriage.

Neuda, as the wife of a respected rabbi, was accorded quite some respect herself. Research has yet to be done on the role of the rabbi's wife as para-rabbi, but we do see, at the beginning of the twentieth century, the emergence of Jewish women as leaders of social and religious movements, equipped by the campaigns of the nineteenth century to improve the education of Jewish girls. Hannah Solomon, for example, was invited to represent Jewish women at one of the conferences accompanying the World Parliament of Religions in 1894,[17] and founded the Jewish Women's Congress in the United States. Bertha Pappenheim (1856–1939) founded the Judische Frauenbund in Germany, and a series of orphanages and schools. Lily Montagu formed the Jewish Religious Union (later to become Liberal Judaism in 1902). She started her own synagogue and founded the World Union of Progressive Jews, a major international body, in 1928.

One of the fundamentals of Reform Judaism is that men and women are equal in the sight of God. As far back as 1842, the Revd. D.W. Marks had proclaimed,

> Woman, created by God as a 'help meet for man' and in every way his equal; woman, endowed by the same parental care as man, with wondrous perceptions, that she might participate (as it may be inferred from Holy Writ that she was intended to participate) in the full discharge of every moral and religious obligation, has been degraded below her proper station. That power of exercising those exalted virtues that appertain to her sex has been withheld from her; and since equality has been denied to her in other things, as a natural consequence it has not been permitted to her in the duties and delights of religion. It is true that education has done much to remedy this injustice in other respects; yet does memory live in the indifference manifested for the religious instruction of females.[18]

The question of women's ordination to the rabbinate was first raised in the 1880s,[19] though it took nearly fifty years for the first woman to be ordained.[20] Today, among Liberal, Reform and American Conservatives, it is commonplace.

Women in Orthodox Judaism

Jewish feminism has long been divided into two camps. The demand for equality within the religious sphere is one of them, but as women in the progressive movements accepted their place as equals, a new question arose: are women any

17. Internal arguments about the inclusion of women meant, however, that in the end she did not in fact take part.

18. D.W. Marks, *Sermons Preached on Various Occasions* (London: Groombridge & Sons, 1851), p. 18.

19. P.S. Nadell, *Women who would be Rabbis* (Boston, MA: Beacon Press, 1998).

20. Regina Jonas in Berlin in 1934. Cf. E. Klaphek, introduction to Fraülein Rabbiner Jonas, *Kann die Frau das rabbinische Amt bekleiden?* (Teetz: Hentrich and Hentrich, 1999), pp. 15–86.

more religiously fulfilled than they had been before? Does this 'male-formed religion' actually meet the needs of a woman's spirituality? Many women who have become rabbis have not been content simply to follow the rules. They ask different questions when interpreting texts and define different priorities in the ministry. But the other route of Jewish feminists, in which women seek their own individual and specifically feminine spirituality, may ultimately prove the more successful. It is also one that cuts across the religious divide and enables Orthodox and non-Orthodox women to work together more easily. As well as reclaiming *miqveh* and creating new liturgy, there is *Rosh Chodesh*, the festival of the new moon, long dropped from the Jewish cycle, but one associated in rabbinic and mediaeval times as a holiday specifically for women. Today, women meet together in *Rosh Chodesh* groups to study and explore their Judaism without the filter of men's interpretation. The fact that many of these groups are cross-denominational suggests that the religious divisions are simply another male construct and also raises the possibility that Orthodoxy's strict division between the sexes enables women to explore their own religious identities more easily. Women's prayer groups and study groups are popular, led by women who in many ways function as rabbis.

On the face of it, in Orthodoxy, women do appear to have a rough deal. They have little say in the running of their communities and separation in synagogue worship usually results in complete segregation: a *meḥitsa*, or divider, between the sexes has the effect of cutting off women from the scene of religious action. Yet the education of women in the traditionally male texts of Talmud and *halakha* has had a revolutionary effect here also. Some of the greatest teachers in the Orthodox world today are women, and in the synagogue, where once, women would accept a rabbi's dictum 'It is forbidden', they are today more likely to ask, 'Where is it written?' This puts the onus on the rabbi to argue his case properly and convincingly and changes have resulted where what were once perceived to be God-given injunctions have proved to be simply the force of habit.[21]

To all appearances, Orthodox women cannot become rabbis. The formula recited at the point of *semikha* (the laying on of hands symbolizing the passing on of the tradition) authorizes the candidate to teach and to judge – the two prime activities of a rabbi. While teaching does not pose a problem, the question arises as to whether or not she is qualified to judge in matters of religious law where she herself is not obligated. Nevertheless, some women have been ordained as Orthodox rabbis. This has been by private *semikha*, the rabbi and teacher of the individual showing his satisfaction that the woman has gained sufficient knowledge to act as judge and teacher. Such *semikha* is not generally recognized; nevertheless, a precedent has been set, and as the number of these women grows, recognition may come.

21. An example of this is *Kaddish*, the mourners' prayer. It was assumed to be forbidden to women till their persistence resulted in research which showed that this was not the case. Many Orthodox communities now make provision for women to say *Kaddish* either alongside or in addition to the men.

But there is another and perhaps more profound way in which the Orthodox woman's role is changing. One of the greatest injustices relating to Jewish women is the situation of the woman whose husband refuses to grant her a religious divorce (the *get*). Jewish law requires that the man give it, and the woman receive it. But in this day of civil divorce, it is necessary for a couple to be divorced according to the law of the land first. This is a situation ripe for blackmail. A man who is divorced civilly can refuse his wife a *get* out of spite or malice, or sheer inertia. This prevents her from marrying again in a religious ceremony. She is in effect an *aguna* (a chained woman). Should she remarry in a civil ceremony, any subsequent children will be declared the children of an adulterous union and therefore illegitimate, with grave consequences for their status in the community. Should he remarry, the same rule does not apply since rabbinic Judaism recognized the polygamy of our biblical ancestors. The great rabbinic minds of our age seem unable to find a solution to this problem. Instead, in Israel, the rabbinic court sees women on a case-by-case basis and hopes to alleviate the misery of some, but by no means all of them, by finding grounds for annulment. In the last few years, the rabbinate has trained a few specially selected women in the intricate details of divorce law in order that they may act as advocates for the women, who, coming from a deeply religious background, may not feel happy to relate the intimate details of their marriages to the male rabbis who take on their cases. The experiment has been a great success and it is possible that as these advocates gain in confidence, they will see their way to interpret, as well as simply follow, the law. This would indeed be fulfilling a truly rabbinic function but within a structure that is exclusively theirs.

The process may be slow, but it is happening. Orthodox women may well find a place and a voice within the male establishment while retaining the uniquely female aspects of their religious practice. If so, they could have the edge over their Liberal and Reform sisters, who have yet to find a way of integrating specifically women's needs with the overarching principle of equality.

Homosexuality

Similar challenges face the gay and lesbian community and a similar process seems to be developing. Thirty years ago, it was possible for a leading rabbi to announce, 'There is no such thing as a Jewish homosexual.' Today, few would make such a statement, even if a majority would consider such practices to be wilful sin rather than a basic orientation. The Levitical injunction appears unequivocal,[22] yet study of the text offers many differing interpretations relating to context and intent. The ambiguity of Genesis 1.27 offers the possibility that homosexuality is indeed God's creation and God's will, while stories of David and Jonathan, and Ruth and Naomi, provide role models for gay and lesbian couples.

22. Leviticus 18.22.

While education is happening, the ensuing changes have yet to take effect. Within the progressive movements, gay and lesbian Jews have been welcomed simply as Jews. However, the question of gay commitment ceremonies is contentious and, while permissible, they remain a matter of conscience for individual rabbis. Within Orthodoxy, a small but vocal movement has arisen. A film released four years ago has had an impact in opening the debate in modern Orthodox circles.[23] It shows starkly the struggle of committed Orthodox Jews, who hold a great and sincere love for a religion that rejects them for who they are.

Comparisons have been made between gay rights and the women's movement, but the issue of homosexuality within Judaism does have strong differences. While the two movements share the goal of changing perceptions, there is no need for gays and lesbians, as there is for women, to change religious structures to be accommodated: the male homosexual is obligated in all aspects of masculine Judaism, the lesbian in all female ones. But social structures are another matter. The issue brings to the fore one of the great strengths – or perhaps weaknesses – in Judaism today, its focus on family life. As people marry late, or not at all, as people have fewer children or none at all, Judaism will need to focus more on the single person and on other lifestyle choices if it is to retain the devotion of many of its adherents.

A Midrash to Leviticus 18.5 gives us insight: 'I call heaven and earth to witness that whether one be a gentile or an Israelite, a man or a woman, a slave or a handmaid, according to their deeds will the divine *Shekhina* rest upon them.'[24]

23. *Trembling before G-d*, dir. S.S. Dubowski (2001).
24. Sifra 89a.

Gender from a Christian Perspective

Marcus Braybrooke

The subject of gender and sexuality in Christianity is, as John Macquarrie has said, 'dynamite'.[1] He quotes Linda Woodhead, who has written about 'woman/femininity' in *The Oxford Companion to Christian Thought*, as saying that 'what is needed is fresh and creative reflection on the mystery of human sexual difference which is as responsibly related to the Christian tradition as it is to contemporary concerns'.

Three main areas of such reflection are discussed here. First, it is asked whether the language used of God, which has in the past been almost entirely male, could include the female. Secondly, traditional Christian attitudes to sexuality are described and the development of a more positive attitude to sexuality is noted. Thirdly, the various aspects of what has been called 'the sexual revolution' are identified. This has led some Christians to look anew at the teaching and example of Jesus and Paul, to reconsider Christian teaching about premarital and extramarital sex and homosexuality, and to support the ordination of women to the priesthood.

Critics accuse the Christian Church of being one of the last bastions of male dominance, of seeking to preserve outmoded sexual mores and of regarding sexual pleasure as, if not actually sinful, at least an impediment to a holy life. Friedrich Nietzsche said that 'Christianity gave Eros poison to drink. He did not die from it but he did degenerate into a vice.'[2]

Changes, however, are taking place. The two-thousand-year-old link of sex with procreation has been broken and sexual pleasure is celebrated and seen as reflecting the image of God in human nature. Some churches are now willing to ordain women as priests and have adopted inclusive language. Attitudes to divorce, extramarital sex and homosexuality have become more permissive – thereby attracting criticism from more conservative Christians.

1. J. Macquarrie, review of A. Hastings, A. Mason and H. Pyper (eds.), *The Oxford Companion to Christian Thought*, *Church Times*, 29 December 2000, p. 15.
2. F. Nietzsche, *Beyond Good and Evil* (Munich: de Gruyter, 1968), V, p. 102.

The Language Used of God

The Christian Church is frequently criticized today for the masculine nature of the language it has used of God. It is claimed that the Church has thereby reflected and reinforced a patriarchal society which has shut out female forms of self-representation and has seen women in terms of male desire. For example, Luce Irigaray, a French feminist psychoanalytical philosopher with a deep interest in Catholicism, has written, 'Monotheistic religions speak to us of God the Father and God made man; nothing is said of a God the Mother or of God made woman or even of God as a couple or couples ... Not all the quibbling over maternity and neutrality (neuterness) of God can succeed in erasing the one reality that determines identities, rights, symbols and discourse.'[3] Although in Christian thought God is beyond gender, the Christian Trinitarian picture of God can seem masculine: Jesus the '*Son* of God' took human form as a *male*, and the most common way for Christians to address God is as 'Father'.

Christians speak of God as one God in three persons: Father, Son and Holy Spirit. Occasionally, the Holy Spirit, like Wisdom in the book of Proverbs,[4] has been spoken of as feminine, as for example in Syrian Christianity prior to the fourth century.[5] This, however, has not been the dominant tradition, and many hymns to the Holy Spirit are not gender-specific. It could be said that the neglect of the Spirit in much Christian theology parallels the neglect of the feminine. Although the three persons of the Trinity are co-equal, talk of the Father begetting the Son and of the Spirit proceeding from the Father and, in the Western tradition, from the Son, may suggest that the Godhead resides principally in the Father – the sole monarch who is never co-dependent or co-related until he so chooses and who seems all too like a Byzantine emperor.[6]

Again, when God took human flesh in the person of Jesus of Nazareth, he was incarnate in a male body. For Irigaray, therefore, the incarnation in Jesus is only partial. For women to be redeemed, God needs also to be incarnate in a female body.[7] Jesus is for her not the only incarnation of God. But is the masculinity of Jesus more important than his humanity? Is there not 'masculinity' and 'femininity' in every person and is not undue emphasis being placed on anatomical differences? For example, I find Margaret Argyle's woven tapestry, *Bosnia Christa* (1993), in which the naked figure of Jesus on the cross is female – in identification with the women of Bosnia who had been raped –

3. L. Irigaray, 'Equal to Whom?', in G.J. Ward (ed.), *The Post-Modern God* (Oxford: Blackwell, 1997), pp. 198–213 (209).

4. Proverbs 8.1.

5. See G. D'Costa, *Sexing the Trinity* (London: SCM Press, 2000). He refers to S.A. Harvey, 'Feminine Imagery for the Divine: The Holy Spirit, the Odes of Solomon and the Early Syriac Tradition', *St. Vladimir's Theological Quarterly* 37.2–3 (1993), pp. 111–39.

6. See D'Costa, *Sexing the Trinity*, pp. 16–20. He refers to T.G. Weinandy, *The Father's Spirit of Sonship: Reconceiving the Trinity* (Edinburgh: T&T Clark, 1995).

7. Irigaray, 'Equal to Whom?', p. 207.

illuminating rather than shocking. Yet, I am conscious that I write as a male who remains, albeit at times uneasily, a priest of the established Church of England, and I have not experienced the pain and alienation of many women who feel rejected by a male religion.

A further complaint is that Christians are in the habit of addressing God as 'our Father'. Interestingly, the use of the term 'Father' for God is not common in the Hebrew Bible and only occurs about twenty times. God, as Paul Ricoeur points out, is not designated as Father in relation to the creation of the world.[8] The Hebrew Bible was clear that the world is not an emanation from the divine, and sexual imagery is avoided in accounts of the origins of the world – unlike much of the mythology of the ancient Near East. Compared to other ancient gods, the God of the Old Testament does not have a female consort and God's masculinity refers to power and authority rather than to procreation. The Old Testament reflects the struggle between the worshippers of Yahweh – originally a nomadic people – and the Canaanites, who as tillers of the soil were devotees of Baal, a goddess of fertility. Indeed, some Christians are still uneasy with the phrase 'Mother Earth'.

Israel, God's chosen people, is spoken of as a son and in this context God is called Father, but Israel is also called a daughter.[9] It is the prophets Hosea,[10] Jeremiah and Third Isaiah who speak of God as Father, often with reference to the future and a 'new creation'. In the New Testament, use of the word 'Father', which was also used by the Pharisees, is common. It is to be found more than one hundred times in John's Gospel and forty-two times in Matthew's. This probably reflects Jesus' own use of the term *Abba*, or Father, for God. Wolfhart Pannenberg even says that 'On the lips of Jesus, "Father" becomes a proper name for God.'[11]

To many Christians, speaking of God as 'Father', despite Ricoeur, says something about God as creator and our dependence on God for the gift of life and for our sustenance. The use of 'Mother' would be equally appropriate. Oliver Quick saw in the language of 'Father' a way of highlighting God's nature as *agapē* or self-giving love.[12] But the images of father and especially king may suggest control and punishment and perhaps abuse. The language has reinforced male dominance in church life. Even though the term 'Father' was sanctified by Jesus, I see no reason why God should not be addressed as Mother or 'Mother/Father God'. Archbishop Anselm wrote a prayer which

8. P. Ricoeur, 'Fatherhood: From Phantasm to Symbol', in D. Ihde (ed.), *The Conflict of Interpretations: Essays in Hermeneutics* (Evanston, IL: Northwestern University Press, 1974), pp. 468–97 (486).

9. Psalm 45.10.

10. Some writers think that the picture of God in Hosea 11 is of God as a mother caring for her child. See, for example, K. Keay (ed.), *Laughter, Silence and Shouting: An Anthology of Women's Prayers* (London: HarperCollins, 1994), p. 26.

11. W. Pannenberg, *Systematic Theology* (Edinburgh: T&T Clark, 1991), I, p. 262.

12. O.C. Quick, *Doctrines of the Creed* (London: James Nisbet, 1938, Fontana edn 1963), pp. 59–68.

begins, 'Jesus, as a mother you gather your people to you.'[13] Perhaps in addressing the divine, we might use non-gender-specific terms such as 'the Holy One' or 'God our Parent'? Psalm 18 speaks of God as 'my Rock' and 'my Shield'. The new Church of England service book, *Common Worship*, continues to address God as 'Father' although one of the eucharistic prayers compares God's love to a mother's tender care:

> How wonderful the work of your hands, O Lord.
> As a mother tenderly gathers her children,
> you embraced a people as your own.
> When they turned away and rebelled
> your love remained steadfast.[14]

New insights relate not only to gender in our language about God but also to our understanding of God's nature. If sexuality is part of the image of God in human beings, it is appropriate to speak of God as a 'cosmic lover'. Equally, human beings were made to be 'lovers', because that was what the image was an image of.[15] Moreover, as Adrian Thatcher says, nowadays it is common to find theologians saying that the image of God in humankind is a Trinitarian one. 'God is love, "calls us to love"; is a communion of love.'[16]

The feminine is most evident in the high place that the Virgin Mary has occupied in Catholic and Orthodox devotion. Mary is seldom mentioned by the earliest Church fathers (not mothers), except in contrast to Eve. Mariology (devotion to Mary) probably owed much of its growth to the widespread opinion in the early and mediaeval Church that celibacy and virginity were superior to the married state, and also to the increasing removal of Jesus from the human level. The tradition of Mary's perpetual virginity (that she remained a virgin after giving birth to Jesus) became established and, rather later, the doctrine of the immaculate conception, according to which Mary was without stain of original sin from the moment that she was conceived. By the fifth century, especially in the Eastern Church, Mary was spoken of as 'theotokos' or Mother of God. The doctrine of her bodily assumption into heaven was first formulated by Gregory of Tours (d. 594) and was defined as Catholic doctrine in 1950.

As Christ became more austere and remote in Christian worship, Mary became the representative of humanity in heaven and the focus of popular piety.

13. Quoted in M.C.R. Braybrooke (ed.), *1,000 World Prayers* (Alresford: John Hunt Publishing, 2002), p. 68. See further M. Furlong (ed.), *Women Pray* (Woodstock, VT: Skylight Paths Publishing, 2001), and Keay (ed.), *Laughter, Silence and Shouting*.

14. *Common Worship: Services and Prayers for the Church of England* (London: Church House Publishing, 2000), p. 201. See also J. Morley and H. Ward (eds.), *Celebrating Women* (London: SPCK, 1995).

15. These terms were particularly used by the process theologian Norman Pittenger.

16. A. Thatcher, 'Intimate Relationships and the Christian Way', *Modern Believing* 44.1 (2003), pp. 5–14 (6).

Eventually, she became known in the Western Church as 'mediator of all graces' and 'co-redemptress', although this title has not been officially approved. Gavin D' Costa, in his book *Sexing the Trinity*, argues that the doctrine of Mary as 'co-redeemer' (his term) should be developed to include all Christians in the Marian community who bring the work of redemption to its completion.[17] Leonardo Boff, a Brazilian liberation theologian, even suggests that the Holy Spirit (feminine) is incarnated in Mary, whom, he says, should be seen as divine.[18]

At the Reformation, there was a strong reaction against Marian devotion, and hostility to mariolatry persists in much of the Protestant Church, although the Ecumenical Society of the Blessed Virgin Mary was founded in 1967. Some theologians, influenced by Carl Jung (1875–1961), see Mary as a valued way of expressing a feminine element in God, although some feminist writers see Mary as a model of harmless feminine passivity created by a male-dominated Church.[19]

Attitudes to Sexuality

In terms of Christian attitudes to human sexuality, there has been an uneasy tension between the Hebrew influence which accepts human sexuality, rightly used, as good and a gift of God in creation, and a Hellenistic dualism which saw the body, with its appetites, ensnaring the soul. Plato, for example, wrote that 'purification ... consists in separating the soul as much as possible from all contact with the body'.[20] This attitude was adopted by the Church. As Mark Jordan puts it, 'The original Christian ideal for sex was of a new life beyond it – of a life in which there had never been sexual relations or in which sexual relations had been renounced.'[21] In reaction to the sexual laxity of the times, later Greek philosophers often proclaimed an asceticism, which involved mortification of the flesh. This was also practised by the desert fathers. Celibacy became the ideal. Monks and nuns took a vow of chastity – even if it was not always observed. Clergy, too, were required to be celibate, as is still the case today for Catholic priests.

This attitude was reinforced by the spread of Gnostic and Manichaean ideas. Augustine of Hippo was much influenced by the latter. Augustine also held that Adam's sin – original sin – was transmitted from parent to child through 'concupiscence', that is, the sinful excitement which accompanies procreation.

17. D'Costa, *Sexing the Trinity*. Although I am not persuaded by D'Costa's main argument, I am much indebted to the wealth of scholarship that his book contains.

18. L. Boff, *Trinity and Society* (trans. P. Burns; London: Burns & Oates, 1988), pp. 210–11.

19. Some of this information is taken from J.W. Bowker (ed.), *The Oxford Dictionary of World Religions* (Oxford: Oxford University Press, 1997), p. 624.

20. Plato, *Phaedo*, section 66 (trans. H. Tredennick; London: Penguin, 1954), p. 86.

21. M.D. Jordan, *The Ethics of Sex* (Oxford: Blackwell, 2002), p. 47.

The human race thus became a 'lump of sin', *massa damnata*, shown for example in the practice of including an exorcism in the baptism of new-born babies. Augustine's views were never fully accepted. According to present-day Catholic teaching, original sin is the loss of sanctifying grace, as a result of which humans experience concupiscence. Luther and Calvin, if anything, were more pessimistic about human nature than Catholic teaching. Liberal theologians, on the other hand, if they speak of original sin, see it as a recognition that throughout human history, people have been under the influence of a bias toward evil and, prior to any responsible act of choice on their part, lack full communion with God.[22]

Traditional teaching about sin has produced a legacy which suggests a fear of human sexuality and of the body – unmarried male confessors forbidding masturbation, fellatio, coitus from behind, anal coitus and coitus during menstruation. Moreover, sexual intercourse and bodily emissions were sometimes seen as rendering a person ritually impure. Women were often seen, like Eve, as tempting men to turn away from the spiritual path and to enjoy the pleasures of the flesh. Women were encouraged by religious teachers to be submissive and to serve the needs of men. The relation of the soul, always feminine, to Christ, the bridegroom, was often spoken of in the language of romance. The Song of Songs was a popular book for mediaeval sermons, while physical sexual imagery was used to describe mystical rapture.[23] Courtly love, of which the troubadours sang, separated love from marriage and celebrated sexual pleasure. These views, however, were condemned at the Second Lateran Council in 1139. Mark Jordan wonders whether some mediaeval heretics unabashedly affirmed the goodness of sex.[24]

Gradually, some Christian writers began to affirm that sexual intercourse was not merely 'a remedy for sin' but was good in itself, apart from procreation. Francis of Sales, in his *Introduction to the Devout Life*, wrote, 'Marital intercourse is certainly holy, lawful and praiseworthy in itself and profitable to society.' 'Love,' he added, 'wedded to fidelity gives birth to a confident intimacy.'[25] Jeremy Taylor, in his *Rule and Exercises of Holy Living* and in *Ductor Dubitantium*, discussed the pleasures of sexual intercourse, which include lightening and easing the cares and sadness of household business and endearing the couple each to the other. Sherwin Bailey, an Anglican scholar, some forty years ago, said that this was probably the first overt theological recognition of the relational aspects of coitus.[26]

22. See *Doctrine in the Church of England: A Report Published in 1938* (London: SPCK, 1957), pp. 60–64.

23. See G. Parrinder, *Sex in the World Religions* (London: Sheldon Press, 1980), p. 218.

24. Jordan, *Ethics of Sex*, p. 71.

25. F. De Sales, *Introduction to the Devout Life* (London: Darton, Longman & Todd, 2001), p. 25.

26. D.S. Bailey, *The Man-Woman Relationship in Christian Thought* (London: Longmans, 1959), quoted in J. Dominian, *Let's Make Love: The Meaning of Sexual Intercourse* (London: Darton, Longman & Todd, 2001), p. 8.

The Sexual Revolution

In the last forty years, dramatic changes have been taking place in Christian attitudes to sexuality. In part, these reflect the changes in society. Sigmund Freud (1856–1939) showed that sexuality is an essential component of human personality. Havelock Ellis (1859–1939) challenged the Victorian suppression of sexuality. In 1886, Kraft-Ebing (1840–1902) wrote *Psychopathis Sexualis* which is still an essential text about abnormal sexuality. The Dutch gynaecologist, Theodoor Hendrik van de Velde (1873–1937), in his *Ideal Marriage*, informed many couples about sexuality in marriage. More recently, Alfred Charles Kinsey (1895–1956) astonished Americans with his statistical studies on male and female sexuality. Then in 1966, Masters and Johnson clarified the inner world of the orgasm in their book *Human Sexual Response*.

Moreover, from the sixties onwards, reliable contraceptives became more widely available. This created, in Jack Dominian's words, 'a permanent transformation in sexual behaviour'.[27] Coitus could be separated from procreation. In Mark Jordan's words, 'effective contraception separates sexual pleasure from reproduction for heterosexuals in a way that biology has always separated it for homosexuals'.[28] Increasingly, women asserted their full place in society and refused to accept a subordinate role on the basis of physical differentiation. In the West, many sexual taboos disappeared and sex was freely discussed. At the same time, pornographic literature increased and the advertising and entertainment industries trivialized sex.

These changes have dramatically affected the context in which Christians think about sexual behaviour.[29] Underlying the debate about particular issues is the bigger question of whether Christian teaching is, as some believers think, unchangeable, or whether, as others hold, it can be modified in the light of new knowledge, especially in this case about human sexuality. This also reflects different attitudes to the authority of scripture. Mark Jordan also emphasizes the significance for the Church of its loss of control in this area. Increasingly, the state took on responsibility for population control, healthy reproduction and eugenics. What Foucault called 'bio-power' passed to secular authorities from the Churches which, in some countries, had continued to exercise sexual surveillance and marriage control into the twentieth century.[30]

In Christian discussion, new voices began to be heard, including those of gay and lesbian people, as well as voices from outside Europe. In Christian thinking,

27. Dominian, *Let's Make Love*, p. 34.

28. Jordan, *Ethics of Sex*, p. 141.

29. Examples of writing which takes the new context seriously are K.T. Kelly, *New Directions in Sexual Ethics* (London: Chapman, 1998); G. Moore, 'Sex, Sexuality and Relationships', in B. Hoose (ed.), *Christian Ethics* (London: Cassell, 1998), pp. 223–47; and E. Stuart and A. Thatcher, *People of Passion* (London: Mowbray, 1997).

30. Jordan, *Ethics of Sex*, pp. 133–34.

procreation ceased to be seen as the primary purpose of sexual intercourse,[31] and Christians began to see sexual pleasure as God-given and in part a reflection of the divine image. Pope John Paul II, in his *The Theology of the Body*, described the created readiness of the male and female bodies for sexual intercourse. 'In sexual self-donation the couple indeed speak a "language of the body", expressing in a manner far more profound than words, the totality of the gift of each other.'[32] The Anglican statement *Marriage and the Church's Task* says,

> the polyphony of love finds expression in the lovers' bodily union. This is not to be comprehended simply in terms of two individuals' experience of ecstatic pleasure. Such it certainly may be, but it is always more. It is an act of personal commitment that spans past, present and future. It is celebration, healing, renewed pledge and promise ... Above all, it communicates the affirmation of mutual belonging.[33]

The Methodist report *A Christian Understanding of Human Sexuality* says, 'Sexual love, including genital acts when they express love, shares in the divine act of loving with every human activity which is creative, dedicated and generous.'[34] Jack Dominian speaks of the home as a domestic church. In sexual intercourse, the couple 'enter the very heart of the Trinity. Through sexual intercourse they enter a recurrent act of love through which the love of God joins their human experience of love. As embodied people, they live the very centrality of the incarnation in the love of their bodies.'[35]

In the light of this new and positive valuing of human sexuality, some Christians are looking again at the scriptural authorities and at traditional moral discipline. In particular, many writers now stress the Hebraic roots of the faith, with its valuing of the body, and in affirming the equality and full dignity of women, they look to the example of Jesus. Although Jesus lived in a patriarchal society governed by androcentric language, and his choice of twelve male disciples as representatives of the new Israel fitted these conventions, women play a surprisingly large part in the narrative of his ministry and, in his preaching, he used images drawn from the lives of women. Jesus healed numerous women, including Mary of Magdala, the daughter of the Syro-Phoenician woman and, defying purity laws, the woman with an issue of blood. Some women travelled with him during his ministry, and Jesus defended both the woman who anointed him with a very expensive perfume, and the

31. The Second Vatican Council dropped the terms 'primary' and 'secondary' ends for marriage; see Dominian, *Let's Make Love*, p. 37.

32. John Paul II, *The Theology of the Body* (London: Daughters of St. Paul, 1994), quoted in Dominian, *Let's Make Love*, p. 5.

33. *Marriage and the Church's Task* (London: CIO Publishing, 1978), quoted in Dominian, *Let's Make Love*, p. 37.

34. *A Christian Understanding of Human Sexuality* (London: Methodist Publishing House, 1990), article 28, quoted in Dominian, *Let's Make Love*, p. 37.

35. Dominian, *Let's Make Love*, p. 174. See also Thatcher, 'Intimate Relationships', pp. 12–13.

woman taken in the act of adultery.[36] He spoke of women grinding grain together, of a woman searching for a lost coin, and of prostitutes entering the kingdom of heaven before the religious elite.[37] Jesus' empathy for women seems typical of his sensitivity to others especially to those marginalized by society, but should not be used to draw a false contrast between Jesus and his Jewish contemporaries.[38]

In his teaching, Jesus, who it is generally assumed was unmarried, affirmed the place of marriage in God's purposes in creation. 'From the beginning of creation, "God made them male and female." "For this reason a man shall leave his father and mother and be joined to his wife, and the two shall become one flesh." So they are no longer two but one flesh.'[39] This is a strong affirmation of marriage and of sexual union as expressing and effecting the most intimate union of husband and wife. Indeed, the physical union may be spoken of as sacramental – the bodily union strengthening the spiritual union of marriage partners. Jesus, in his emphasis on love, also dignified marriage and Christians have come to see the love of a couple for each other as the primary reason for marriage – it is more than a contract or an arrangement between families.

Paul echoed Jesus' words about marriage and urged husbands to love their wives 'just as Christ loved the church and gave himself up for her, in order to make her holy'.[40] He expected a wife to submit to her husband, but also said that distinctions of Jew and Greek, slave and free, and male and female had been transcended in Christ.[41] His more negative statements may be coloured by his expectation of the imminent return of Jesus, because he was not himself married and because he was conditioned by the culture of his time.

The Church has traditionally opposed sexual intercourse outside marriage. This opposition is partly the legacy of mediaeval fears of human sexuality and also the treating of women as if they were the property of men; but now, extramarital sex is usually seen as a threat to relationships. Modern Christian writers, as Mark Jordan has said, see adultery 'as a sin … against unity, against honesty, against continence'.[42] Dominian rejects attempts to judge who is the 'innocent' and who the 'guilty' party. 'We are all wounded people who often let each other down … Jesus, who knew the heart of humanity, did not condemn.'[43] Dominian, however, makes clear the destructive effect of unfaithfulness. Sexual intercourse affirms identity and a mutual feeling of uniqueness.

36. Luke 8.2–3; Mark 14.3; and John 7.53–8.11.
37. Luke 17.35; Luke 15.8–10; and Matthew 21.31.
38. This is a point made in G. Theissen and A. Metz, *The Historical Jesus* (London: SCM Press, 1988), p. 221. My discussion of Jesus' attitude to women is largely based on pp. 219–25 of this book.
39. Mark 10.6–8, citing Genesis 1.27 and 2.24.
40. Ephesians 5.25–26.
41. Galatians 3.28.
42. Jordan, *Ethics of Sex*, p. 127.
43. Dominian, *Let's Make Love*, p. 114.

When it is 'discovered that this unique message has been conveyed to someone else, there is a massive sense of being let down'.[44]

The attitude of Christians toward premarital sex, like that of society at large, is changing. A number of teenagers have experimental relationships, but although they have the biological and physical capacity to have sex, few have the maturity for real love, which is different from infatuation and physical attraction. Too easily, the physical aspects of sex are emphasized at the expense of loving relationships. Cohabitation, however, is different, especially if it leads to a permanent relationship. Cohabitation may be an exclusive, committed and enduring relationship and has many of the characteristics of marriage.[45]

Casual sexuality undermines the high value of bodily union, which involves the whole person. Physical self-giving should promote a total self-giving, the union of love. The Church affirms a high ideal – marriage indeed is said to point to Christ's union with the Church or the soul. Several contemporary writers put the emphasis on the quality of a relationship rather than its legal status. The Argentinian scholar Marcella Althaus-Reid, in what she calls 'indecent theology', is perhaps the sharpest critic of legalistic views of marriage. These, she says, discourage intimate friendship. 'Adultery may not be a divine commandment but, in a real sense, intimacy with others has a divine nature.'[46]

The balance between legal considerations and an emphasis on relationship is particularly acute in attitudes to divorce. Further, should Jesus' answer to a question about divorce – reported differently in Matthew and Mark[47] – be binding on church attitudes to divorce today? While maintaining the Christian ideal of marriage as a life-long union, I have been willing, as the Church of England now allows in certain circumstances, to officiate at the marriage of persons who are divorced, as I believe this can witness to the gospel of forgiveness, and certainly some such marriages seem to have been richly blessed.[48] Another question is whether a homosexual relationship has the marks of a marriage. Clearly a homosexual partnership is not open to procreation, but neither are heterosexual marriages which take place when a woman is too old to have children. If sexual pleasure is a God-given blessing, then it would seem to be so in faithful and loving relationships, whether they are homosexual or heterosexual. I doubt whether it is helpful to speak of a homosexual partnership as a marriage, but in my view it may be right to ask God's blessing

44. Dominian, *Let's Make Love*, p. 112.

45. See further, A. Thatcher, *Living Together* (Cambridge: Cambridge University Press, 2002), and D.J. Dormor, *Just Cohabiting? The Church, Sex and Getting Married* (London: Darton, Longman & Todd, 2004).

46. M. Althaus-Reid, *Indecent Theology: Theological Perversions in Sex, Gender and Politics* (London: Routledge, 2000), p. 143, quoted in Thatcher, 'Intimate Relationships', p. 10.

47. Matthew 19.1–12 and Mark 10.1–12.

48. I have been much helped by the writings of Jack Dominian, especially *Marriage, Faith and Love* (London: Darton, Longman & Todd, 1981).

on such a partnership and the Churches should help to see that homosexual couples do not suffer from legal discrimination or popular prejudice.[49]

The focus for discussion of gender issues in many churches has been the divisive question of the ordination of women to the priesthood and the episcopate. Those for whom the priest represents Jesus Christ in his maleness have opposed such ordinations. Others believe that, in Christ, gender differences are transcended. I have always supported the ordination of women to the priesthood, although I have been afraid that emphasis on this issue has made ordination too important and has inhibited the development of the ministry of the whole people of God. I wonder also, whether, rather than bringing new and particular gifts to the ordained ministry, the expectation has been that women priests should replicate the pattern of ministry of their male colleagues. This copies secular society's understanding of gender equality as meaning that men and women should, if they wish, perform identical tasks – such as fighting in the armed forces. If, however, one starts from the Christian conviction that God loves each person totally as an individual, then the ideal may be equality of dignity and respect, not identity of function. If, as some secular writers are now recognizing, 'men are from Mars and women are from Venus',[50] perhaps we can find in the relationship of the persons of the Trinity a model for human relationships which give full worth to each person in his or her particularity. Indeed, Luce Irigaray, with whom we began, objects to the search for equality because it still defines women in terms of men. Instead, she argues that women need to discover their own subjectivities and become persons in their own right, not in relationship to men.[51] Rather than seeking equality, do we need to balance, like Yin and Yang, the 'masculine' and the 'feminine' in each of us, in the Church and in society?

Conclusion

Linda Woodhead, as we saw at the beginning, called for a 'fresh and creative reflection on the mystery of human sexual difference'.[52] There are signs that this is happening in the Churches. If God is pictured as a cosmic lover and human beings, made in the divine image, as lovers, then, as Adrian Thatcher says, 'the "holy life" for most Christians will not be the way of renunciation, but rather the integration of sex and sexuality into the loving which seeks God and the neighbour'.[53] Equally, as Jack Dominian says, the Christian contribution is to

49. See further, T. Bradshaw (ed.), *The Way Forward: Christian Voices on Homosexuality and the Church* (London: SCM Press, 2nd edn, 2003), and S. Bates, *A Church at War: Anglicans and Homosexuality* (London and New York: I. B. Tauris, 2004).

50. To use the title of J. Gray's book, *Men are from Mars, Women are from Venus* (London: HarperCollins, 1993).

51. See D'Costa, *Sexing the Trinity*, pp. 5–6.

52. See n. 1.

53. Thatcher, 'Intimate Relationships', p. 12.

embrace sexuality and critically to assess it in terms of love. The Church should seek to counteract the trivializing of sex and also offer a community of love to the many people who are sexually wounded.[54] Indeed, in the mutuality of human love, the Church should see the 'drawing of all created good toward Christ and the transfigurative union in Christ of apparent opposites'.[55] The new Christian appreciation of human sexuality and desire may indeed bring new life to theology and, as Jack Dominian hopes, revitalize the evangelization of the young.[56]

54. Dominian, *Let's Make Love*, p. 181.
55. Jordan, *Ethics of Sex*, p. 164.
56. Dominian, *Let's Make Love*, p. 173.

Gender from a Muslim Perspective

Tim Winter

> The Prophet said that woman prevails exceedingly over the wise and intelligent. While on the other hand, ignorant men prevail over woman, for in them the fierceness of the animal is imprisoned.
>
> They lack tenderness, kindness and affection, because animality predominates over their (human) nature.
>
> Love and tenderness are human qualities, anger and lust are animal qualities.
>
> She (woman) is a ray of God, she is not that (earthly) beloved: she is creative, you might say she is not created.[1]

The 'Gender' of God

Classical Muslim theology (*kalām*) confronts us with the demanding absence of a gendered Godhead. The Muslim God is not 'Father', still less 'Son'. A theology which discloses the divine through incarnation in a body also locates it in a gender. A theology which reveals it in a book makes no judgement thereby about gender, since books are unsexed. For *kalām*, the divine remains divine, that is, the only genderless entity, even when expressed in a fully saving way on earth.

This does not mean that gender is absent from Muslim metaphysics. The *kalām* scholars, emphasizing God's transcendence, banished it from the superlunary world. But the mystics, as immanentists, read it into almost everything. We might say that while in Christianity, relationality is in the triune Godhead, and is explicitly male, in Islam, relationality is absent from the Godhead but exuberantly exists in the Names. To use the Kantian distinction, the noumenal God is neutral, whereas the phenomenal God is manifested in not one but two genders. As they interact to weave creation into being, the Names, of Rigour and of Mercy, traditionally identified with male and female activities, become like the androgens and oestrogens of the cosmos.

1. R.A. Nicholson (trans.), *The Mathnawí of Jalálu'ddín Rúmí* (London: Gibb Memorial Series, 1926), II, pp. 122–23.

By far the most conspicuous of the divine Names in the Qur'ān is *al-Raḥmān*, the All-Compassionate. The explicitly feminine resonances of this name had been remarked upon by the Prophet himself, who taught that *raḥma*, loving compassion, had an etymology in the word *raḥim*, meaning a womb.[2] As in many ancient systems, the cosmic matrix from which differentiated being is fashioned seems to be feminine, although the essence of God remains outside qualification by gender.

This 'female' aspect of the merciful God allowed many of the major Sufi poets to refer to the celestial beloved as *Laylā*. *Laylā* (meaning 'night') is the veiled, darkly unknown God who brings forth life, and whose beauty once revealed dazzles the lover. In one branch of this tradition, the poets use frankly erotic language to convey the rapture of the spiritual wayfarer as he lifts the veil – a metaphor for distraction and sin – to be annihilated in his Beloved.[3] Hence the *kalām* ignores gender; Sufism deploys it exuberantly as metaphor. This tension supplies the ground against which the outward forms of religion are to be interpreted, forms which in turn recognize and affirm gender as a fundamental quality of existence, as expressed in many provisions of Islamic law and the norms of Muslim life.

Some Inequalities in Islamic law

The pattern of life decreed by Islam is implicitly primordial and non-peccatist, and hence biophiliac and affirmative of the hormonal, sexual and genetic dimensions of humanity. For Muslims, body, mind and spirit are aspects of the same created phenomenon, and are all gendered through their interrelation.[4]

Postmodernism and post-structuralism have tended to problematize the idea of 'nature'. Even traditional feminists can regard it as essentialist, recalling the undesirable biologism of Freud, which the constructivist paradigms which spread during the 1960s took to be discredited. According to these paradigms, the female mind is simply the site of 'cultural inscription', so that awakening from a patriarchally induced false consciousness is no more than a heuristic exercise. This is the paradigm with which many Muslim feminists work today, and which drives their project to restore authenticity by levelling *sharīʿa* gender disparities. It is an approach which, however, is highly reductive, as it neglects theological and cosmological context, thereby implicitly delegitimizing the

2. Bukhārī, Adab, 13.

3. See T.J. Winter, '*Pulchra ut Luna:* Some Reflections on the Marian Theme in Muslim-Catholic Dialogue', *Journal of Ecumenical Studies* 36 (1999), pp. 439–69.

4. Against this background, it is unsurprising that although the mediaeval jurists disagreed over the punishment to be applied for homosexual acts (ten lashes according to some, the death penalty according to others), there is consensus in classical Islam, and apparently today, on the status of homosexual practice as a defiance of the created purposes of the human body: see the (unsigned) article 'Liwat', in *The Encyclopedia of Islam* (Leiden: E.J. Brill, 2nd edn, 1960–2002), V, pp. 776–79.

sacred *telos* of the non-Western other. In comparison with Christian feminism, it is shallow; like many 'fundamentalist' apologists' countermoves in vindication,[5] its reduction of the topic to a simple issue of praxis and identity is surely a profoundly secularizing move, which neglects to identify the qualities of God which might shape values and institutions in the here-below.

I have no space to review the detailed provisions of the *sharīʿa*, and to assess, in each individual instance, the traditional case that gender equality, even where the concept is meaningful, can be undermined rather than established by enforced parity of roles and rights. Such a project would require a separate volume of the type attempted by many Muslim apologists;[6] and we must content ourselves with surveying a few representative issues.

Built into the archetypal patterns of Islam is a characteristic emendation to existing Semitic purity laws. Feminists have often identified these as a major sign and strengthener of misogyny. Islam has preserved the memory of the ancient (and also specifically Semitic) hesitation over bodily emissions, but in an attenuated form. So in Qur'ān 2.220, we read: 'They will question you concerning the monthly course: Say, it is a hurt. So go apart from women during the monthly course and do not approach them until they are clean.'

What this means becomes clearer in the *sunna*. A *hadīth* reports that: 'ʿĀ'isha said: "During my menstruation, I would drink, and would then pass the drink to the Blessed Prophet, who would place his mouth at the place from which I had drunk."'[7]

There are echoes here of this primordial human unease, but they are very reduced. The naturalism of Islam appears to insist that holiness does not emerge from the suppression of bodily norms, but from their affirmation through regulation, so that the natural rhythms of the body and the awe with which we regard them are not ignored, but are commemorated in religious ritual. Hence a woman is granted a suspension of formal prayer and fasting for several days in every month. Some feminists see this as a diminution of female spirituality; female Muslim theologians regard it as a reverent acknowledgment; others interpret it as a relief from religious duties at a difficult time. The dispensation is easily deconstructed by either suspicious or benign hermeneutics, and resists total interpretation.

What Muslims do stress is that Islam valorizes women by making the cardinal duties of the faith, including even the arduous ḥajj pilgrimage, equally incumbent upon both sexes: the suspension from formal prayer for a few days each month is seen as a pragmatic and generous dispensation which does not vitiate this basic principle. Similarly, Islam does not establish sacred spaces inaccessible to women. Women may enter the Kaʿba; and there is no gender

5. S. Zuhur, *Revealing Islamist Gender Ideology in Modern Egypt* (Albany, NY: State University of New York Press, 1992).

6. For example, H. Jawad, *The Rights of Women in Islam: An Authentic Approach* (Basingstoke and New York: Macmillan, 1998).

7. Muslim, Ḥayḍ, 14.

differentiation during the seven circumambulations of Islam's greatest shrine. In Jerusalem, the Muslim conquerors threw the Temple open to both sexes. Hence the Dome of the Rock is allocated on Fridays exclusively to women, so that men pray in the nearby al-Aqṣā mosque hall. Here, as elsewhere, the sexes are segregated during congregational prayers, and the reason given for this is again the pragmatic one that a commingling of men and women during a form of worship which entails a good deal of physical contact would readily lead to distraction.

Women may penetrate the *sacratum*; but what of the ambivalent privilege of leadership? Here, Islam extends its feminizing of sanctuaries to its own epiphany of the Word which resonates within them. For the *sharīʿa*, the word made Book is open to female touch and cantillation. Symbolically, perhaps, the custodianship of the first copy of the Qur'ān was entrusted to the Prophet's wife Ḥafṣa, not to a man.

Regarding collective celebration of the divine word, it is clear that there can be no Islamic equivalent to the debate over women's ordination, for the straightforward reason that Islam does not ordain anyone, whether male or female. Our recollection of the primordial covenant has already conferred priestly orders upon us all, which are valid to the extent of our recollection.

The imam does not mediate; but the spiritual director may do so, by counselling and praying for the disciple, and by prescribing techniques of divine invocation and meditation. It is a manifestation of the inescapably antifeminine harshness of modern Wahhābī activism that the Sufi shaykh is for such activists a figure not to be revered, but to be abolished. Sufism, and certain other forms of Muslim initiatic spirituality, have frequently accommodated women in ways which purely exoteric forms of the religion have not: the Sufi shaykh, for instance, who exercises such influence on the formation and guidance of the disciple, and is often a more significant presence for the individual and for society than the person of the mosque imam, may be of either gender. Frequently in those Muslim societies where the mosque is a primarily male space, the tomb of a prophet or a saint supplies a sacred place for women, responding to an affective spirituality which flourishes in the embrace of closed circles (the shrine) rather than in the straight lines characteristic of mosque worship.[8] Wahhābīsm, with its nervousness about any public visibility for women, seeks to suppress such contexts, with the exception only of the tomb at Medina, which it construes not as paradigm but as exception.

Nonetheless, the issue of a possible female imamate has been raised in several communities in recent years. The debate is a fairly muted one, perhaps because few women currently seem to aspire to this ambivalent position. The imam of a mosque can claim none of the mediating authority of a priest: he does not stand *in loco divinis*; but is mainly present to mark time, to ensure that the

8. N. Tapper, '*Ziyaret*, Gender, Movement and Exchange in a Turkish Community', in D.F. Eickelman and J. Piscatori (eds.), *Muslim Travellers: Pilgrimage, Migration and the Religious Imagination* (London: Routledge, 1990), pp. 236–56.

worshippers' movements are co-ordinated, and to represent the unity of the community. While in some cultures he may have the added function of a pastoral counsellor, this is not a canonical requirement. All four law-schools of Sunnī Islam affirm that the imam must be male if there are males in the congregation. If there are only females, then many classical scholars permit the imamate of females.[9] But women cannot lead men in worship. There are in fact no Qur'ānic or *ḥadīth* texts that explicitly lay this down: it is a product of expert consensus. In the mediaeval period, only a few sought to query this consensus, the best-known being the jurist al-Ṭabarī (d. 923) and the mystic Ibn ʿArabī (d. 1240), both of whom defended the right of women to lead men in the canonical prayer.[10] In practice, women activists in the Muslim world appear to have little concern for this, again, because of the absence of inherent prestige and authority in the imamate. A Muslim female chaplain in the US army carries out her duties without needing to lead congregations in this way.[11] In a culture which vests authority in scholarship irrespective of liturgical function, one can, indeed, be a religious leader without being imam of a mosque, as is shown by the most recent study of mediaeval Muslim female academicians, which notes:

> If U. S. and European historians feel a need to reconstruct women's history because women are invisible in the traditional sources, Islamic scholars are faced with a plethora of source material that has only begun to be studied … In reading the biographies of thousands of Muslim women scholars, one is amazed at the evidence that contradicts the view of Muslim women as marginal, secluded, and restricted.[12]

Women's functions vary widely in the Muslim world and in Muslim history. In peasant communities, women work out of doors; while among urban elites, womanhood is more frequently celebrated in the home. Recurrently, however, what Westerners would define as the public space is rigorously desexualized, and this is represented by the quasi-monastic garb of men and women, where frequently the colour white is the colour of the male, while black, the colour of interiority, of the Kaʿba and hence the celestial *Laylā*, denotes womanhood.

9. Ibn Qudāma, *al-Mughnī* (Cairo: Dār Hajr, AH 1407/1987), III, pp. 37–42 (for the Ḥanbalīs); and ʿAlā' al-Dīn al-Kāsānī, *Badā'iʿ al-ṣanā'iʿ fi tartīb al-sharā'iʿ* (Beirut: Dār Iḥyā' al-Turāth al-ʿArabī, AH 1421/2000), I, p. 388 (for the Ḥanafīs and Shāfiʿīs). The Mālikīs, by contrast, forbid the practice: Aḥmad al-Dardīr, *al-Sharḥ al-ṣaghīr ʿalā Aqrab al-masālik* (Cairo: Dār al-Maʿārif, 1972–74), I, p. 458.

10. For Ṭabarī's position (shared with another important early jurist, Abū Thawr [d. 854]), see Ibn Rushd, *The Distinguished Jurist's Primer: A Translation of Bidāyat Al-Mujtahid* (trans. I. Nyazee; Reading: Garnet, 1994), I, p. 161; for Muḥyī al-Dīn Ibn ʿArabī, see his *al-Futūḥāt al-Makkiyya* (Cairo: al-Maṭbaʿa al-Miṣriyya, AH 1293/1876), I, pp. 562–63.

11. *Army Times*, 24 December 2001, www.army.mil/usar/news/2002archives/January/femalecleric.html.

12. R. Roded, *Women in Islamic Biographical Collections* (Boulder, CO and London: Lynne Riener, 1994), p. viii. For women saints, see Abū ʿAbd al-Raḥmān al-Sulamī, *Early Sufi Women: Dhikr An-Niswa Al-Muta'abbidat As-Sufiyyat* (trans. R.E. Cornell; Louisville, KY: Fons Vitae, 1999).

In the private space of the home, these signs are cast aside, and the home becomes as colourful as the public space is austere and polarized. From the Muslim perspective, modernity, refusing to recognize gender as sacred sign, and tolerant of casual erotic signalling, renders the public space 'domestic' by colouring it, and makes war on all remnants of gender separation, which it crudely construes as judgemental.

Perhaps the most immediately conspicuous feature of Muslim communities is the dress code traditional for women. It is often forgotten that the *sharīʿa* and the Muslim sense of human dignity require a dress code for men as well: in fully traditional Muslim societies, men typically cover their hair in public, and wear robes exposing only the hands and feet. In Muslim law, however, this is not quite an obligation: men have to cover themselves from the navel to the knees as a minimum. But women, on the basis of a *ḥadīth*, are to cover everything except the face, hands and (according to some) the feet.[13]

Again, the feminine dress code, known as *ḥijāb*, forms a largely passive text available for a range of readings. For some Western feminist missionaries to Muslim lands, it is a symbol of patriarchy and of woman's demure submission.[14] For Muslim women, it may proclaim their identity: many deeply secular women who demonstrated against the Shah in the 1970s wore it for this reason, as an almost aggressive flag of defiance.[15] Twenty years earlier, Franz Fanon had reflected on a similar phenomenon among Algerian women protesting against French rule, which had assumed that 'every veil that fell, every body that became liberated from the traditional embrace of the *haik*, every face that offered itself to the bold and impatient glance of the occupier, was a negative expression of the fact that Algeria was beginning to deny herself and was accepting the rape of the colonizer'.[16]

For still other women, however, such as the Egyptian thinker Safinaz Kazim, the *ḥijāb* is to be reconstrued as a quasi-feminist statement.[17] A woman who exposes her charms in public is vulnerable to what might be described as 'visual

13. A.S. Roald, *Women in Islam: The Western Experience* (London: Routledge, 2001), pp. 254–94.

14. Much feminist criticism originated in Christian missionary attitudes to Muslim women's dress, for which see E.L. Fleischman, 'Our Moslem Sisters: Women of Greater Syria in the Eyes of American Protestant Missionary Women', *Islam and Christian-Muslim Relations* 9 (1998), pp. 307–23 (314). The equation of *ḥijāb* with appurtenance appears to neglect the fact that in Islamic law, slave women are not required to cover their heads (Ibn Qudāma, *al-Mughnī*, II, pp. 331–35), so that *ḥijāb* is a signal of free status, not of ownership.

15. Cf. N. Yeganeh and N.R. Keddie, 'Sexuality and Shiʿi Social Protest in Iran', in J.R.I. Cole and N.R. Keddie (eds.), *Shiʿism and Social Protest* (New Haven, CT and London: Yale University Press, 1986), pp. 108–36 (132).

16. F. Fanon, *A Dying Colonialism* (New York: Monthly Review Press, 1965), p. 42. For a critique, see R.A. Faulkner, 'Assia Djebar, Frantz Fanon, Women, Veil and Land', *World Literature Today* 70.4 (1996), pp. 847–55.

17. S. Hutchinson, 'The Issue of the *Ḥijāb* in Classical and Modern Muslim Scholarship' (unpublished doctoral thesis, School of African and Oriental Studies, University of London, 1987), p. 67.

theft', so that men unknown to her can enjoy her visually without her consent. By covering herself, she regains her ability to present herself as a physical being only to her family and sorority. This view of *ḥijāb*, as a kind of moral raincoat particularly useful under the inclement climate of modernity, allows a vision of Islamic woman as liberated, not from tradition and meaning, but from ostentation, and from subjection to arbitrary visual possession by men.[18] The feminist objection to the patriarchal adornment or denuding of women, namely that it reduces them to the status of vulnerable, passive objects of the male regard, makes no headway against the *ḥijāb*, responsibly understood.

There are other aspects of the *sharīʿa* which deserve mention as illustrations of our theme, not least those which have been largely forgotten by Muslim societies. Frequently, the jurists' exegesis of the texts is plurivocal. Domestic chores, for instance, appear as an aspect of interior sociality, but this is not identified with purely female space, since they are regarded by some schools of Sunnī law as the responsibility of the man rather than the wife. ʿĀ'isha was asked, after the Prophet's death, what he used to do at home when he was not at prayer; and she replied: 'He served his family: he used to sweep the floor, and sew clothes.'[19] On this basis, jurists of several schools defend the woman's right not to perform housework. For instance, one fourteenth-century Shāfiʿī jurist could insist: 'A woman is not obliged to serve her husband by baking, grinding flour, cooking, washing, or any other kind of service, because the marriage contract entails, for her part, only that she let him enjoy her sexually, and she is not obliged to do other than that.'[20] The Ḥanafī school, by contrast, considers these acts as the wife's obligations – another sufficient reminder of the difficulty of generalizing about Islamic law, which remains a diverse body of rules and approaches.[21]

Conclusion

Islam's theology of gender thus contends with a maze, a web of connections which demand familiarity with a diverse legal code, regional heterogeneity, and

18. For the 'liberative' veil, see C. Delaney, 'Untangling the Meanings of Hair in Turkish Society', *Anthropological Quarterly* 67.4 (1994), pp. 159–72; and L. Abu Odeh, 'Post-Colonial Feminism and the Veil: Thinking the Difference', *Feminist Review* 43 (1993), pp. 26–37.

19. Bukhārī, Adhān, 44.

20. N.H.M. Keller (trans.), *Reliance of the Traveller* (Brattleboro, VT: Amana, 3rd edn, 1997), p. 948.

21. Another important area, which cannot be detailed here, is the law of child custody: the Ḥanafīs prefer boys to leave a divorced mother at the age of seven or eight, to live with the father; girls remain with her until the menarch (Kāsānī, *Badā'iʿ al-ṣanā'iʿ fī tartīb al-sharā'iʿ*, III, p. 459). For the Mālikīs, the boy lives with the mother until sexual maturity (*iḥtilām*), and the girl until her marriage is consummated (Dardīr, *al-Sharḥ al-ṣaghīr ʿalā Aqrab al-masālik*, II, p. 755). Among the Shāfiʿīs, the child chooses between its parents when it is old enough to do so (Ibn Rushd, *Distinguished Jurist's Primer*, II, p. 66).

with the metaphysical no less than with the physical. This complexity should warn us against offering facile generalizations about Islam's attitude to women. Journalists, feminists and cultivated people generally in the West have harboured deeply negative verdicts here. Often these verdicts are arrived at through the observation of actual Muslim societies; and it would be perverse to suggest that the modern Islamic world is to be admired for its treatment of women. In some respects, the situation is deteriorating due to strategies of 'Islamization' being launched in several countries today by activists driven by resentment and committed to an anthropomorphized and hence andromorphic God, in apparent detachment from traditional *fiqh* discourse and the revelatory insistence on justice. This imbalance may continue unless actualized religion learns to revive neglected possibilities in classical Muslim law, and also, more profoundly, to reincorporate the dimension of Sufism, which can valorize the feminine principle, and which also obstructs and ultimately annihilates the ego which underpins gender chauvinism. We need to distinguish, as many Muslim women thinkers are doing, between the expectations of the religion's ethos as legible in scripture, classical exegesis and spirituality, and the actual asymmetric structures of post-classical Muslim societies, which, like Christian, Jewish, Hindu and Chinese cultures, contain much that is in need of reform.

Gender in Jewish, Christian and Muslim Thought

Norman Solomon, Richard Harries and Tim Winter

Sybil Sheridan has written in her paper that Judaism is 'a supremely gendered faith, defined and practised by men, and written down for future generations, with women possibly defining and practising their own version: separate, but not necessarily equal'.

Although within Judaism there are feminine images of the divine (so that, for example, God is like a mother who cares for her child), and feminine qualities such as mercy and wisdom are attributed to God, this seems to make no difference to the way in which women have been regarded as significantly subordinate and excluded from certain crucial, religious functions. Feminine imagery is in fact quite strong, and Jewish mysticism abounds in female imagery, while the relationship between the people of Israel and God is seen in terms of the imagery of male and female love. Despite all this, women have not had an equal place.

This does not mean to say that women have not had their own distinctive religious experience. They have, particularly in relation to the *miqveh*, and in their home-making role, as well as in special forms of prayer and piety. It is also likely that rabbis' wives have had a significant religious function, although this is not well documented at the moment. A great deal of this has changed in the Liberal, Reform and American Conservative traditions, most obviously in the way in which they allow women to become rabbis. In recent years, changes have been taking place in Orthodox Judaism as well. The most significant change has been that women now have access to the intellectual tradition of Judaism: women can study the Torah in places of learning. There have consequently been private ordinations to the rabbinate, with women working incognito as hospital chaplains. There have been a few specially trained women to act as advocates over the question of obtaining a religious divorce, the *get*. Indeed, Sybil Sheridan comes to a rather surprising conclusion that if such changes continue to occur within Orthodox Judaism, a specifically female religious experience may develop, which could be regarded as on a par with that of men and not simply imitative of it. In other words, it would be equal but distinctive.

Marcus Braybrooke sets out the negative attitude to women which has characterized so much of Christian history. God is addressed as Father, and the incarnation is thought of as having taken place in the Son of God. Although Jung saw the image of the virgin as a way in which the feminine side of God could be expressed, and there is a highly developed devotion to the Virgin Mary in the Catholic and Orthodox traditions, this is viewed with great suspicion by feminists who in Mary's idealized, virginal status, see women being honoured not as they really are, but as a male projection.

As far as sexuality is concerned, again, Christian history has been characterized by an excessively negative attitude, a Manichaean strain which entered the tradition through Augustine. This began to change in the twentieth century, in which very positive assessments of Jesus' relation to women have been recovered. The change is reflected in new marriage liturgies, which see marriage primarily in terms of a relationship – a relationship which rejoices in physical expression – rather than simply in terms of procreation. Another expression of this new attitude is the way in which many churches now welcome the ordination of women to the priesthood.

All this having been said, Braybrooke ends up, like Sheridan, wondering if women now need to discover their own subjectivities and become persons in their own right, rather than simply try to achieve what men enjoy. In other words, rather than seek equality, should we not look for balance, both within each one of us, and within the Church and in society?

Tim Winter argues that, in contrast to the Christian understanding of God who is addressed as Father, there is in Islam the 'absence of a gendered Godhead'. While the pre-eminent name for God, Allah, in Arabic is masculine, the other names of God which describe God's attributes or qualities indicate the importance both of relationship and of the feminine. Like Sheridan, Winter points out that the Semitic root for the word 'mercy', which is so important in Islam as well as in Judaism and Christianity, means a womb. In short, the cosmic matrix on which differentiated being is fashioned seems to be feminine. This female aspect of the merciful God finds expression in some of the major Sufi poets, who often sing of their passion for *Laylā*, a female name frequently applied to the divine Beloved, who brought the world into being out of pure compassion, seen as a pre-eminently feminine quality. In pre-modern Sunnī Islam, this valorizing of the female principle was commonplace, and although with the rise of Wahhābī-style fundamentalism in recent years it has been driven into the background in some Muslim cultures, it would seem to be a promising basis for the development of feminist Muslim theologies.

Islamic law is very often criticized in the West for reinforcing a subordinate role for women, but Tim Winter argues that some of what is said is open to different interpretations, and that both in law and in Muslim tradition, women can have a significant role: for example, they are encouraged to take part in the ḥajj pilgrimage, and they are allowed to enter the Kaʿba. There is no debate over women's ordination, primarily because Islam does not ordain anyone. It seems, nevertheless, that women are not allowed to be imams (although there is a female Muslim chaplain in the US army who carries out duties which do not involve leading a male congregation in worship or prayer). As far as women's dress code is concerned, some feminists welcome the headscarf as a way of preserving private space and avoiding the 'visual theft' by which men unknown to a woman can enjoy her visually without her consent. It is true that in many Muslim countries, women are both subordinate and subjugated. But this is a feature of the culture, not enjoined by Islam itself. Reform is needed, as reform is needed in many countries that are not Islamic. Nevertheless, Islam, properly understood, has a distinctive affirmation of women, even though in some respects this may mean having a different role to that of men.

A number of themes emerge from this consideration of gender in the three religions. First of all, although it is widely assumed that there is a relationship between the understanding a religion has of the divine reality and the way it treats women, this is not necessarily so. For example, Athens had as its deity Athena, a female God, but women in Athens were given a very inferior role. It is not proven that the relative paucity of female images of God in the three religions is a factor in the way in which women have been treated in cultures dominated by those religions. There may be a very proper, strong movement for greater equality, particularly equality of opportunity, in cultures that have a dominant monotheistic religion, but this does not necessarily entail that there should be any fundamental shift in the way God's gender is understood. It may be that male images of God have seemed oppressive because they have been used in cultures where male power has been both dominant and oppressive. If we move towards societies in which there is greater equality of power between the two sexes, and where the use of that power is not oppressive, it could be that there would be a much more relaxed attitude as to which images are or are not used of the divine. In short, it may be morally more effective to change social conditions than to change theology.

All three great monotheistic religions have been criticized by feminists for reinforcing a traditional view of women in which they are held, either explicitly or implicitly, to be inferior. The record of these religions in this respect is certainly hard to defend. Nevertheless, as all three contributions to this section indicate, there may be wisdom in these traditions that has yet to be fully appreciated by feminists. It may be that women do have a distinctive perspective on human existence, with different gifts and needs, and therefore some difference of role in religion would be entirely appropriate. Indeed, this essentialist view of gender seems to be supported by the findings of modern sociobiology. All three religions agree in affirming the spiritual equality of women, their equality with men in the eyes of God. How this has translated into political, economic and social forms has varied from culture to culture. All would agree that this spiritual equality needs to take shape in tangible ways in both religious communities and society as a whole, but it may be that society needs to be more critical about the way in which equality has been defined in exclusively male terms. So it may be necessary for women to be more explicit about what their role should be, particularly in religion, without in any way being complicit in some form of subordination. This is a risky argument, since it can be used by some to avoid making the kind of changes in both society and religious institutions that are necessary. Yet, aware of that danger, it is likely that feminists from within the three religions will be able to make a distinctive contribution to the larger feminist debate as it further unfolds and transforms society.

Chapter 8: The Environment

The Environment from a Jewish Perspective[1]

Norman Solomon

The word 'ecology', from the Greek *oikos* ('home'), may be loosely interpreted as 'the science of understanding and looking after our home'. There *is* only one home; we must conserve our planet and share its resources peacefully, or else perish!

What has religious faith to contribute to this? Jews and Christians share a biblical tradition on creation; and though Muslims draw on different written sources, all three faiths can jointly affirm a wide range of values relating to the created world. In the first part of this paper, I will define and illustrate six leading values in the Judaeo-Christian attitude to nature; in the second part, I shall indicate some of the problem areas; and then I shall make brief recommendations for teaching and preaching.

Six Principles

The First Principle: Creation is Good; it Reflects the Glory of its Creator

'God saw everything that he had made, and indeed, it was very good.'[2] Judaism affirms life, not just human life but the biosphere as a whole.

So is Judaism, or for that matter Christianity or Islam, biocentric? Certainly not. Faith focuses not on the *bios*, but on God. We are *theo*centric, not *bio*centric; to set anything other than God in the centre constitutes idolatry. Nature bears God's 'signature', mirrors God's glory; yet to *equate* God with nature is pantheism. Therefore we rejected Spinoza, deism and *deus sive natura*; therefore we now reject careless talk of *gaia* as an 'earth-goddess', a divinity in her own right; there is only one God, and only the one God may command.

Rabbi Abraham Isaac Kook (1865–1935), drawing on Jewish sources from the psalms to Lurianic mysticism, beautifully acknowledged the divine significance of all things:

1. This chapter is based on a paper read in Athens on 28 July 1994 to the Biopolitics International Organization, at the International Sakharov Festival.
2. Genesis 1.31.

> I recall that with God's grace in the year 5665 [1904–1905] I visited Jaffa in the Holy Land, and went to pay my respects to its Chief Rabbi [Rabbi Kook]. He received me warmly ... and after the afternoon prayer I accompanied him as he went out into the fields, as was his wont, to concentrate his thoughts. As we were walking I plucked some flower or plant; he trembled, and quietly told me that he always took great care not to pluck, unless it were for some benefit, anything that could grow ... Everything that grew said something, every stone whispered some secret, all creation sang.[3]

Kook heard the hymn that nature sings to God. He sang not *in praise of* nature, but *with* nature in praise of God, in line with psalms such as 104 and 148.

The Second Principle: Biodiversity, the Rich Variety of Nature, is to be Cherished
Genesis describes how everything is created 'according to its kind'; Adam then names each animal. Noah conserved in the ark a viable population of males and females of each species.[4]

Several biblical commandments stress the distinctness of species. Nowadays, we should read the dietary lists,[5] the laws prohibiting mixtures of seeds,[6] or of wool and linen,[7] or forbidding the cross-breeding or yoking of different animals,[8] as demonstrating the religious duty to maintain biodiversity.

Under this heading, we should also consider the diversity of habitats. Vast areas have been affected by desertification and other forms of land degradation; forests have been seriously depleted in the past century; wetlands and other special habitats have been lost, and with them numerous irreplaceable plant and animal species. Clearly, this is contrary to biblical teaching.

The Third Principle: Living Things Range from Lower to Higher, with Humankind at the Top
Genesis 1 depicts the creation of order out of primaeval chaos. The web of life encompasses all; human beings, both male and female, created 'in the image of God',[9] stand at the apex of this structure. There is a hierarchy in created things.

The hierarchical model carries practical consequences. First, the higher bears a responsibility toward the lower, traditionally expressed as 'rule', latterly as 'stewardship'. Second, in a competitive situation, the higher has priority over the lower. Humans have priority over dogs so that, for instance, it is wrong for

3. Reminiscence by Aryeh Levine in *Lahai Ro'i* (Hebrew) (Jerusalem: n. p., AM 5721/1961), pp. 15–16.
4. We would not today regard a single pair as a viable population, but presumably viability is what the biblical text meant to convey.
5. Leviticus 11; Deuteronomy 14.
6. Leviticus 19.19; Deuteronomy 22.9.
7. Leviticus 19.19; Deuteronomy 22.11.
8. Leviticus 19.19; Deuteronomy 22.10.
9. Genesis 1.27.

a man to risk his life to save that of a dog, though right, in many circumstances, for him to risk his life to save that of another human.[10]

The Spanish Jewish philosopher Joseph Albo (1380–1435) placed humans at the top of the earthly hierarchy, and discerned in this the possibility for humans to receive God's revelation.[11] According to Albo, just as clothes are an integral part of the animal, but remain external to people, who have to make clothes for themselves, so are specific ethical impulses integral to the behaviour of particular animals, and we should learn from their behaviour: '[God] teaches us from the beasts of the earth, and imparts wisdom to us through the birds of the sky.'[12] The superiority of humans lies in their unique combination of freedom to choose and intelligence to judge, without which the divine revelation would have no application. Being in this sense 'higher' than other creatures, humans must be humble towards all. Albo, in citing these passages and commending the reading of *Pereq Shira*,[13] articulated the attitude of humble stewardship towards creation which characterizes rabbinic Judaism.

The Fourth Principle: Human Beings are Responsible for the Active Maintenance of All Life

Setting people at the top of the hierarchy of creation places them in a special position of responsibility towards nature. Adam is placed in the garden of Eden 'to till it and keep it',[14] and to 'name' (that implies, understand) the animals. We are not to sit idly by and see the forests destroyed, but must act to prevent the destruction, and actively seek understanding of our environment.

The Fifth Principle: Land and People Depend on Each Other

In the past, Jews and Christians parted company in interpreting those sections of the Bible concerned with the land. Jews read them literally, of the land of Israel, but Christians rejected the plain meaning. Today, in the awareness of our common responsibility for the planet, Jews can apply the principles universally, and Christians can regain appreciation of their relevance.

10. I am not aware of any Jewish theologian who challenges the priority of human over animal life.

11. J. Albo, *Sefer Ha-Ikkarim: Book of Principles* (ed. and trans. I. Husik; 5 vols.; Philadelphia, PA: Jewish Publication Society of America, 1929–30), III, pp. 1–13.

12. Job 35.11 (my translation, in accordance with Albo's reading of the verse, which derives from the Babylonian Talmud, *Eruvin* 100b). Mediaeval commentators such as Rashi, followed by modern translators, correctly understood the verse to say, 'who teaches us more than [he teaches] the animals of the earth, and makes us wiser than the birds of the air'.

13. *Pereq Shira*, the 'Chapter of Song', may be as old as the fourth century, and was popularized by the *Hasidei Ashkenaz* in the twelfth. Each of its five or six sections comprises from ten to twenty-five biblical verses, each interpreted as the 'song' or saying of some individual creature. Francis of Assisi's *Cantico del Sole*, composed in the early thirteenth century, has much the same flavour.

14. Genesis 2.15.

The Bible refers to the land of Israel as *eretz ha-tzvi*,[15] translated by some as 'the fairest of lands'. Judaism has developed within a specific context of chosen people and chosen land; it has emphasized the interrelationship of people and land, the idea that the prosperity of the land depends on the people's obedience to God's covenant. For instance:

> If you will only heed his every commandment that I am commanding you today – loving the Lord your God, and serving him with all your heart and with all your soul – then he will give the rain for your land in its season ... and you will gather in your grain, your wine, and your oil; and he will give grass in your fields for your livestock, and you will eat your fill. Take care, or you will be seduced into turning away, serving other gods and worshipping them, for then the anger of the Lord will be kindled against you and he will shut up the heavens, so that there will be no rain and the land will yield no fruit; then you will perish quickly off the good land that the Lord is giving you.[16]

How can we apply this link between morality and prosperity to the contemporary situation?

The Bible stresses the intimate relationship between people and land. The prosperity of a land depends on (a) the social justice and moral integrity of its inhabitants, and (b) a caring, even loving, attitude to land with effective regulation of its use. Conservation demands the extrapolation of these principles from ancient or idealized Israel to the contemporary global situation; we need education in social values together with scientific investigation of the effects of our activities on nature.

There are religious circles in Israel today which observe the sabbatical year by refraining from agricultural work and by cancelling debts.[17] The analogy between the sabbath (literally, 'rest day') of the land and that of the people communicates the idea that land must 'rest' to be refreshed and regain its productive vigour; land resources must be conserved through the avoidance of over-use.

The Bible links this to social justice. Just as land must not be exploited, so slaves must go free after six years of bondage. The sabbatical year (in Hebrew *shemitta*, which means 'release') cancels private debts, thus preventing the accumulation of debt and the economic exploitation of the individual. We must work out how to apply these ideas to reform our contemporary social and economic structures.

The Sixth Principle: Respect Creation: Do Not Waste or Destroy

Bal tashḥit ('not to destroy', derived from Deuteronomy 20.19) is the Hebrew phrase on which the rabbis base the call to respect and conserve all that has been created. Some of the best illustrations of rabbinic exegesis and development of *halakha* (law) relate to aspects of environmental pollution.

15. For example, Daniel 11.16 and 41.
16. Deuteronomy 11.13–17.
17. Leviticus 25.2–4. AM 5768 (2007-8) and 5775 (2014-5) will be sabbatical years.

Deuteronomy 23.13 and 14 insist that refuse be removed 'outside the camp', that is, collected in a location where it will not reduce the quality of life. The Talmud and codes extend this concept to the general prohibition of dumping refuse or garbage where it may interfere with the environment or with crops. The rabbis forbade the growing of kitchen gardens and orchards around Jerusalem on the grounds that the manuring would degrade the local environment;[18] they would have been deeply concerned at the large-scale environmental degradation caused by traditional mining operations, the burning of fossil fuels and the like. Other specific environmental hazards for which the rabbis sought to legislate included smell, atmospheric pollution and smoke, and water pollution. Modern Israeli law, such as the Hazards Prevention Law, passed by the Knesset on 23 March 1961, draws on traditional Jewish formulations.[19] This well-founded Jewish tradition supports action today to safeguard the world's water, clean up the seas, and dispose cleanly of radioactive and toxic chemical wastes.

Sample Ethical Problems Relating to Conservation

I shall now briefly review some of the areas where religious teaching risks conflict with secular conservation practices. There will be more questions than answers.

Animal versus Human Life

Judaism consistently values human life more than animal life. If I am driving a car and a dog runs into the road, it would be wrong to swerve, endangering my own or someone else's life, to save the dog. But is it right to take a human life, for example, that of a poacher, to save not an individual animal but an endangered species? I can find nothing in Jewish sources to support killing poachers in any circumstances other than those in which they directly threaten human life. If it be argued that the extinction of a species would threaten human life because it would upset the balance of nature, it is still unlikely that Jewish law would countenance homicide to avoid an indirect and uncertain threat of this nature.

Even if homicide were justified in such circumstances, how many human lives is a single species worth? How far down the evolutionary scale would such a principle be applied? After all, the argument about upsetting the balance of nature applies equally with microscopic species as with large, appealing vertebrates like the panda, and with plants as much as with animals. The tsetse fly is no less part of the interdependent fabric of nature than the whale. Judaism,

18. Babylonian Talmud, *Bava Qama* 82b.

19. See, for example, M. Sichel's admirable paper 'Air Pollution: Smoke and Odour Damage', *Jewish Law Annual* 5 (1985), pp. 25–43. He provides a translation of the Israeli legislation referred to.

true to the hierarchical principle of creation, consistently values human life more than that of other living things, but at the same time stresses the special responsibility of human beings to 'till and keep' the created order.[20]

Procreation versus Population Control

Thomas R. Malthus (1766–1834), early in the Industrial Revolution, explored the consequences of the truism that population cannot exceed that which can be sustained by available resources. If there is insufficient food to feed everyone, someone will die; but whereas resources increase only arithmetically, population increases geometrically.[21] If population doubles every 25 years, in 500 years we would require 2 to the power of 20 times as much food to be produced, that is, 1,048,576 times as much – clearly an unattainable requirement. Statistics from the International Data Base indicate that between 1950 and 2004, the population of Nigeria grew from 31.8 million to 137.3 million, that of Kenya from 6.12 million to 32.02 million, and that of the Gaza Strip from less than a quarter of a million to 1.33 million;[22] from 1990–2000, the population of the Gaza Strip increased by 5.7% a year, which means that it would double in 14 years, or increase 242-fold in a century. Of course, these rates cannot continue, and in some affluent countries, populations have declined slightly in recent years; nevertheless, the pressures from rapidly increasing population lead to economic, social and environmental problems.

During the expansionary phase of the Industrial Revolution, the European nations over-exploited resources and engaged in mass migration and imperialistic ventures to cope with 'excess' population. Such methods are no longer available or acceptable. In Malthus' day, the world population reached one billion. It has now passed six billion. As populations increase still further, will the world be able to avoid massive deaths from starvation and disease? Increased food production already causes environmental degradation. Redistribution may temporarily alleviate local famines, but in the long run cannot sustain an exponentially increasing population.

What has Judaism to say on this matter? There is general agreement that at least some forms of birth control are permissible where a potential mother's life is in danger, and that abortion is not only permissible but mandatory up to full term to save a mother's life.[23] Even though contraception may be morally questionable, it is preferable to abstinence where danger to life would be involved through normal sexual relations within a marriage.[24] Such matters are not just questions of 'permitted' and 'forbidden', but require sensitive personal counselling.

20. Genesis 2.15.

21. Malthus published his *Essay on the Principle of Population* anonymously in 1798. He revised and enlarged it in 1803.

22. Available online from the US Census Bureau at www.census.gov/ipc/www/idbnew.html.

23. For an excellent treatment of these issues, see D.M. Feldman, *Marital Relations, Birth Control and Abortion in Jewish Law* (New York: Schocken Books, 1974).

24. Feldman, *Marital Relations*, p. 302.

Halakha places the basic duty of procreation above personal economic hardship. But what about general economic hardship, which can arise (a) through local or temporary famine and (b) through the upward pressure of population on finite world resources? The former situation was in the mind of the third-century Palestinian sage Resh Laqish when he ruled: 'It is forbidden for a man to engage in sexual intercourse in years of famine.'[25] Upward pressure of population on world resources is a concept unknown to the classical sources of the Jewish religion, and not indeed clearly understood before Malthus. Feldman remarks, 'It would be just as reckless to overbreed as to refrain from procreation.'[26] In my view, as the duty of procreation is expressed in Genesis 1.28 in the words 'be fruitful and multiply, and fill the earth', it is not unreasonable to suggest that 'fill' be taken as 'reach the maximum population sustainable at an acceptable standard of living but do not exceed it'. In like vein, the rabbis utilized Isaiah's phrase '[God] did not create [the earth] a chaos, he formed it to be inhabited' to define the minimum requirement for procreation – a requirement, namely one son and one daughter, which does not increase population.[27]

Of course, there is room for local variation among populations. Although as a general rule, governments nowadays should discourage population growth, there are instances of thinly populated areas or of small ethnic groups whose survival is threatened where some population growth might be acceptable even from the global perspective.

Nuclear Energy, Fossil Fuel and Solar Energy

Can religious sources offer guidance on the choice between nuclear and fossil, and other energy sources?

Some religious leaders have expressed strong condemnation of nuclear energy production, but it is hard to understand what *theological* justification there is for, say, preferring windmills to nuclear reactors. The choice among energy sources rests on estimates of cost effectiveness, environmental damage caused by production, operational hazards, clean disposal of waste products, and long-term environmental sustainability. Religious considerations have no part to play in assessing these factors; they are technical matters, demanding painstaking research and hard evidence, but have nothing to do with theology. Windmills *may* indeed do less harm to the environment than nuclear reactors, though this is less obvious than it seems, but theology becomes relevant only once the facts of the case have been scientifically demonstrated.

There could be a religious viewpoint on overall strategy. Moral theology might suggest that scientists should pay more attention to finding out how to

25. Babylonian Talmud, *Taanit* 11a. The ruling was adopted in the codes (*Shulhan Arukh: Orah Hayyim* 240.12 and 574.4), but its application was restricted to those who already have children.

26. Feldman, *Marital Relations*, p. 304.

27. Isaiah 45.18; Babylonian Talmud, *Yevamot* 62a.

use less energy to meet demands for goods than to finding out how to produce more energy. However, unless such advice stems from asceticism, it is merely the counsel of prudence, not dependent on any characteristically religious value.

Who Pays the Piper?

Who should *pay* for conservation? The dilemmas involved in this are exceedingly complex. Should rich nations pay to 'clean up' the technology of poorer nations (for example, should Western Europe pay for Eastern Europe, but not at the expense of India)? Should governments distort the free market by subsidizing lead-free petrol and other 'environment-friendly' commodities? How does one assess environmental efficiency and social costs, and how should such costs be allocated between taxpayer, customer and manufacturer? Much progress has been made in recent years in making industry bear its own environmental costs; ultimately the customer pays, through increased prices. At all levels, the religious have an input to make from the aspect of social justice.

Directed Evolution

After writing about the progress from physical evolution through biological evolution to cultural evolution, Edward Rubinstein continues:

> Henceforth, life no longer evolves solely through chance mutation. Humankind has begun to modify evolution, to bring about non random, deliberate changes in DNA that alter living assemblies and create assemblies that did not exist before.
>
> The messengers of directed evolution are human beings. Their messages, expressed in the language and methods of molecular biology, genetics and medicine and in moral precepts, express their awareness of human imperfections and reflect the values and aspirations of their species.[28]

These words indicate the area where religions, Judaism included, are most in need of adjusting themselves to contemporary reality, the area in which modern knowledge sets us most apart from those who formed our religious traditions. Religion as we know it has come into being only since the neolithic revolution, and thus presupposes some technology. But can it cope with the challenges posed by modern information technology and molecular biology? I do not know, but I expect that religious communities working together will make a better response than any could alone.

Summary and Conclusion

Six principles emerge from the Bible to govern our attitude to the biosphere in which we are placed:

28. E. Rubinstein, 'Stages of Evolution and their Messengers', *Scientific American* (June 1989), p. 104.

1. Creation is good; it reflects the glory of its creator. 'God saw everything that he had made, and indeed, it was very good.'[29] Judaism affirms life, and with it the creation as a whole.
2. Biodiversity, the rich variety of nature, is to be cherished. In Genesis 1, everything is said to be created 'according to its kind'. Genesis 9 tells the story of the flood, how Noah conserved in the ark a male and female of each species of animal, so that they might subsequently procreate.
3. Living things range from lower to higher, with humankind at the top. Genesis 1 depicts a process of the creation of order out of primaeval chaos. The web of life encompasses all; human beings, both male and female, 'in the image of God', stand at the apex of this structure.
4. Human beings are responsible for the active maintenance of all life. Setting people at the top of the hierarchy of creation places them in a special position of responsibility towards nature. Adam is placed in the garden of Eden 'to till it and keep it', and to 'name' (that implies, understand) the animals.
5. Land and people depend on each other. The Bible is the story of a chosen people and a chosen land; prosperity of the land depends on the people's obedience to God's covenant. In the global context, this means that conservation of the planet depends on (a) the social justice and moral integrity of its people and (b) a caring, loving, attitude to land, with effective regulation of its use.
6. Respect creation: do not waste or destroy. *Bal tashchit* ('not to destroy', derived from Deuteronomy 20.19) is the Hebrew phrase on which the rabbis base the call to respect and conserve all that has been created.

These principles are based on Jewish sources, largely shared with Christians, and they must guide the way we preach and teach scripture. We must call for the production of new scriptural commentaries, textbooks and catechisms which interpret with sensitivity to bio-issues, and we must train our clergy and teachers to use them.

Concern for the *bios* is, moreover, an ideal enterprise to stimulate religions to work co-operatively. They have a common interest, some common scriptures and many common values. Therefore, in educating better for the environment, we will also educate better for a world which can accommodate many religions peacefully. Concern for our common home should lead us to set aside the mutual antagonisms which in the past have led to religious wars and human destruction.

The prophet Isaiah proclaimed, 'The wolf shall live with the lamb ... and the lion shall eat straw like the ox';[30] he perceived clearly the link between the harmony of nature and the peace of humankind.

29. Genesis 1.31.
30. Isaiah 11.6–7.

The Environment from a Christian Perspective

Kallistos Ware

'Love the Trees'

When I was living in the Monastery of St. John the Theologian on the Greek island of Patmos during 1965–66, I had the happiness of frequently meeting the *geronta* or 'elder' of the island, Father Amphilochios. One of his outstanding characteristics was a reverence and love for the created world. 'Do you know,' he used to say, 'that God gave us one more commandment, which is not recorded in scripture? It is the commandment "Love the trees."' Whoever does not love trees, he believed, does not love God. 'When you plant a tree,' he affirmed, 'you plant hope, you plant peace, you plant love; and you will receive God's blessing.' An ecologist long before ecology had become fashionable, it was his practice, when hearing the confessions of the local farmers, to assign to them, as a penance, the task of planting a tree. Under his influence, many parts of the island have been transformed: on the path up to the monastery, where photographs taken eighty years ago show a bare and stony hillside, today there is a flourishing wood of pine and eucalyptus.[1]

Fr. Amphilochios was expressing a conviction shared by Jews, Christians and Muslims. All three religious traditions are in full agreement that the world around us is God's creation, and as such it reflects the goodness and glory of its creator. They are agreed also in affirming that we human beings share together a special responsibility to tend and watch over the divine creation.

Christians, no less than Jews, appeal to Genesis 1.31: 'God saw everything that he had made, and indeed, it was very good.' In the Septuagint (the Greek translation of the Hebrew Old Testament that is used in the Orthodox Church), the final words of this scriptural verse are rendered *kala lian*, which is much stronger than the anodyne English phrase 'very good'. The Greek can best be paraphrased 'exceedingly good and beautiful'. The word *kalos* means in Greek

1. On Father Amphilochios and the material environment, see P. Nikitaras, *O Gerontas Amphilochios Makris: Mia synchroni morphi tis Patmou (1888–1970)* (Athens: Eptalophos, n.d. [1984]), pp. 47–49; and I.L. Triantis, *O Gerontas tis Patmou Amphilochios Makris 1889–1970* (Patmos: Evangelismos, 1993), pp. 138–40.

not only morally good but aesthetically beautiful; and this spiritual beauty of the cosmos is something that as human beings we are required to cherish and proclaim. The adjective *kalos* is related to the verb *kaleo*, meaning 'I call out, summon, invite'. That is exactly the effect that the beauty of the created world has upon us: it calls out to us, it draws us to itself, it is immediately attractive. If we do not feel this, we are not genuinely human.

Exploring the way in which Christians understand this goodness and beauty of the created world, let us first consider the basic teaching concerning the creation to be found in the New Testament, and the struggle of the early Church against Gnostic dualism. This will lead us to examine two further aspects of creation theology: how the world is the expression of God's free love, and how the divine creator is both immanent and transcendent ('panentheism'). In the light of this, we can then evaluate our relationship as human beings to the physical environment. What is to be our attitude towards our own bodies? And in what way does our psychosomatic unity empower us to act as priests of the creation?

'O Lord, how Manifold are your Works!'

An affirmative attitude towards the creation is implied, first of all, by our belief as Christians in God's incarnation. At his human birth from the Virgin Mary, Jesus Christ took integral humanness, not only a human soul but equally a human body. Through this human body, he related to the material world around him, which through his sense-perceptions became part of his inner life. In this human body he was transfigured on the mountain, crucified on Golgotha, and raised from the dead on the third day; in this human body he ascended into heaven, and will come again in glory on the last day. By making human physicality his own and appropriating it in this way, Christ bears witness to the sacredness of all human bodies and all material things.

From his Jewish upbringing, Jesus inherited the conviction that the world is 'exceedingly good and beautiful'. In the Sermon on the Mount, he spoke about the marvels of nature: 'Consider the lilies of the field ... even Solomon in all his glory was not clothed like one of these.'[2] He also taught that God cares for every living creature, however seemingly insignificant: 'Are not two sparrows sold for a penny? Yet not one of them will fall to the ground apart from your Father.'[3]

Faith in God as maker and sustainer of the world was a firm and clear element in the preaching of the apostolic Church. 'The God who made the world and everything in it,' stated Paul to the Athenians in his speech on the Areopagus, 'he who is Lord of heaven and earth ... "In him we live and move

2. Matthew 6.28–29.
3. Matthew 10.29.

and have our being."'[4] Moreover, Jesus Christ was seen not only as the saviour of humankind but more broadly as God's agent in creation. In the words of the prologue to the fourth gospel, 'In the beginning was the Word [Logos] ... All things came into being through him, and without him not one thing came into being.'[5] Paul was even more explicit in assigning a cosmic role to Christ: 'in him all things in heaven and on earth were created, things visible and invisible ... all things have been created through him and for him ... and in him all things hold together.'[6] Christ is the 'togetherness' of the cosmos, its unity and coherence.

Reflecting further on the role of Christ in the universe, early Christian thinkers from the second century onwards saw creation as a Trinitarian act: God the Father creates through the Son in the Holy Spirit. They discerned a Trinitarian pattern in the opening of the creation story in Genesis: 'God said, "Let there be light"' – God created through his Word or Logos Jesus Christ – and at the same time 'the spirit of God swept over the face of the waters'.[7] The same triadic scheme is to be found in Psalm 33.6: 'By the word of the Lord the heavens were made, and all their host by the breath [or Spirit] of his mouth.'

More specifically, writers such as Theophilus of Antioch (late second-century) and Irenaeus of Lyons (c. 130 – c. 200) envisaged the creation of the human person as a Trinitarian act. Appealing to the use of the plural in Genesis 1.26 – 'Let *us* make humankind (*adam*) in *our* image, according to *our* likeness' – they considered that here, God the Father is taking counsel with the Son and the Holy Spirit. The creation of the human person is thus 'conciliar' in character, the shared work of all three members of the Trinity; and so the divine image bestowed on humankind is specifically a Trinitarian image.[8] Thus the created world as a whole, and above all the human race, are a reflection of the mutual love – the *perichoresis* or reciprocal indwelling – of the three divine persons of the uncreated Trinity.

As long as early Christians remained within a predominantly Jewish setting, there was little need to insist upon the intrinsic goodness of the world, for this was something that almost every Jew would take for granted. But as soon as Christianity moved out from a Jewish to a Hellenistic milieu, the situation was dramatically altered. The *Zeitgeist* of contemporary Graeco-Roman civilization was deeply marked by global pessimism. The material world was widely regarded either as itself evil, or at any rate as subject to the dominion of evil powers. In particular, the human body was seen in sharply negative terms. 'You are a poor soul carrying about a corpse,' said Marcus Aurelius (121–80 CE);[9] and Philo of Alexandria (d. c. 50 CE) – himself Jewish, but much influenced by

4. Acts 17.24 and 28.
5. John 1.1 and 3.
6. Colossians 1.16–17.
7. Genesis 1.3 and 2.
8. On the image of God, see Alison Salvesen's paper, 'The Image of God in Humanity from a Christian Perspective', in this volume.
9. *Meditations* 4.41.

Hellenism – went so far as to describe the body as a 'foul prison house', 'evil by nature and treacherous towards the soul'.[10] There were, however, a few Greek philosophers, such as the neo-Platonist Plotinus (205–69/70 CE), who upheld the goodness of the material world: although standing on the lowest level of reality, it is, according to its own mode of existence, as good and beautiful as it is possible for it to be. This prevailing anti-cosmic dualism came to a head in the amorphous movement or group of movements known to modern scholarship as 'Gnosticism'. In the second century, there was a serious possibility that Gnosticism might have taken over the Church, but this did not in fact happen. In its teaching concerning creation, early Christianity remained faithful to its Jewish roots. Opposing the Gnostics, Irenaeus insisted that the Father of our Lord Jesus Christ is also the creator of the world, and that the material order, including our physical bodies, is essentially good. 'It is right,' he stated, 'that we should start with the first, most important proposition, that is to say, with God the creator, who made heaven and earth and everything in them ... He alone is God, alone Lord, alone creator, alone Father, and alone contains all things and bestows existence on them.'[11]

Yet, while reaffirming the Jewish belief in the goodness of the created world, Christian writers have not emphasized the interdependence between people and land in the way that Judaism does. They have tended, on the contrary, to see their Christian allegiance as signifying that they are citizens of the entire world; or, rather, that their true citizenship is in heaven alone. In the words of the second-century *Letter to Diognetus*, 'Christians live in their own countries, but as strangers ... Every foreign country is their fatherland, and every fatherland is foreign ... Their existence is on earth, their citizenship in heaven.'[12]

The repudiation of Gnosticism represents a decisive turning-point in Christian history. It is true that the spirit of Gnosticism, while officially rejected, has continued to maintain an underground existence within the Church. All too often, it has to be admitted, Christians have spoken in negative terms about the material world and their own physicality. Asceticism has tended to be seen as a struggle, not merely against the flesh – that is, our fallen human impulses – but against the body as such. Distinguishing the two, the Russian theologian Sergei Bulgakov (1871–1944) used to say, 'Kill the flesh ... to acquire a body';[13] but the distinction has frequently been forgotten.

Nevertheless, in principle, the Christian Church remains firmly committed to a positive view of the created order. The Nicene-Constantinopolitan Creed

10. *On the Migration of Abraham* 9; *Allegorical Interpretation of the Laws* 3.71.

11. *Against the Heresies* 2.1.1. On the early Christian doctrine of creation, see R.A. Norris, *God and World in Early Christian Theology: A Study in Justin Martyr, Irenaeus, Tertullian and Origen* (London: A. & C. Black, 1966); and D.S. Wallace-Hadrill, *The Greek Patristic View of Nature* (Manchester: University Press, 1968).

12. *Letter to Diognetus* 5.

13. Quoted by Metropolitan Anthony of Sourozh, 'Body and Matter in Spiritual Life', in A.M. Allchin (ed.), *Sacrament and Image: Essays in the Christian Understanding of Man* (London: Fellowship of St. Alban and St. Sergius, 1967), pp. 33–41 (41).

(325/381), accepted by virtually all Christians, states without compromise: 'We believe in one God, the Father all-powerful, maker of heaven and of earth, and of all things both seen and unseen; and in one Lord Jesus Christ ... through whom all things came to be.' At its evening worship daily throughout the year, except in Easter week, the Orthodox Church begins the new day by reading Psalm 103/104: 'O Lord, how manifold are your works! In wisdom you have made them all.'[14]

An Act of God's Free Love

Why did God choose to create the world? To this unanswerable question – and yet it is a question that we cannot avoid asking – Christianity, in common with Judaism and Islam, replies that the world, and human persons within it, were created in order to worship and glorify the creator. 'The heavens are telling the glory of God; and the firmament proclaims his handiwork';[15] in the words of Irenaeus, 'God's glory is a human being fully alive' (*gloria Dei vivens homo*).[16] More particularly, the reason for the world's existence can be spelt out in terms of joy and love. According to Maximos the Confessor (c. 580–662), God brought the world into existence so that God and the creation might rejoice in one another: 'God, full beyond all fullness, brought creatures into being not because he had need of anything, but so that they might participate in him in proportion to their capacity, and that he himself might rejoice in his works through seeing them joyful.'[17]

What Maximos expressed in terms of mutual joy can be propounded also in terms of God's outgoing love. As Dionysios the Areopagite (c. 500) put it, 'Divine love is ecstatic',[18] in the literal sense of the Greek word *ekstasis*, meaning 'standing outside oneself'. God created the world because God's love is supra-abundant, overflowing and self-diffusive, and without this self-diffusive love, the world would not exist. As the fourteenth-century English anchorite Julian of Norwich recorded in one of her 'showings':

> [Our Lord] showed me ... a little thing, the size of a hazelnut, on the palm of my hand, round like a ball. I looked at it thoughtfully and wondered, 'What is this?' And the answer came, 'It is all that is made.' I marvelled that it continued to exist and did not suddenly disintegrate; it was so small. And again my mind supplied the answer, 'It exists, both now and for ever, because God loves it.' In short, everything owes its existence to the love of God.[19]

14. Verse 24.
15. Psalm 19.1.
16. *Against the Heresies* 4.20.7.
17. *Centuries on Love* 3.46.
18. *On the Divine Names* 4.13. The word used here for 'love' is *erōs*, not *agapē*.
19. Julian of Norwich, *Revelations of Divine Love* (trans. C. Wolters; Harmondsworth: Penguin Books, 1966), p. 68.

In Christian theology, it is customary to speak of God creating the world *ex nihilo*, 'out of nothing'. So far as I am aware, this concept of creation *ex nihilo* is found only once in scripture, in 2 Maccabees 7.28: 'look at the heaven and the earth and see everything that is in them, and recognize that God did not make them out of things that existed'. While this doctrine is not found explicitly in the New Testament, it is taken up in second-century texts such as *The Shepherd of Hermas*: 'First of all, believe that there is only one God, who created and set in order all things, bringing them out of non-existence into existence.'[20]

The phrase 'out of nothing' is a way of asserting the total transcendence of God, God's absolute freedom and sovereignty in relation to the created world. God did not simply fashion the world out of pre-existent matter, as many Greek philosophers maintained, but is the sole and exclusive source of all that exists. There is nothing and no one outside God that determined or influenced God's act of creation. In unconditioned divine freedom, God *chose* to create. God is necessary to the world, but the world is not necessary to God. Yet, while acknowledging the positive truth that the words 'out of nothing' are in this way intended to safeguard, at the same time we may regret the negative form that the phrase possesses. Rather than say 'out of nothing', it would be more illuminating to say, with Julian of Norwich, that God created *out of love*.

Immanent yet Transcendent

So as to preserve a balanced view of God's relation to the created world, there are two ways of speaking that it is wise to avoid. First, many modern writers – chiefly Western, but sometimes also Eastern Orthodox – tend to speak as if God the creator were somehow external to the creation. They have envisaged the universe as an artefact, produced by the divine maker from the outside. God has been likened to an architect, a builder or engineer, a potter, or even a clock-maker who does no more than set the cosmic process in motion, winding up the clock but then leaving it to continue ticking away on its own.

This 'deist' approach overemphasizes God's transcendence at the expense of God's immanence. If the doctrine of creation is to mean anything at all, it must surely signify that God is on the *inside* of everything, not on the outside. Creation is not something upon which God acts from the exterior, but something through which God expresses God's self from within. Our primary images should be of indwelling and omnipresence. To use a phrase often applied to Christ or to the Holy Spirit in Orthodox worship, God is 'everywhere present and fills all things'. In the words of the second-century *Gospel of Thomas*, 'Cut the wood in two, and I am there; lift up the stone, and there you will find me.'[21] While above and beyond the creation, God is also its true inwardness, its 'within'.

20. *Mandatum* 1.1.
21. *Gospel of Thomas* 77.

In this context, it is perhaps legitimate to speak of 'panentheism', as distinct from pantheism.[22] The pantheist says that God is the world, and that the world is God; but the panentheist says that God is *in* the world, and that the world is *in* God. Pantheism – the identification of God and the world, the collapsing of divine transcendence into divine immanence – is not, I believe, a viable option for Christianity, any more than it is for Judaism or Islam. At times, it is true, members of all three traditions, especially mystical writers, have seemed to come close to the pantheist position; it is, however, a disputed point how literally their statements should be interpreted. But, while pantheism is to be set aside, panentheism can be understood in a sense acceptable to the Christian faith (and, I imagine, also to Judaism and Islam). Antinomic and dialectical in its approach, yet not self-contradictory, panentheism allows full scope to divine immanence, yet without thereby excluding divine transcendence. In the presence of each person and each thing, the panentheist responds, in the words of the Anglican poet Charles Williams (1886–1945), 'This also is Thou; neither is this Thou.'[23] God, that is to say, is more intimate to us than we are to our own selves; God is at the centre of everything, the heart of its heart, the core of its core, closer to us than the jugular vein, as the Qur'ān puts it.[24] Yet at the same time God is, in the phrase of Rudolf Otto (1869–1937), 'the Wholly Other',[25] ultimate Mystery surpassing everything that exists, beyond understanding and participation.

A second manner of speaking that is best avoided is the common practice of talking about God's act of creation in the past tense, as if it were a once-for-all event occurring only 'in the beginning', an initial deed that constitutes a

22. 'Panentheism' is a slippery word, employed in a number of different senses, as is made clear in M.W. Brierley, 'Naming a Quiet Revolution: The Panentheistic Turn in Modern Theology', in P. Clayton and A.R. Peacocke (eds.), *In Whom We Live and Move and Have Our Being: Panentheistic Reflections on God's Presence in a Scientific World* (Grand Rapids, MI and Cambridge: Eerdmans, 2004), pp. 1–15, and N.H. Gregersen, 'Three Varieties of Panentheism', in Clayton and Peacocke (eds.), *In Whom We Live and Move and Have Our Being*, pp. 19–35. For my own use of the term, see my article 'God Immanent yet Transcendent: The Divine Energies according to Saint Gregory Palamas' in the same volume, pp. 157–68 (at 166–68). In adopting the word, I do not wish to endorse panentheism of a Whiteheadian type, whereby God is envisaged as dependent upon the world. I understand the word simply in the sense 'that the Being of God includes and penetrates the whole universe, so that every part of it exists in Him, but (as against pantheism) that His Being is more than, and is not exhausted by, the universe' (F.L. Cross and E.A. Livingstone [eds.], *The Oxford Dictionary of the Christian Church* [Oxford: Oxford University Press, 3rd edn, 1997], p. 1213).

23. See, for example, C. Williams, *Seed of Adam and Other Plays* (London, New York and Toronto: Oxford University Press, 1948), p. 12. Williams saw the double phrase as an asymptote: see C. Williams, *The Image of the City and Other Essays* (ed. A. Ridler; London: Oxford University Press, 1958), p. xl. He implied that the phrase is a quotation, but did not indicate the source. Similar language can certainly be found in Hindu texts.

24. Qur'ān 50.16.

25. R. Otto, *The Idea of the Holy* (Oxford and London: Oxford University Press, 6th edn, 1936), p. 25.

chronological starting-point. Once more, this will not do. Creation is to be seen not as a past event but as a present relationship – as something that is occurring here and now, at this moment and at every moment. We are to think and speak not in the aorist but in the present tense. We are to say, not 'God *made* the world, once upon a time, long ago', but 'God *is making* the world, and you and me in it, at this very instant and always'.

In this sense, it is appropriate to employ the phrase 'continual creation'. At each and every instant, God is the constant and unceasing source, principle and sustainer of all that has being. Without the active and uninterrupted presence of God in every part of the cosmos, nothing would remain in existence for a single moment. If the divine maker did not exert a creative will at each split second of time, the universe would immediately disappear into the void of non-being. In the words of Philaret, Metropolitan of Moscow (1782–1867), 'All creatures are balanced upon the creative word of God, as upon a bridge of diamond. Above them is the abyss of the divine infinitude, below them that of their own nothingness.'[26]

During the early Christian and Byzantine periods, Greek patristic authors employed two ways in particular by which to articulate this double truth of God as transcendent yet immanent, as beyond and above, yet everywhere present. In both of these cases, the relationship between creator and creation is presented in a dynamic rather than a static manner. The act of creating, understood in terms of divine indwelling and omnipresence, is seen as a continuing reality in the present, not as a unique event in the remote past.

First, Maximos the Confessor, among others, understood God's relationship to the world in terms of Logos and *logoi*. Christ the creator Logos has implanted in every created thing a characteristic *logos*, a 'thought' or 'word', which is God's intention for that thing, its inner essence, that which makes it to be distinctively itself and which at the same time draws it towards God. By virtue of these indwelling *logoi*, each created thing is not just an object but a personal word addressed to us by the creator. The *logoi* are described by Maximos in two different ways, sometimes as created and sometimes as uncreated, depending upon the perspective in which they are viewed. They are created, inasmuch as they inhere in the created world; but, when regarded as God's intention for each thing – as the divine 'predetermination' or 'preconception' concerning that thing – they are not created but uncreated. The divine Logos, the second person of the Trinity, the Wisdom and Providence of God, constitutes at once the source and end of the particular *logoi*, and in this manner acts as an all-embracing and unifying cosmic presence.[27]

26. Quoted in V. Lossky, *The Mystical Theology of the Eastern Church* (London: James Clarke, 1957), p. 92.

27. For further bibliography on Maximos' teaching concerning Logos and *logoi*, see A. Louth, 'The Cosmic Vision of Saint Maximos the Confessor', in Clayton and Peacocke (eds.), *In Whom We Live and Move and Have Our Being*, pp. 184–96.

In the second place, other Greek Fathers – in particular Gregory Palamas (c. 1296–1359) – adopted another approach, not contrary to the first but complementary: they made a distinction between God's transcendent essence (*ousia*) and God's immanent energies or operations (*energeiai*). In essence, God is infinitely transcendent, utterly surpassing all circumscribed being and totally beyond all participation from the side of creation. God's essence is and will always remain unknowable to all created beings, to both angels and humankind, alike in this present age and in the age to come. But in God's energies, which are inseparable from God's essence – and which are nothing less than God's own self in action – God is inexhaustibly immanent, maintaining all things in existence, animating them, making each of them a sacrament of God's personal presence. While permeating created reality, these energies are not themselves created but uncreated and eternal. When the three disciples saw Christ transfigured by light upon the mountain,[28] this was a revelation of his uncreated energies; and the saints experience these same energies through the vision of divine light during prayer. These energies, omnipresent throughout the universe, transform it into a cosmic burning bush, incandescent with the fire of the Godhead yet unconsumed.[29]

All that has been said about the indwelling presence of the divine *logoi* or energies will be gravely misleading if we do not also add something else. The world is indeed a sacrament of God's presence, and as such it is 'exceedingly good and beautiful'. Yet at the same time, it is a *fallen* world. I am not sure how far the notion of the Fall of humankind and of nature is accepted in Judaism and Islam. Even in Christianity, there is no single and universally accepted understanding of what is signified by the Fall and original sin. Some Western writers, such as Augustine and Calvin, are strongly pessimistic, whereas the Christian East adopts on the whole a less sombre view. But, disregarding these differences, it may be said that the doctrine of the Fall is a way of stating that the world and in particular our own human nature, as we know them in our present experience, are not as God intends them to be. There is a radical discrepancy, a tragic gap, between the divine plan and our actual situation. Something has gone wrong. We have within us a nostalgia for a lost paradise, but we are all too conscious that the world around us is not paradise. We feel ourselves to be exiles from our true home. The world is still beautiful, but its beauty is flawed.

Just as the Fall involves both humankind and the created order as a whole, so also salvation extends not only to human beings but to the total realm of nature.

28. Matthew 17.1–8.

29. Cf. Exodus 3.2. The basic work on Palamas, now much in need of updating, is J. Meyendorff, *Introduction à l'étude de Grégoire Palamas* (Patristica Sorbonensia, 3; Paris: Seuil, 1959); English translation, *A Study of Gregory Palamas* (trans. G. Lawrence; London: Faith Press, 1964), where the essence-energies distinction is discussed on pp. 202–27. For more recent treatments of the distinction, see J. Lison, *L'Esprit repandu: la pneumatologie de Grégoire Palamas* (Paris: Cerf, 1994), pp. 101–32; and A.N. Williams, *The Ground of Union: Deification in Aquinas and Palamas* (New York and Oxford: Oxford University Press, 1999), pp. 137–56.

We humans are not saved *from* but *with* the world; our salvation involves also the transfiguration of the cosmos. We are saved in our entirety, body, soul and spirit together. In the future life that we await, we look forward not just to the immortality of the soul but more specifically to the resurrection of the body. This Christian expectation of bodily resurrection rests on our belief in the already accomplished resurrection of Jesus Christ on the third day after his crucifixion. He is the forerunner, opening up the path that we are to follow; he is the first-fruits, and we are the harvest.[30]

Moreover, in the age to come after our bodily resurrection, we shall exist not in isolation but within a transformed material creation, with rocks, rivers, trees and animals. The Jewish prophecies concerning the messianic age are in this way applied by Christianity to the *eschaton*.[31] We look forward to a 'new earth',[32] to a future transformation of the natural world. At present, said Paul, the whole creation is in 'bondage to decay' and 'groans in labour pains', as it awaits the 'revealing of the children of God'; but in the future age, as a result of our salvation, the environment also will be saved, and will obtain 'the freedom of the glory of the children of God'.[33] Such are the cosmic dimensions of our all-embracing future hope.

Priests of the Creation

In the light of these beliefs concerning the creation of the world, the Fall, the incarnation, and the final resurrection of humankind, how do Christians understand their relationship to the physical environment? Let us begin by considering our attitude towards our own physical bodies; for it is our bodies that constitute our immediate environment, and it is through them that we relate to the rest of the natural world. Here our key term will be *unity*. Second, let us next ask what is to be our attitude towards the realm of nature as a whole. Here our key term will be *offering*.

First, then, as regards the human body, it is necessary to apply here what was said earlier about the creation in general: along with the rest of creation, the body is God's handiwork, and as such, it is in its basic essence 'exceedingly good and beautiful'. In its present state, the body often seems to be an enemy, a cause of inner conflict, an instrument of temptation; but that is because, in our fallen situation, it exists in a condition that is not natural but highly unnatural.[34]

30. Cf. 1 Corinthians 15.12–28.
31. Isaiah 11.6–9 and 41.18–20, etc.
32. Revelation 21.1.
33. Romans 8.19–22.
34. See K. Ware, '"My Helper and My Enemy": The Body in Greek Christianity', in S. Coakley (ed.), *Religion and the Body* (Cambridge: Cambridge University Press, 1997), pp. 90–110. Cf. from the same volume, L. Jacobs, 'The Body in Jewish Worship: Three Rituals Examined', pp. 71–89; A. Louth, 'The Body in Western Catholic Christianity', pp. 111–30; and A. Schimmel, '"I Take Off the Dress of the Body": Eros in Sufi Literature and Life', pp. 262–88.

The next step, after affirming the goodness of the body, is for us to recognize its unity with the soul. The view of human personhood to be found in the New Testament is, like that of the Old Testament, fundamentally unitary and holistic. I do not simply 'have' a body or 'use' a body, but I *am* my body and my body is *me*. The body is not a part or constituent element of the human person, but it is the total human person considered from one point of view, just as the soul is also the total human person, considered from another point of view.

Significantly, Paul frequently contrasted spirit and flesh, but scarcely if ever did he make a contrast between soul and body (or, for that matter, between head and heart).[35] Many later Christian writers, often under Platonic influence, have asserted a sharp dichotomy between soul and body. But this does not reflect the true Christian standpoint – the standpoint of the Bible – which thinks of human personhood in terms of interdependence and integration. This holistic anthropology entails a holistic soteriology: the body is redeemed and sanctified together with the soul. Sanctification does not signify the escape of the soul from the body, but the transformation of both of them, through the action of divine grace, in unbroken solidarity with each other. This is clear, as already emphasized, from the example of Christ himself. Just as Christ was transfigured, suffered, rose from the dead, and ascended into heaven in his material body, so likewise those who believe in him are called to serve and worship him through their bodies. As Paul insisted, 'your body is a temple of the Holy Spirit within you ... glorify God in your body'; 'present your bodies as a living sacrifice, holy and acceptable to God'.[36] The spiritual value of the body is evident from the sacramental practice of the Church: at baptism the body is immersed in water, at the eucharist the body feeds upon the consecrated bread and wine that are the body and blood of Christ, and at services of healing the body is anointed with consecrated oil. In the words of J.V. Taylor, 'Our retrieval of mystery is dependent upon our reinstatement of the body, with its rhythms and dreams and ways of knowing.'[37]

Turning now to our second point, the relationship of human beings to the physical environment in general, the first thing to be said is that the misuse of material things is to be regarded as a *sin*. This may seem obvious, but it has in fact been widely disregarded by Christians in the past. We have tended to assume that sin involves only what we do to other human persons. This way of thinking has had disastrous consequences. We Christians have frankly to admit that in significant respects, we ourselves are responsible for the contemporary ecological catastrophe, which many believe to be now irreversible. We cannot simply blame modern secularism and economic greed; the environmental

35. On this, see the discussion by J.A.T. Robinson (as relevant today as when it was first written), *The Body: A Study in Pauline Theology* (London: SCM Press, 1952), pp. 11–33.

36. 1 Corinthians 6.19–20; Romans 12.1.

37. J.V. Taylor, *The Go-Between God: The Holy Spirit and the Christian Mission* (London: SCM Press, 1972), p. 45.

crisis also has Christian roots. Let us as Christians confess that, in the words of Edward Echlin, 'our present behaviour is unsustainable'.[38]

I have just used the familiar words 'environmental crisis'. But such a phrase is actually inaccurate. What confronts us is not a crisis in the environment but a crisis in the human heart. The fundamental problem lies not outside but inside ourselves, not in the ecosystem but in the way in which we ourselves think. The issue is not primarily technological or economic but, much more profoundly, spiritual. If we are destroying the forests and rendering poisonous the air we breathe and the water we drink, this is because we have forgotten our true relationship as human beings to the world that is God's gift to us. Our 'world image' has become distorted because our 'human image', our human self-understanding, has become grievously twisted.[39] Our most urgent need is not for more sophisticated scientific skills but for an act of ecological repentance, of *metanoia* in the literal sense of the Greek word – an ecological 'change of mind'. We have to recognize how deep within the heart of every one of us there lies greed and the lust for power.

So where shall we begin with this ecological 'change of mind', with this combat against our destructive greed and our deep-seated lust for power? A good point at which to start is a proper understanding of hierarchy. In common with Judaism and Islam, Christianity believes that the universe is hierarchical, in the sense that it is a unified whole existing on many interdependent levels, an ordered system in which the diverse parts are all organically connected. Since to many people today, the word 'hierarchy' has an unattractive sound, it is important to underline its true religious significance. Hierarchy is concerned, not with subjection and oppressive subordination, but with the transmission of divine grace and the drawing of all things into harmony with God. In the words of Dionysius the Areopagite, 'The goal of hierarchy is to enable all beings to be made as like as possible to God, and to be united with him.'[40]

Within this divinely ordained hierarchy, the human person occupies a unique position, by virtue of the fact that human beings alone are created according to the image and likeness of God. As such, we humans are authorized to use the rest of creation for our own benefit: 'Then God said, "Let us make humankind in our image, according to our likeness; and let them have dominion over the fish of the sea, and over the birds of the air, and over the cattle, and over all the wild animals of the earth."'[41] Yet at the same time, it is clearly stated in the Bible that, in our utilization of created things, we should display a sense of respect and reverence, acknowledging that these created things exist not merely in relation to us but in their own right.

As regards domestic animals, for example, this means that, when employing them in our service, it is our duty to treat them with kindness, not overworking

38. E.P. Echlin, *Earth Spirituality: Jesus at the Centre* (New Alresford: Arthur James, 1999), p. 130.

39. See P. Sherrard, *Human Image, World Image: The Death and Resurrection of Sacred Cosmology* (Ipswich: Golgonooza Press and Friends of the Centre, 1992), pp. 1–10.

40. *Celestial Hierarchy* 3.2.

41. Genesis 1.26.

them, not inflicting pain upon them, but providing them with food and warmth. Most Christians, citing biblical authority,[42] believe that it is permissible to kill animals and eat them. There is, however, a significant minority that chooses to be vegetarian, on strongly held grounds of principle; and in many monasteries, both Roman Catholic and Orthodox, meat is not eaten (but fish is generally allowed, so such monastic communities are not strictly vegetarian).[43] Whatever our viewpoint on this particular issue, we are bound always and everywhere to recognize with awe and gratitude the characteristic 'isness' of each existing thing, whether animate or inanimate. To borrow Martin Buber's terminology, nature is to be treated not as an 'It' but as a 'Thou'.

Three words are commonly used by Christians to describe the relationship of human beings to the world: *king*, *steward* and *priest*. The first of these, although justified by the words of Genesis, 'Let them have dominion', has today become unpopular; for it is seen as implying an arrogant attitude towards creation, such as has led directly to the present ecological crisis. It should not be forgotten, however, that in the Genesis account this granting of dominion is directly linked with the creation of humankind according to God's image. Our exercise of kingship and dominion, that is to say, is to reflect the tender-hearted compassion of God's own self. It is to be a humble and kenotic kingship, not selfish and arbitrary. Dominion does not mean domination.

Sensitive to the manner in which this language of kingship, albeit in itself defensible, can easily be misinterpreted, some Christian ecologists prefer to speak of our stewardship of creation. This has the advantage of stressing that our authority over the created world is not absolute but delegated. We are not the owners or proprietors of creation, for the world belongs to God and not to us. It is merely given to us in trust. Such language, however, also has disadvantages. To speak of stewardship could suggest a managerial, utilitarian approach to nature, as if it were an 'asset' to be developed and exploited. We must not allow ourselves to objectify and depersonalize the world around us.

Because of possible misunderstandings of the terms 'king' and 'steward', it may be wise to choose a third model: it is our human vocation to be priests of the creation.[44] The essence of priesthood, as the Bible makes clear, is to offer,

42. Genesis 9.3–5; Acts 15.20.

43. On the Christian attitude to animals, see in particular the books of A. Linzey, such as *Christianity and the Rights of Animals* (New York: Crossroad, 1987), and *Animal Theology* (Urbana, IL: University of Illinois Press, 1995); cf. S.R.L. Clark, *Animals and Their Moral Standing* (London: Routledge, 1997). For evidence from the early Church, consult R.M. Grant, *Early Christians and Animals* (London and New York: Routledge, 1999). R. Murray, *The Cosmic Covenant: Biblical Themes of Justice, Peace and the Integrity of Creation* (Heythrop Monographs, 7; London: Sheed & Ward, 1992), pp. 94–125, is an excellent assessment of the Old Testament evidence by a Roman Catholic scholar.

44. When speaking of priesthood in this context, I am not thinking of the ministerial priesthood, conferred by ordination and exercised by a limited group of people, but of the universal priesthood bestowed on every human being by virtue of the fact that each is created in the divine image.

to give thanks, and to bless. As a creature fashioned according to the divine image, the human animal can best be described, not just as a logical or political animal, but as a eucharistic or doxological animal, endowed with the ability to offer the world back to God in thanksgiving, and so to call down the divine blessing upon each created thing. In the words of the Greek Orthodox Metropolitan John Zizioulas of Pergamum:

> The priest is one who, freely and as himself an organic part of it, takes the world in his hands to refer it to God, and who, in return, brings God's blessing on what he refers to God. Through this act, creation is brought into communion with God himself. This is the essence of priesthood, and it is only the human being who can do it, namely, unite the world in his hand in order to refer it to God, so that it can be united with God and saved and fulfilled.[45]

To appreciate the true meaning of this image of priesthood, two things need to be added. First, there can be no genuine act of offering without *sacrifice*. The ecological crisis cannot be resolved – if, indeed, a resolution is still possible – without self-restraint, without voluntary self-limitation in our consumption of food and natural resources, without making a distinction between what I *want* and what I *need*. Only through constructive self-denial, through the willingness to forgo and to say 'no', will we rediscover our proper place in the universe. As the Ecumenical Patriarch Bartholomew affirmed at the closing ceremony of the Fourth International Symposium on Religion, Science and the Environment in Venice on 10 June 2002, this element of sacrifice constitutes the 'missing dimension' in our ecological programme: 'Without sacrifice there can be no blessing and no cosmic transfiguration.'[46]

Secondly, and yet more important, there can be no genuine act of priestly offering without *love*. It is love that lies at the heart of the human mystery, love that expresses the divine image within us, love that enables us to act as priests of the creation, offering back the world in eucharist to God. Fr. Amphilochios was right to say, '*Love* the trees'. We cannot save what we do not love.

As members of the three 'Abrahamic' religions, sharing a common belief in the intrinsic goodness of the material world, we can and should work closely together in seeking to protect the environment.[47] A start has already been made, but it requires to be carried much further. Of course, in order to secure global agreement, religious leaders and theologians have to be in dialogue also with scientists, economic experts and political leaders. Above all – and this is where the chief difficulty lies – there is an imperative need to involve the heads of the

45. Speech delivered at the Fourth International Symposium on Religion, Science and the Environment (5–11 June 2002).

46. Ecumenical Patriarch Bartholomew, 'Sacrifice: The Missing Dimension', in J. Chryssavgis (ed.), *Cosmic Grace, Humble Prayer: The Ecological Vision of the Green Patriarch Bartholomew I* (Grand Rapids, MI and Cambridge: Eerdmans, 2003), pp. 304–308 (308).

47. Needless to say, we should also co-operate with Hindus, Buddhists, and indeed with members of all faiths.

great international corporations. Yet, indispensable though the involvement of politicians and business people undoubtedly is, in the end it is spiritual values, not economic factors, that should determine the ecological agenda. It is precisely here that inter-religious co-operation has a vital role to play.

Divine Sparks

In conclusion, to complement the 'panentheistic' theology of Maximos the Confessor and Gregory Palamas, let us quote some words from a Western visionary, Hildegard of Bingen (1098–1179). 'All living creatures,' she said, 'are, so to speak, sparks from the radiation of God's brilliance, emerging from God like the rays of the sun.'[48] She recorded the memorable words addressed to her by the Holy Spirit:

> I, the highest and fiery power, have kindled every living spark ... I flame above the beauty of the fields; I shine in the waters; in the sun, the moon and the stars, I burn. And by means of the airy wind, I stir everything into quickness with a certain invisible life that sustains all. For the air is alive in its green power and its blossoming; the waters flow as if they were alive. Even the sun is alive in its own light ... I, the fiery power, lie hidden in these things and they blaze from me, just as human beings are continually moved by their breath, and as the fire contains the nimble flame ... I am the whole of life ... Every living thing is rooted in me.[49]

48. *Book of Divine Works* 4.1, in F. Bowie and O. Davies (eds.), *Hildegard of Bingen: An Anthology* (London: SPCK, 1990), p. 33 (translation adapted).
49. *Book of Divine Works* 1.2, in Bowie and Davies (eds.), *Hildegard of Bingen*, pp. 91–92 (translation adapted).

The Environment from a Muslim Perspective

Lutfi Radwan

The End of the World is Nigh!

> When the sun is shrouded in darkness, when the stars are dimmed, when the mountains are set in motion, when pregnant camels are abandoned, when wild beasts are herded together, when the seas boil over, when souls are sorted into classes, when the baby girl, buried alive, is asked for what sin she was killed, when the record of deeds are spread open, when the sky is peeled away, when hell is made to blaze and paradise brought near; then every soul will know what it has brought about.[1]

Traditional readings of the above verses emphasize the reference to infanticide – a pre-Islamic practice. Contemporary readings, however, cannot fail to notice the relevance of references to disorder in the natural world: some of the verses might be interpreted in terms of global warming, ozone depletion and even a 'nuclear winter'. In both cases, traditional and contemporary, the reader should still conclude that the activities of humankind are in need of moral reform. The essential message of the passage is that individuals are intensely responsible for their deeds, while at the same time God's plan for humankind will be fulfilled, despite individuals but by their own hands.

While each of the Abrahamic faiths focuses on the personal spiritual development of the individual, it is in the created world that individuals exercise their freedom to act in accordance with God's law. It is beyond dispute that the created world is finite, and it is increasingly likely that our own deeds will play no small part in the partial or complete destruction of the earth. The Qur'ān, along with the Bible and Torah, contains abundant references to cataclysmic events prior to our resurrection and judgement, so Islam clearly has something to say about the current abuse of the natural environment.[2] In its simplest form, such abuse is regarded as a sign of moral corruption and spiritual imbalance. This is hardly

1. Qur'ān 81.1–14.
2. 'When the Earth is shaken to her utmost convulsion. And the Earth throws up her burdens from within. And man cries, "What is the matter with her?" On that day will she declare her tidings: For that thy Lord hath given her inspiration' (Qur'ān 99.1–5). For an introduction to modern Muslim writing on ecology, see R.C. Foltz, F.M. Denny and A. Baharuddin (eds.), *Islam and Ecology: A Bestowed Trust* (Cambridge, MA: Harvard University Press, 2003).

a controversial position and few in modern times would question the assertion that there is something fundamentally wrong in our relationship with the natural world, and moreover that the magnitude of the impact we are having is potentially life-threatening. While for some, there would be no direct link between our moral behaviour and the state of the environment, for many more our current obsession with the economic valuation of resources has simply allowed us to sideline any serious discussion of the moral dimensions of our actions.[3]

Secular and religious approaches to understanding the natural environment broadly concur that we inhabit and form part of an ordered system. Like constituents of a living organism, each of the individual parts plays a role, and interacts with and reacts to the other parts. However, this is often where the agreement ends; important divergences occur concerning how this natural environment came into being. Our perspectives on this will shape our responses to further questions concerning the purpose and ultimate destination of the creation, including the role or station occupied by humanity in the natural world and humanity's concomitant rights and responsibilities.

The following essay therefore attempts to outline the main features of an Islamic approach to the environment and seeks to indicate why a theocentric view is so urgently needed if we are to address both the moral and environmental crises which threaten the continued existence of humanity on earth.

The Unity of God

Muslim scholars, especially in the third and fourth centuries AH (ninth and tenth centuries CE), developed sophisticated cosmologies to enable them to conceptualize the relationship between the creator and the objects of creation. These conceptions drew upon earlier traditions, the authenticity of which was measured by their convergence with Qur'ānic precepts, in particular the concept of the unity of God or '*tawḥīd*'.[4] In many respects, advances in observation and understanding have superseded these physical classifications of the natural order. However, the underlying beliefs remain as pertinent now as then: namely, that we form part of a contingent creation united by a shared origin and governed by the 'laws of nature' that bind us. These basic precepts are firmly rooted in the Qur'ān, as indicated in the following verses:

3. See S.H. Nasr, *The Encounter of Man and Nature: The Spiritual Crisis of Modern Man* (London: Allen & Unwin, 1968).

4. For example, one group of such scholars, the Ikhwān al-Ṣafā, interpreted *tawḥīd* in accordance with Pythagorean and Hermetic influences, which are discernible in their doctrines; while the interpretation of another scholar, al-Bīrūnī, involved rejecting much of the rationalistic philosophy of Aristotle and peripatetic views on the eternity of the world. A good introduction to Islamic cosmology is S.H. Nasr, *Religion and the Order of Nature* (Oxford: Oxford University Press, 1994), and *idem*, *An Introduction to Islamic Cosmological Doctrines: Conceptions of Nature and Methods Used for Its Study by the Ikhwan al-Safa', al-Biruni, and Ibn Sina* (Bath: Thames & Hudson, 1978).

> There is no moving creature on earth but its sustenance dependeth on God: He knoweth the time and place of its definite abode and its temporary deposit. All is in a clear record.[5]
>
> Say, who is it that sustains you from the sky and from the earth? Or who is it that has power over hearing and sight? And who is it that brings out the living from the dead and the dead from the living? And who is it that regulates all affairs? They will say, 'God'. Say, 'Will ye not then show piety (to Him)?' Such is God your real cherisher and sustainer. Apart from truth what remains but error? How then are you turned away?[6]

Within this natural order, God has raised humanity and jinn above the rest of creation, imbuing them with both a moral consciousness and a freedom of will. 'Let there be no compulsion in religion. Truth stands out clear from error. Whoever rejects evil and believes in God has grasped the most trustworthy handhold that never breaks. And God heareth and knoweth all things.'[7]

In addition to elaborating a Muslim classification and hierarchy of being, Muslim enquiry in this period also established a link between the study of the natural sciences and worship. All intellectual endeavours could be considered worship, provided that the primary goal was living in harmony with the created world and upholding, within its multiplicity, the unity of its maker.

The Unity of the Created World

All knowledge and enquiry in an Islamic perspective proceeds from the presupposition of an omnipresent and all-powerful God. The essential monotheism of Islam is summed up in one of the closing passages of the Qur'ān: 'Say he is God the one, God the eternal, he begets not nor is he begotten and there is none like unto him.'[8]

Thus God is placed beyond the limitations of the created world: God is the truth, '*Ḥaqq*', reflected in the creation, '*Khalq*'; God is both immanent and transcendent. While it is impossible for the created fully to comprehend the creator, we are able to approach God-consciousness through the manifestations of God's majesty in the created world. In our combination of physical and spiritual attributes, we human beings and to a lesser degree all of creation, have been imbued with an aspect of divinity variously referred to in the Qur'ān as the '*rūḥ*' or spirit (of God) or the '*fiṭra*' or natural state. This innate spirituality, linking all creation, forms what can be regarded as the collective consciousness or the universal soul.[9] 'Do not those who reject faith see that the heavens and

5. Qur'ān 11.6.
6. Qur'ān 10.31–32.
7. Qur'ān 2.256.
8. Qur'ān 112.
9. The Ikhwān al-Ṣafā described the universal soul as 'the spirit of the world ... Nature is the act of this universal soul. The four elements are the matter, which serve as its support. The spheres and the stars are like its organs, and the minerals, plants and animals are the objects which it makes to move' (cited in Nasr, *Introduction to Islamic Cosmological Doctrines*, p. 47).

earth were joined together as one unit of creation before we clove them asunder? And we made all living things of water. Will they not then believe?'[10]

This concept of the unity of creation, referred to in Arabic by the term *waḥdat al-wujūd*, denotes the shared spiritual insight held by all creation and, by extension, it affirms the unity of the creator. As a conceptual framework, it enables the believer to identify the power of the creator through features of the creation; indeed, this is the ultimate aim of all enquiries – drawing closer to the One. 'We shall show them our signs upon the horizons and within themselves until it becomes clear to them that it is the truth.'[11]

When correctly understood, the concept provides a bridge between seemingly polytheistic faiths and the staunch monotheism of Islam. Indeed, such a veneration of the natural order is an important feature of the environmental ethic of Islam.[12] Occurring within finite space and time, nature offers a limited reflection of the true perfection that is God. The ultimate truth is represented in the interconnectedness of nature, with each constituent, in its own fashion, reflecting the divine light. This is an important condition of scientific enquiry in Islam, as it shapes the mind towards the object of study. Much modern understanding of the cosmos regards it as inert matter from which life (on earth) came forth. Within Islam, the created world contains a 'breath' of the eternal and, individually and collectively, is spiritual as well as physical. This understanding shapes one's actions in the world, and represents an individual journey of enlightenment. Material advantage from the study of nature is a secondary benefit and should never be sought at the expense of spiritual knowledge. An important theme resulting from this is the perception of humanity as a microcosm of the cosmos. Rather than the cosmos being viewed as an exterior object, it must be seen as a reflection of one's own reality. Thus harmony (or sustainability) is both a practical and spiritual goal in the Muslim's life.

Following the Natural Law

Within the matrix of Islam, harmony can be achieved through conforming one's whims and desires not only to the revealed guidance in the holy scriptures but also to the natural law accessible to every heart.[13] 'God, there is no god but he, the living, the self-subsisting and eternal. It is he who sent down to you in truth the book, confirming what went before it; And he sent down the Torah and the

10. Qur'ān 21.30.

11. Qur'ān 41.53. The pronoun 'it' may refer to God, or to the Qur'ān.

12. 'Were a Muslim to know what an "idol" is, he would know that all religion is idol worship' (Shaykh Mahmud Shabistari, in J. Nurbaksh [ed. and trans.], *Gulshan-i raz* [Tehran: Khaniqah-i Nimatullahi, 1976], p. 5).

13. Revelation and natural law, properly interpreted, should present no conflict as indicated in the following prophetic tradition: 'None amongst you truly believe until his natural inclination is in accordance with that with which I have come' (Yaḥyā al-Nawawī, *Forty Hadith* [trans. D. Johnson-Davies and I. Ibrahim; Beirut: Dār al-Koran al-Kareem, 1980], 41).

Gospels before, as a guide to mankind; And he sent down the criterion [of distinguishing right and wrong].'[14]

The criterion (*al Furqān*) is referred to separately from revelation and is more akin to the intuitive knowledge of a moral agent endowed with free will; it guides not only people's social interactions but also their relationship with the environment.[15] This source of God's revelation, 'the book of the natural world', is in the above verse placed on a par with textual revelations insofar as both, while serving differing functions and accessed through different senses, ultimately lead to the same truth. Parallels to this universal criterion can be drawn with the Platonic 'ideas'; and Muslim philosophers of the Middle Ages readily adapted this model to incorporate the 'names' of God (the divine attributes referred to in the Qur'ān and central to devotional prayer). These attributes imbue all creation and are the stable and unchangeable essences of all things. 'They neither come into being nor do they pass away, but everything that can or does come into being and passes away is formed in accordance with them.'[16]

The Qur'ān guides us to consider the divine attributes of God by reference to the *āyāt*, or signs, placed in the created environment around us.

> Verily in the creation of the heavens and earth, in the alternation of night and day, in the sailing of ships upon the ocean for the profit of mankind, in the rain which God sends down from the skies and the life he gives therewith to earth that is dead; in the beasts of all kinds that he scatters through the earth, in the change of the winds, and the clouds which they trail like slaves between the sky and the earth: here indeed are signs for those who are wise.[17]

All cosmic reality can be viewed as reflections and combinations of these divine names, as there is no reality in the cosmos that does not reflect a divine attribute. As the thirteenth-century Sufi and philosopher Ibn ʿArabī put it, 'there is no property in the cosmos without a divine support and lordly attribute'.[18] Or, as found in the Qur'ān, 'To God belong the east and the west: Wheresoever you turn, there is the face of God. For God is all-embracing, all-knowing.'[19]

These immutable attributes, names or 'ideas' are the link between cosmic manifestations of reality and the divine reality itself. Thus investigation of the processes of the environment is also the sight of the face of God, and therefore worship. Similarly, abusing the environment in a manner that obscures the

14. Qur'ān 3.3.
15. For the mediaeval debate on natural intuition, see K. Reinhart, *Before Revelation: The Boundaries of Muslim Moral Thought* (Albany, NY: State University of New York Press, 1995).
16. E. Gilson, *The Christian Philosophy of Saint Augustine* (New York: Random House, 1960), p. 19.
17. Qur'ān 2.164.
18. Cited in Nasr, *Introduction to Islamic Cosmological Doctrines*, p. 21.
19. Qur'ān 2.115.

essential unity of creation is evil. There is thus both a law and also a moral framework which issue from the same divine reality and govern humanity and animals, while being significantly different for humanity than for the rest of creation, particularly with reference to free will. Our relationship with nature should be guided by recognition of these laws of nature and of the moral choice for humanity within its parameters.

> The sun and the moon follow their calculated courses; the planets and the trees submit to His designs; He has lifted the sky. He has set the balance in order for you not to exceed it – weigh with justice – and not fall short in it. He laid down the Earth for His creatures, with its fruits, its palm-trees with sheathed clusters, its husked grain, its fragrant plants. Which, then, of your Lord's gifts do you both deny?[20]

The Hierarchy of the Created World

While all of God's creation is imbued with God's spirit, that is not to say that all is equal and there is no hierarchy. Humanity is constantly reminded of its role as a trustee and of its greater ability for spiritual insight. 'He it is that has made you his representatives on earth. Whosoever subverts this trust does so to the harm of his own soul.'[21]

However, reference is also made in the Qur'ān to the spiritual value and ecological importance of the 'lower order' of creation: animal, vegetable and mineral. 'There is not an animal on earth, nor a bird that flies on the wing, but that they are communities like you.'[22] 'The seven heavens and the earth and all things therein declare his glory. There is not a thing but celebrates His praise: and yet you understand not how they declare His glory.'[23]

The above verses imply that even inanimate objects possess an ability to praise their creator and thus a degree of spirituality. This is certainly something above the evolutionary qualities of instinct and intuition. Indeed, God even speaks in the Qur'ān of communication with the lower order of creation in terms of '*waḥy*' or revelation, a term usually reserved for God's communication with the prophets. The principal distinction is the absence of free will: all created things other than humanity and jinn are 'Muslim' in the broader sense of the word, of submitting to the will of that which pervades the whole.[24]

We therefore have no claim to superiority over the other natural kingdoms by token of our reason, science, art or other material achievements, as all such kingdoms are fulfilling the purpose for which they were created. Humanity can, however, demonstrate a higher spiritual capacity through the exercise of free will. Our task is to seek the path of justice in our interactions with the created

20. Qur'ān 55.5–13.
21. Qur'ān 35.39.
22. Qur'ān 6.38.
23. Qur'ān 17.44.
24. See, for example, Qur'ān 99.5 and 16.68.

world, ensuring that our impact is proportionate to our needs and maintains the right to survival of our fellow beings.

The prophet Muhammad always exhorted compassion in the treatment of the natural world, stating, 'All creatures are like a family of God; and he loves the most those who are the most beneficent to their family.'[25] A higher spiritual station implies a stewardship of the natural world, rather than its domination. The station of humanity is substantively different, yet we are all component parts of the same unified creation, dependent on one another for our continued existence. While our basic needs may take precedence over the right to survive of some of creation, for instance in obtaining sufficient nourishment, we are required to show respect and compassion in our treatment of the created world. This obligation requires that we seek sufficient knowledge of the physical world and its processes to ensure that we live to the best of our abilities in harmony. With knowledge comes greater responsibility, and it is essential that humanity does not lose sight of the underlying motivation for its enquiries, namely, recognizing God's presence through God's handiwork.

Furthermore, our own physical and spiritual well-being are linked insofar as they are a product of our actions. Individually and collectively, we possess the capacity to render our physical environment unsustainable and our spiritual value lower than the rest of creation. 'We have indeed created man in the most perfect constitution; then we have lowered him to the lowest of the low, except such as believe and do righteous deeds, for they shall have a reward unfailing.'[26] And with reference to those who ignore the revelation of natural law, it is said that 'they have hearts wherewith they fail to comprehend and eyes wherewith they fail to see and ears wherewith they fail to hear. They are like cattle; nay, even less aware of what is right. Such [humans] are far from the straight path.'[27]

The Need for an Islamic Cosmology

The impact of an Islamic cosmological doctrine on the individual Muslim is a heightening of his or her awareness of the interconnectedness of all creation. An Islamic cosmology emphasizes the rights of creation and the need for humanity to exercise compassion and restraint, and all this within a concept of study as a worshipful act, laden with instructive lessons to draw the individual to God. Modern scientific (post-Enlightenment) enquiry, on the other hand, has tended to isolate and reduce components of the natural world to closed systems and divest their study of any spiritual and moral concerns. This has allowed phenomenal 'progress' in the understanding of these studied components but at the cost of losing sight of the ultimate objective. Furthermore, despite our

25. Al-Tabrizi, *Mishkat al-Masabih* (trans. J. Robson; Pakistan: Sh. Muhammad Ashraf, 1999), p. 1392.
26. Qur'ān 95.
27. Qur'ān 7.179.

endeavours to isolate and fully to understand any particular process, from the cross-pollination of plants to gene-coding and the manipulation of genetic material, we are increasingly shown that no system is closed and that connections we could never have imagined come back to haunt us.[28]

In reality, the diverse and intricate bonds that tie our ecosystems into a unified creation are only fully comprehensible to the creator. The key contribution of a theocentric environmentalism is that, proceeding from knowledge of the creator, it places moral questions at the heart of enquiry. In the current context where crude economic and political imperatives have been shaping environmental interactions, resulting in a backlog of environmental crises requiring our attention, it is precisely such a holistic and integrative approach that is required. However, the complexity that the concept of *waḥdat al-wujūd* conveys (the underlying unity of the multiplicity of creation) should make us realize that this is no easy task. In almost every activity, we impact upon our environment, and at different times in human history the same practices can shift from being of little impact to threatening the sustainability of a species or ecosystem. What is required is balanced judgement and the measuring of needs against impacts, both of which are inevitably constrained within the sum total of human knowledge at a particular point in time.

There is little doubt that we live in a period of heightened environmental stress assuming global proportions unimaginable to earlier civilizations. Water and land resources are under pressure worldwide with many nations facing deficits and quality constraints. Atmospheric pollution is threatening human health and possibly inducing climate change; and animal welfare standards have been allowed to fall so low under 'conventional' farming systems that they have 'created' new forms of viral and genetic disorders capable of crossing barriers between species. The list is endless and the total absence in 'free market' economics of any meaningful mechanisms to alleviate these problems is frightening. The role of contemporary Muslim environmentalists and ecologists, therefore, is to evaluate the impacts within a holistic framework and to engage with the moral and spiritual debates. These will inevitably lead beyond the boundaries of science into the realm of social, economic and political considerations. 'Corruption has appeared on land and sea as a result of people's actions and He will make them taste the consequences of some of their own actions so that they may turn back.'[29]

This brings us back to the point that science is never neutral. It is intimately linked to questions of morality either in its endeavour or in its application. In

28. The history of the development, use and subsequent restriction of organo-phosphates in agriculture provides an illustration of a preoccupation with economic returns driving scientific research and commercial production, at a high cost to the environment and the social systems of those involved. See, for example, P.B. Thompson, *The Spirit of the Soil* (London: Routledge, 1995), and R.B. Noorgard, *Development Betrayed: The End of Progress and a Coevolutionary Revisioning of the Future* (London: Routledge, 1994).

29. Qur'ān 30.4.

the endeavour of science, our insights or inspiration are inevitably constrained by the conditions of the social environment within which we are located. Similarly, the application of science will reflect the desires and aspirations of society. Thus an Islamic environmentalism must succeed in reintroducing the moral choices of good and evil into the practice of science at both these levels if we are to contribute to ameliorating the current global environmental crisis.

The Failure of Techno-centric Market-led Resource Management

While a stark contrast can be drawn between a theocentric concept of interactions between humanity and the environment, and short-term economic self-interest, we need to recognize that the latter view, while dominant in practice, is defended by few as a sound and rational position.

Weiskel comments that:

> For those from religious traditions who consider the created order to be a manifestation of the sacred and for those research scientists who consider nature to be the rich and wondrous outcome of a four billion year evolutionary experiment, the current attempt to commodify nature's biodiversity in monetary prices to be assigned in today's transitory and fluctuating currencies is silly beyond belief.[30]

Indefensible as it may be, the unenlightened self-interest of contemporary economic theory is an objective reality and its philosophical basis is rarely questioned. Early capitalist industrial theory paid little attention to social justice, and as a result, far less to 'environmental externalities'. When it did, it justified its position with reference to a future economic utopia in the mature stages of industrial society. Rostow, for example, asserted that the eventual 'take off into self-sustaining growth' of industrial nations would lead to a degree of affluence permitting investment in, and the regeneration of, 'natural capital'.[31] Allied with narrow economic criteria and the history of apparently successful Western economies, this optimism led to planning approaches which justified the depletion of resources on a global scale on the assumption of a future willingness to make amends.

This supposed relationship between economic development and resource management is given a conceptual basis in the writings of Beck and Giddens, who argue that postmodern society of the late twentieth century has indeed entered a stage of reflexive modernity.[32] Reflexivity is said to exist when a social

30. T.C. Weiskel, *Selling Pigeons in the Temple: The Danger of Market Metaphors in an Ecosystem* (Harvard Divinity School Occasional Papers, 8, 1997), p. 5.

31. W. Rostow, *The Stages of Economic Growth: A Non-Communist Manifesto* (Oxford: Oxford University Press, 1960).

32. U. Beck, *Risk Society: Towards a New Modernity* (trans. M. Ritter; London: SAGE Publications, 1992); A. Giddens, *The Consequences of Modernity* (Stanford, CA: Stanford University Press, 1991).

grouping becomes concerned by the undesirable and unintended consequences of its actions, such as environmental degradation caused by industrialization. It therefore seeks to limit these consequences by developing coherent strategies, policies and regimes to effect the necessary changes – the corollary of course also being true, that if there is no reflexivity, then consumption of environmental capital will continue until such time as ecological catastrophe occurs. Sadly, it is this latter trajectory which humanity appears to be following, with many nations set to reach a point of crisis in the availability of natural resources in the next twenty years.[33]

Stewardship of Water Resources in the Middle East

If we were expecting the nations of the Middle East to embody features of a holistic and sustainable stewardship of their natural-resource endowment, by token of their monotheistic heritage, we would be sorely disappointed. Indeed, it is sadly the case that nowhere are the impacts of short-term planning more apparent, and in this, Muslims, Jews and Christians share the blame as perpetrators.[34] The region is in fact the most water-stressed in the world, with almost all states maintaining water-use patterns well above sustainable yields, often through the mining of groundwater resources. Yet this pattern of resource depletion runs hand-in-hand with high levels of wastage and low productivity. Overall efficiencies of conveyance and distribution systems are low, at between 50–60%. Technology-led, politically motivated land-development schemes result in large allocations of water to marginal lands, often incapable of generating sufficient economic returns. Considerable exports of generally low-value agricultural commodities result in a virtual export of water resources. And, last but not least, national consumption patterns over-emphasize livestock, requiring greater inputs of land and water to feed the same population.

Therefore the crisis is not really one of availability but rather one of use. Human interactions with environmental systems clearly need to be judged in relation to a broad set of criteria including other non-economic values alongside spiritual and moral implications. The dominant theories of political economy over the last two centuries have not developed a language to incorporate such seemingly abstract notions of value. Indeed, they have served to confine debate to economic 'realities', to the exclusion of other perspectives, with nature seen

33. Various statistics from international agencies such as the UNDP, UNEP, FAO and WHO indicate environmental and health concerns which could reach crisis proportions in the next twenty to fifty years. See, for example, http://www.fao.org/ag/agl/aglw/aquastat/main/index.stm.

34. See, for example, M. Karshenas, 'Environment, Technology and Employment', *Development and Change* 25 (1994), pp. 723–57, and M. Karshenas and J.A. Allan, 'Managing Environmental Capital', in J.A. Allan (ed.), *Water, Peace and the Middle East: Negotiating Resources in the Jordan Basin* (London: Taurus Academic Publications, 1996), pp. 121–35.

not as an interactive ecosystem but rather as a marketplace of commodities. The power of the economic argument is not in its substance but rather in its ability to have dislodged all other valuations. Spiritual and moral values, or even other values such as aesthetic quality or future potential, are ignored in favour of a transient valuation based on short-term gains.

Islamic Cosmology and Contemporary Ecological Critiques of Development

An Islamic cosmology stresses the moral and spiritual dimensions of humanity's position in the created world. It directs us towards a recognition that, in practical terms, the human economy needs to be understood as a subset of the physical ecosystem and not the other way around. Islam bestows an intrinsic spiritual value upon the biodiversity of earth, so that it should be protected for its own sake, not simply for the economic advantage it presents. Failure so to protect it leads humanity towards arrogance and a separation from nature, where humanity sees itself as unconstrained by the basic laws of interdependent or co-evolutionary development. In adopting this co-evolutionary stance, Islam can be aligned with a broad range of contemporary ecological thinking, most of which is highly critical of the current hegemony of economic discourse. Environmental theorists such as Lovelock recognize the inherent tendency of capitalist production systems to externalize environmental impacts.[35] Naess argues for a broader understanding of the environment, which utilizes social, economic and cultural analysis in order to show how human agents may contribute to the achievement of a balanced social order when engaged in a symbiotic exchange with the wider environment.[36] An understanding of the interrelatedness of all creation led Margulis to assert that symbiosis and co-operation have been at least as central to biological evolution as the competitive conflict for survival that marks Darwinian theory.[37] Islamic cosmology therefore provides fertile ground for developing a co-evolutionary understanding of life on earth, linking it to a moral philosophy, which unites us all. The purpose of human endeavour is to strive for a path of moderation between utilitarianism and passivity: what could be termed a 'positive engagement' with the natural order. Human morality and ethics thus become an articulated manifestation of the natural interdependency in which, through affinity and empathy, we recognize the rights of other constituent elements of the created world and find ways in which interrelation becomes co-operative and mutually life-enhancing for both sides.

35. J.E. Lovelock, *Reintegrating God's Creation: A Paper for Discussion* (Church and Society Documents, 3; Geneva: World Council of Churches, Programme Unit on Faith and Witness, Sub-Unit on Church and Society, 1987).

36. A. Naess, *Ecology, Community and Lifestyle* (Cambridge: Cambridge University Press, 1989).

37. L. Margulis and D. Sagan, *Microcosmos: Four Billion Years of Evolution from Our Microbial Ancestors* (New York: Summit Books, 1986).

Such an approach seeks to counter traditional dualisms that have had such deleterious consequences for both humanity and nature. In the Qur'ān, we find this put more simply: 'God changes not the conditions facing any community until they change that which is within themselves.'[38]

38. Qur'ān 13.11.

The Environment in Jewish, Christian and Muslim Thought

Norman Solomon, Richard Harries and Tim Winter

Norman Solomon stresses that, in Judaism, creation is good and the variety of the biosphere is to be cherished. Humans stand at the apex of creation, but this gives them a responsibility towards nature. It is not to be wasted or destroyed. Within Judaism, there is a special understanding of the relationship between land and people. The flourishing of the land depends upon a right moral ordering of human life. While animal life is to be respected, human life takes priority in any clash. Although Judaism is associated with the command to multiply and fill the earth, this is not to be taken as implying unlimited procreation. It is reasonable to suggest that the earth has now been filled or nearly filled, and that the growth in the population of the world should be taken under control. When, however, it comes to different kinds of energy, nuclear, fossil fuel or solar, Judaism has nothing distinctive to contribute to the debate. These are technical issues, and their solution is to be guided by the widely shared moral principle that we should minimize damage to the earth. When it comes to the question as to who should bear the cost of conservation, again, the widely shared values of social justice should guide our answers. Momentous decisions are already being made in relation to the future of evolution because of our capacity to make changes in DNA. There is much scope for inter-religious co-operation here, as there is more generally, in the teaching and preaching that now needs to be done about the environment.

Bishop Kallistos, in his contribution from a Christian point of view, affirms the basic principles of Judaism on this matter. He points out, however, that the Greek word '*kalos*', normally translated 'good', also means 'beauty', and is related to the Greek root for 'call'; so creation is not only good, it also has a beauty that draws us to itself. Christianity had to fight for this fundamental insight, derived from Judaism, when it went out into the classical world. It encountered religions and philosophies that believed that the material world was evil, something from which one had to escape.

Christianity teaches that God creates the world out of love; that creatures might rejoice in God and God in them. Although most Christianity rejects pantheism, many strains affirm panentheism, namely the belief that God, though transcendent, dwells within creation and that creation dwells within God. God is the constant and unceasing source of every moment and every thing. This creative word of God which holds all things in being and indwells all things is a 'bridge of diamond' between divine infinitude and nothingness.[1]

Although the divine logos is implanted in every created thing and the divine energies animate all things, Christianity also holds that the world is fallen. The whole world is in bondage to decay, and needs to be liberated. There is a tragic gap between what God plans and the actual situation of the world. The implication of this theology is that human beings should see themselves as priests of creation. This means, first of all, having a particular attitude to one's own body, regarding it as a temple of the Holy Spirit, and then, secondly, offering the physical world to God in thanksgiving and praise. This also means that the so-called ecological crisis is first and foremost a crisis of the human heart, for it is humanity's attitudes that are wrong and flawed. We need to repent, that is, to change our whole outlook. Instead of exploiting nature for short-term ends, we need to have a sense of stewardship; but this concept might imply a utilitarian or managerial approach to nature and therefore it is better to think in terms of being priests of creation. All human beings, as part of creation, are called to relate to God the physical world with which they are in touch, and thereby bring it into union or communion with God. This has two further implications. First, personal sacrifice is involved. We need to give up our inordinate desires and focus only on what we need. Secondly, the priestly offering of creation involves loving creation, a creation which is deeply imbued with the radiance of the divine Spirit.

If the emphasis in Judaism and Christianity is on the goodness of creation, within Islam, according to Lutfi Radwan, the emphasis is on the unity of creation as reflecting the unity of God's own self. There is an interdependence in the created world and this means that it can point, or act as a witness, to the creator. More particularly, the ninety-nine attributes of God, though they are eternal, are also reflected in creation. Thus, in trying to understand the processes of creation, we can also see something of the face of God.

As in Judaism and Christianity, humanity is seen as the apex of creation, with a particular responsibility to the natural world. Human beings have a spiritual nature which calls them to submit to the divine order and act as stewards of creation. If they fail to do this, not only do they create havoc in the natural world, they also fall below the beasts themselves. The moral dimension is thus crucial. Too much planning in recent decades has been on the basis of short-

1. For panentheism, see M.W. Brierley, 'Naming a Quiet Revolution: The Panentheistic Turn in Modern Theology', in P. Clayton and A.R. Peacocke (eds.), *In Whom We Live and Move and Have Our Being: Panentheistic Reflections on God's Presence in a Scientific World* (Grand Rapids, MI and Cambridge: Eerdmans, 2004), pp. 1–15; P. Clayton, 'Panentheism Today: A Constructive Systematic Evaluation', in Clayton and Peacocke (eds.), *In Whom We Live and Move and Have Our Being*, pp. 249–64; and M.W. Brierley, 'Panentheism', in *The Encyclopedia of Christianity* (Grand Rapids, MI and Cambridge: Eerdmans, and Leiden: Brill, 2005), IV, pp. 21–25.

term economic interests, ignoring the fundamental principles which should have guided our approach to the natural order. According to some economic theorists, a period of unbridled growth without attention to moral principles should be followed by a period of 'reflexive modernity' when the danger of this situation comes home and steps are taken to relate to the natural world in a sustainable way; but there is no evidence that this has happened. For example, in the Middle East, there is an ever-increasing crisis in relation to water supplies. Islam urges the return to fundamental moral principles and a spirit of co-operation, rather than unrestrained competition.

All three religions are totally one in asserting that the natural environment is God's creation. It comes from God, by divine *fiat* alone, as God's gift, and it is to be respected in its own right. Humans, as moral beings, have a responsibility towards the environment and therefore moral values are absolutely fundamental. There is a direct relationship between human beings observing moral values in their dealings with the environment and the environment's flourishing. This is made quite explicit in Judaism with its integral link between observing the Torah and the prosperity of the land. But the same point is affirmed in Christianity and Islam in more general terms. Human beings have a role as stewards of the natural world and this means that they are ultimately accountable for how they act towards it. The dominant strands of all three religions agree that while creation is to be respected in its own right, it is also God's purpose that it exists for the benefit of human beings. This means that it is a proper part of the vocation of human beings to intervene in, manipulate and use the processes of nature, provided that this is done in a responsible manner. At the same time, many affirm that there is an accumulated wisdom in nature, the product of billions of years of evolution.

It has become increasingly apparent in recent decades that certain kinds of human intervention in natural processes can unbalance or even destroy whole ecological systems, as, for example, was seen in the case of excessive use of pesticides. So intervention in nature needs to go alongside respect for it. Furthermore, nature is not simply 'red in tooth and claw': there is also a co-operative element in nature. For many people, this whole issue is focused most sharply in the question of the proper human attitude to animals. All three religions unite in believing that animals can be used by human beings and that they do not have absolute rights. This is sometimes challenged today by radical ethicists within all three traditions, such as Andrew Linzey from within the Christian tradition; nevertheless mainstream thinking within them would emphasize the need to avoid cruelty, to minimize pain and preserve the variety of the species, rather than put non-human animals on a moral par with humanity.

Radical monotheism, as it has emerged in Judaism, Christianity and Islam, has often had to struggle against pagan nature religions. It has resisted any idea that nature, or elements of nature, are divine. Traditional monotheism has asserted a radical divide between the uncreated source of all that exists, and the whole created order. Moreover, it has also held a hierarchical principle: that human beings are accountable to God but able to use the natural order for their own benefit. Much of this has been challenged in the modern world by 'new age' religions which have sometimes thought in terms of an earth goddess, Gaia, or a world soul, and which have certainly wanted to attribute something of divinity to the natural world. Such approaches have therefore claimed to be more sympathetic to environmental issues than traditional monotheism. However, the theological emphases of the 'new age' religions do have some resonance within Judaism, Christianity and Islam and can to some extent be incorporated in entirely orthodox terms. The mystical traditions in all three religions have sometimes had a much stronger sense of the presence of God in all things, including nature, than the purely dogmatic forms of the religion of which they are a part. The idea that God is not simply the ground of all being but is in and through all things and who aims to fill all things with divine presence, that is to say panentheism, is, again, not inimical to these religions. While they might reject the metaphor that God is the world soul, the idea of God being present in the length and breadth of creation, within as well as behind and beyond all things, is perfectly compatible with traditional monotheism. Again, the concept of the divine Spirit, the breath of God on creation (what many Muslims call 'the breath of the All-Compassionate'), bringing it to life and reflected in its every aspect, is again part of mainstream thought. It may be true that many interpretations of Islam would wish strongly to qualify this kind of language, but the qualifications, as well as the affirmations, belong to all three religions.

Christianity has traditionally taken the view that all of nature is fallen. Neither Judaism nor Islam have this emphasis; and modern people find it very difficult to make sense of such a belief. Suffering and death, which trad-itionally have been seen as a consequence of the Fall, clearly belonged to the animal world long before human beings came on the scene. Perhaps the only way of making sense of such a belief is through an understanding of the centrality of language in our apprehension of all objects, including nature. As we emerge into consciousness we are shaped by language, and if the society into which we are born is 'off centre', askew in some way, then this will be reflected in the language which shapes and forms us. The natural environment, like everything else, will be understood and apprehended by us in terms of words and concepts. If these from the outset represent a partially distorted view of what it is to be a human being, then our very apprehension of nature will be distorted as well.

When it comes to the future of nature, all three traditions have emphasized the centrality of humanity in God's redemptive purpose; though as Christianity has thought of nature as fallen, so it has believed it will be ultimately redeemed. Again, it is very difficult to make sense of this, though C.S. Lewis sought to do so, in a view which is referred to in a later essay.[2] All three religions, however, use imagery from nature to depict that ultimate state of affairs where God is all in all, so at least in that sense, nature is taken up into the redemptive purpose of God.

2. See the paper by Richard Harries, 'Life after Death from a Christian Perspective', below.

As Bishop Kallistos brought out within the Christian tradition or one important strand of it, human beings can be seen as priests of nature. Thus in eucharistic prayer G of the Church of England liturgy *Common Worship*, there are the words:

> From the beginning you have created all things
> and all your works echo the silent music of your praise.
> In the fullness of time you made us in your image,
> the crown of all creation.
> You give us breath and speech, that with angels and archangels
> and all the powers of heaven
> we may find a voice to sing your praise.[3]

This is a theme which finds expression in a good number of Christian poets. Everything in nature worships God in its own way, by being itself. Human beings are called to articulate that silent praise. Islam, however, might be concerned that this gives too great a role of mediation to humanity. Nature needs guarding and protecting more than being 'offered' or 'lifted', because God is already present within it.

Whatever variations of emphasis there may be between the religions in their different understandings of nature, nevertheless they are firmly united in giving a positive place for it within the purpose of God, which calls for respect for the environment and for the observance of moral law in relation to it. The world is faced by a series of major crises concerned with the environment. The three religions can co-operate more than they have done in the past in urging governments, international institutions and transnational corporations to pay more attention to the moral dimensions of issues, which need to be given greater weight in a world that is dominated by short-term economic gain.

3. *Common Worship: Services and Prayers for the Church of England* (London: Church House Publishing, 2000), p. 201.

Chapter 9: Life after Death

Life after Death from a Jewish Perspective

Norman Solomon

From at least the time of the fifth dynasty, well before the period of 'Israel in Egypt', Egyptian priests taught that there was an afterlife for all. Egyptian and perhaps Indian beliefs reached Greece not later than the time of Pythagoras, in the sixth century BCE. In this essay, I shall review Israelite and Jewish ideas on life after death, commencing with the scriptures, summarizing mediaeval debates on resurrection, the nature of the afterlife and reincarnation, and then moving on to modern critiques and some personal reflections. The surprise is that the Bible (that is to say, the Hebrew scriptures) has no clear statement on the subject, and that the constant affirmations of reward and punishment in a book such as Deuteronomy seem concerned entirely with life on earth.

There are more than sixty references in the Hebrew scriptures to 'Sheol', akin to the Greek Hades. Not much should be read into this. Often, as in Genesis 37.35, it is no more than a poetic term for 'death' or 'the grave', and may be translated as such; even the solemn meditation on 'the abode of worms and decay' in Job 17.13–16 does not portray a coherent doctrine of the afterlife. The scriptures' silence may be polemical, designed to focus attention on the urgent needs of this world.

The earliest Jewish sources to speak openly of an afterlife belong to the second century BCE, the Maccabaean period. Daniel and late additions to Isaiah,[1] together with several apocryphal books, testify to the bodily resurrection of the faithful; the apocryphal story in 2 Maccabees 7 of the mother and her seven sons who submitted to torture and death for their faith links this to the concept of martyrdom. Ecclesiastes, on the other hand, voices scepticism.[2]

It may be that the open declaration of belief in an afterlife was born out of the desperation of the times; or it may owe something to Iranian influence. It is a markedly different concept, at this stage, from popular Greek notions of Hades or from the Platonic concept of the immortal soul.

1. Daniel 7.2 and 12.2–3, and Isaiah 26.19 and 66.24.
2. Ecclesiastes 3.21.

The Rabbis on Life after Death

Sadducees and Pharisees both laid claim to the mantle of authentic tradition. The first-century CE Jewish historian Josephus Flavius wrote, of their differences,

> The Pharisees live modestly, in accordance with reason, respect the elderly and believe in divine providence, freedom of the will and personal immortality; they are held in esteem by the people, who are guided by them in prayer and sacrifice. The Sadducees deny life after death, following only the explicit provisions of scripture.[3]

The rabbis, who regarded themselves as the true heirs of the Pharisees in an unbroken line going back to Moses, inherited from the Pharisees the belief in life after death that has remained a firm principle of Judaism to this day. As they were certain that this was correct doctrine, they struggled with indifferent success to discover 'hints' of the afterlife concealed within the words of scripture.[4]

Why were the rabbis so strongly committed to a doctrine which scripture all but ignores? It helped them to explain suffering and apparent injustice in this world; without such rationalization, it would have been difficult to uphold the integrity of scripture, which promises reward to the faithful and punishment to the guilty. Also, the promise of future eternal bliss offered comfort and reassurance to their followers, while the threat of punishment deterred them from disobedience.

Day of Judgement

The term *yom ha-din*, 'day of judgement', is an alternative name for the New Year festival. It is also a designation for the 'Day of the Lord', which in Amos 5.18 is a day on which God will punish the wicked among the nations and in Israel. In Jewish apocalyptic writings and rabbinic eschatology, it became the day at the end of time when God would gather the souls of the living and the dead and pronounce judgement on each one in accordance with their deeds.

> Antoninus said to Rabbi, 'The body and soul could exonerate themselves from judgment. How is this so? The body says, "The soul sinned, for from the day that it parted from me I have lain like a silent stone in the grave!" And the soul says, "The body is the sinner, for from the day that I parted from it I have flown in the air like a bird."' He answered him, 'I will give you a parable. What is this like? A king of flesh and blood had a beautiful orchard in which were lovely early figs, and he placed two watchmen over it, one lame and the other blind. The lame said to the blind, "I see delicious early figs in the orchard. Come and carry me and we will fetch and eat them." The lame rode on the back of the blind man and they fetched and ate them. After a while the owner of the orchard came and said to them, "Where are my delicious early figs?" The lame answered, "Do I have legs to go?" The blind

3. Josephus, *Antiquities* 18.1.2–4.
4. Babylonian Talmud, *Sanhedrin* 90b and 92b.

> answered, "Do I have eyes to see?" What did he do? He placed the lame on the back of the blind man and judged them as one – so also the Holy Blessed One brings the soul and casts it into the body and judges them as one.'[5]

This tale might be read as a polemic against Gnosticism, for it rejects the idea of the body as evil and the soul as good. Body and soul together make up the human personality, which can be judged only as a whole. At any rate, the story reinforces the belief that individuals will be called to account after death for their sins in this life.

Bodily Resurrection or Spiritual Afterlife?

Most rabbinic sources equate the afterlife with resurrection. Souls are restored to the bodies of the resurrected, and they rise from their graves fully clothed;[6] the picture is perhaps inspired by the vision of the valley of dry bones in Ezekiel 37.1–14. Occasionally, this is tempered by a more spiritual interpretation. The third-century CE Babylonian teacher Rav, against his colleague and rival Shmuel, argued that the prophets spoke only of worldly reward, for no eye but that of God had beheld the ultimate reward of the righteous in the world to come: 'Above, there is there neither eating, nor drinking, nor begetting of children, no bargaining or jealousy or hatred or strife, but the righteous sit with their crowns on their heads and enjoy the radiance of the [divine] Presence.'[7]

The debate of Rav and Shmuel echoed through succeeding centuries. Almost a thousand years later, Moses Maimonides (1138–1204) included belief in bodily resurrection among his thirteen articles of the faith, but held that this was not the ultimate state of the person. The ultimate afterlife, in his view, was entirely spiritual, of soul and in no way of body; though the rabbis had indeed spoken of material rewards and a resurrected body, such remarks were addressed to simple folk who could not conceive the true spiritual bliss.

Maimonides' view was forcefully attacked by Nahmanides,[8] who could not bring himself to abandon a literal understanding of the rabbinic concept of the resurrection as the rejoining of body and soul. However, Nahmanides was adamant that at the resurrection the body will be transfigured into a superior material, free from physical desires and from decay.

Another mediaeval debate that has had significant repercussions arose when Jewish philosophers sought to harmonize rabbinic soul-talk with Aristotle's contention that the soul was the 'form' of the body and inseparable from it. If the soul was not a separate entity, but perished with the body of which it was the form, it made no sense to talk about life after death. Maimonides therefore distinguished between two souls. On the one hand, there is the soul that humans have in common with all living beings, which is the form of the body

5. Babylonian Talmud, *Sanhedrin* 91a–b.
6. Babylonian Talmud, *Ketubot* 111b.
7. Babylonian Talmud, *Berakhot* 17a.
8. In *Shaar ha-Gemul*, the final chapter of his *Torat ha-Adam*, a work on the laws of sickness, death and mourning.

and inseparable from it. On the other hand, there is an independent soul that is 'from God, from the heavens';[9] this soul survives the body and 'knows' its creator forever.[10]

This apparent quibble about the nature of the soul turned out to be far more significant than Maimonides realized. It points directly to the main problem that most modern people have with the whole concept of the afterlife. Like Aristotle, modern science is uncomfortable with the notion of 'soul' as an independent substance. There is compelling evidence that mind, or soul, is an aspect or consequence of bodily processes; memory, for instance, previously thought to be a distinctively mental and therefore non-material function, is now seen to be embodied in physical structures including that of the brain. Some philosophers of religion continue to uphold the traditional dualism of body and soul,[11] but the idea of the disembodied soul enjoying eternal bliss is increasingly difficult to render coherent.

Reincarnation

Though most strongly associated with Indian religions, the concept of reincarnation was well known in the ancient Mediterranean. The Greek philosopher Pythagoras was said to have claimed that he had been Euphorbus, a warrior in the Trojan War, and that he had been permitted to bring into his earthly life the memory of all his previous existences.

Neither the Bible nor the Talmud acknowledges a doctrine of reincarnation in this sense. The doctrine that the soul, after death, is transferred to a body other than its original one was introduced to Judaism at a later date by the Karaites,[12] and was attacked and ridiculed by the 'Rabbanite' philosopher Sa'adia (c. 882–942).[13]

Nevertheless, the concept of *gilgul neshamot*, literally the 'rolling of souls', that is, reincarnation, was vigorously espoused by the Spanish Kabbalists of the thirteenth century. Their most influential work, the *Zohar*, commented:

9. Genesis 19.24 applied to Genesis 2.7.

10. Maimonides, *Mishneh Torah: Yesodey ha-Torah* 4.8–9.

11. The Christian Richard Swinburne is one of the staunchest defenders of this view. In *The Evolution of the Soul* (Oxford: Clarendon Press, 1986), he seeks to demonstrate that it is at least logically possible for the soul to continue to exist after the body has been destroyed: 'continuing matter is not [logically] essential for the continuing existence of persons' (p. 153). The argument, which he regards as a restatement of Descartes' position, is formalized in an additional note (pp. 314–15).

12. Anan ben David is credited with having founded Karaism in the eighth century, though he probably served only as a focus for tendencies within Judaism to reject non-biblical elements within Judaism, including the rabbinic tradition. It is surprising that this sect should have introduced the decidedly non-biblical doctrine of reincarnation.

13. Sa'adia Gaon, *Book of Beliefs and Opinions* 6.8, pp. 214–17 in Y. Kafiḥ's Arabic and Hebrew edition, published jointly by the Sura Institute in Jerusalem and Yeshiva University, New York, but undated.

> 'These are the judgments ...' [Exodus 21.1] The Targum translates:[14] 'These are the judgments you shall set in array for them ...' – these are the arrays of *gilgul*, the judgments of the souls, each of which is judged to receive its punishment. 'When you acquire a Hebrew slave he shall labor for six years and in the seventh he shall go out free.' [Exodus 21.2] – Brethren! Now is the time to reveal to you many of the hidden secrets of *gilgul*.[15]

Zohar viewed reincarnation as a punishment for sin, or in the case of superior souls, as an opportunity to enable them to fulfil those divine commandments that they had been unable to fulfil in their previous incarnations.

Among those outside the mainstream of Kabbala, Menasseh ben Israel (1604–57) is perhaps the staunchest advocate of reincarnation, elaborating on it at length in his *Nishmat Ḥayyim*, a work in which he collected, from every available source, reports and anecdotes pointing to the independent existence of the soul, as evidenced in apparitions, possession and the like. Menasseh is rather better known for his intervention with Oliver Cromwell to secure the readmission of the Jews to England in 1656. His learned but uncritical theology, with its stress on independence of the soul from the body, was a reaction to 'modern' ideas such as those of his erstwhile pupil Spinoza who appeared to deny traditional teaching on the soul and the afterlife.

Belief in reincarnation is nowadays common among the Orthodox, many of whom seem to regard Kabbala as mainstream tradition. It is a belief that helps them come to terms with the suffering of the apparently innocent, such as children, or the victims of the Holocaust.

Immortality of the Soul

Strictly speaking, immortality implies life before birth as well as after death; it is linked to belief in the soul as distinct from and superior to its temporary home, the body. Although pre-existence of the soul was denied by Sa'adia and others, it appealed to neo-Platonist Jewish philosophers such as Joseph ibn Zaddik (d. 1149), according to whom the soul is incorporeal, existed within the 'world soul' before its conjunction with the body, and continues to exist after the passing of the body. If the soul attains the necessary level of knowledge, it returns after death to its place of origin within the world soul; but if it remains ignorant, it is like a traveller who cannot find the way back to their homeland, and is pulled by the motion of the celestial sphere and tortured by fire.[16] Clearly, ibn Zaddik was strongly influenced by Plato's theory of learning as recollection of the soul's knowledge before birth.

Ibn Zaddik, like the Aristotelians, saw human perfection and ultimate human bliss in terms of perfection of the intellect. Later, Ḥasdai Crescas and others argued that it was the love of God, rather than knowledge of God, which

14. The Jewish Aramaic version of scripture.
15. *Zohar*, Exodus 94a. The 'Hebrew slave' is the soul enslaved to the body.
16. On some elements in Ibn Zaddik's philosophy, see J. Guttman, *Philosophies of Judaism* (New York: Schocken Books, 1973), pp. 129–34.

brought life after death in the form of an ever-strengthening bond with the *Shekhina*, or divine presence.[17]

Through neo-Platonism, the concept of the pre-existent, immortal soul migrated to Kabbala. Kabbalists regard the soul as a spiritual entity originating in the supernal worlds and from the divine emanation; it enters the body only in order to fulfil a specific task or purpose. Its special spiritual essence guarantees its immortality after death. Its reward consists in its ascent or return through the heavenly paradise and from there into even higher spiritual worlds until it reaches its original anchorage in the world of creation and in the world of emanation. Whether or not some Kabbalists believe the soul loses its individuality and is absorbed, in a mystic union, into the divine essence, is a matter of debate among scholars.[18]

Modern Attitudes

The Orthodox remain committed to a belief in the persistence after death of the individual soul. Belief in both bodily resurrection and reincarnation are widespread even though it is difficult to reconcile the two. Others have increasingly questioned traditional positions in the light of modern scientific and philosophical perspectives. The concept of bodily resurrection was already under attack in the Middle Ages; people who thought deeply about the matter either conceived of a 'transfigured' body (Nahmanides), or downgraded bodily resurrection in favour of some form of immortality of the soul (Maimonides).

Enlightenment philosophers, especially those who accepted Descartes' sharp distinction between body and soul, promoted the notion of immortality rather than resurrection. One of the most influential works of Moses Mendelssohn (1729–86) was his *Phaedon oder ueber die Unsterblichkeit der Seele*, a set of three Socratic dialogues published in 1767 in which he portrayed how Socrates might, in terms of 'modern philosophy', have argued for immortality of the soul.[19] The whole world, Mendelssohn argued, was created for the sake of the existence of rational beings who progressively increase their perfection, and herein lies their bliss. It is unthinkable that beings who are prepared to sacrifice their lives for social justice, freedom, virtue and truth,[20] should be frustrated in these efforts in the next. Surely it was not in vain that the creator instilled in humanity a desire for eternal bliss. It is both possible and necessary that this desire should be fulfilled, despite all the setbacks and obstacles.

17. Crescas, *Or Hashem* 3.3.

18. M. Idel (*Kabbala: New Perspectives* [New Haven, CT and London: Yale University Press, 1988], pp. 59–73), *contra* G. G. Scholem, argues that *unio mystica* is a significant element in Jewish mysticism.

19. M. Mendelssohn, *Gesammelte Schriften*, III, bk 1 (ed. F. Bamberger and L. Strauss; Berlin: Akademie-Verlag, 1932), pp. 5–128.

20. Mendelssohn, *Gesammelte Schriften*, p. 116.

From the foundation of the Jewish Reform movement in the early nineteenth century until the latter half of the twentieth century, Mendelssohn's ideas held sway. Here is the seventh principle of the 1885 Pittsburgh Platform:

> We reassert the doctrine of Judaism, that the soul of man is immortal, grounding this belief on the divine nature of the human spirit, which forever finds bliss in righteousness and misery in wickedness. We reject as ideas not rooted in Judaism the beliefs both in bodily resurrection and in Gehenna and Eden (Hell and Paradise) as abodes for everlasting punishment or reward.

In more recent times, Reform pronouncements have been less forthcoming; the 1976 San Francisco Platform rather hedged its bets on the afterlife, stating merely that 'amid the mystery we call life, we affirm that human beings, created in God's image, share in God's eternality despite the mystery we call death'.[21]

Another Enlightenment trend, more difficult to reconcile with religious tradition, was denial of the existence of the soul as an independent metaphysical entity. This trend has been strengthened in recent times by physiological evidence suggesting the congruence of 'mental' or 'soul' states with bodily states. How is it possible to make any sense of life independent of those bodily sensations which are the foundation of all our knowledge?

Some liberal and many secular Jews have accordingly accepted the finality of death. Others deny its finality, reinterpreting the 'myth' of life after death either as a metaphor for the continuing influence of the deceased, or in an eschatological sense, as an assertion that the life of the virtuous is eternally treasured by God as fulfilment of God's victory over death. The philosopher Hermann Cohen (1842–1918) built on what he considered a biblical foundation by interpreting life after death in a collective sense. The people (*das Volk*, in the sense of humankind as a whole) never dies, but rather has an eternal, continuing history: 'To the eternity of God corresponds ... the eternity of man. Liberated of the anthropomorphic setting, this eternity of man means only the infinite continuation of the correlation of man and God.'[22] The individual soul is perpetuated by means of this history, and is real only within the context of the continuity of the people. Individual immortality, which belongs in the realm of mythology, means that the individual is constantly required to strive to effect the eternal principles of truth and morality in the world. This is perhaps a surprisingly earth-centred doctrine for an idealist philosopher who denied the ultimate reality of anything but thought.

21. See M.A. Meyer, *Response to Modernity: A History of the Reform Movement in Judaism* (New York and Oxford: Oxford University Press, 1988). The text of the Pittsburg Platform is on pp. 387–88, and that of the San Francisco Platform on pp. 391–94; the citation is on p. 392. Meyer's perceptive account of the genesis and significance of these statements may be found in the body of the work.

22. H. Cohen, *Religion of Reason out of the Sources of Judaism* (trans. S. Kaplan; New York: Frederick Unger, 1972), p. 337. The whole of chapter 15 of Cohen's work (pp. 296–337) is devoted to the theme of immortality and resurrection.

A Personal View

I should like to conclude with some personal musings on 'afterlife talk'.

First, the problems I have with the naïve traditional view:

- It depends on the notion that the human person consists of two separable parts, soul and body, the former of which is the 'organ' of reason, love, etc. This notion needs drastic revision in the light of modern understanding of brain function.[23]
- The notion of a resurrected body, that is to say, one reunited with a soul, persisting in a state of eternal bliss, is incoherent. The idea that it may persist in eternal torment is not only incoherent but morally unacceptable.
- All the experience I have is through the senses, and I can conceive of no other (which is not to deny that there may be other ways of being).

These are not new problems, and have led in the past to profound modifications of traditional doctrine, for instance placing the afterlife 'beyond' time and space (Maimonides); but this made it even less coherent, since human beings cannot imagine anything other than within a space-time framework.

Religious language about life after death is metaphor. That is why there is so much confusion about what it 'refers' to, whether this-worldly resurrection or other-worldly immortality of the soul. It is why attempts to portray it, whether as 'the righteous sitting with crowns on their heads and absorbing the divine radiance' or in grosser terms of two regions, one inhabited by angel harpists and the other by pitch-forked devils, lapse into childishness and absurdity.

To explain the 'meaning' of the metaphor results only in another metaphor. Yet to dismiss traditional ways of talking about the afterlife entirely, and to speak of death simply as the final end, fail to do justice to the sense that many people have of being part of what lies beyond each of us as individuals. The 'Yizkor' ceremony that takes place in many Jewish rites on certain festivals conveys this powerfully: as parents and others are remembered, one feels a bond that binds the 'community of saints' (to use a Christian term) and transcends the generations. But even a phrase like 'what lies beyond' is a spatial metaphor; it seems that any attempt to articulate 'life after death' in words comes up against a language boundary that cannot be crossed.

Humility is necessary to see oneself not as an independent, disconnected individual, but as a focus of limited self-awareness within an inconceivably vast universe, every part of which interacts with every other. Death is a melting back, a re-absorption, into this wholeness. The notion of an afterlife conveys several value judgements about 'normal' life:

- Life is meaningful, not 'a tale Told by an idiot, full of sound and fury, Signifying nothing'.[24]
- The best in human endeavour – love, wisdom, beauty – is of enduring significance.

23. G. Edelman, *Bright Air, Brilliant Fire: On the Matter of the Mind* (London: Penguin Books, 1992), is a masterly summary at the popular level.

24. Shakespeare, *Macbeth* V.5.26–28.

- Life is to be taken seriously (there is a 'Day of Judgement'), not in the self-indulgent attitude of the revellers of Jerusalem: 'Let us eat and drink, for tomorrow we die!'[25]
- There is continuity between the individual life and that which 'lies beyond', including other lives, past and present.

The physiological finality of death must be accepted, and literal theories of resurrection abandoned. Death ends a process, but it does not cause it not to have existed. It may be likened to the completion of a journey, the crossing of a barrier, a 'going home'. Such metaphors bring comfort to those who find finitude difficult to bear, and offer the genuine consolation that my life story is part of a story that is bigger than me or than any individual human being.

Belief cannot be justified solely on the grounds that it generates a positive attitude to life; a belief not grounded in reality is worthless. The reality conveyed by afterlife talk is of the totality and interconnectedness of creation, and of the enduring significance of the life-work of the individual.

25. Isaiah 22.13.

Life after Death from a Christian Perspective

Richard Harries

In the modern world, every element in the traditional Christian schema for life after death has been called into question. The schema has been criticized from a philosophical, scientific, psychological, sociological, moral and political point of view. It is therefore necessary to assert at the outset that Christian propositions are stated in the form of a symbolic realism. In other words, they are not literal assertions but neither are they empty metaphors. There is a spiritual dimension and reality, which includes life after death, which can only be pointed to with the help of analogies, metaphors and symbols. This spiritual dimension is, from a Christian point of view, as real as the world of electrons and atoms. The traditional Christian schema is therefore best seen in terms of safeguarding certain fundamental truths and thereby helping people to relate to God in a true and appropriate way, that is, in faith and hope and love. This paper examines such truths as they are found in the Christian doctrines of the soul and resurrection, death and judgement, purgatory, hell and heaven.

The Soul and Resurrection of the Dead

Christianity arose in a Jewish matrix and, within that matrix, both Jesus and Paul affirmed the Pharisaic concept of the resurrection of the dead. When the Sadducees, who did not believe in the resurrection, asked Jesus a trick question, he replied, 'Is not this the reason you are wrong, that you know neither the scriptures nor the power of God?'[1] He then referred to God's words to Moses in the story of the burning bush, 'I am the God of Abraham, the God of Isaac, and the God of Jacob.'[2] Jesus concluded from this that God 'is God not of the dead, but of the living'.[3] In other words, Abraham, Isaac and Jacob have a continuing relationship with God. Similarly, Paul, when he addressed the Jewish council in Jerusalem, aligned himself with the Pharisees: 'When Paul noticed that some were Sadducees and others were Pharisees, he called out in

1. Mark 12.24.
2. Mark 12.26; cf. Exodus 3.6.
3. Mark 12.27.

the council, "Brothers, I am a Pharisee, a son of Pharisees. I am on trial concerning the hope of the resurrection of the dead."'[4]

The sense of defeat and despair for the first followers of Jesus after his death was transformed into courage and hope because they believed that God had raised him from the dead. The Christian movement was driven forward into history on the basis of this conviction. It is not surprising, therefore, that the concept of resurrection should have been central to early Christian preaching. For Paul and other New Testament writers, the resurrection of Jesus was the beginning of the end, when all would be raised: 'Christ has been raised from the dead, the first fruits of those who have died.'[5]

The concept of resurrection was controversial and difficult to believe in the ancient world, as it is in ours. Paul had to argue in its favour with a series of analogies, while guarding against literalism by asserting that we are raised as 'a spiritual body'.[6] When Paul engaged in some Christian apologetics with Athenian philosophers, finding common ground with them in the idea of a creator who is close to each one of us, he lost some sympathy when he referred to the resurrection. 'When they heard of the resurrection of the dead, some scoffed; but others said, "We will hear you again about this."'[7]

The ancient world felt much more at ease with the idea of human beings having an eternal soul, a spark of divinity within them, a share in the divine rationality that orders the universe. It is not surprising, therefore, that as Christianity moved out into the Graeco-Roman world, the idea of the soul should have been taken on board, as it was in the Judaism of the time. There is also some basis for this in the New Testament itself, where there is no uniform view of the afterlife. Jesus told a parable about a rich man who neglected a pauper called Lazarus at his gate. Both died: 'The poor man died and was carried away by the angels to be with Abraham. The rich man also died and was buried. In Hades, where he was being tormented, he looked up and saw Abraham far away with Lazarus by his side.'[8] Jesus said to the penitent thief being crucified with him, 'Truly I tell you, today you will be with me in Paradise.'[9]

The Church sought to combine this belief with hope of the resurrection of the dead. Thus, as paragraphs 1051 and 1052 of the *Catechism of the Catholic Church* put it, 'Every [person] receives [their] eternal recompense in [their] immortal soul from the moment of [their] death in a particular judgement by Christ ... On the day of resurrection, death will be definitively conquered, when these souls will be reunited with their bodies.'[10] Nevertheless, the distinctive

4. Acts 23.6.
5. 1 Corinthians 15.20.
6. 1 Corinthians 15.44.
7. Acts 17.32.
8. Luke 16.22–23.
9. Luke 23.43.
10. *Catechism of the Catholic Church* (London: Geoffrey Chapman, 1994), p. 240.

belief of Christians, as of Jews, is the idea of resurrection, which is affirmed in both the Apostles' Creed and the Nicene Creed. In the catacombs where Christians buried their dead until the end of the fourth century, one of the familiar frescos is of Jesus raising Lazarus. They buried their dead in trust and hope that Christ, the resurrection and the life, would raise them to an eternal existence with himself.[11]

The concept of the resurrection of the body safeguards four fundamental insights. First, whatever lies on the other side of death is, like this life, sheer gift. We have no right to a life after death. We do not automatically live on. Moment by moment, we are held in existence by the ground of all being. That is true now and that will be true in the hereafter. Secondly, the human person is a psychosomatic unity. Body, mind and spirit are bound up together as the book of Genesis makes clear where God is pictured breathing life into clay.[12] If we are a unity now, with the person-we-are expressed in and through what is outward, the same will be true in the hereafter. We have no idea of what 'the stuff of glory' consists. Here we are flesh and blood, expressing ourselves in and through physical bodies; but as Paul said, flesh and blood cannot inherit the kingdom of God.[13] 'We will be changed. For this perishable body must put on imperishability, and this mortal body must put on immortality.'[14]

Thirdly, bodily life is good. We are not, as some thought in the ancient world, souls trapped in a prison, from which death releases us. The material world has been created good by God and we are an essential part of that material world. Finally, whatever lies ahead will not be less rich or satisfying than material existence. Sheol, the place of the departed in early Israelite history, was thought of as a wispy, weaker form of life; a grey existence which had no appeal. But in the hereafter, we will be more truly and richly ourselves than we are now. The environment will be more glorious still. C.S. Lewis had very suggestive ideas about how this might be so, in terms of the taking up of 'matter' into 'soul'; but, as he was the first to admit, this was speculation.[15]

Language about the soul has come in for severe philosophical criticism in recent decades and has also been undermined by neurological studies of the brain. Clearly, we can no longer think of the soul as a kind of box within a box within a box, or as a spiritual entity essentially independent of the body and loosely joined to it. On the other hand, language about the soul serves a vital purpose in resisting all forms of reductionism. In particular, it resists any idea that the mind is simply certain electrical impulses in the brain. Language about

11. Cf. John 11.21–27.
12. Cf. Genesis 2.7.
13. 1 Corinthians 15.50.
14. 1 Corinthians 15.52–53.
15. C.S. Lewis, *Prayer: Letters to Malcolm* (London: Fountain Books, 1977), pp. 121–24; cf. R.D. Harries, *C.S. Lewis: The Man and His God* (London: Fount Paperbacks, 1987), pp. 80–88. Among other thinkers, 'process' theists interpret the hereafter in terms of 'memory', but do not agree on whether or not individuals are conscious of this existence, and therefore whether immortality is 'objective' or 'subjective'.

the soul points up the fact that as human beings we have an inescapable spiritual orientation and destiny. We are made to grow in the knowledge and love of God. We come from God and go back to God. This is a dimension of all that we are and do, not an isolatable entity within us.

Putting the concepts of soul and resurrection together, we might say that when we die, everything does indeed seem to come to an end. But God's knowledge of us does not end. Moreover, God knows us through and through; God knows which is our truest self. That true self, which is, as it were, lodged in God's heart and mind of love, is recreated or reformed in a form and manner appropriate to an eternal existence. Gerard Manley Hopkins composed a poem about the resurrection in which he wrote,

> Across my foundering deck shone
> A beacon, an eternal beam. Flesh fade, and mortal trash
> Fall to the residuary worm; world's wild fire, leave but ash:
> In a flash, at a trumpet crash,
> I am all at once what Christ is, since he is what I am, and
> This Jack, joke, poor potsherd, patch, matchwood, immortal diamond,
> Is immortal diamond.[16]

In that poem, Hopkins considered the human person from a range of points of view. We are a joke, nothing more than a bit of broken pottery or matchwood. But we are also immortal diamond, and in the resurrection, it is that immortal diamond which emerges.

Death and Judgement

The Christian schema includes not only talk about soul and resurrection, but also death, judgement, purgatory, heaven, hell, the communion of saints and Christ in glory. Each of these, from a Christian point of view, safeguards some essential aspect of truth.

Death is regarded by one strand in the Bible as an enemy. It came about as a result of the sin of Adam and Eve and has, as it were, to be overcome. So Paul continues in the great fifteenth chapter of his first letter to the Corinthians: 'When ... this mortal body puts on immortality, then the saying that is written will be fulfilled: "Death has been swallowed up in victory." "Where, O death, is your victory? Where, O death, is your sting?" The sting of death is sin, and the power of sin is the law. But thanks be to God, who gives us the victory through our Lord Jesus Christ.'[17]

16. 'That Nature is a Heraclitean Fire and of the Comfort of the Resurrection', in W.H. Gardner and N.H. Mackenzie (eds.), *The Poems of Gerard Manley Hopkins* (London: Oxford University Press, 4th edn, 1970), p. 105.

17. 1 Corinthians 15.54–57.

Significantly, there has been a powerful element in twentieth-century secular thought which has also thought of death as an enemy. When his father died, Dylan Thomas, in a famous poem, urged him to 'rage against the dying of the light'.[18] When Simone de Beauvoir's mother died, she wrote an essay saying that whenever death comes it is an outrage.[19] Yet death is part of the natural order; it belongs to the animal creation as such, of which we are a part, and in no way can be regarded as a consequence of human sinfulness. Death pre-existed human beings on this planet by millions of years. So we must see death within the providence of God, as part of God's original purpose for God's creatures. The analogy of an artist working with particular materials can perhaps help. A sculptor works with a particular piece of stone, a painter with canvas of a definite size. It is in and through the particular that his or her vision is realized. The boundaries are necessary. If someone is to produce a work of art then it has to be done through particular materials in a particular way. We human beings are also works of art, the work of the divine artist who works with us. The boundaries with which we have to work are living as particular people in particular places at particular times within limited life-spans. If we literally lived for ever on this earth, then it is doubtful that we would ever get anything done, or achieve anything. All could and probably would be put off and off. But the fact that we have limits and boundaries both of space and time creates, as it were, the artistic materials in and through which we give our lives a particular shape. In this, death has a defining function. For it is the point at which we finally surrender ourselves into the hands of a loving God or the point at which we finally lock ourselves away from God. Because human life is flawed and skewed, the tendency is to approach death in the wrong way, which is why Paul talked about the sting of death being sin. The sting is that far from being the point of yielding to God, it can be the point of resisting God. Because human life is still ambiguous, the idea of death as an enemy still captures something of the reality. On the other hand, for those who see it in terms of a final act of trust, it can be seen as a friend, as it is in the canticle of the sun attributed to Francis of Assisi.[20] In a fine hymn of Charles Wesley, one verse reads,

> Ready for all thy perfect will,
> my acts of faith and love repeat;
> till death thy endless mercies seal,
> and make the sacrifice complete.[21]

18. 'Do Not Go Gentle into That Good Night', in P. Larkin (ed.), *The Oxford Book of Twentieth-Century English Verse* (Oxford: Clarendon Press, 1973), p. 474.

19. See R.D. Harries, *Questioning Belief* (London: SPCK, 1995), p. 36.

20. See verse 6 of the hymn 'All creatures of our God and King', in, for example, *Common Praise* (Norwich: Canterbury Press, 2000), no. 250.

21. From the hymn 'O thou who camest from above', in, for example, *Common Praise*, no. 191.

Here, death is seen as a mercy, the seal of God's endless mercies, in which the surrender of our whole lives comes to its proper fulfilment. So it is that in Luke's picture of Jesus, Jesus dies with words from a psalm on his lips, words which every Jewish mother taught her child: 'Father, into your hands I commend my spirit.'[22]

According to the traditional schema, the individual soul is judged after death; but this is a prelude to the last judgement when all things shall be judged. In early Christian art, the emphasis was on Christ in glory. It was in the Romanesque period, the height of which was between 1050 and 1150, that the concept of judgement came to the fore, as can be seen for example in the Tympanum in the churches at Conques and Autun. Thereafter, it was the theme of many mediaeval doom wall-paintings. All this can seem rather grim. So two points need to be borne in mind. First, behind this belief is the conviction that as human beings we are accountable, and that is a crucial feature of our dignity as human beings which is not to be lost. Furthermore, if we are asked to give an account of ourselves, that is a sign that the person who asks for this cares for us, cares enough to want to know how we have got on. If we contrast two families, one in which the parents are totally indifferent to how their children get on at school and the other family in which, when the child returns, they ask how the day has gone, the second clearly expresses far more than the first a proper sense of care. In asking how we have got on, what we have made of our lives, God expresses care for us.

Secondly, from a Christian point of view, it is Christ himself who is the judge. He came into the world to save it and that is still his eternal purpose.[23] He is the good shepherd who looks for the one lost sheep, the woman who scrabbles all over the floor to search out the lost coin[24] – parables which Jesus lived out in his own ministry to the marginalized. 'Everything that the Father gives me will come to me, and anyone who comes to me I will never drive away.'[25] Christ is the one who asks us to give an account of ourselves to him, and it is he who loves us and who has died for us.

Purgatory

According to the classical Catholic picture, judgement of the soul is followed by purgatory. This belief came in for very severe criticism at the Reformation, quite rightly, in that it had become associated with money-making indulgences and was conceived in a very crude, literalistic manner. Furthermore, the Reformers wanted to emphasize the all-sufficiency of the sacrifice of Christ and the necessity of faith in him. But, as always, people are more usually right in what they affirm than in what they deny. The Reformers were right to

22. Luke 23.46.
23. Cf. John 3.17.
24. Cf. Luke 15.1–10.
25. John 6.37. Cf. the Authorized Version: 'I will in no wise cast out.'

emphasize the sheer graciousness and all-sufficiency of the love of Christ; they were right to reject corrupt and mechanistic views of purgatory. Yet the essence of a belief in purgatory can be found in Paul's corpus where he writes about Jesus Christ being the foundation of the Church:

> Now if anyone builds on the foundation with gold, silver, precious stones, wood, hay, straw – the work of each builder will become visible, for the Day will disclose it, because it will be revealed with fire, and the fire will test what sort of work each has done. If what has been built on the foundation survives, the builder will receive a reward. If the work is burned up, the builder will suffer loss; the builder will be saved, but only as through fire.[26]

Dante pictured purgatory as a mountain which we have to ascend. More in tune with contemporary sensibility, T.S. Eliot wrote about it in terms of a psychological state: purgatory, properly understood, is central to his great poem 'Four Quartets'. In it, he wrote about old age not as a time of serenity but of painful self-knowledge and re-evaluation: a time when even our best actions and thoughts look flawed, 'of motives late revealed'.[27] In the same poem, he used the image of fire to indicate both God's love and the way that that love brings painful purgation.[28] When we experience the fire of God's love, it brings self-knowledge, and that self-knowledge is a purging which is at once pain and bliss.

Hell

Hell, which was regarded as a fundamental tenet of Christian belief until the nineteenth century, has come in for increased criticism since then on moral grounds. F.D. Maurice was sacked in the nineteenth century from his position as a professor at King's College, London, for denying the everlastingness of hell. Few today dare even mention the subject. Yet, if we believe in the reality of human free choice, then hell might seem to be a logical possibility. That is, we can always lock ourselves into ourselves in self-pity, resentment and malice. If we can do that now, it is arguable that we can do that in the hereafter, which would be hell. It is difficult to think of the God revealed, for example, in the parable of the prodigal son,[29] *sending* anyone to hell. For God's love continually reaches out to us, trying to break down our barriers of suspicion, pride and hate. But if we are free, then it would seem logical that we can always freely choose to create hell even in the midst of heaven. Will all in the end be saved? The great fourteenth-century mystic Julian of Norwich teetered on the edge of universalism;[30] but faced

26. 1 Corinthians 3.12–15.

27. 'Little Gidding', in *The Complete Poems and Plays of T. S. Eliot* (London and Boston, MA: Faber and Faber, 1969), p. 194.

28. 'Little Gidding', in *Complete Poems and Plays of T. S. Eliot*, p. 196.

29. Luke 15.11–32.

30. See R.D. Harries, 'On the Brink of Universalism', in R.C. Llewelyn (ed.), *Julian: Woman of Our Day* (London: Darton, Longman & Todd, 1985), pp. 41–60.

by the sheer evils of the twentieth century in the Holocaust, the purges of Stalin, the genocide of Pol Pot, and the ethnic cleansing in Rwanda, to mention just a few, we need to be very wary about any easy talk of forgiveness. Because of the difficulty of reconciling the mercy of God with everlasting hell, and at the same time facing up to the reality of evil, some modern thinkers have thought instead of God simply extinguishing certain lives, no longer holding them in being. Perhaps that is so, but it is difficult to think of a God of infinite love and infinite time ever giving up on anyone. In William Golding's remarkable novel *Pincher Martin*, the central character has to face the knowledge of himself as a pair of greedy, grasping claws. But he is conscious of these claws being eaten into by a kind of divine lightning: 'The lightning came forward. Some of the lines pointed to the centre, waiting for the moment when they could pierce it. Others lay against the claws, playing over them, prying for a weakness, wearing them away in a compassion that was timeless and without mercy.'[31]

Heaven

The prospect and possibility of heaven still remains fundamental to Christian belief, however often it has been caricatured and disparaged. For heaven is nothing less than God's own self and the communion of saints. This is not to be seen in terms of a reward, like a medal stuck on the chest, but as the destination of the road of godliness. Of course we cannot imagine now what heaven will be like; there can only be hints and guesses taken from the most fulfilling and worthwhile human experiences. But heaven remains, because, as Paul said, nothing, not even death itself, can separate us from the love of God in Jesus Christ.[32] Heaven is inseparable from the glory of God in God's saints. For the great goal is not simply human fulfilment but a community of persons upheld and bonded together within the love of God. In the New Testament, the risen Christ is inseparable from his body, the Church, with every Christian being a limb or member of that body. So the abiding reality of heaven is the glory of God, which is that sublime conjunction of love, truth and goodness, glimpses of which we have in this life and which point to their source and standard in God's own self. Above all, this glory is revealed in the self-emptying of Jesus Christ, a theme which is profoundly explored in the Gospel of John. The glory irradiates and suffuses the whole communion of saints.

Karl Marx criticized religion in general and Christianity in particular for offering a misplaced hope. Instead of getting people to change this world for the better and hoping for a new future, religion directed their hope to another world. That is a salutary criticism, which many churches have taken on board. The kingdom of God is not limited to this world but we have nevertheless to strive to make it a reality within this world. Christians pray daily, 'Our Father

31. W. Golding, *Pincher Martin* (Harmondsworth: Penguin Books, 1962), p. 184.
32. Romans 8.38–39.

in heaven, hallowed be your name, your kingdom come, your will be done on earth as in heaven.' The kingdom of God has, as it were, to be built up in this world, even though it has its consummation beyond space and time.

Freud criticized the hope of heaven as wishful thinking. Or, as Iris Murdoch put it in a lapidary statement, 'almost anything that consoles us is a fake'.[33] But that itself is an assumption. Why should all that consoles be fake, however suspicious we might rightly be of the power of wishful thinking? Most Christians join with Jews and Muslims in believing that this hope of heaven is not an optional extra to the faith but is fundamental to it. This is not so much because of any individual's desire for an afterlife, but because all three religions have at their heart a concern for the establishment of true justice, divine justice. All through the Hebrew scriptures, there is this great hope and longing that God will act to put right everything that is wrong in the world. Jesus made this hope his own and Christians have carried it into history, believing that while in a profound sense the just and gentle rule of God in human affairs has already been inaugurated in the life, death and resurrection of Jesus Christ, nevertheless its consummation lies in the future. The hope of a utopia on this earth is not enough for all the outraged innocence and injustice in history, all those who have died for the truth's sake or in tragedy and who still cry out, 'How long, O Lord, how long?'[34] As the Vatican document on liberation theology put it, 'true justice must include everyone; it must bring the answer to the immense load of suffering borne by all the generations. In fact, without the resurrection of the dead and the Lord's judgment, there is no justice in the full sense of the term. The promise of the resurrection is freely made to meet the desire for true justice dwelling in the human heart.'[35]

Conclusion

Christians believe that God created the universe out of love and wisdom. So much that happens in the world seems directly to contradict this meaning and purpose. Christians, like Jews and Muslims, hold out the hope that, in the end, God's loving wisdom will prevail. For us, the humility of the self-emptying God revealed in Jesus Christ will be revealed in all its glory in those who share Christ's character and purpose whether they are aware of it or not. In the words of Julian of Norwich, quoted by T.S. Eliot,

> And all shall be well and
> All manner of thing shall be well.[36]

33. I. Murdoch, *The Sovereignty of Good* (repr., London and New York: Routledge, 2001), p. 58.
34. Cf. Revelation 6.10.
35. Congregation for the Doctrine of the Faith, *Instruction on Christian Freedom and Liberation* (London: Incorporated Catholic Truth Society, 1986), p. 35.
36. 'Little Gidding', in *Complete Poems and Plays of T. S. Eliot*, p. 198.

Life after Death from a Muslim Perspective

Yahya Michot

Many are the ways the theologians, philosophers, spiritual masters, and other thinkers of Islam, classical and modern, have approached the often very suggestive eschatological data found in the Qur'ān and the prophetic traditions. In their divergences as much as in their similarities, as this paper will show, they aid understanding not only of Muslims' fears and hopes but also of their conception of God and humanity.

Doubts and Certainties

In one of his most controversial works, Avicenna (d. 1037) developed a hermeneutic that led him to doubt that the Qur'ān, when speaking of the hereafter, the garden, and the fire, set up and validated a theological doctrine of bodily resurrection and bodily torments or pleasures after death.

> How then will the outer meaning of the Laws be an argument in this matter [i.e. concerning the hereafter, the resurrection of bodies, paradise and hell]? If we were supposing the hereafter matters to be spiritual, not made corporeal, and their true essence to be far from being perceived a priori by the minds, the way followed by the religious Laws to call people to accept these [spiritual matters] and to warn about them would not consist in drawing their attention by furnishing evidence about them but, rather, by expressing them through various likenesses (*tamthīl*) that would bring them closer to their wits. How then will the existence of one thing[1] be an argument in favour of the existence of another thing[2] when, if this other thing was not as it is supposed to be,[3] the first thing would still be as it is?

1. I.e. the literality of the Qur'ānic statements concerning the hereafter.
2. I.e. a corporeal hereafter.
3. I.e. spiritual rather than corporeal.

> All this is said to make known, to somebody wanting to be a member of the elite (*khāṣṣ*) of humans, not of the commonalty (*ʿāmm*), that the outer meaning of the religious Laws cannot be used as an argument in matters like these.[4]

For the great Iranian philosopher, Muslim theologians were mistaken in basing their eschatology on a literal reading of the revelation, as its fundamental purpose was not to teach such an eschatology but, rather, to guide the masses or, in other words, to encourage and maintain stability within human societies by frightening people with threats and attracting them with promises; just as, one way or another, a donkey is led on the right path with carrot and stick.[5] 'It appears from all this that the religious Laws come to address the crowd about things that they understand, bringing things that they do not understand closer to their estimative faculties by striking likenesses (*tamthīl*) and similitudes (*tashbīh*). If matters were otherwise, the religious Laws would be of no use at all.'[6]

Philosophy, Avicenna explained, demonstrates the impossibility of a physical return (*maʿād*) of the bodies, the purely immaterial nature of the human soul, its immortality, and the immense superiority of spiritual pleasures and pains over their sensorial equivalents. The elite of those who possess knowledge are therefore not interested by the Qur'ānic eschatological promises and threats, in which they only see, at best, images and allegories of the intelligible realities to which reason gives them access. As for the masses who follow the outward meaning of the revelation without having any idea of its meaning for the philosophers, the closer they adhere to it, the better it is as it secures social peace and order. This being so, the Prophet, whose mission is from this point of view marked by complete success in that his descriptions of the afterlife were more willingly accepted by the crowd than other religious messages, is by no means a liar. When they die, simple, naïve people indeed live in imagination all that in which they believed – the garden, the fire, etc. – just as in a dream. And one knows how real, from within sleep, dreams or nightmares can be.[7]

In the famous *Self-Destruction of the Philosophers (Tahāfut al-falāsifa)*, one of the three doctrines for which al-Ghazālī (d. 1111) – Algazel to the mediaeval Latins – condemned Avicenna and his like is their 'denial of the resurrection of bodies, their denial of corporeal pleasures in the Garden and of corporeal pains in the Fire, and their denial of the existence of the Garden and of the Fire as it is described in the Qur'ān'.[8] One may indeed wonder what is left of the

4. Avicenna, *Risāla Aḍḥawiyya*, in Y. Michot, 'A Mamlūk Theologian's Commentary on Avicenna's *Risāla Aḍḥawiyya*: Being a Translation of a Part of the *Dar' al-Taʿāruḍ* of Ibn Taymiyya, with Introduction, Annotation, and Appendices', part 1, *Journal of Islamic Studies* 14 (2003), pp. 149–203 (177).

5. On Avicenna's prophetology, see Y. Michot, *La destinée de l'homme selon Avicenne: Le retour à Dieu (*maʿād*) et l'imagination* (Louvain: Peeters, 1986), pp. 35–43.

6. Avicenna, *Aḍḥawiyya*, in Michot, 'Mamlūk Theologian's Commentary', p. 177.

7. On Avicenna's doctrine of an imaginal hereafter for simple believers, see Michot, *Destinée*, pp. 43–54.

8. al-Ghazālī, *Tahāfut*, quoted in Michot, *Destinée*, p. 214.

message of the Prophet in the philosopher's two-tier eschatology – purely immaterial for the elite, imaginal for the *vulgum pecus*.

Particularly vivid are indeed the depictions that the Qur'ān, the traditions of the Messenger, and the creeds composed during the classical age of Islam provide of the afterlife, the interrogation in the tomb, the resurrection of bodies, the day of judgement, the torments of hell and the pleasures of paradise.[9]

The state between death and resurrection, while the body rests in the tomb, is described as a barrier, or as an isthmus (*barzakh*): 'Then He caused him to die, and put him in a tomb. Then, when He wills, He will bring him to life again.' 'And there behind them is an isthmus until the day they will be raised.'[10] According to one of the Ḥanbalite creeds reproduced by Ibn al-Farrā' (d. 1066), 'the punishment of the tomb is a reality; a person will be questioned about his religion and his Lord, and about Paradise and Hell. Munkar and Nakīr are a reality; they are the two interrogators of the tomb.'[11]

The names of the day of resurrection are many: 'the day of the anastasis' (*yawm al-qiyāma*), 'the hour' (*al-sāʿa*), 'the day of requital' (*yawm al-dīn*), 'the day of reckoning' (*yawm al-ḥisāb*), 'the last day' (*al-yawm al-ākhir*), etc. This day will be unimaginably cataclysmic and there is no doubt that it will come.

> Surely what you are promised will befall. Then when the stars become dim, when the sky is cleft asunder, and when the mountains are blown away, and when God's messengers are brought together on the appointed day; for what day is the time appointed? For the day of judgment.[12]
>
> How can you deny God when you were dead and He made you live! Then He will make you die and then He will make you live [again], and unto Him you will be returned![13]
>
> Say: 'God makes you live, then He makes you die, then He gathers you together for the day of the anastasis, about which there is no doubt.'[14]

For the Ḥanafite al-Ṭaḥāwī (d. 933), Sunnis 'believe in the resurrection after death and in the recompensing of [a person's] works on the day of resurrection, in the scrutiny and the reckoning, in the reading of the book [recording

9. On Qur'ānic eschatology, I often follow M.M. ʿAli, *The Religion of Islām: A Comprehensive Discussion of the Sources, Principles and Practices of Islam* (Cairo: National Publication and Printing House [, 1972?]), pp. 264–314; and D. Masson, *Monothéisme coranique et monothéisme biblique: Doctrines comparées* (Paris: Desclée De Brouwer, 1976), pp. 679–764. See also J.I. Smith and Y.Y. Haddad, *The Islamic Understanding of Death and Resurrection* (Oxford: Oxford University Press, 2002).

10. Qur'ān 80.21–22 and 23.100. The Qur'ānic translations are free quotes of *The Holy Qur'ān with English Translation* (Istanbul: Ensar Neşriyat, 1996). Only a few of the Qur'ānic verses referring to the various subjects analysed can be quoted here. See Masson, *Monothéisme*, for a complete study.

11. Ibn al-Farrā', quoted in W.M. Watt, *Islamic Creeds: A Selection* (Edinburgh: Edinburgh University Press, 1994), p. 35.

12. Qur'ān 77.7–13.

13. Qur'ān 2.28.

14. Qur'ān 46.26.

deeds], in reward and punishment, in the Bridge and the Balance'.[15] The Ḥanbalite creed quoted earlier is more specific: 'The Bridge is a reality. It is set stretching over Gehenna. People pass over it and Paradise is beyond it. We ask God for safety [in crossing]. The Balance is a reality. In it are weighed good deeds and evil deeds, as God wills they should be weighed.' This creed also speaks of a basin and a trumpet:

> The Basin of Muḥammad (pbuh) is a reality; his community will go to drink there; there are vessels with which they will drink from it ...
>
> The Trumpet is a reality. Isrāfīl blows on it and created beings die. Then he blows on it a second blast and they are raised before the Lord of the worlds for the reckoning and the decree, and reward and punishment, and Paradise and Hell.[16]

'The Sovereignty on that day belongs to God. He will judge between them. Then those who believed and did righteous deeds will be in the Gardens of Delight. And those who disbelieved and denied Our Signs, for them will be a shameful torment.'[17] 'Paradise and Hell,' explained al-Ṭaḥāwī, 'are [already] created, and will never disappear or cease to exist. God created Paradise and Hell before the creation [of the world], and [then] created for each of them a people; some He willed for Paradise out of His grace, and some He willed for Hell out of His justice.'[18]

> ... and when We drive the criminals to Hell like thirsty cattle.[19]
>
> As for those who disbelieve, garments of fire will be cut out for them, while boiling water will be poured down on their heads. Whatever is in their bodies and skins is melted by it and for them are goads of iron. Whenever they desire to go forth from Hell in distress, they are returned to it. And it will be said: 'Taste the torment of burning.'[20]

Just as the torment of hell is made of fire, flames and boiling water, the pleasures and delights of paradise take the form of various terrestrial enjoyments, including sensual and sexual ones.

> The Garden that has been promised to the righteous is such that rivers will be flowing in it, of unpolluted water, and rivers will be flowing in it of milk of unchanged flavour, and rivers will be flowing in it of wine which will be delicious to the drinkers, and of honey, clear and pure. In it there will be fruits of every kind for them, and pardon from their Lord.[21]
>
> ... on lined couches, reclining therein face to face. There wait on them immortal youths, with bowls and ewers, and a cup from a pure spring that will neither pain

15. al-Ṭaḥāwī, quoted in Watt, *Creeds*, p. 54.
16. Ibn al-Farrā', quoted in Watt, *Creeds*, pp. 35–36.
17. Qur'ān 22.56–57.
18. al-Ṭaḥāwī, quoted in Watt, *Creeds*, p. 54.
19. Qur'ān 20.86.
20. Qur'ān 22.19–22.
21. Qur'ān 47.15.

> their heads nor take away their reason; with fruits of their choice and flesh of fowls that they desire, and Ḥouris with wide, lovely eyes, like unto hidden pearls, as a reward for what they used to do. There they will hear no idle talk, no sinful speech, but only the greeting, 'Peace! peace!'[22]

These pleasures are an effect of God's benevolence, of God's grace and favour, and a sign of God's mercy. Their essence and reality nevertheless remain covered with some mystery. 'No soul knows what is kept hid for them of delights of the eyes, as a reward for what they used to do.'[23] An authentic tradition of the Messenger states: 'God said: "I have prepared for My upright servants what neither eye has seen, nor ear has heard, nor has ever passed into the heart of any human."'[24]

The Qur'ān also evokes kinds of bliss in the afterlife that are of a higher nature than sensual pleasures. 'For those who do good is the greatest good, and yet more' (*ziyāda*).[25] According to various commentators, this complement (*ziyāda*) of beatitude consists in seeing God. Someone 'seeking only the Face of his Lord Most High will indeed be satisfied'.[26] The 'encounter' (*liqā'*) with God and God's 'satisfaction' (*riḍwān*) can also be understood in relation to this ultimate happiness. 'Whoever hopes to meet his Lord, let him work righteousness, and let him not associate anyone with Him in worship.' 'God is satisfied with them and they with Him. That is the great triumph.' 'O you the soul at peace, return to your Lord, satisfied and satisfying! Enter among My servants, and enter My Garden.'[27]

Hedonism and Contemplation

Although various Qur'ānic verses suggest that life in paradise is 'the starting-point for a new advancement, in which man shall continue to rise to higher and higher places',[28] many are the Muslims who have seen or continue to see the garden and the fire as places where they will be physically rewarded or punished. As the Qur'ān puts it about paradise, 'therein you shall have all that your souls desire, therein you shall have all that you call for.'[29] For many, this must mean, among other things, the fulfilment of sensual expectations or even sexual appetites.

22. Qur'ān 56.15–26.
23. Qur'ān 32.17.
24. al-Bukhārī, quoted in W.A. Graham, *Divine Word and Prophetic Word in Early Islam: A Reconsideration of the Sources, with Special Reference to the Divine Saying* or Ḥadīth Qudsī (The Hague and Paris: Mouton, 1977), p. 117.
25. Qur'ān 10.26.
26. Qur'ān 92.20–21.
27. Qur'ān 18.110; 5.119; and 89.27–30.
28. ʿAli, *Religion*, p. 303.
29. Qur'ān 41.31.

Aḥmad Bahgat, one of the best contemporary Egyptian humorist writers, illustrates this perfectly in his *Memoirs of Ramaḍān*. He remembers a day when he was hesitating to break his fast: 'Then the Garden appeared to me with its rivers of wine, milk and honey. So I decided to have patience.' He also evokes one of his friends, a drunkard, who was telling him: 'Do you know what makes me sad in the thought that I will not enter the Garden? ... The rivers of wine ... Just think: the bottle which we empty every day disappears before we fill the glass, before we start enjoying ourselves and before we get drunk ... Imagine yourself in front of a river of wine!'[30]

As for Abdelwahab Bouhdiba, in his controversial but acclaimed *La sexualité en Islam*, he did not hesitate to describe the Islamic vision of paradise as an 'infinite orgasm'. He notably quoted statements of the great Mamlūk religious scholar Jalāl al-Dīn al-Suyūṭī (d. 1505) that 'an inhabitant of the Garden espouses seventy Ḥouris besides the legitimate wives he had on earth' and that his 'erection is eternal'.[31] There is some bravado in the Tunisian sociologist's analysis, as he well knows how Muslim sexuality and eschatology have been judged 'immoral' by orientalists and, before them, generations of Christian polemicists since the mediaeval period. '*Hoc non erit paradisus, sed lupanar et locus obscenissimus*,' the Cordoban abbot Speraindeo wrote during the ninth century about the garden described in the Qur'ān.[32] More recently, in order to invite Muslims to 'rethink about the divine origin of Islam', the apostate of Pakistani origin Anwar Shaikh (b. 1928) reduces Islam to 'sex and violence' and speaks of 'sex-after-death' as 'a speciality of Islam': 'Islam exploits the psychological weakness of man for sex, and prescribes Jehad as the sure way of getting into paradise, the abode of the most luxurious sex.'[33]

Without, obviously, indulging in such extreme opinions, a number of Muslim classical thinkers or spiritual masters also expressed concerns or reservations about too explicitly literal, materialistic, or hedonistic readings of the afterlife described in the Qur'ān and the *ḥadīths* of the Prophet. Or they managed to make such descriptions lose their 'controversial' character by developing an *ad hoc* hermeneutic. Avicenna's criticisms were not the first to have circulated. The very force with which the creeds of various orthodox theological schools insist on the reality of not only the bridge, the balance, the basin, etc., but also the garden and the fire themselves, is indicative of the intensity of the attacks to which these physical aspects of the afterlife and the latter's nature as corporeal reward or punishment have been sometimes subjected since the early period of Islam, by Muʿtazilī rationalists or others. Famous, in this regard, is the way in

30. A. Bahgat, *Mémoires de Ramadan (Mudhakkirāt ṣā'im)* (trans. Y. Michot; Paris: L'Harmattan, 1991), pp. 27–28.

31. A. Bouhdiba, *La sexualité en Islam* (Paris: Presses Universitaires de France, 1975), pp. 91 and 95–96.

32. Cited in N. Daniel, *Islam and the West: The Making of an Image* (Edinburgh: Edinburgh University Press, 1960), p. 126.

33. A. Shaikh, *Islam: Sex and Violence* (Cardiff: Principality Publishers, 1999), p. 91. On this author, see www.secularislam.org/skeptics/anwar.htm.

which Rābiʿat al-ʿAdawiyya, the great female Baṣrian Sufi of the eighth century, understood the Arabic proverb *al-jār qabla l-dār*, 'The neighbour [comes] before the house': she was exclusively interested in God, not in God's garden.[34] In an anecdote that the French chronicler of St. Louis, Joinville, transmitted to the Latin Middle Ages, she is portrayed as a madwoman going around with a bucket of water and a torch: as she had no love for anything but God, she was ready to extinguish the flames of hell and to set fire to paradise.[35]

One of the most important Sufi masters of the ninth century, Abū Yazīd al-Bisṭāmī, declared himself ready to plant his tent at the door of hell. 'I know,' he used to say, 'that if Hell sees me, it will stop burning and I will be a mercy for the creatures.' He would only accept as his disciple 'someone who, on the Day of resurrection, would stand up, take by the hand every monotheist condemned to the Fire, and lead him into Paradise'.[36]

The same al-Ghazālī who, in his *Tahāfut*, condemned the denial of the resurrection of the bodies by the philosophers, in other works distinguished three different modes of realization of the eschatological promises and threats of the Prophet: sensory, imagined and intellectual.[37] He had therefore no problem with the doctrine of an imaginal afterlife developed by Avicenna in respect of the mass of naïve believers. In his *Fayṣal al-tafriqa*, he went as far as to accept five modes of existence for the realities of the hereafter: concrete, sensory, imaginal, intellectual and analogous.[38]

In a way, the objections often raised against the eschatology of the Qur'ān and the Sunna in Islam are part of a broader questioning manifest, in various measures and expressions, among spiritual masters as well as rationalist scholars, about the real purpose of the religion. The garden with its sensual pleasures can indeed be regarded by some thinkers as exclusively destined for the commonalty (*ʿāmma*) of those followers of the Prophet, the 'Muslims' naïvely or blindly submitting to his religious law (*sharīʿa*), whose mental universe is essentially limited to the realm of bodies (*jism*) and whose virtuous actions (*ʿamal*) result from their fear of the fire or are some kind of commercial transaction (*tijāra*) aiming at the obtaining of a future reward (*ajr*). As for themselves, such thinkers most often expect to see and contemplate (*mushāhada*) God in the hereafter and prefer such a favour (*faḍl*) rather than living the sensual delights of a resurrected body in paradise. They indeed see their human essences as pure immaterial souls (*nafs*) or spirits (*rūḥ*). They consider that, among believers (*mu'min*), they form an elite (*khāṣṣa*) possessing knowledge (*maʿrifa*) or gnosis (*ʿirfān*). They think that they can therefore dispense with religious

34. See R. Caspar, *Cours de mystique musulmane* (Rome: Pontifical Institute of Arabic Studies, 1976), p. 37.

35. See Caspar, *Cours*, p. 38.

36. See Caspar, *Cours*, p. 58.

37. See Michot, *Destinée*, p. 212.

38. See S.A. Jackson, *On the Boundaries of Theological Tolerance in Islam: Abū Ḥāmid al-Ghazālī's* Fayṣal al-Tafriqa Bayna al-Islām wa al-Zandaqa (Karachi: Oxford University Press, 2002), pp. 94–96.

obedience (*ṭāʿa*) and virtuous action. They claim to have accessed the realm of esoteric truth (*bāṭin*) and reality (*ḥaqīqa*) beyond the limitations of the exoteric law (*ẓāhir*). They pretend to be living in a universe of sainthood (*wilāya*) supposedly superior to the realm of prophethood (*nubuwwa*), and to have no other preoccupation than a pure love (*ḥubb*) of God.

An All-encompassing Bliss

The contrast between these two types of religiosity is immense. For the great Damascene Shaykh al-Islām Ibn Taymiyya (d. 1328), it involved a dichotomy and a contempt for the Prophet that are totally unacceptable. Outward and inward dimensions must accompany one another rather than be separated. As a middle way between Judaism and Christianity, the Mamlūk reformist theologian explained, Islam is a service of God (*ʿibāda*) – one would now say a *Gottesdienst* rather than a *religion* – that includes both love (*ḥubb*) for the Lord and a humble and obedient submission (*dhull*) to the divine commands and prohibitions.[39] Someone whose religious practice would not be enriched by spirituality would not be a real believer (*mu'min*), and someone claiming to live a deep religious reality without adhering to the way of the Prophet (peace be upon him) would not be a Muslim.[40] The *sharīʿa* of the Prophet is complete and perfect. It constitutes the best way to draw nearer to God, and is broad and deep enough to accommodate much. There is no reason to limit its usefulness to the crowd and develop an alternative, innovative, path for any kind of elite. Similarly, concerning the afterlife: to distinguish and oppose to one another the garden and the vision of God is a mistake. The paradisiac bliss is all-encompassing and there is nothing beyond it.

> The Most High said: 'Those whom they invoke seek the way of approach to their Lord – which of them shall be the nearest; they hope for His mercy and they fear His torment. Lo! the torment of your Lord is to be shunned' (Q. 17. 56–57). He also said: 'Those who believe, who emigrate and who fight in the way of God, these have hope of God's mercy' (Q. 2. 218). His 'mercy' (*raḥma*) is a word encompassing every good, and His 'torment' (*ʿadhāb*) a word encompassing every harm. The abode of pure mercy is the Garden, the abode of torment the Fire. As for this world, it is the abode of amalgam.
>
> Even if hope is [only] attached to entering the Garden, the 'Garden' is a word encompassing every felicity and the highest felicity is to see the Face of God. So, in Muslim's *Ṣaḥīḥ*, it is reported about the Prophet, God bless him and grant him peace, according to ʿAbd al-Raḥmān b. Abī Laylā, according to Ṣuhayb, that he said: 'When the people of the Garden enter the Garden, a herald interpellates them: "O the people of the

39. See the Taymiyyan pages translated in Y. Michot, 'Textes spirituels d'Ibn Taymiyya. XVI: La réalité de l'amour (*maḥabba*) de Dieu et de l'homme (suite)', *Le Musulman* 29 (1998), pp. 20–25 (20).

40. Ibn Taymiyya, *Majmūʿ al-Fatāwā* (ed. ʿA. R. b. M. Ibn Qāsim; 37 vols.; Rabat: Maktabat al-maʿārif, AH 1401/1981), VIII, p. 316; translation in my forthcoming *Ibn Taymiyya: Le sang et la foi d'al-Ḥallāj* (Paris: Elbouraq, 2006).

Garden! You have, from God, a promise that He wants to fulfil completely for you." They will say: "What is it? Has He not whitened our faces? Has He not made our balances heavy? Has He not made us enter the Garden? Has He not saved us from the Fire?" He will lift the veil and they will see Him. He will indeed not have given them anything more loved by them than seeing Him. This is the "complement".'[41] Therefore obviously disappears the confusion which is present in the words of someone saying 'I did not worship You out of desire for Your Garden, nor out of fear of Your Fire. I have only worshipped You out of desire to see You'.[42] Someone saying that is of the opinion – he and who follows him – that in what is named 'the Garden' nothing is included but eating and drinking, clothes and coition, hearing and similar matters in which one enjoys created things. With him also agree, about this, those who deny the [future] seeing of God – the Jahmites[43] – or who confess it but maintain that one does not enjoy the seeing of God itself, as said by a group of doctors of *Fiqh*. These are agreed on saying that, in what is named 'the Garden' and 'the hereafter' nothing is included but the enjoyment of created things. This is why, when hearing God's words 'Some of you want this world and some of you want the hereafter' (Q. 3. 152), one of the shaykhs who are mistaken said: 'And where are those who want God?' About these words of the Most High 'God has bought from the believers their persons and their wealth by giving them the Garden' (Q. 9. 111), someone else said: 'If our persons and our wealth entitle us to the Garden, what about seeing Him?' All this because they were of the opinion that, in 'the Garden', to see [the Face of God] is not included.

The truth is that the Garden is the abode encompassing all felicity and that the highest [felicity] that one finds there is to see the face of God. This is part of the felicity that the [servants] attain in the Garden, just as the Scriptures have told us. And similarly for the people of the Fire: in relation to their Lord, they are under a veil when they enter the Fire.

This being so, if he who says these words knows what he says, what he means is only this: 'Even if You had created no Fire, or even if You had created no Garden, one would necessarily have to worship You and one would necessarily have to draw nearer to You and to see You', what is meant here by 'the Garden' being what the creature enjoys.[44]

41. See Muslim, *al-Ṣaḥīḥ*, Īmān, bāb 80 (8 vols.; Constantinople: n.p., AH 1334/1916), I, p. 112; Ibn Ḥanbal, *al-Musnad* (6 vols.; Cairo: al-Bābī l-Ḥalabī, AH 1313/1896), IV, p. 332. On the 'complement', see the Qur'ānic verse 10.26 quoted above.

42. Cf. the saying of Rābiʿat al-ʿAdawiyya (d. Baṣra, 801): 'Je ne L'ai adoré ni par crainte de Son Enfer, ni par amour de Son Paradis. Car j'aurais été alors comme un mauvais serviteur qui travaille quand il a peur ou quand il est récompensé. Mais je L'ai adoré par amour et par passion de Lui' (*Rābiʿa: Chants de la recluse* [trans. M. Oudaimah and G. Pfister; Paris: Arfuyen, 1988], p. 9).

See also Abū Yazīd al-Bisṭāmī (d. 874 or 857): 'J'ai vu les hommes ici-bas prendre plaisir à boire, à manger, à convoler. De même dans l'au-delà. J'ai mis alors mon plaisir en Son invocation ici-bas, en Sa contemplation dans l'au-delà' (*Les dits de Bisṭāmī: Shaṭaḥāt* [trans. A. Meddeb; Paris: Fayard, 1989], pp. 173–74, no. 423).

43. The followers of the theological doctrines of Jahm b. Ṣafwān, Abū Muḥriz (d. 746); see W.M. Watt, 'Dj̲ahm b. Ṣafwān' and 'Dj̲ahmiyya', in *Encyclopedia of Islam* (11 vols.; Leiden: E.J. Brill, 1986–2002), II, p. 388.

44. Ibn Taymiyya, *Majmūʿ al-Fatāwā*, translated in Y. Michot, 'Textes spirituels d'Ibn Taymiyya. XV: La réalité de l'amour (*maḥabba*) de Dieu et de l'homme', *Le Musulman* 28 (1996), pp. 24–27 (24–25).

'I Will Forgive You Whatever Comes From You'

Bouhdiba is right in saying that, 'of the life *post mortem*, Islam has provided with a remarkable continuity a vision which is so total and so detailed that it constitutes a real creed'.[45] Centuries of theological and mystical endeavour have led to a very wide spectrum of readings of that creed, from the most literally faithful to the Qur'ān and the *ḥadīth* to the most deleterious. A 'personal' approach – and, admittedly, a quite widespread and traditional one – could include the following elements.

Our trial in this life has an end at an appointed term. 'I do not hesitate about anything I do,' God says in a famous *ḥadīth qudsī*, 'as I hesitate [to take] the soul of the believer. He hates death and I hate to harm him.'[46] However, as confirmed in the Qur'ān, 'every soul will taste death'. 'Lo! we are God's and lo! unto Him we are returning.'[47] There is no transmigration (*tanāsukh*).

Faith in the afterlife is one of the fundamental principles of the religion, like faith in the one God and the prophethood of the Prophet (peace be upon him). We do not survive death because of some everlasting essence of our soul but exclusively thanks to the will, the power, the providence, the justice and the mercy of God. 'As He originated you, so you shall return.' 'Have they not seen that God, Who created the heavens and the earth and was not wearied by their creation, has the power to bring life back to the dead?'[48]

Humans are servants accountable to their divine Lord, 'Who created death and life that He may try you, which of you is best in action'.[49] Their deeds are weighed on the day of judgement and 'whoso does good an atom's weight will see it then, and whoso does ill an atom's weight will see it then'.[50] Ethics, which are at the core of revelation and prophethood, would have no meaning without the final reckoning leading to a reward or a punishment. For sure, everything comes about by the will, knowledge, decree and predestination of God. God, however, does not command evil nor approve of it but forbids it and commands good. Although all our acts, good or bad, are the creation of God, we acquire them and will be judged for them.[51] We do not investigate this secret of God but have faith in God's justice, wisdom and mercy.

> The hereafter will be better for him who fears God; and you will not be wronged, even [in the weight of] a date-thread.[52]
>
> Say: 'O my servants who have transgressed against their souls! Do not despair of God's mercy. God indeed forgives all sins. Lo! He is the Forgiving, the Merciful.'[53]

45. Bouhdiba, *Sexualité*, p. 99.
46. al-Bukhārī, quoted in Graham, *Divine Word*, p. 173.
47. Qur'ān 3.185 and 2.156.
48. Qur'ān 7.29 and 46.33.
49. Qur'ān 67.2.
50. Qur'ān 99.7–8.
51. See the creed of al-Ashʿarī translated in Watt, *Creeds*, pp. 42–44.
52. Qur'ān 4.77.
53. Qur'ān 39.53.

> God does not forgive the giving of partners to Him. He forgives what is beneath that to whom He wills.[54]
>
> He said: 'I smite with My torment whom I will, and My mercy embraces all things.'[55]
>
> If You torment them, they are Your servants; and if You forgive them, You, only You, are the Mighty, the Wise.[56]

We also assert the intercession of the Messenger on behalf of the great sinners of his community. As al-Ghazālī wrote, 'monotheists will be taken out of Hell after punishment. As a result, by the grace of God no monotheist will remain in Gehenna and no monotheist will be everlastingly in Hell.'[57] This being said, 'the affair of these [people] belongs to God; if He wills, He punishes them, and if He wills, He forgives them'.[58]

In the present life, the religion – its rituals as well as its *art de vivre* – involves our complete being, with its bodily, sensory, emotional and affective aspects as well as all our other human dimensions, everything being put in its right place, which is the condition for harmony and balance. Of this world, the Messenger (peace be upon him) said that he loved three things: women, perfume and prayer, which was the delight of his eyes.[59] Seeing no incompatibility between a normal sexual life and worship, he also forbade all kinds of ascetic monasticism or celibacy.[60] Similarly for the hereafter, as properly explained by Bouhdiba:

> In fact we have the feeling that the vision of God constitutes the essence itself of the delights of the Muslim Paradise. But it is not exclusive. It looks like the extension of the other delights, in some way physical, promised to the Elected ... It is not by chance that Hell is solitude, non-presence to the others, in a word absence of love. Paradise on the contrary is total love, full and infinite. It is unity and accord with the world, with oneself and with God. Paradise is first of all the reconciliation of man with nature, i.e. with matter. Which explains this material profusion that characterizes the *Janna*. It is a feast for all the senses ... The meaning of paradisiac enjoyment is surely that one must take his own body seriously. Far from de-realizing our desires, Islam teaches us to realize them better ... Islam is thus not an economy of pleasure. It is its superconscious valorization. To integrate the sexual into the sacral, these are finally, we believe, the great lesson and the great merit of this Islamic vision of the hereafter.[61]

54. Qur'ān 4.48.
55. Qur'ān 7.156.
56. Qur'ān 5.118.
57. Quoted in Watt, *Creeds*, p. 78.
58. Al-Ashʿarī, quoted in Watt, *Creeds*, p. 44.
59. On this tradition, see Ibn Ḥanbal, *al-Musnad*, III, pp. 128, 199 and 285.
60. On the tradition attributed to the Prophet 'No monasticism in Islam', see L. Massignon, *Essai sur les origines du lexique technique de la mystique musulmane* (Paris: J. Vrin, 1954), pp. 145–53. See also Y. Michot, 'Un célibataire endurci et sa maman: Ibn Taymiyya (m. 728/1328) et les femmes', in *La femme dans les sociétés orientales* (ed. C. Cannuyer; Brussels: Société Belge d'Études Orientales, 2001), pp. 165–90 (182–87).
61. Bouhdiba, *Sexualité*, pp. 102–106.

Whatever be their exact nature and modalities, future reward or punishment that would not suit our human condition, by being exclusively immaterial, spiritual or intellectual, would be absurd, as they would in fact mutilate us. Inversely, a modulation, progression and hierarchization of the delights of the garden, according to the states of consciousness and the spiritual development or expectations of its various inhabitants, should not be excluded. Various degrees and abodes are indeed traditionally distinguished within paradise. Moreover, it would be quite strange that the company of the prophets, the saints (*walī*), and the virtuous (*ṣāliḥ*), to which Muslims aspire to be introduced there,[62] not to speak of their vision of God, would have no effect on their souls.

As often, Avicenna is right: there is no such thing as a scientific eschatology. There is rather a faith in the revelation conveyed by the Prophet (peace be upon him) and a trust in God, which, without excluding some fear of God's judgement and wrath, principally means reliance on God's promises and hope in God's mercy. Apart from that, the hereafter essentially belongs to the unknown (*ghayb*). As Ibn ʿAbbās, the famous companion of the Prophet, is reported to have said: 'In Paradise, there are no foods of this life except the names.'[63] As was noted above, from the Qur'ān: 'No soul knows what is kept hid for them of delights of the eyes, as a reward for what they used to do.'[64] We can diverge and dispute with one another about our eschatological hypotheses and analyses, doctrines, dogmas and creeds. 'Had God willed He could have made you one community. But that He may try you by that which He has given you, [He has made you as you are]. So vie one with another in good works. Unto God you will all return, and He will then inform you about that concerning which you were differing.'[65] Just as for many other matters!

> Son of Adam, as long as you call on Me and hope in Me, I will forgive you whatever comes from you [of wrong actions] and I do not care. Son of Adam, even if your wrong actions were to reach to the clouds of the sky and then you seek forgiveness of Me I will forgive you. Son of Adam, even if you were to come to Me with nearly the earth in wrong actions and then later you meet Me, not associating anything with Me, then I will definitely bring you nearly as much as [the earth] in forgiveness.[66]

62. See, for example, the prayer of Joseph in Qur'ān 12.101: 'Make me die as a Muslim and join me to the virtuous.'
63. See ʿAli, *Religion*, p. 292.
64. Qur'ān 32.17.
65. Qur'ān 5.48.
66. *Ḥadīth qudsī*; see al-Nawawī (d. 1277), *The Complete Forty Ḥadīth* (trans. A. Clarke; London: Ta-Ha Publishers, AH 1419/1998), p. 145.

Life after Death in Jewish, Christian and Muslim Thought

Norman Solomon, Richard Harries and Tim Winter

Although there are certainly some differences of emphasis between Jewish and Christian understandings of life after death, it is noteworthy that both Norman Solomon and Richard Harries are primarily concerned with a defence of traditional beliefs in the face of modern scepticism. In short, however important inter-religious dialogue may be, religions affected by the culture of modern science and philosophy see the prime challenge as one of credibility for a religious view of any kind.

Within both Judaism and Christianity, different adherents give different weightings to belief in an afterlife. As Norman Solomon points out, such a belief grew up comparatively late, in the second century BCE, and while it has been as essential for historic Judaism as it has been for historic Christianity and was regarded as such by Maimonides, in the modern world a good many liberal and reformed Jews, without ceasing to regard themselves as good Jews, who typically have a passionate belief in God and the Torah, have personally sat light to or even explicitly denied any concept of the afterlife. This would not be the case with a vast majority of Orthodox Jews, who for example would refuse to be cremated, since they believe in the resurrection of the body. Similarly, while literalistic understandings of language about life after death can be rejected and regarded as metaphor or symbol, such metaphors can be treated very differently. For some, they convey value judgements about normal life, highlighting and underlining the value and importance of the way we live now. For others, these metaphors and symbols point to a dimension or realm which, while it cannot be described in any straightforward or literal way, is none the less 'real'. For some, they are metaphors about this life. For others, they are metaphors about the consummation of this life beyond space and time.

While in the modern world, both Judaism and Christianity have tended to react to the criticisms of Marx and Freud and others by stressing the importance of this life and downgrading any thought of the hereafter, certainly by way of contrast with the mediaeval world, it is probably true that the Jewish emphasis on this life antedates any modern criticism and is an essential feature of that faith. So, for example, in discussing how far life in extreme old age should be prolonged, the late Lord Jakobovits argued in the House of Lords that because this life is intrinsically valuable, it is wrong to shorten it, even as a side effect of pain-reducing drugs. This is in contrast to the Christian view, officially stated by the Vatican for example, that there is no obligation to prolong life unnecessarily when it has become a burden.

There is no sign that most modern Muslim thinkers have been influenced by the criticism of Marx, Freud and others by downplaying the importance of a life after death. On the contrary, the concept of an ultimate judgement is as central as ever. As Michot makes clear in his paper, there is no way in which Islam either has in the past downplayed, or could in the future downplay, the significance of a life after death. It is as fundamental to Islam today as such a belief has been for Christianity and Judaism in previous centuries. Michot points out how Avicenna (d. 1037) drew a distinction between literalistic readings of the afterlife and more philosophical ones. The literal meaning of resurrection, judgement, heaven and hell were, Avicenna maintained, quite properly taught by Muhammad, for this was the only way in which the great majority of people could understand and accept profound spiritual truths. These themes enabled people to lead the good life and kept society stable. Moreover, the literalistic reading has its place even in the hereafter, for simple-minded people will live out the truth of the metaphors in their imagination, as in a dream, and as we all know, dreams can be real enough.

Al-Ghazālī (d. 1111) took issue with Avicenna in making these distinctions and, affirming the literal truth of these ideas, stood within the mainstream of Islam. However, he, like the Qur'ān, also evoked bliss in the afterlife that is of a higher nature than sensual pleasures. 'For those who do good is the greatest good, and yet more.'[1] According to mainstream Muslim belief, the highest beatitude consists in seeing God. Someone 'seeking only the Face of his Lord Most High will indeed be satisfied'.

Norman Solomon brings out the important strand within certain traditions of Judaism of belief in reincarnation – a fact which comes as some surprise to most Christians and Muslims. Only one major Christian theologian, Origen in the second century, taught the pre-existence of the soul, and he was condemned for his views. Otherwise, belief in reincarnation is unusual and regarded as something of an individual quirk. However, in the modern world there have been some Christians who believed it, for example W.R. Matthews, a dean of St. Paul's cathedral. Furthermore, John Hick, emphasizing the metaphorical nature of the language, has suggested that reincarnation might point to the possibility of further stages of growth and development after death, a taking of different forms not within this life but beyond this life in another sphere of existence altogether. Yahya Michot makes it clear that reincarnation or the concept of transmigration of souls has no place within mainstream Islam. The concept of purgatory, an intermediate state between death and the final

1. For quotations, see Yahya Michot's paper, 'Life after Death from a Muslim Perspective', above.

judgement in which the soul is 'purged', is present in all three religions but is accorded different degrees of significance. In Judaism, the *Kaddish*, a prayer declaring the holiness of God, is said for a set period after a person's death, perhaps up to eleven months. Saying this prayer, which affirms in a dignified, accepting way the absolute sovereignty of God, is said to avail for the departed in the hereafter but the doctrine associated with this is not developed. In Islam, the widespread custom of visiting the graves of the departed, and saying prayers there, is again said to have benefits for the departed in the next life. Within Islam, there is also a belief in a temporary purgation of some souls in hell, which are then released by the Prophet's intercession. In Western Europe at least from 1193 until the Reformation, the concept of purgatory was central to the Christian schema. It has taken noble literary forms from Dante's *Purgatorio* to Newman's *Dream of Gerontius*. It became increasingly associated with crude, prudential calculations of days or years of purgatory. This was linked with financial contributions, and as such decisively rejected by the Reformers, who asserted the sufficiency of Christ's atoning sacrifice alone. In Christian Orthodoxy, the word purgatory is not used, but there is the idea of *kathartein*, or cleansing of the soul after death. In modern Christian thought, the concept of purgatory, if retained at all, would be seen in terms of the painful self-knowledge that comes about through knowledge of the absolute love of God for us, as expressed, for example, in T.S. Eliot's 'Four Quartets'.

It is doubtful whether there is any significant difference in the way that both Judaism and Christianity have sought to hold together a belief in the resurrection of the body on the one hand and belief in the immortality of the soul on the other. Traditionally, as Norman Solomon brings out, many people have found it difficult to believe in the idea of a resurrection of the body and therefore they have been drawn to the concept of the immortality of the soul. But in the modern world, both views are equally problematic. On the one hand, we know that we are embodied beings and the concept of resurrection is congruous with that. But many can no longer conceive of people being raised from their graves like those in a Stanley Spencer painting. If true, it will be as a 'transfigured' body, as suggested by Nahmanides, or to use Paul's term, 'a spiritual body'. But whereas thinkers in the past have sometimes sought relief from difficulties of believing in the resurrection of the body by turning to belief in an immortal soul, the latter is equally difficult for those shaped by modern culture.

While the concepts of an immortal soul and an afterlife conceived in a purely spiritual way appear in some Muslim thinkers, the main emphasis of that tradition is on the sensual, even the sexual, delights of the hereafter. The modern Tunisian writer Bouhdiba has not hesitated to describe paradise in graphic sexual terms, such as an inhabitant having seventy ḥouris in addition to the legitimate wives he had on earth. This kind of picture has been very strongly criticized by Christian thinkers down the years, as much has been made of the idea of paradise full of 'Ḥouris with wide, lovely eyes' as a reward for religious obedience on earth. However, for Islam, there is no shyness about affirming the goodness of sensual pleasures, including sexual ones: they are part of the goodness of God's creation, and their affirmation is to be preferred to a false asceticism. This means that there need be no hesitation in conceiving paradise in terms of such joy for both sexes. But within Islam itself, there has also been a reaction against such imagery and an emphasis on a more spiritual way of understanding paradise.

Michot quotes Ibn Taymiyya (d. 1328) with approval, in refusing to accept that kind of dichotomy. Paradise does indeed include every kind of felicity; this is indeed a garden of all delights. But this is also a garden in which, within and beneath those delights, there is the delight of God's own self for God's own sake. 'He will lift the veil and they will see Him. He will indeed not have given them anything more loved by them than seeing Him.'[2] 'The truth is that the Garden is the abode encompassing all felicity and that the highest [felicity] that one finds there is to see the face of God. This is part of the felicity that the [servants] attain in the Garden, just as the Scriptures have told us. And similarly for the people of the Fire: in relation to their Lord, they are under a veil when they enter the Fire.'

Religions which emphasize rewards and punishments in the afterlife, traditionally all three monotheistic religions but perhaps especially Islam today, are criticized for inculcating a purely prudential morality: do good now in order to obtain good in the hereafter, avoid evil now in order to avoid punishment in the world to come. But this criticism was not unknown to believers in all three religions. So it is that in all of them, there is a strong strand of doing good for its own sake and loving God for God's sake. So, to quote Ibn Taymiyya again, 'Even if You had created no Fire, or even if You had created no Garden, one would necessarily have to worship You and one would necessarily have to draw nearer to You and to see You.'

There is also the criticism, both modern and ancient, that a God who sentences people to eternal punishment is immoral. Against this can be set not only the equal or often greater emphasis upon the mercy of God but also the tradition of saints or holy people willing to draw near to hell to save others. A Sufi saint of the ninth century quoted by Michot adopted this attitude. He said he was ready to plant his tent at the door of hell: 'I know that if the Hell sees me, it will stop burning and I will be a mercy for the creatures.' He would only accept as his disciple 'someone who, on the Day of resurrection, would stand up, take by the hand every monotheist condemned to the Fire, and lead him into Paradise'.

All three religions today show a growing desire to emphasize the sheer grace and mercy of God and draw on those aspects of their tradition which hold out the possibility of salvation for all. As a previous paper brings out, Judaism has

2. For quotations, see Yahya Michot's paper, 'Life after Death from a Muslim Perspective', above.
3. See Norman Solomon's paper, 'Pluralism from a Jewish Perspective', above.

never confined salvation to Jews.[3] In Islam, though there is punishment, it has not universally been regarded as everlasting.[4] Within Christianity, Cardinal Bellarmine in the sixteenth century said that while it is necessary to believe in hell, it is not necessary to believe that anyone is in it. Thinkers in the East, such as Isaac the Syrian, and in the West, such as Julian of Norwich, have come very close to being universalists.

Again, all three religions today would want to emphasize the mystery of life after death and the inadequacy of all images drawn from temporal life. There is no railway line running straight through death to any station beyond, that we can describe. Images such as that of 'the beatific vision' are useful in indicating the experience of being so taken out of ourselves by sublime beauty, truth and goodness, that any concept of 'before' and 'after' seems to fall away. The resurrection is, indeed, the 'last day'. In short, although we know one thing following another in this life, in the hereafter there is no successivity. On the other hand, some scholars urge that although time in the hereafter is of a different order from the time we know, nevertheless images that draw on the concept of time are still appropriate, and perhaps essential.

4. 'Just as the dominant contemporary understanding is that some form of intercession will obtain on the last day, so the great majority come down firmly on the side of ultimate extinction of the fires of torment' (J.I. Smith and Y.Y. Haddad, *The Islamic Understanding of Death and Resurrection* [Albany, NY: State University of New York Press, 1981], p. 143).

Index of References

Bible

Old Testament

Other Ancient References

Pseudepigrapha

Targums

Mishnah

Babylonian Talmud

Jerusalem Talmud

Tosefta

Midrash

CLASSICAL AND EARLY CHRISTIAN LITERATURE

Index of Modern Authors